TO A BRIGHTER FUTURE

The Pankow Family Story

The children ... how we love and cherish
them! To live for them, to provide for them,
to nurture and protect them, is our sacred
duty. That they may go forward to face a
brighter future is my constant prayer.

.....Else Pankow

by Ursula (Pankow) Delfs

i

Note for Librarians: A cataloguing record for this book is available from Library and Archives
Canada at www.collectionscanada.ca/amicus/index-e.html
ISBN 1-4120-7288-3

*Printed in Victoria, BC, Canada. Printed on paper with minimum 30% recycled fibre. Trafford's print
shop runs on "green energy" from solar, wind and other environmentally-friendly power sources.*

TRAFFORD
PUBLISHING

Offices in Canada, USA, Ireland and UK

This book was published *on-demand* in cooperation with Trafford Publishing. On-demand
publishing is a unique process and service of making a book available for retail sale to the
public taking advantage of on-demand manufacturing and Internet marketing. On-demand
publishing includes promotions, retail sales, manufacturing, order fulfilment, accounting and
collecting royalties on behalf of the author.

Book sales for North America and international:
Trafford Publishing, 6E–2333 Government St.,
Victoria, BC v8t 4p4 CANADA
phone 250 383 6864 (toll-free 1 888 232 4444)
fax 250 383 6804; email to orders@trafford.com
Book sales in Europe:
Trafford Publishing (uk) Limited, 9 Park End Street, 2nd Floor
Oxford, UK ox1 1hh UNITED KINGDOM
phone 44 (0)1865 722 113 (local rate 0845 230 9601)
facsimile 44 (0)1865 722 868; info.uk@trafford.com
Order online at:
trafford.com/05-2183
10 9 8 7 6 5 4 3 2

Table of Contents

Acknowledgments

If I could say "Thank you," my first words would go to my mother and father, who so diligently kept family history alive in the form of saved letters and journals.

Thank you to:
Dieter Anders for deciphering many pages of old German script; Gordon Boutcher for his patient computer lessons; my good friend Marion McNaught for proof-reading; Violet Pankow for the family genealogy charts; my siblings Dieter, Gerta, Heidi and Irma for assistance with pictures; Thanh Van of Priority Printing Ltd. for her friendly professional assistance. Thank you to my children Ellen, Brenda, Eric, Dwayne, and their families for their help and encouragement and their belief in "You can do it, Mom!" My heartfelt thanks goes to my husband, Hans Delfs, who, throughout this project, has been a driver, a cook, an understanding critic, proof-reader, photo scanner, computer operator, and best friend. Without his help and loving support these memoirs would not have been completed.

> *Dedicated to the memory of my parents, Günther and Else Pankow, and written with love and affection for my siblings, my children and grandchildren, nieces and nephews.*

Sources

Letters: Written by:
- Günther Pankow to his fiancée and relatives in Germany.
- Else Pankow to her husband in internment camp, and to relatives in Germany
- Relatives in Germany to the Pankow family in Canada.

Journals: Written by: Emilie(Pisch) Pankow
Anna Pankow
Günther Pankow.

1. **Frank P. Thomas.** How to Write the Story of your Life.
Cincinnati, Ohio. Writer's Digest Books. 1984.

2. **Woking & Area Historical Society**, Burnt Embers, A History of
Woking & District in the Burnt River Valley.
Friesen Printers, Altona, Manitoba 1985

On the Threshold

Foreword

These memoirs were written with the hope that they would not only provide interesting reading, but that they would give us all a better understanding of our roots and the history that led to our Canadian citizenship. Hopefully your ancestors will come to life as real people, experiencing joys and sorrows, successes and setbacks, as we all do. I have tried to describe the homestead days as I remember them, so that you may feel a part of that era.

Parts of this memoir would not have been possible, had it not been for the scores of letters that were not only written but also organized and saved over a period of several decades. The majority of the old letters were written in the old German script, which we find very difficult to read, and I feel deeply grateful to Dieter Anders. He is related to us only in that his Uncle Hellmut Anders married our Aunt Anneliese Pankow. He spent many, many hours to print old letters into readable form for us. I am glad that Dieter himself derived a great deal of pleasure out of this task. Being a history buff , he was fascinated by the rich personal histories that he saw emerge as he deciphered each letter.

Our father, Günther, was an excellent writer. Substantial contributions to these chapters come from his letters to his family and to his fiancée in Germany, as well as from his two journals. Mother's family, the Gesiens, were not prolific writers like the Pankow family, but Mother's weekly letters to Father in internment camp were so warm, so down-to-earth and newsy, that they portrayed a very real picture of homestead life during the war. Her later travelogues and Christmas letters to Germany served as useful "time lines." I am truly grateful for all this family correspondence, because it made my task easier. Numerous actual letter excerpts have been used (in italics) because I felt this was the best way to convey the true mood of the time. Some photos are of poor quality, but the decision had to be made. Do we use what is available or have no picture?

In attempting this large task of writing our family story, I hope that I have brought to you, my dear family, some enjoyment and pleasure, something memorable and worthwhile. Sorting materials out, setting priorities and organizing was a difficult task. So much had to be translated from the German, otherwise it would have been of little use to the majority of you. To get the translation just right sometimes required a great deal of time and thought. Naturally, the personal bias of the writer will always creep in, perhaps subconsciously, but it was my honest intent to "tell it like it was." Affected by individual hopes and dreams, and by the ruthless passage of time, memory can only be an imperfect witness. It is my fervent hope that I have offended no one. There are bound to be errors and differences in perception. For these I ask your indulgence and forgiveness.

Ursula Delfs
June, 2003, Woking, Alberta

Introduction

The rhythmic beat of the shipboard band punctuated the murmur of harbour waves as the ocean liner D. Derfflinger slid ponderously out of its moorings. It was March 18th, 1928 as the port of Bremen faded gradually into the distance.

The tall lanky young German standing on deck waved, for the last time, to the lonely figures who followed the shoreline as long as they could, then gradually disappeared from his view. Strains of the German national anthem echoed from the deck, and the young passenger was surprised by its effect. The music touched the very core of his being, stirring a patriotism never felt so strongly before. A lump filled his throat as he turned his back on the homeland. God willing it would not be forever. For a long time he stood quietly at the railing, lost in thought, and watched the coastline disappear.

That young man was Günther Pankow and he was to become our father. Because he had, in the year 1928, made the momentous decision to take this ocean voyage, he would set the stage for many other lives. His offspring and future generations, though of German heritage, would be Canadians.

Günther Pankow's heritage was steeped in the rich culture and good life of early twentieth century Germany. East Prussia, the province of his birth, is rich in history, dating back to the Teutonic Knights of the twelfth century. It was a battleground of Napoleon's campaign in 1806, and then of both world wars. His ancestry was made up largely of relatives engaged in either professional or business careers. His paternal grandparents were teachers and headmasters, his father a dentist. His maternal grandfather was a successful businessman, as was his Uncle Max. His siblings chose dentistry, teaching and nursing. Why then did he choose non-conformity? What was the appeal and challenge in embarking on something so different and uncertain? How enthusiastically, or not, did his family accept his decision? Certainly it could not have been easy.

To understand, even partially, the circumstances which would prompt such a decision, it is necessary to retrace some of this young adventurer's footsteps, and those of his ancestors, so we will leave him on deck for now and go back to an earlier time.

Chapter 1 A Remarkable Great-Grandmother

*Life is what we make it, always has been, always will be. ...Grandma
Moses.*

This woman, born in the nineteenth century, left behind for all of us to enjoy,
her memories, some poetry and many anecdotes from her childhood. Her
daughter Anna, in turn, recalled her own childhood years in a manuscript
entitled "Erinnerungen". I feel very fortunate to have access to these
treasured documents as they have enabled me to feel a closeness to my
ancestry and to relate with greater credibility something of their lives.

Great Great Grandparents Pisch

Emilie Pisch was born in Berlin on
January 25, 1836, to Friedrich
Wilhelm and Emilie (nee Henke)
Pisch. Her father descended from a
family of French immigrants and
during his twelve years as a
merchant in Berlin he also served
as a sexton of a French monasterial
church. This position made it
possible for him to secure lodging,
including a large garden, on the
premises. It was here that the
children were born. In that era of
high infant mortality this family,
too, was not spared. Five infants
died at birth or shortly thereafter,
leaving Emilie, her sister Julie and
brothers Franz and Louis. Emilie,
too, was a weak child, fearfully
sheltered, in bed for weeks at a
time, and dosed with countless evil-tasting medications.

It is not difficult then to understand that there were many sad times in
Emilie's childhood. Another depressing aspect was the fact that her father
suffered from epilepsy, and in the spring of 1844 was forced to apply for a
disability pension. This necessitated a move from the beloved old house and
garden and a change in lifestyle which was not for the better. Emilie's Uncle
Louis, her mother's brother, owned a textile business in another part of the
city. Louis was a bachelor at the time, so the family moved in with him and
Friedrich was able to help out with the bookkeeping and secretarial duties in
the business.

In 1849 Uncle Louis Henke got married, and this changed his life as well as that of the Pisch family. Their financial situation worsened as the support of their dear uncle was no longer available, and forced them twice more to seek new lodgings and more "belt-tightening".

Emilie received her education at the Berlin "Höherin Tochterschule" and decided at an early age to make teaching her career. With this goal always in mind, she enriched her curriculum with sewing classes, lessons in conversational French and music. Even during her elementary school days she often suffered from debilitating headaches which forced her to miss classes frequently. However, at the age of sixteen, shortly after confirmation, armed with a letter of commendation from principal Fournier, she applied for her first position as governess, a lifestyle that would fill her life for the next number of years.

Emilie's first place of employment was at Gross Klonia in West - Prussia for the family of Baron Hiller and proved to be a very difficult initiation to her desired career. She was required to be available to the family from six in the morning till ten at night, sometimes more. Her duties included the education of four children, which meant preparing lessons for four different ages. Her desire to maintain her letter-writing, her daily journal, and complete the fancy-work expected of young women at that time, often saw her working late at night by the dim light of a candle. This schedule took its toll. After only one year, with an extremely hoarse throat and badly inflamed eyes she was forced to abdicate her position and return to the parental home for several months.

After her convalescence, Emilie sought a second position and soon started working at Herwigsdorf, Niederschlesien for the owner of a manor who needed a governess for his two daughters, aged seven and eight. This proved to be a much better experience and she held this job from 1853 to 1859, at the yearly salary of 100 Taller. She felt obliged to send some of this home, although she knew even then that her contribution was like "a drop on a hot stone." Her employer, Herr Franke, was not only a good hearted man, but also well-educated. The home was a very large house which had stood for two hundred years and bore vestiges of the old surrounding wall and moat of a castle. In this home and social circle she was able to enrich her knowledge in the well-stocked family library and had free time to pursue her own interests — sketching, writing poetry, enjoying nature.

During this time Emilie carried on an active correspondence with Rudolf Heger, a student of architecture in Berlin, whom she described as the "best, the kindest, the most irresistable human being she had ever met." In 1855 Emilie and Rudolf were engaged to be married. But fate intervened when

Rudolf became seriously ill with pulmonory tuberculosis. Four months after their engagement Emilie stood at her fiance's deathbed. Beside her was Rudolf's best friend Fritz Pankow, also saying his last painful words of farewell.

Tired of living, but sure now that she would be able to deal with anything life handed her, she returned to the Franke household. With a broken heart, she carried out her duties mechanically, plagued by frequent headaches and sleepless nights. She buried herself in her books, for only these could so captivate her that her death-wish torture would be somewhat alleviated.

For three years Emilie carried on a somewhat irregular correspondence with Fritz Pankow, about philosophical or scientific themes, about their work, his studies, and of course, the loss of their mutual friend whom neither could forget. But time heals. Fritz gave up his position in Berlin and broke off his engagement to music teacher Emilie Fischer. It soon became clear to both that fate had brought them together, and as of October 30, 1858 Fritz Pankow and Emilie Pisch considered themselves to be engaged. Neither of them was in a hurry to get married as they wished to accompish their personal goals first. Fritz had become a home-tutor in Koslowo and was also working towards his grammar-school teacher exams. Emilie went to Berlin for a year to add to her knowledge of English and to complete the program of studies required for her teacher's diploma.

At the end of this term she was offered a teaching position in Finland which included her two-way passage and an annual salary of 300 rubels. She found this opportunity to explore the North and its people very tempting, and since her fiancé was in agreement, she quickly signed a two-year contract. In October 1860 the last steamer of the season took her from Lübeck to Helsingfors. Shortly upon arrival at the predominently Swedish city of Fredriksham, the northern winter set in with all its vigor as well as wonderful natural beauty — endless sparkling white snowfields, shimmering ice palaces and magical borealis.

She was hired as a teacher of languages at a private school founded by Gustava Forsblom and lived at the boarding school under conditions which were surprisingly primitive. Teachers had the "luxury" of their own rooms, sparsely furnished, but the students slept in the classrooms. At night the desks were removed, and mattresses, pillows, blankets, water jugs and basins transformed the space into sleeping quarters. The air was dry and short of oxygen, and the food, prepared in the not-too-clean institutional kitchen was unappetizing and hard to digest.

Teaching methods were a mixture of German and English, and all students participated in the compulsory Swedish "Heilgymnastik." Her job made heavy demands on her time, the pace for all teachers set by the energetic head-mistress herself. Apart from learning the Swedish language which she mastered very quickly, Emilie had little time for her own pursuits. The spartan environment of the boarding school was brightened several times during the term by various activities to which the public was invited. These were meant to foster the student's use of the foreign language in music, literature and drama, as well as in social interactions.

During school holidays Emilie travelled and was able to visit many parts of Finland to see it's majestic natural beauty, including the falls at Imatra. She found the Finns, though generally reserved in nature, to be most cordial and proud to show visitors their beautiful northern land. Her two - year sojourn here (1860 -1862), though sometimes fraught with discomfort and difficulty, would be forever etched in her memory as a worthwhile chapter in her life.

In 1862 Emilie began her last job as governess. This was with the three Falkenberg children at Kobieliner Mühle, Posen. Returning to this "home - schooling" atmosphere, she missed the daily camaraderie of colleagues that she had become accustomed to in Finland and in Berlin. But in this home she was treated like one of the family and participated fully in their social circles. She was to remember this governess position as a most pleasant and rewarding one. Much of her spare time was spent in sewing for her dowry from materials she had purchased with money she had saved from her Finland employment.

Great Grandparents Fritz and Emilie Pankow

In the meantime Fritz Pankow had written his exams to qualify him as a headmaster, and he accepted a position in Michalis in 1863. Finally he and Emilie started making plans for their life together. Emilie reluctantly gave notice to her beloved Falkenberg family in April, 1864 and left them with an excellent letter of commendation in her hands. This, along with earlier documents, which always spoke of excellence, were most valuable in obtaining government permission to establish the private girl's school which would become her life's mission.

After an engagement of nearly six years, Fritz Pankow and Emilie Pisch were married in Thorn on May 16, 1864. They made their first home in Gnesen where together they established a highly-rated private girls school.

Who was this man who became our great grandfather? Friedrich Johann (Fritz) Pankow was born October 27, 1833 in Thorn, West Prussia, to Christian and Henriette (Güttner) Pankow. An unfortunate childhood accident affected his life by leaving him lame. When only two years old, a maid left him unattended, sitting on a cold entryway floor for sometime. When she returned, his one leg had become crippled by some kind of stroke. Throughout his early years he had to be taken to elementary school in a wheelchair. Later he learned to walk with crutches. During his university years in Berlin he took therapeutic treatments, and with the help of a specially built boot with a higher heel, he graduated to walking with a cane. Although cheerful by nature, this handicap depressed him and made him despondent at times. How one act of negligence can have such dire consequences!

Fritz attended university in Berlin, majoring in Greek and Latin studies, and became a teacher. He served as home-tutor in Koslowo, then wrote exams to qualify him as headmaster, which he accepted in Michalis in 1863. In 1864 he, together with his new bride, founded the Hohern Tochter Schule in Gnesen. Fritz inherited the indestructable zest for life which is a genuine Pankow heritage, was known to be good-hearted and was dearly loved by all who knew him. He also had a tendency to be quite a socialite, even when his finances didn't allow it. He sometimes had to borrow money and didn't always get around to repaying it, causing his wife Emilie some worrisome times. They were poor. Neither came into the marriage with any capital. Fritz's father Christian Pankow of Thorn had provided a loan to help with the furnishings for the new school.

Fritz, Marie and Anna Pankow

Three children were born to this union: Anna in 1865, Marie in 1866, and Fritz (our grandfather) in 1867. It was remarkable that Emilie, having borne a child in each of the two previous years, being extremely busy at the newly-established school, and having just survived cholera, was able to give birth to this healthy boy. Her incredible energy seemed to see her through any crisis.

In 1866 the cholera epidemic struck Gnesen. Whole households were wiped out. Tante Julie nursed countless students, teachers, household staff and family members. Both Fritz and Emilie were stricken with the disease and

survived. But Fritz was never strong thereafter. In 1867 his body could not withstand the typhus germ which he is believed to have contracted while visiting a sick student.

Fritz died on September 26, 1867, when his youngest child Fritzchen was only two months old. As a result the children grew up with no direct memories of their father; this becomes apparent in Anna's journal ERINNERUNGEN. It now became Emilie's task, as a widow with three very young children, to carry on as head-mistress of the school.

Julie Pisch

The school became her whole life. The principles and methods which governed the school seem surprisingly advanced and broadminded for an educational institution of the 19th century. Along with a program of studies, curriculum and timetable, Fritz wrote a brochure outlining the basic philosophy of the school. He believed that its mandate was not just training for a career, but also the awakening, development and cultivation of the whole human being — the nature and the spirit, to the extent that character building would have a foundation in truth, and to preserve capabilities which would lend themselves to any life situation.

In his brochure Fritz then went on to deal with individual school subjects, one of which was religion. "Whenever, as here, people of different denominations are in contact with each other, it behooves this institution to strengthen a child's belief, but with evangelical leniency, towards an atmosphere of tolerance and reconciliation. Acceptable social behavior, friendly accommodation, including a loving association between older and younger students, shall always be fostered and maintained." Other subjects included the languages: German, English, French, Polish; history, geography, botany, zoology, physics, mathematics, needlework, sketching, choir, handwriting and physical education. Fritz taught history and geography and Emilie was the instructor for French and music.

The school building actually housed a combination of facilities including classrooms, a boardinghouse and a family home. Teachers were often boarders and renters. Tante Julie, Emilie's sister, lived with the family for many years, serving in many capacities, but mainly in the care of the Pankow children because their mother was so fully occupied with teaching and administration. Tante Lina Pankow, Fritz's sister, was also a young teacher at the school for a time. The physical structure existed on three different locations in Gnesen, the first being a large two- story building on Stomianka Street (1864-1867), then a three-story house with several dormers on Wilhelmstr. (1867-1877) surrounded by a large garden with pear trees, raspberries, gooseberries, vegetables and lilacs. In 1877 the school was moved to Klosterhaus, a convent that had been occupied for forty years by the Ursuline Order of nuns.

A well-stocked library was considered essential to the school and included insect, egg, shell, rock, butterfly collections, stuffed birds and animals, in addition to the treasury of books and printed materials. Although Emilie was almost miserly when it came to spending money on herself, diligently paid her debts and operated a spartan household, she always had something left for the library which she valued highly. Anna, Marie and Fritz had ready access and exposure to the classics and every literary genre during their formative years. Often the family, the resident teachers and the household staff would meet in the evenings for readings, literary discussions, piano recitals, theater, games, singing and dancing, as well as the regular sessions of knitting, sewing and fancywork.

Twice a year the daily routine of the home and school would be brightened by the visit of a travelling man to Gnesen. He carried a large sack containing a variety of grains, cereals and dried fruits. Emilie always purchased some of his wares for the school kitchen and the children looked forward to his visits because it meant they'd each have a prune for a treat. With the same regularity, a Silesian woman came with a backpack of textiles, including handwovens, and Emilie replenished her supply of materials for clothing, bedding and tablecloths. Her goods also included small kegs of Hungarian wine, which Emilie always bought as that was the beverage of choice for special celebrations.

The Christmas holiday season at the school was special in many ways. The school put on an annual theater performance to raise money for Christmas treats for poor children. The resident teachers often stayed because their homes were too far away, and they joined in with the baking of marzipan and pfeffernüsse, sang carols with the family and staff, made advent decorations and joined in seasonal readings. Every Wednesday and

Saturday every one in the household was engaged in knitting and sewing for the poor. The postman brought many packages at this time —pfefferkuchen arrived from the Pankow grandparents in Thorn, and Emilie had ordered myriad books, many of the classics, for the teachers. On Christmas Eve the ringing of a bell signified time for the opening of the parlour door and the magical appearance of the candlelit tree. Supper was a simple affair — open faced sandwiches with tea, followed by wheatlets served with milk, poppy-seed, sugar and cinnamon.

A very special occasion was in the 1870s when Emilie and the three children, all dressed in new outfits, travelled to Thorn for the golden wedding anniversary of the grandparents Christian and Henriette Pankow. The children were excited by all the food (much of which they had never seen before), by the dancing and the gifts. Grandmother wore a golden tiara and

Johann Christian Pankow
Anna Carolina Henrietta (Güttner) Pankow

Grandfather carried a golden bouquet. It was a happy occasion which united the family, although at other times the "Thorner Pankows" were not famous for their unity. The relationship between Emilie and her in-laws was always somewhat cool and strained. Supposedly Christian had said that he never wanted "that French woman" in his family. When Emilie's Fritz died, her father-in-law, like he would have done with any stranger, demanded full payment with interest of the debt that had been incurred for the furnishing of the school. Great-grandfather Pankow was a brick-layer and building contractor, also sexton at his church and was not a poor man. In letters to her mother-in-law Emilie addressed her in the formal "Sie" instead of "Du" usually used for someone on intimate or familiar terms, and signed "your obedient daughter." Even Henriette's own daughters addressed their mother this way so perhaps this was part of the etiquette of the day.

Emilie's children had little individual love and attention from their mother. She was matron of the boarding house, principal and teacher of the school, head of the housekeeping staff, and extremely conscientious in all these positions. She filled the material needs of her family in every way, but there was never **time** for personal or emotional needs. They were well brought up, with few words, punished by ear cuffs when their mother considered it necessary. Essentially it was the daily regimen of the institution that disciplined them. Here they automatically learned respect for other people, to expect nothing more for themselves than for others, to be modest and undemanding, because their mother was all these things. Emilie despised gossip, and though good-natured jokes were told about others, any trace of judgemental or racist remarks were strictly taboo in her home. Anna felt more fear than love towards her mother and even as an adult, she felt a constant need to seek her mother's approval, and this was rarely expressed. Emilie set an example almost impossible to follow. In addition to all her work, she kept up an active correspondence with former colleague Dr. Meier, regarding educational issues; she read all the pedagogical journals that seemed pertinent to her work and kept abreast of scientific, political and literary achievements. But she scorned any public recognition, being a firm believer in the axiom "Actions speak louder than words." Even her severe headaches, sometimes accompanied by vomiting, failed to keep her down for more than a few hours.

Franz Pisch (Emilie's Brother)

Two members of the Pisch family emigrated to the United States. Emilie's brother Franz completed his apprenticeship in plumbing in Berlin. Then to avoid the military draft he secretly sought passage on an ocean liner and sailed for New York. Here he built up a successful plumbing business, married a beautiful German -American girl and had a family of one son and two daughters. Emilie's children called him "Uncle America" and wrote letters to him. The youngest Pisch brother, Louis, handsome and adroit, shifted from job to job, left his wife Tante Jettchen in Berlin and joined his brother in New York. But he prospered no better in America than he had in Germany. The brothers parted and Louis went to Chicago. His unhealthy life-style eventually led to tuberculosis and admittance to a hospital where he was one of many who perished in a fire.

After the death of her husband, Emilie, as headmistress, led the school with great energy and efficiency. Utter simplicity reigned in her home. Exceptionally neat and orderly in her personal appearance and with her belongings, only high-quality clothing or materials were purchased, but these were diligently cared for and worn for years. For visiting or for school festivals she wore black silk or wool cashmere. Her daily dresses were almost always dark brown, with occasional grey. Without exception every outfit included a black apron, woolen for daily wear, silken for Sundays. Her soft black hair was always parted in the middle, drawn back and held in place with pomade so that not a wisp would be out of place.

Her head was covered with a black veil of genuine lace, secured with a hatpin. This is how family, employees and friends would remember the small

Emilie (Pisch) Pankow

woman with the indomitable spirit who led Gnesen girls school until the year 1888.

In 1897 she sold the school and spent the last years of her life living together with her sister Julie Pisch in Grünau near Berlin. She lived to witness great sorrow in the death of her only son, our grandfather, in 1913. Emilie Pisch Pankow died February 15, 1915 at the age of eighty and left to mourn were her two daughters Anna and Marie Pankow.

Marie Pankow and Anna Pankow

Chapter 2   The Dentist Of Bergplatz 15

If our lives shall be such that we shall receive the glad welcome of "Well done good and faithful servant," we shall then know that we have not lived in vain. ... Peter Cooper.

Christian Friedrich (Fritz) Pankow was born in Gnesen, Germany on July 29, 1867, the third child and only son of Johann Friedrich and Emilie (Pisch) Pankow. His childhood years were spent at the private school which his parents had founded in 1864. Fritzchen was only two months old when his father died. His mother's time and energy were severely taxed as teacher and headmistress, so Tante Julie, Emilie's sister, and Oma Hencke played a large part in his early upbringing. The little boy became so attached to his loving grandmother, that when she died in 1870, it was as though, in his grief, he would follow her. All day long he perched in his Oma's chair by the window, daydreaming and crying, refusing to eat or drink and visibly failing. Finally his attendance at a playschool, under the care of an understanding teacher, brought him out of his suffering.

Fritz was a handsome, well-behaved child, well liked by all — the household staff, other students and teachers. He was an average student, finding Latin and mathematics especially difficult because he thought these to be entirely useless and boring subjects. His upbringing was by example. Emilie was not only his mother but his mentor. He had an exceptionally close relationship with his mother and carried her ideals, her philosophies into his own adult life as husband, father and career person.

In the summer holidays of 1885, eighteen-year-old high school student Fritz Pankow travelled from his home in Gnesen to visit relatives in Göttingen. Enroute he stopped in Goslar to visit Uncle Ernst Breithaupt who had established a dental practice there in 1871. Uncle Ernst proudly showed off his facilities and gave Fritz an honest appraisal of the positive and negative sides of his chosen career. This aroused a keen interest, and it would seem, planted the seed which determined Fritz's future.

In 1886 Fritz became a student of dentistry and commenced classes at Breslau. In his first year he observed under Dr.Bruck, mostly in a clinic for the poor. He interned with Dr.Riegner whom he greatly admired and credited with teaching him everything he knew about dentistry — indeed, Riegner became his mentor. Compulsory subjects included hygiene, surgery, pathology and pharmacology. General anatomy was not on the curriculum; instead a very intensive study of the anatomy of the head was required.
Fritz felt he needed something apart from the academic classes and practical internships, so he joined the "Scientific and Academic Association of

Odontology," even though his mother expressed some doubt as to its desirability. Wasn't it just for drinking and fencing and parties? He insisted that the fellowship and support of other students, the dentistry-related speakers and presentations were the main purpose of the organization.

It is interesting to note that in March 1887, the rush of exam preparations was interrupted by the death of Kaiser Wilhelm I. Throughout the week there was feverish excitement in Breslau, and every bit of news from Berlin was followed with great interest. When the death was announced, all major businesses were closed immediately, signs were draped and black flags hung at half mast and from the windows. Huge numbers of wreaths were piled in the florist's shops, ready to be sent to Berlin.

During the month of May the state exams took up nearly two weeks — a gruelling schedule of five to six hours daily of written work, then the practical exam: fillings, extractions, and other surgical techniques. At the end of it all, Fritz could proudly report to his mother that he had been successful.

As a result of Regnier's recommendation, Fritz secured the position of assistant to Doctor Müller in Vienna which he began in June 1888. A very large practice with international clientele, kept him extremely busy, working

Friedrich Wilhelm (Fritz)
Pankow 1867 - 1913

daily from nine in the morning till six at night for fifteen months. Many times over he silently thanked Dr.Regnier for teaching him so well, especially in careful cavity preparation and precise fillings.

In October 1889 Fritz was called to begin his one year of compulsory military service. This was short-lived when a gymnasium accident resulted in serious injury and weeks of convalescence. Between hospital stays and upon recovery, he opened his own practice of dentistry in Gnesen.

In 1893 Dentist Fritz Pankow, together with seven German colleagues, sailed from Hamburg to attend an International Congress of Dentists in Chicago, U.S.A. Some eleven hundred dentists from many countries were in attendance. The huge hall at the Chicago Dental College was equipped with some forty dental chairs, where demonstrations of various techniques were

Else Sürth and Fritz Pankow

given by practitioners from around the world. By befriending a German New York dentist, Fritz was able, for nine weeks, to observe in several practices in New York City. During this time he was able to stay with his uncle, Franz Pisch (Emilie's brother) who owned a large light-fixture business in New York.

Apart from being a most enriching and valuable experience career wise, Fritz's trip to America had a momentous personal affect on his future. On his return voyage to Germany, a shipboard romance blossomed. Fritz met Else Sürth, who together with her sister, was returning from her brother Max's wedding in America. On November 17, 1893, upon their arrival at the port of Bremen, Fritz and Else celebrated their engagement in the Ratskeller, a wine-cellar in the city hall. (This locale has assumed special significance for the Pankow family ever since, and has been visited by several family members.)

On March 6,1895, Fritz Pankow and Else Sürth were married in Cologne. After investigating many possibilities all over Germany, the doctor was able to secure an established dental practice in Königsberg and hung up his shingle at BERGPLATZ 15. His practice thrived, had six dentist chairs, and always one or two assistants. His patients included dignitaries and nobility from his city and throughout East Prussia. Often he would load a treadle drilling machine into a cab and head for the railroad station, in order to provide dental treatment to rural people on their estates or to nobility in their castles. Fritz also had a close working relationship with the surgical clinic at the

Dentist Fritz Pankow in his Practice

University where he was especially skilled and in demand for cases of broken jaws, or following serious head operations where restoration of entire jaws, nose or ear was required.

Fritz and Else (Sürth) Pankow

In spite of his obvious excellence and dedication to his work, his involvement and executive positions in societies relating to dentistry, Fritz was a devoted and loving family man. He and Else made their first home in a rented house in Amalienau, a suburb of Königsberg. Here their six children were born and enjoyed a happy childhood . A large garden and an adjacent undeveloped lot provided lots of room to play. In the evening they often awaited the arrival of their father at the corner of Kastanienallee as he came home from work by streetcar, from his downtown office. He was never too tired to play with his children. Sunday walks with their father took them along the Pregel River, exploring many a hidden path, away from the crowded city. In 1912 Fritz purchased his own home on Louisenallee 31.

Back l to r – Lotte, Else holding Hans Jürgen, Erika. Front - Werner, Anneliese, Günther, Fritz Pankow.

Summer holidays were sometimes spent on the beaches of the Baltic at Cranz. A man of sunny disposition and a lover of nature, he shared this with

Pankow Home on Kastanienalle Königsberg, East Prussia

his children. The happy childhood of the six siblings was soon marred by tragedy. The younger ones especially (Günther was only nine) were not aware that their father had been ailing. His trip to Egypt to seek medical help for a kidney ailment met with failure. On June 17, 1913, husband, father, and highly respected Doctor of Dentistry, Fritz Pankow died at the young age of forty – six years. These Königsberg Newspaper items, printed upon the death of Dr. Fritz Pankow, give an indication of the love and respect in which he was held, not only by his family:

This morning, after long suffering, my dear associate and colleague, Doctor of Dentistry, Friedrich Pankow, died. During our years of working together, I learned to appreciate and love the deceased as a colleague of great capability and a human being of rare golden quality. His heart-warming ways and sunny disposition, even in deep suffering, and integrity of his character, have earned him our eternal remembrance.

And from the technical staff at his dental office:

At two o'clock this morning, after long suffering, our highly esteemed employer, Doctor of Dentistry Fritz Pankow died. The dear deceased was, to us, a kind, loving, and concerned teacher and mentor. In spite of his deep suffering, he was a shining example of true loyalty to duty.

Fritz Pankow, 1913

(Information was gleaned and condensed from an article entitled "Aus der Geschichte der Zahnheilkunde". This had been submitted by Dr. Werner Pankow, son of Fritz Pankow, and was featured in a Dentistry paper "Zahnärtzliche Beteilungen." Uncle Werner had compiled the article from letters that his father Fritz had written home to his mother Emilie Pankow, during his student years. This contains a wealth of information pertaining to dentistry at the end of the nineteenth century, in addition to family history. These letters are contained in the Pankow family archives.)

Chapter 3   Grandmother, The Dentist's Widow

On that fateful day, June 17,1913, a mother was left alone to raise her six young children. Perhaps Else (Sürth) Pankow was better equipped to do this than some might have been.

Johann (Jean) Sürth
and son Max

Marie (Leopold) Sürth

She was born Elizabeth Mathilde Alverda (Else) Sürth, on May 12, 1870 in Cologne, Germany, to Johann Baptist Bruno (Jean) Sürth and Marie Henriette Dorothea Erdmuthe Louise (Leopold) Sürth. In 1882 Else's mother had become physically and mentally ill and had to be institutionalized. As a result, Else, at sixteen years of age and her sister Anning, had been forced to manage the large household in Cologne. Else had two brothers, Max and Fred, and two sisters, Anning and Ida.

Now at forty-three, with a family of her own, she displayed great courage and resourcefulness, and was determined to provide her children with a happy childhood home. The deep sadness of her husband's death had hardly subsided when the Great War broke out on August 1, 1914, bringing with it many changes for the family. High school students, including her oldest son Werner, volunteered for military service; soldiers were among the boarders in their home and the school had "coal holidays," closed to conserve fuel, also holidays to celebrate major battle victories; teachers were predominantly female. Food became scarce or unavailable. Posters of Hindenburg, statesman born in East Prussia and revered as a saviour and protector could be seen in homes and schools.

During these difficult years, Else gratefully received help from her sister-in-law, Anna, Fritz's sister. Perhaps because she never married and had none of

her own, this woman took a very personal interest in her brother's children. Tante Anna held a special place in the hearts of her nieces and nephews. They often spent their holidays with her and carried on a regular correspondence with her for life. Being a teacher without dependents, she was in a position to help financially as well. From her, Günther received an interest- free loan to help him get established on his Canadian homestead. He was never able to repay her. I can remember writing letters to Great-aunt Anna in the forties.

Anna Pankow

Else also received support from her (Sürth) side of the family. Her brother Max warrants special mention here. Max was born in St. Louis, Missouri in 1861, during the short time that his parents sought their fortune in the U.S.A., but upon their return, he grew up in Germany. As a young man he emigrated to the States, also spent some years in Japan, and became a rich entrepreneur. He married Jessica Gaetz, originally from Japan, and they had one daughter, Dorcas. Uncle Max had come to the aid of his nephew Günther, not only financially by paying his ship's voyage to Canada but also with immigration information, advice and encouragement. Again, the loan could not be repaid — indeed Günther never met his benefactor. Uncle Max died in 1937, a relatively poor man as a result of the great stock market crash. Our grandparents met aboard ship because of Uncle Max's wedding in the U.S.A. Our father came to Canada aided by a loan from Uncle Max. Was not our destiny shaped at least partly by this great-uncle?

Our grandmother Else Pankow's home in Königsberg was always a "haven" where family members gathered, in happy times and in times of sadness. She stood by them, wrote countless letters, sometimes moralizing or admonishing, but always loving and encouraging. These missives went with great regularity, often weekly, to Lotte in her training to become a deaconess; to Werner in the military or school of dentistry; to Anneliese in teacher training; to Erika struggling to hold down a job; to Günther during his agricultural apprenticeship, then to Canada; and to Hansi who seemed to be "the eternal student." A typical ending to her letters might be: "So many good wishes for you are always in my heart, that you must feel it almost palpably. In whatever you do, make sure that your conscience is always clear in the sight of God and self. You will face so much that is evil and mean. You must stand strong and steadfast to remain pure of heart."

She struggled with the day-to-day problems of just making a living. Her dentist husband had provided well and left her a rich legacy — they had been able to live on the interest alone. That, however, was all in vain, when the economics of the time caused a complete breakdown. As a result of inflation, the Pankow family, along with thousands of others, lost everything. Else was forced to sell the house on Louisenallee 31 and move to a rental house. Here she sublet rooms and took in boarders. She no longer had a housekeeper and looked after the household herself.

Her letters of 1923 give a brief insight into the situation when she writes:

> *Inflation seems to have reached its peak. It's enough to make you dizzy. As of yesterday we pay 9000 Mark for a liter of milk. I wish I had a piece of land for a garden because a pound of potatoes costs 4000 M. I can't provide a meal for four for under 10,000 -- 15,000 M. I must walk to market because the fare would be 5000 M. I had the opportunity to sell my bronze light fixture for 20,000 M. Rental rates for furnished rooms have gone up, so we have something to keep us going again.*

But worse was yet to come. Later that year Hansi writes as follows: "My suit cost me 7 million M., a pound of butter 1 million M., one kilowatt hour 250,000 M., two tickets to the symphony 44 million M. I worked one week for Werner and earned 800 million M. I did after-school tutoring every day and came home with 3 billion M."

Standing l to r: Anneliese & Hellmut Anders, Hans Jürgen, Erika, Lena. Sitting l to r: Lotte, Günther, Else, Werner Pankow.

In spite of these constant financial struggles, every effort was made to perpetuate the concept that "the soul too must be fed." Else found peace and inner strength in music and made it a part of their home. She played the piano and soloed for herself or for the enjoyment of others. She had an extraordinarily beautiful voice, enhanced by several years of voice lessons in her youth. She was often invited to solo in churches, at Christmas concerts, parties and other functions. In her letter to Günther on December 5, 1921, she writes:

> *Your mother will perform Christmas songs composed by Cornelius at the "Verein der Studenten" (Student Association) concert. What do you say to that!? I'll be doing the same at the Labtauer Church. But I'm getting stage-fright. Imagine your mother at her age performing in public! Keep your fingers crossed for me, because I've caught a cold too."*

Many of the young people played recorder duets, participated in four - part

Grandmother Else Pankow

singing and choral groups. On at least one occasion, our two uncles, Werner Pankow and Ernst Gesien enjoyed singing duets in harmony. The family attended concerts, the opera, theater productions, speaker and discussion seminars, dances and masquerades. Some took piano lessons and dance instruction. They were church-goers and attended related social functions; all were confirmed, with the accompanying confirmation dinner and family gift-giving. Apart from these cultural pursuits, a very common form of recreation for all ages, one which cost nothing, seemed to be hiking, or just going for a walk (spazieren gehen), whether alone, with a friend, or with a large organized school group.

Hans Jürgen, Nora, Anneliese, Hellmut.

As the children left home to make their own life, Else kept the home-fires burning, always there for their needs and their visits. Now she more often assisted in their homes — moving, house-sitting during holidays, laundry and mending. On one such occasion, at Werner and Lena's house in Cranz, she had

Werner's replacement dentist perform a fairly major dental procedure. Complications arose, causing much pain and discomfort. When her children returned from holidays, they found her very ill. She was hospitalized for several weeks in early June. It was believed that infection around the heart had developed as a result of the dental procedure. Considerable improvement was soon evident, she was able to go home, and then travelled to her daughter's home in Tilsit.

Here she happily anticipated the task of looking after the two young expectant mothers — her own daughter, Anneliese Anders, and her daughter-in-law Nora Pankow, Hansi's wife. Although now she would not be able to provide the physical help she had hoped to, she would be there for emotional support.

Alas, the events of the next fortnight turned out to be quite different, and for Else, totally devastating. After a terribly long and difficult labor, during which Else assisted, Nora's fully-developed baby girl was still-born. Again Else's hopes of becoming a grandmother were cruelly shattered. She had witnessed the many miscarriages of Lena (Werner's wife). But unselfishly she put her own sorrow aside and tried to comfort the young parents in their anguish. During the next few days she persevered with great determination, helping with household tasks and caring for Nora. But no one could relieve her of the terrible fear and anxiety: "How would things evolve now with the other young mother-to-be?"

When Anneliese went into labor, she entreated, then ordered her mother to leave the room, wishing to spare her any more suffering. From that moment, it seems, a terrible conflict took place in Else's psyche. She felt possessed by dark forces which reproached her with: "You are no longer needed in this world. What are you doing here?" The sleepless nights of inner conflict must have seemed like an eternity to the suffering woman. In the morning she set up a telegram for Hansi to send to Lotte: "Come at once." Then she ordered him to "take me out of this house" so that the two young women would "suffer no damage by my presence." It is believed that she never regained the ability to fully enjoy or realize that she was indeed a grandmother to Elizabeth, Anneliese's healthy baby. No one at that time could even imagine the extent of her mental and spiritual anguish, accompanied by such extreme agitation and unrest, that she could not be held in bed. Hansi by himself was unable to subdue her. In a state of collapse, she, accompanied by Hansi, was taken by three-hour ambulance, to the hospital in Königsberg. Lotte interrupted her vacation in Switzerland to be by her mother's side.

The darkness of depression, the mental anguish, the fear of a fate similar to that of her own mother who had been institutionalized at an early age — all this threatened to overwhelm her. She had lost the will to live, and was determined not to be a burden to her children. All this made it difficult for her weakened body to withstand the physical problems which now arose; weakness in the heart muscle, malnutrition and dehydration because she would accept no food, then severe inflammation of the bladder and kidney.

With her daughter and faithful nurse at her side, Else quietly passed away at 6:05 p.m. on Monday, August 12, 1929, at the age of 60 years. On August 15, Else Sürth Pankow, our grandmother, was buried beside her husband Fritz in the Luisen Church cemetery in Königsberg.

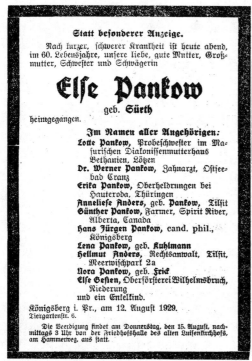

In a letter of condolence after Grandmother's recent death, Anneliese wrote this to her brother Günther in Canada:

Our Mütterlein is well off. We children would have wished to provide her with many more pleasures, to share much more with her, and we will miss her terribly. But we must tell ourselves that God knows best. She had a rich full life, and until recently our active, energetic mother was granted good health and strength. That's why it never occured to us that we could lose her at such an early age. But for her who could never sit idle, a slow wasting away would have been torture. All we can do is be still and be truly thankful for all the goodness that was ours through this very special woman. Her soul will continue to live among us

The household goods were divided among the siblings, and in September the home, which had witnessed so much love and living, also sorrow and sadness, was forever closed to the Pankow family. Each would go forth to establish his own nest, but would never forget the warm, loving, mother-centered haven.

The six children of Fritz and Else Pankow were born in Königsberg, East Prussia, Germany, now Kaliningrad, Russia. They became our aunts and uncles.

The Children of Fritz and Else Pankow		
Lotte ....9 – 01 – 1896,	deceased ....3 -- o5 – 1945,	at age 49
Werner...............2 – 02 – 1897,	deceased .....6 – 09 – 1983,	at age 83
Erika ....8 – 10 – 1898,	deceased .....8 – 10 – 1982,	at age 84
Anneliese ....26 – 02 – 1901,	deceased ...26 – 12 – 1969,	at age 68
Günther ....8 – 01 – 1904,	deceased ...11 – 05 – 1948,	at age 44

Lötzen, Ostpr.   Diakonissen-Mutterhaus Bethanien

Lotte, the first-born, took nurse's training during World War I in Tenkitten, worked in hospitals, became a deaconess and served as matron or Sister Superior in the Mutterhaus in Lötzen, East Prussia. Her work also included giving courses in infant care, which took her to many parts of the province. Though never married, she led a very full and active life. All written accounts indicate that here, in her plain grey attire, was a true philanthropist, a deeply spiritual person, who made her whole life one of service to others. A colleague writes lovingly of "Schwester Lotte's" life, citing *"When they walk through the vale of tears, it will become a place of springs where pools of blessing and refreshment collect after rain, Psalm 84 Verse 6"* as a perfect metaphor for the life of the deaconess.

Deaconess Lotte Pankow

In a 1928 letter to her brother Günther, this was Lotte's reaction to his decision to become a farmer in Canada, and says something about her outlook on life, one of simplicity: *"You have chosen fine travel companions: Mother Nature and Mother Earth, both of whom have opened the eyes of many. Return to nature and simplicity, for thus is man's greatest happiness assured."*

By a strange twist of fate, the only bomb that fell on Bramstedt during World War II, dropped there one day before the end of the war, apparently by accident, as there was no strategic target here. It struck the nurse's residence which a number of the sisters of service called home. Seriously injured, her last words expressing concern for others, Sister Lotte Pankow died on May 3, 1945 at the age of 49.

Werner, the second born, experienced the responsibilities of being the oldest boy in a fatherless home at an early age. He joined the army during World War I, earning the rank of lieutenant at the age of eighteen. After the war he followed in his father's footsteps and studied at the school of dentistry, then set up his practice in Cranz, a Baltic Sea resort town. In 1932 he lost his first wife Lena Kuhlmann in childbirth, after many previous miscarriages. Werner was somewhat politically active, being a strong supporter of Hindenburg and Ludendorff. He married Margarethe Wagner and had four daughters - - Gisela, Ingrid, Gudrun and Karin. He loved his daughters dearly, but never quite lived down the disappointment of not producing a son, an heir to the Pankow name. In World War II, Werner again joined the military, achieved the rank of colonel, was awarded the Ritterkreuz medal, was wounded twice and spent five years in a Russian prisoner of war camp. After the war, at the age of 53, he made a fresh start and resumed his dental career by setting up a new practice in Helstorf, where he had found his wife and children after they fled East Prussia. In the seventies he took a big trip to the U.S.A. and Canada to visit his sister-in-law Else and Günther's children, his nieces and nephews. After suffering for some time with Parkinson's disease, Uncle Werner Pankow died in Helstorf on September 6, 1980, at the age of eighty three.

Werner Pankow 1914

The Werner Pankow Family 1951
Back: Ingrid, Gisela, Gudrun
Front: Margarete, Karin, Werner

Uncle Werner on his 75th Birthday in his Library of Archives

Erika , the third child, was born in 1898, it would seem with a slight physical and mental handicap. She sometimes suffered from depression, nervousness, a deep apathy towards life in general. This showed itself in lack of ambition and a somewhat sullen nature. On the other hand, she quite capably wrote long interesting letters to her brother in Canada, and during her youth she helped her mother a great deal with the younger siblings. She was sporadically employed as housekeeper or baby-sitter, but never seemed to hold a position for any length of time. Other family members always appeared to make special concessions, especially regarding finances, "for Erika." Erika married Fritz Seidler, an older man, in what

Erika Pankow 1936

Erika & Fritz Seidler

some believe was an arranged marriage. She spent her final years in a home for the aged in Neustadt near Helstorf, where she died in 1982 at the age of 84.

Anneliese was the fourth child, born in 1901. For ten years she went to a private

Back l to r: Gunthard, Kriemhild, Ingrid
Front: Elizabeth, Anneliese, Reintraud Anders

school for young girls in Tragheim, and later took teacher training. She was briefly employed as a governess on a family estate, also teacher at a girl's school. In 1928 she was married to Hellmut Anders, a lawyer, and they made their home in Tilsit, East Prussia. Five children were born in five years: Elizabeth (1929), Gunthard (1930), Ingrid (1931), Kriemhild (1932),

Reintraut (1934). Hellmut died during active military service in 1943, leaving Anneliese with five young children. As a result of the Russian invasion of East Prussia, she, with the children, was forced to flee from their homeland in a harrowing trek. They settled for some time in Tiefenort, where she was able to support her family by teaching for a number of years. She ended her career at the Waldorf School in Munich. Anneliese suffered from asthma, which often left her in fragile health. It would seem that she had a philosophical tendency. She did a lot of philosophizing in her letters, making it harder for those of us with a limited grasp of the German language, to understand some of her ideas. Tante Anneliese Pankow died in Frankfurt in 1969, at the age of 68.

Gunther Pankow 1904

Günther, our father, was the fifth child, and of course his life will be covered in much greater detail.

Hans Jurgen and Gunther Pankow

Hans Jürgen was the last child and was only six years old when his father died. He and Günther, the two youngest, growing up together, became very close, and judging from the many letters, they remained that way as adults. Here was a young man who loved life and lived it to the fullest. He had a great sense of humor, often self-deprecating, which indicated no lack of self-esteem. He loved sports of all kinds: bicycling, hiking, skiing, snowshoeing, rowing, fencing, and especially gymnastics, and was quite proficient in all of them. He was also fond of music, drama and dancing, as participant or audience. All this sometimes took place to the detriment of his studies, and to his mother's consternation.

Hansi was especially fond of hiking, and even more, cycling, taking extended country-wide tours, either by himself, with a friend, or with youth groups. Perhaps this mode of transport was taken more out of necessity than

Gunther and Hans Jurgen Pankow

sheer pleasure, because only the well-to-do owned automobiles. These trips would cover miles of shoreline, sand dunes and beautiful forested areas, visiting bird sanctuaries, museums, castles and myriad natural wonders. Included in the camaraderie would be outdoor meals, campfires, music, singing, folkdancing; overnight stays in youth hostels, barns or forestery stations. The family was poor after inflation had wiped out their inheritance, and it was a constant struggle for Hansi, as a student, to reach his goal of becoming a Phys. Ed. teacher. He earned money wherever he could, was not afraid of work, and no task was too menial. He hauled all types of fuel — coal, coke, briquettes, peat, sawed and split wood. He worked at the harbour and on surrounding farms, and helped on moving days. While studying in Freiburg he was business manager for the Student Loan Board, for which he received a token salary, and sometimes did after-school tutoring.

Hansi was very involved with the German Youth Organization of the time (Deutsche Jugend), serving as leader of the branch and was prone to volunteering for more than he had time. For example, in 1924, for a large concert staged by this group, in addition to having a part in it, he was solely responsible for the rather elaborate lighting.

In 1929, Hansi, while still a student, married Nora Frick whom he had been seeing for some time. Fortunately he was loved and accepted by his wife's family and received financial help from his father-in-law for years. Their first baby, a girl, was still-born in 1929 while Nora, during her pregnancy, stayed with Anneliese and Hellmut Anders in Tilsit. The sadness of this event was heightened when Hansi had serious guilt

**Hans Jurgen (Hansi) Pankow
1927**

feelings that this tragedy may have precipitated his mother's breakdown.

In 1932, after many semesters of study, writing countless term papers, taking

**Nora, Inga, Hansi, Helga
Pankow 1941**

oral exams, Hansi passed his qualification exams and began student-teaching in Preuss Eylaw, three quarters of an hour train ride out of Königsberg. Then he started working on his Doctorate of Philosophy, spending some time at the Berlin Archives to help him with his treatise. But after the many semesters of academic studies, and the constant lack of income, it became painfully obvious that the prospects for getting a job were very poor. There was a surplus of teachers.

After much serious soul-searching, Hansi made a career change and began training in a bank. Though he did not find his job truly satisfying, he was now able to build a small house of his own, and finally become almost financially independent. Their second daughter, Helga, died at the age of eleven years. The youngest, Inga, was born in 1938. She is married to Wilfried Kuntze and is presently living in Erfurt.

Hansi's many prolific letters to his brother Günther are a delight to read, and give a lively commentary of his days as a student — indeed of life in Germany in the early 1900s. His writing, at fifteen years of age, shows an amazing maturity, and excellent style, outstanding vocabulary. His letters exhibit humor and a deep patriotism. In a letter of congratulation on one of

**Back l to r: Hans Jurgen, Werner Pankow
Front: Anneliese Anders, Lotte Pankow
Erika Seidler,1934**

our births, he writes: "We wish for you that your children will become honest, good, upright human beings, and that they will uphold the German culture of their parents, even though they are growing up on Canadian soil."

Just when the life of this young man had reached a level of stability and greater ease, World War II broke out, and every able-bodied young man became a member of the

29

military. In 1945, Hans Jürgen Pankow was declared missing in action during the fighting in East Prussia. The loss of this life seemed particularily poignant and tragic. There was so much potential, so much more to do and give, and he was only 38 years old. I wish I had known him!

We, Günther's children, have often felt that we missed a great deal by never knowing a grandmother or a grandfather, an aunt or an uncle, never being near an extended family. We had letters and parcels, but not even the long-distance telephone connections of today. But that is the fate of many children of immigrants who left their roots for a new future in Canada.

Chapter 4   Growing Up in East Prussia

Günther John Pankow, the fifth child of the dentist Fritz Pankow and his wife Else, was born on January 8th, 1904, in Königsberg, East Prussia, now Kaliningrad, Russia.

Else Pankow with Günther

His early childhood was a time of happy memories, playing with his brother Hansi, holidaying on the beaches of the Baltic Sea, hiking in the dunes and woodlands. Often he would run to greet his father as he returned home from his downtown dental practice. Those happy times came to a tragic end with the death of his father on June 17, 1913, at the age of 46. Death to a nine-year-old is a frightening and mysterious concept. He sat on the stairway for a long time, sobbing inconsolably. He always remembered the funeral, with its long line of vehicles, the many wreaths and so many sad people. Somehow he understood that his father would never again be among them.

Soon after, came the great war. For the young boys who did not yet understand the serious implications and the full meaning of the word **war**, this time held a degree of excitement and great interest. They got to watch military bands and parades; to interact with real soldiers who roomed at their house. It was especially exciting when their uniformed older brother Werner or Uncle Fred came "home on leave" from military duty. At fourteen Günther was a member of a youth group which participated in some military training (without the weapons) and took outings which included war maneuvers. With the war-time scarcity of food, it was always a good thing when Günther was invited to the home of a rural friend during holidays. Here at the Selbstaedt farm he was able to

Günther Pankow 1907

enjoy plenty of good country food, and familiarize himself with life on the farm. He loved it. Was this the beginning of a dream?

Further fuel was added to this budding idea when Günther, at the age of fifteen, spent one of several summer holidays with Tante Anna at Detmold, a village near Berlin. He got to know several of the neighboring farmers and helped them with their tasks whenever he could. He found this work to be enjoyable and satisfying. The thought of returning to the classroom and cramming for exams was most unappealing. Furthermore, he reasoned, there would be no need for further academics. He now considered agriculture his future, and began to dream of someday farming on his own land, not to be a wage-earner or just a farm employee. Perhaps this was still in the realm of possibility. His father's estate money was not yet in jeopardy at this time. It was during the inflation of 1923 that the entire inheritance was lost.

With some trepidation, Günther approached his mother and other kin with this dream of his. Would a family of professionals accept him as a farmer? After some hesitation and consideration, they agreed, even giving him their blessing. Registration for his final year of high school was cancelled. He was immediately broken in as he worked on a nearby farm at harvest time, its busiest and most taxing season.

Then for two years he was employed on the farm of Meyer Biesen in Lippe, where he learned about many facets of agriculture, and although he was only a trainee, received a small wage. His employer had a water-mill, that, as well as grinding wheat, also powered the threshing machine, wood saw, electric generator and feed cutter. He learned to operate them all. On occasion he was able to bring his mother flour which he himself had ground. When hauling grain or potatoes to town, or on his Sundays off, he often stopped to visit Tante Anna, only seven and a half kilometers from the farm.

Inspector Günther at Linkenau

When his two years at Biesens were completed, he took his apprenticeship exam on a farm in East Prussia, then took a position with a large farming operation in Linkenau until July 1924. The most remarkable part of this time was working with the grossly inflated and dizzying figures (billions) involved in salary statements and record keeping. Inflation was at its peak.

In August,1924, Günther volunteered for military service, a dream he'd had since childhood and probably influenced by his brother Werner. He joined the 3rd Infantry Regiment in Allenstein. Extreme discipline and strenuous training such as battle practices and long marches, abetted by extra-curricular sports, gymnastics and swimming, soon made him strong and very fit. Target-shooting was his one weakness, due to his eye-sight. The young volunteers were paid 45 Mark per month, plus free uniforms, room and board. Much as he enjoyed this time, his military experience was short-lived, only three months, when all the young volunteer recruits were discharged on short notice. Apparently some allied body, an inspections commission, had discovered that Germany had surpassed its official quota of infantry personnel.

In January, 1925, Günther enrolled in the "Senior Institution for Practical Agriculture" in Landsberg to get some of the theory courses for his chosen career. He was grateful to his brother Werner for making this financially

The winning Oarsmen, Günther Sitting Second from Left.

possible.The dental practice in Cranz was doing well, and as the oldest brother in a fatherless home, Werner had always felt somewhat responsible for his younger siblings.

The school in Landsberg provided good experience, intensive study, also farm visits, practicums, and a class field trip to the German Agricultural Exhibition in Stuttgart. In addition to school, there were many recreational activities, including bicycle tours, swimming, theater and movies, dancing and pubbing. Although it was the practice among students to go from pub to pub to see who could drink the most beer, Günther seemed to know his limits and still have a good time. The best part of the school year proved to be his participation in the "Landsberger Rowing Society" where he became part of the competative team. They trained almost every evening, and took part in several regattas on the Warthe and the Oder Rivers during the summer. These outings to regattas were most enjoyable and the cost was small. The club paid for lodging, food and transportation, and the oarsmen gave their all to win for the team and the school. Competing in both the four-man and the eight-man events, Günther was involved in six victories and proudly came home with his silver cups.

In mid-December, 1925, it was time to "hit the books" seriously and Günther successfully passed both the written and oral exams at Landsberg, and could now call himself a graduate agriculturist. After a most memorable happy family Christmas in Königsberg at his mother's house, he accepted a position as Class 2 Agriculturist at Seepathen in order to get some more practical experience. At twenty-two years of age

The competitive Team Landsberger Rowing Society. Günther Pankow 2nd from right.

some doubts had begun to creep in. Had his decision to go into agriculture been the right one? He liked the life very much, but his family was not one of the land-owning gentry and had lost all its assets during the inflation. He realized that, in Germany at least, he would never be able to farm on his own, even as a renter. During his apprenticeship on large estates, he had witnessed first-hand the plight of poor farm workers, living and working under impoverished, undignified conditions, while the landlord prospered in his castle. With all this in mind, Günther penned a letter to Uncle Max, his mother's older brother, who was a prosperous business man in the United States, asking for information and advice. Would there be a future for a German agriculture student if he immigrated to America? Correspondence flowed back and forth. No decision was made at the time, but Günther applied himself even more vigorously to his English lessons.

In what he already presumed would be his last employment in Germany, Günther went to work in January, 1927, for "Domaine Langebogen," part of a large well-to-do farming operation with an excellent

Fencing, Günther Pankow, right.

reputation, near Halle. This enterprise included a sugar factory, a distillery, a potato-chip factory and a dryer, so there were many new learning experiences. It was also modern enough to have tractors and trucks, and one of his jobs was to haul pigs to the slaughterhouse in Leipzig, so he was able to observe the operation of a huge packing plant. On weekends he made a point of seeing as much of the country as possible, as though knowing he would never have the opportunity again.

He was already thinking of that piece of land in Canada which would be his very own. For Uncle Max had advised him to go to Canada rather than the U.S. Efforts at mastering English were stepped up, sometimes with help from Tante Anne who was a teacher of the language. The last family Christmas in Königsberg, everyone was very conscious of the fact that Günther would be missing from this gathering for the next few years. He had booked his passage on the ocean liner for March 17. Uncle Max, as promised, had sent money to pay for the voyage, and only two and a half months remained until departure time.

Günther Pankow 1927

There was not enough time left to start another job, so Günther volunteered at a farm machinery factory to learn a bit about tractor and other machine repairs, cycling daily from his mother's home. He also spent a good deal of time with Werner and Lena in Cranz, as he had a close, warm relationship with his brother and his sister-in-law. And it was through them, as fate would have it, that he met the most important person in his life, and as a result, also in our lives.

**Else Gesien, Günther Pankow
1928**

Before leaving for the Canadian north, where he expected to find few modern amenities, Günther thought it imperative that he should have his teeth looked after. Having a brother in dentistry proved rather convenient, and part of a week-end or two in January, 1928, were spent in the Cranz dental practice of Dr. Werner Pankow. In most circumstances this would not be an enjoyable pastime. But it seems in this case, there was a pleasant diversion.

Greeting him at the door was an attractive young blonde dental assistant. Her name was Else Gesien. He was smitten! Further visits to that office became quite frequent, and had nothing to do with his teeth. Whenever the young lady could slip away for a moment, he was waiting, and was glad to help her with the clean-up when all the patients were gone.

On the Baltic Coast

Evenings and weekends were spent walking on the frozen harbour and through beautiful snow-covered spruce forests. It soon became obvious to the two young people, that they were meant for each other. With this discovery came the rather terrifying reality that Günther would be leaving for Canada in six weeks. Many questions loomed. Could he tie the life of another person, a most loved one, to his own uncertain future? Even though he had some training for a chosen career, with good report cards, he had no money. But two people, young and in love, are optimists and are sure they can overcome all obstacles. Their engagement was not a secret for long, and the young man's family was overjoyed. But in his mind a major hurdle remained. How would he approach his future father-in-law? What would this man think of such a hasty engagement? True, the young man was the brother of Doctor Pankow where his daughter worked, but what did that really mean? He had no established trade, or at best a very uncertain one somewhere in Canada. But the step had to be taken.

On an evening in February, Günther, nervous and apprehensive, made his way to Villa Kornblume, the home of the Gesien family. He was greeted warmly. Apparently a little advance "preparation" on the part of Else and her sister Mieze had taken place. Now Mieze sat in an adjoining room and provided a little atmosphere by playing "Largo" on the piano.

Günther, hiding his trepidation, approached gardener Gesien as he sat quietly on the sofa and calmly said: "Sir, I love your daughter Else, and would like to request your permission to make her my wife. I plan to secure land of my own in Canada, to clear it for a farm, and build a home there. There are many optimistic reports about farming in Canada."

Ernst Gesien cleared his throat, then spoke slowly and thoughtfully, "I have no objections, Günther, but, you understand, I must be very sure that you have a nest for her to come to, and some income, before I can send my daughter across the ocean to join you." Then the two men shook hands, and Mother Gesien who had been listening quietly, embraced her future son-in-law. Else's young brother, Werner, grinning impishly, bounced up the cellar stairs with a bottle of old war-time champagne, and the engagement was celebrated, with visiting and talk of the future. Much later Günther made his way home with a great sense of relief, and happy at the warm welcome he had received.

Werner, Lena, Else, Günther

March 17 was approaching all too quickly for two happy people who had really just found each other. There was a frenzy of packing and preparation. On Anneliese's birthday on February 26, there was a family gathering at the Königsberg home. All family members were present except Hansi, who was attending classes in Freiburg. Günther's last Saturday in Germany was spent in Cranz, and after an emotional farewell to Lena and the Gesiens, he and Else travelled to Königsberg. The next morning, at the railroad station, his mother bade him a tearful farewell and waved at the departing train. Little did he know that he would never see her again.

The Königsberg Railroad Station was used often by the Pankow Family

In order that the betrothed could say their final farewells, Else accompanied Günther as far as Marienburg, where they spent their last day together. They did some sight-seeing, visited the fortress, listened to patriotic band music in the market square, and walked along the Weichsel River. Their pleasure was muted by the painful awareness of the impending separation. A faithful promise to write, one last embrace at the station, and the long lonely hours of pining and waiting had begun.

Werner, Lotte and Tante Anna came to Bremen for the send-off. During the last two days on German soil, the foursome enjoyed the beautiful old city of Bremen, reminisced of the past, and tried to look into the future. At the now well-known wine cellar in City Hall they drank a farewell toast, and all too soon it was time for Günther to board ship for the first leg of his big adventure. So it is time for us to meet again with the young man whom we left on deck at the beginning of our story.

Last Farewell at Marienburg

Günther and his Sister Lotte in Bremen 1928

Werner, Tante Anna, Gunther 1928

38

Chapter 5   New Land, Hard Lessons

I have learned that success is to be measured not so much by the position that one has reached in life, as by the obstacles which he has overcome while trying to succeed. .... Booker T. Washington.

Günther stood quietly on deck. When will I see these shores again he wondered. In his youthful optimism, he dreamed of coming back to marry his beloved, then bringing her back to Canada with him. These thoughts were accompanied by an exciting spirit of adventure, a great anticipation for the months that lay ahead. Plagued by seasickness for the first three days of the voyage, he enjoyed the remaining week.

Günther Boarding the Derfflinger

As he awoke at six o'clock on the morning of March 28, 1928, he saw that the ocean liner had already made its way towards the dock near the port of Halifax. Quickly he got dressed, packed together his personal belongings and hurried on deck, not wanting to miss any great "first impressions." An ice-cold wind greeted him, and snow could be seen on the embankments. But after two days of dense fog, the sun, like a beckoning light, welcomed him warmly to the shores of his new homeland.

The business details regarding customs, immigration papers, and baggage claims caused no difficulties as he stood in the line-ups of newly landed

immigrants. Hundreds of them were setting foot on Canadian soil for the first time, each bringing along his new hopes and dreams. How many of these would be fulfilled? And how many would be disappointed?

Entering Halifax Harbour

After a day or two of sightseeing in Halifax, the first step of his long Canadian journey began with a 78-hour train trip — destination Winnipeg. The long hours passed surprisingly fast and more enjoyably than anticipated. He was impressed by the roomy upholstered seats, which converted into a bed for the night. There was a general atmosphere of

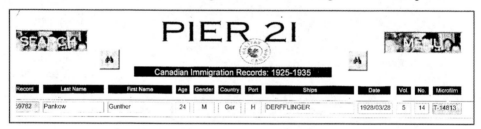

PIER 21

Canadian Immigration Records: 1925-1935

Record	Last Name	First Name	Age	Gender	Country	Port	Ships	Date	Vol.	No.	Microfilm
59782	Pankow	Gunther	24	M	Ger	H	DERFFLINGER	1928/03/28	5	14	T-14813

relaxation. No collar-and-tie dress code here — even slippers were quite acceptable — in contrast to the formality on the ocean liner. The food, too, was of a much simpler nature — cold cuts and bread (horrible soft white stuff, he called it). Nearly all the passengers on that railway car were young Germans. He had developed a friendly liaison with two fellows by the name of Wallenbrink and Nast. The three young men passed hours on the train playing cards, with lively rounds of Skat.

But much of the time his thoughts were back in Germany. As the vast Canadian panorama of forest and farmland unfolded through the train windows, he tried to envision a future here. He saw these Canadian farmsteads through eyes of eager anticipation and hope. In Canada even he could one day, God willing, farm a piece of this great land and call it his very own. This was possible! This was not out of reach! His imagination soared to new heights each time he glimpsed a happy farm family, women and children, waving from their farm home beside the tracks. His mind's eye clearly saw Else, the Cranz gardener's daughter, proudly working beside him as his farm wife, the mother of his children........But there were many obstacles to overcome before this happy reality, and the rocking motion of the train quickly brought him back to reality.

The Ontario countryside still showed evidence of a cold winter — deep snow and ice-covered streams. Snow-capped fence posts were barely visable and even telegraph wires hung close to the snow. The forests of evergreens, birch and smaller bush were beautiful in their hoar-frost covers. But miles and miles of this wintery landscape brought a twinge of uneasiness to the young immigrant. If Canada is like this, still winter in April, and all this bush, it will not be easy to "get a foot-hold" in this Utopia. But perhaps the West will be better? The doubting uneasiness did not last long. Every westbound mile of track inspired optimism, as the snow became less, revealing patches of field and pasture, and beautiful black soil! Even the sun shone warmer on this spring morning and bird-song came through the open window.

At seven in the evening the train rumbled into Winnipeg. After the necessary legal procedures, a large number of immigrants were relayed onward to the West. But Günther and his companion Nast had special letters of recommendation, so were asked to report to the immigration officials the following day. Upon arriving at the employment division of the C.N.R. they were treated with genuine courtesy and given access to long lists of "farmers looking for laborers." An English farmer near Virden, Manitoba was settled upon. The pay would be thirty to forty dollars a month, and this particular farming region had been recommended by Canadian officials, as well as a representative of Norddeutscher Lloyd Liners. Thus after a day of sight-seeing in Winnipeg, they were to set out to their first place of employment in Canada.

The train came to a stop at Virden (Population 1500) where a C.N.R. agent met them, took them to his office, and discussed placements. Manitoba farmer, Robert Burr, his wife and child came to the office and a tentative agreement was reached. Soon Günther found himself bumping over moon-lit country roads in the back seat of the Burr car. Before their fifteen-mile distant destination was reached, they had to be pulled out of a mudhole with the help of a team of horses. So these were Canadian country roads!

It was the fourth of April, 1928. Snow still covered the ground and temperatures dropped below freezing as Günther found himself on the three hundred acre farm of Robert Burr at Lenore, a farming village near Virden, Manitoba. Four children aged from eight months to eleven years, made for a lively household. On his first impression, he sensed that the house was clean and the food was excellent. He would soon find out that the work was hard and there was very little free time. For the first few days his entire body ached from the unaccustomed physical labor, and there was barely enough energy left to write letters as he fell into bed at the end of the day.

Often during the next several weeks, he silently thanked Tante Anna for her English lessons. Here in an English speaking neighbourhood of Manitoba, he heard not a word of German, and though it was often difficult, he knew it was best this way because he would be forced to learn the language.

Easter Sunday, 1928 was one he would long remember. He had made his small attic bedroom, heated by the stove below, as homey as possible. Beside the oil-painting of his beloved, stood two red candles, a farewell gift from his sister Lotte. Ludendorff postcards and Fischer-Friehenhausen poetry adorned the bare walls. As he pondered the "Gemütlichkeit" of his small private domain, he heard footsteps on the stairs. A little girl's voice sang out, "A letter for you, Pank," an announcement that would gladden his heart many times in the months to come.

He even had a few hours off on this day. He didn't have to get up until seven! The Burrs left the farm to go visiting that Easter Sunday, and the new young farm hand was left in charge. The feeding and watering was soon completed, but the dreaded milking awaited him. No position on any German Bauernhof had prepared him for this! Two days previously he had made his first attempts, but managed to milk only one animal in the time that his boss milked four. But now the boss was away and Günther hunched beneath the five hairy bovines, some with poor udders, short hard-milking teats and vicious swinging tails. Two hours later the task was finally accomplished. He trudged to the house. The milk still had to be separated and the calves fed. It was ten o'clock when he crept into his attic retreat. Who would have dreamed he would ever spend an Easter Sunday this way!

This was just a prelude to many more such days, except that he became more experienced, more adept, and thus a better hired man for his hard-driving boss. A typical day started at five-thirty when the alarm clock shattered the silence of his small bedroom. Every day eleven horses had to be fed and watered, twenty-five pigs, thirty head of cattle fed, watered and bedded, five or six cows milked by hand — all this twice a day. He pumped, then carried water in five-gallon pails (no round wooden grips, only wire handles which cut into his hands), often seventy pails a day. Every day manure had to be cleaned out of the cow barn and the horse stables. Every day all the horses had not only to be fed, but also curried, regardless of how busy the day had been. This seemed to be almost a fetish with the boss, and an early indication that here was a man who was going to get what he could out of his hired help, especially a young German greenhorn.

Between daily chores, there were a variety of tasks: hauling and grinding barley, shoeing horses, working newly-broken land. Spreading manure was done by machine, but the loading was by hand — Günther did fifteen loads in one day — alone. The hard physical work and resulting exhaustion at the end of the day was conducive to instant sleep and left little time for sadness, homesickness or brooding. He tried to remain optimistic, always keeping his final goal in mind. He wrote:

> The sun, moon and stars shine here just as they do in the homeland, and that is the one element which we both have in common every day and every night. Right now there's a thin sickle moon in the sky. Do you see it too? Nature here does not seem foreign — this could well be a piece of Germany. Spring on the Burr farm is exciting, in spite of the hard work and having to get up at five. For days now we have had beautiful warm weather. Today we plowed for the first time. What fun that was, to again hold the plow in my own hands and to turn furrow after clean, straight furrow of fragrant, mellow black soil. How I wish you were here. We could go for a walk in the lovely mild spring evening. I'm not sure you would want to walk with me. I smell of manure, my pants are filthy and I'm wearing a stained old blue jacket. My face is unshaven, and my hands would surely not pass salon standards. In Cranz my appearance would create quite a stir and I would get some disapproving looks.

Günther always kept his eyes and ears open, to learn and to plan. He decided there were some things he would, once he had his own farm, do the same as his boss, but others he would do differently. He would be the first one to get up in the morning and light the fires. They would have a vegetable garden and an ornamental garden. Music would be a part of their home, with singing and guitar playing. He often became painfully aware that he still had a great deal to learn, and felt quite inadequate in some situations. All the "school learning" in the world could not make up for "on the spot experience." He also became more and more aware that a tidy sum of money would be required to get a start on a homestead. And that would have to be earned "by the sweat of his brow." During the month of May he certainly did just that. A letter of May 6 gives a fairly graphic description:

> Spring seeding is well underway. Mr. Burr does the plowing and cultivating with five horses. I have to walk behind the harrows, and cover a lot of kilometers in a day. It's very dry and I'm always surrounded by a thick cloud of dust. Using the seed drill is more fun. I stand on a platform on the back, and from here the horses are guided, straight as a string, along the previous track. One really has to pay attention to a number of things all at once. In spite of this, I often find myself singing or whistling a happy tune. I do believe, though, that Mr. Burr is taking advantage of me just a bit too much. It seems that on the neighbouring farms, it is not the practice

to go from five in the morning until nine-thirty at night, without a break, except for twenty minutes to wolf down a meal. And he often insists that, after working all day, then feeding the horses, that I spend another half hour currying them. When he first ordered this I became very angry and almost blew my top, but common sense prevailed. What would be the use of getting into a row with him now, and perhaps being without income? And furthermore, there was still so much to learn, especially now during seeding.

But in July, after spring seeding, it became increasingly clear to Günther that he'd had enough of Robert Burr's outrageous treatment, and he decided to leave before harvest and try his luck elsewhere. When he made his intentions known to the boss, the man became very angry. Instead of the initial agreement that the wage would be between thirty and forty dollars a month, Burr would pay only one hundred dollars for four months. In a Sunday letter of July 22, Günther expresses some of his anger and disillusion:

Now you know how a greenhorn was treated in a strange land. I still feel angry, although I keep telling myself there's no use brooding over it anymore. To have or not to have fifty dollars makes quite a difference in my circumstances. And it's just the idea that I slaved so hard, was a dedicated employee, and this is the thanks I get. I've thought about seeking legal council, but I think there's no point in it. It would cost me more than it's worth. I just have to accept the fact that I paid dearly for what I learned here (teures Lehrgeld), and must put it behind me. After leaving the farm, I spent one night at the Central Hotel in Virden and felt free, free , free! A cheque for one hundred dollars was in my pocket. But Burr showed himself to be a crook and a swindler right to the end. He wanted me to sign a release, saying I had no further claims or demands against him. When I refused to do this, he tried to hand me a cheque without a signature! But I was on my guard.

On August the second, Günther wrote his love letter while sitting in a roadside ditch near Odessa, Saskatchewan, where he had arrived by train from Manitoba. He had made a stop here to look up his friend Wallenbrink at his farm of employment and the two were able to compare experiences. Travelling on to Regina, he attended the exhibition, complete with parade and a military band. The strains of a Prussian army march, and excerpts from Carmen, left him with his first real attack of homesickness. In the midst of thousands of spectators, he felt a lump in his throat and was overcome by a feeling of utter homelessness and loneliness. Then the spectacular fire-works, played against the dark sky, brought back a degree of calm and serenity. The thought of having to find new employment for harvest and winter took over. He looked forward to this with a strange sense of exhilaration. Something about the unknown, the "being entirely dependent on one's own resources" really stimulated him.

On August fourth, the train took him to Saskatoon, where he immediately visited the C.N.R. office, and was able to find harvest employment on an Alberta farm near Oyen. The train rolled into the small town of Oyen in the middle of the night, and after a nine-mile car ride, Günther found himself on the nine hundred acre farm of Nelson Evans. It was probably a very good thing that he happened to land this job, so that not all Canadian farmers would be judged by his Lenore experience. Nelson Evans was an educated man with a dry sense of humor, had a wife and five-year-old son. The home was comfortable and tastefully decorated, with radio, gramophone, electricity and running water! Meals were outstanding. He did have to share a room and bed with a young English man also employed on the farm. After a few days here, he wrote:

> Be happy with me, for the way it looks now, I have hit it very, very lucky here, and Lenore lies behind me like a bad dream. There are no cows to milk, no pigs to feed, no water pails to carry. No big deal is made of currying the horses. I arrived during haying season, and during working hours we work very hard. But it's enjoyable, the meals are better than I've ever had, and I feel like part of the family. I write my letters at the kitchen table amidst radio and conversation, so privacy is somewhat lacking. My salary is sixty dollars a month, and during the hectic harvest season it will increase from four to six dollars a day.

Günther's job in the harvesting operation was running one binder, pulled by four horses, while his boss drove the other. Five men were employed to do the stooking. After three weeks, when the cutting was completed, the men helped with the threshing on neighbouring farms, ate and slept there. Evans and the young Brit operated the threshing machine, while men with teams and five wagons hauled the bundles to the separator. Threshing was completed in three weeks. When asked if he would stay longer, Günther agreed, at two dollars a day.

There was fall field work, rock picking, and manure hauling to be done. He also participated in road-building for eight days, and helped with the painting of the barn and other outbuildings. Wheat had to be hauled to the elevator in Oyen. This could not be accomplished until the end of November because the elevators were plugged. Günther found "turkey slaughtering day" rather interesting. Nelson Evans stabbed the birds, the others plucked them — thirty-seven turkeys averaging twelve pounds each, sold for thirty cents a pound — total income of one hundred thirty three dollars. He put this day's experience in his "for future reference" file. Something else intrigued him. In a November letter from Oyen he writes:

We've had a bit of change in routine here for a few days. Listen and be amazed— a three-day baby-care course ! Every afternoon some ten to fifteen women from the surrounding community arrive by car, and listen carefully to what their leader tells them about the care of babies. This instructor, a pleasant, plumpish, elderly lady with graying hair, reminds me so much of Mother Gesien. For the duration of this course, she is staying here at Evans'. She drives around in her Ford car, giving courses in rural areas.

With winter coming on, we have much more spare time, with the corresponding one dollar a day salary. I don't mind though. Here there is no opportunity for spending, I have good food and a friendly home. I have caught up on all my correspondence. In fact, the Evans tease me about all my "writing", saying I should become a professor or a journalist! I attempted something else. I wrote an article which I entitled "Agriculture in Western Canada" for the German newspaper "Pflug und Feder," I enjoyed doing it and was pleased with the outcome; now I hope they'll print it.

On December 23, 1928, after a heartfelt farewell at the Evans house, the boss took Günther to the Oyen railway station. What a positive memory this would be — the time with this Alberta farm family, and what a contrast to the Manitoba experience.

Now Günther was on his own again, homeless, jobless, alone in a foreign country, on the day before Christmas. Near Calgary, while enjoying breakfast in the dining car, he was thrilled to get his first glimpse of the majestic Rocky Mountains, even a sun-drenched glacier. Upon his arrival in Edmonton, he checked into the Springer, a German hotel. The following day he did some necessary errands: banking, visiting the employment agency to put out some feelers, then some dental work by a pleasant Swiss-German dentist.

And Christmas Eve 1928?   It was spent all alone in a hotel room in Edmonton. Germany parcels were unpacked, letters were read again and again. Photographs, surrounded by nine red candles, were arranged on the simple hotel table. A leisurely cigar smoke attended thoughts of the homeland, and was briefly interrupted by a welcome "Frohe Weihnachten

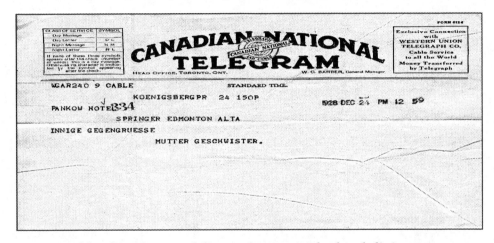

aus Deutschland" telegram delivery. Supper in the hotel dining room was ethnically true and enjoyable. Christmas Eve service in a nearby German church proved to be a big disappointment. It contributed nothing to his vulnerable, lonely mood and was totally lacking in worship. He felt cheated. After the service, he dropped in at a nearby Lutheran Home for immigrants, where, with several other young Germans, he joined in carol singing.

Within a few days, Günther moved into this Lutheran Hospice, because it would cost him only two dollars a week, whereas the hotel cost him that for one night. Some fifteen young Germans lived there. Besides looking for employment opportunities, he studied the twenty-page document outlining the rules and conditions if one were to purchase land through the Canada Colonization Association, and searched out any information he could find regarding the Peace River Country. New Year's Eve '28 was spent at a German Club, then singing folk songs back at the hospice.

Niton, Alberta 1928

On January 7th, 1929, after several visits to the employment agency Günther managed to find a winter job. The next day, which was his twenty-fifth birthday, he, together with two other young Germans, boarded the train to Niton, some one hundred sixty miles west of Edmonton. Here they found, besides the station, a post office and a small general store, and were informed that their tie camp was twenty miles away, into the bush. So the three Germans, along with four Swedes destined for the same camp, spent the first night with their bedrolls spread out on the waiting room floor. The next morning a driver with team and sleigh was hired to drive the would-be tie hackers and their baggage, to the camp. A barely discernible trail winding through beautiful evergreen forests, made

The Cook Shack

Günther Hewing Railroad Ties

for an enjoyable trip, further highlighted when the driver shot two moose along the way! What excitement and first-time experience for the young European passengers!

The camp consisted of three crudely constructed log shelters, one serving as kitchen and dining, the others for sleeping. The crude bunks, thirteen per cabin, were made somewhat more comfortable by laying a spruce-bough "mattress" under the bedroll. A large drum heater in the middle kept the "bedroom" warm. The meals were described as "first class', prepared in the primitive but clean kitchen by a portly chef. It took forty minutes to walk from the camp to the work site. Felling trees, then, axe in hand, transforming them into railroad ties, proved to be very hard work, totally new and unaccustomed. Strength, skill, agility and endurance were required. The first few days were difficult and trying. The pay was thirteen cents per tie, and $1.10 per day was deducted for room and board. At the beginning, the three young men seriously wondered if they would be able to break even, and maybe recover the cost of their tools and the rail fare to Niton. However, they told themselves, this is not wasted time. The work environment is beautiful here in this virgin Canadian wilderness, the food is excellent, and there is no opportunity to spend money. Better to work here than to sit idle in the hospice in Edmonton and spend money. They considered this time a learning experience, an interesting wilderness adventure. However, it proved to be more than that. Through practice their skills improved. Günther managed a record-breaking twenty-nine ties in one day, and his total two and one half months earnings at the camp neared forty dollars.

Knowing that an opportunity like this would not soon arise again, Günther decided to see the Rockies before heading back to Edmonton and serious

Riding the Rails

land searching. Niton was already part way there. No means of transportation out of camp was available until three days later, so he and one of his co-workers walked the twenty miles on the dark, slippery bush road to Niton, a four and a half hour ordeal. Again they slept on the waiting room floor, then caught the train to Jasper. He was over-whelmed by the grandeur, the beauty, the vastness of the Rockies, and so thankful that he had decided to take this side-trip. He described Jasper area as a true paradise of unspoiled natural beauty, the way God had created it. In order to stay here a little longer, he worked for a few days at a construction site for three dollars a day, pushing wheel - barrows of sand and rocks all day.

Against his better judgement, it seems, but tempted by the stories of adventure from other German boys, he decided to go even farther west. Riding the freights through the beautiful spring countryside, along with four others, with always the possibility of being caught, provided an indescribable sense of exhilaration and adventure. On March 29 Günther penned a long letter from Vancouver, to be shared among the relatives. He was anxious to share, as far as this was possible, some of the beauty, the powerful imagery that he had witnessed. His description of "jumping the freights" could be a story in itself. A small portion follows:

> We packed our backpacks with food, and towards evening, made our way furtively to the rear of the railroad station, where other dark forms had already congregated, apparently with similar intentions. Soon the expected freight train pulled into the station, but much to our chagrin, the cars were all sealed. Luckily there was one tank car, and we managed to clamber onto its narrow platform. I played it safe and buckled myself on with my belt. The train sped off into the clear moonlit night. We witnessed a beautiful, unforgettable show — the giant snow-capped mountains, the dark silent forests, rushing mountain streams, pitch black tunnels, steep rocky cliffs and dizzying chasms— all bathed in the silvery light of a full moon, and punctuated by the occasional loud whistle of the locomotive.

> In spite of all this splendor, we began to feel the cold on this drafty platform, and weariness began to set in. At dawn, therefore, we got off, stiff and cold, at the next station, Blue River. We soft-soled our way to the waiting room and breakfast. But "the eye of the law was watching." Soon a policeman stood before us, examined us casually, and gave us a little lecture. A friendly man, he stopped just short of wishing us a good trip to Vancouver! Our next stop was at Kamloops. We had been warned about the station guards at this station, so decided to jump off beforehand and walk into town. This plan did not succeed. Two secret-service men had observed our jump from the train, and nabbed us, triumphantly displaying their badges. We were questioned, our bags examined, and then, with a stern warning, we were allowed to go! It was like a scene from a movie! No sooner were we alone, then our crestfallen "poor fellow" expressions changed to wide grins and laughter. Singing happily, we marched into Kamloops on a warm spring evening, found accomodation at a small Japanese owned inn, and needless to say, slept very well after the day's adventures.

> The next day's freight took us for miles along the Fraser River. It was interesting to observe that a train of the competitor's company (C.P.R.) made its way along the opposite bank of the river. We were on the C.N.R. Again, the scenery was indescribably beautiful and our eyes just couldn't take in enough.

> Nearing Vancouver at six in the evening we left the freight a few stations away from the city and took the streetcar. We had arrived — Vancouver on the Pacific! I had crossed Canada from ocean to ocean. What a feeling!

The next few days were spent sight-seeing in Vancouver and gleaning a wide variety of impressions. A favourite spot was the harbour with its great number of ships from all over the world. But Capilano Canyon with its hanging bridges seemed to have made the greatest impression of all.

The return trip to Jasper was not without its anxious moments. At Kamloops he found himself with the bright glare of a station policeman's flashlight shining in his face as he was heading towards the train. Again he got off with a stern warning and a gruff "Don't ever let me see you again or I'll run you in for two weeks!" On Easter morning at five-thirty he arrived in Jasper

and was later met by hearty hellos and greetings from his friends. Saying good-bye in Jasper was not easy. He loved the beautiful mountain village, had met a number of Germans here, and made a number of friends. Eight of them were there to see him off on his way back to Edmonton. He could not know that he would see the Rocky Mountains again under quite different circumstances.

Chapter 7   The Search For Land

We can build upon foundations anywhere if they are well and firmly laid.
..... Ivy Compton-Burnett

He'd been in Canada for one year now. Mountain adventures and coastal sights still fresh in his mind, Günther, back in Edmonton, began the serious business of trying to find "his" piece of land. He spent his evenings studying information, thinking and calculating. Which was the best route to go? Whenever he thought he had a plan, doubts would begin to creep in. After all, this was the decision of a lifetime, affecting not only his own future, but that of the family he hoped to establish. "What I do right now, could determine the future of coming generations," he mused.

Real estate agents, anxious to make land sales, drove him around Edmonton and area. One day he went fifty-two miles south of Leduc with two young Germans who had purchased land there. A property for sale here really appealed to him, but he couldn't get that much-lauded Peace River Country out of his mind. He'd have to see that before he made any commitments.

The next day he took the four-o-clock train northbound. He would explore for himself this newly opened homesteading area. He had almost made up his mind that taking up a homestead was the way to go, the surest way to "get ahead." After all, there would be no cash payments to make, no interest on loans, no taxes for the first three years. Any money he had could be spent on the actual development of the land. There were disadvantages. A homestead consisted of raw land covered with bush, no house, no fence, no roads, — nothing! Also, after three years he would have to become a Canadian citizen. That did not appeal to his true German nature.

Spirit River, Alberta 1928

Upon his arrival in Spirit River, he heard more about a pioneer settlement making its beginnings some twenty miles south of the town. Several days, from dawn to dusk, were spent walking, exploring, searching. Suddenly the decision became very clear. Günther, too, would take up a homestead in this predominantly German area. (It is a strange twist of fate, that he had originally heard about this new homestead land in the Peace River Country from "a Holsteiner named Otto Delfs" whom he had met in Edmonton. It is interesting to ponder: Would we, Hans Delfs and Ursula Pankow ever have met or married, had it not been for this chance encounter of our fathers?) It seems the advantages of homesteading must have outweighed the disadvantages, for on April 30, 1929, a hastily pencil-scribbled note from Spirit River can barely hide the excited optimism: "Dear girl, I have just taken up land — 160 acres in the Peace River Country! Now we can really get working for our future. Don't be alarmed if you don't get letters for a while. I will have so little time."

Once the momentous decision to take up land was made, the Germany letters which followed were filled with great expectancy and optimism. This spirit can best be conveyed by actual excerpts:

> Taking up a homestead means getting 160 acres of free land from the government, paying only a ten dollar claim fee. It becomes my titled land, if, within three years, I clear and get under cultivation sixty acres of land and erect some buildings. My homestead is well situated. The land has four to six inches of lovely black humus top-soil, underlaid with a clay subsoil. The entire area is covered with fairly dense bush, finger and arm-thick poplars and willows. About twenty-five acres are covered with spruce. My land is crossed by a one-and-a-half to two meter wide stream with beautiful clear water. The banks of the stream are overgrown with lush grass — perfect for pasture. On the banks of this creek I am going to build our house! It's an idyllic setting, in the middle of the bush, beside a rushing stream. Besides the stream valley, the rest of my land is nice and flat.

> How I wish you could have a quick look at this, our land! Perhaps you would be frightened, since everything is still so primitive. But when I bring you home things should look different. In one and a half to two years quite a lot can be accomplished. It will require courage and a pioneer spirit to settle here. I've got lots of that, and I'm sure that my little wife will feel at home in this beautiful, unspoiled natural setting. Better here in a friendly German neighbourhood, than in a densely settled English community. With all this in mind, I can more easily accept the responsibility of having made such a huge decision, on behalf of both of us. Unless I am deceived by all the signs, there is a great future for the Peace River Country. It's true, right now the cultivated acreage is small and there are vast areas of wilderness, but the rate of settler influx is astounding.

> In Spirit River there's a young German pastor who plans to hold occasional services here. He visited us yesterday for the first time. It's no small feat for him to come out here on foot, on these "roads" into this wilderness. From Spirit River, the first six miles heading south, the roads

are fairly good, passing by established farms. But the remaining thirteen miles can only be called "wagon tracks through the bush." During the next year, a road is to be built, as well as to Woking, our twelve-mile-distant railroad station. Once that road is completed, it is likely that a small town will grow there. Can you imagine how full of joy and anticipation I am! The dream of having my own piece of land has become a reality. To make it arable will require lots of sweat and hard work, but I am doing it for us and we will be free people, without any boss telling us what to do!

In this positive frame of mind, work proceeded quickly. First of all, four men cleared a road leading to their adjoining homesteads. Then logs were cut to build one house, which was for Herman Wulf, because he had wife and children. Before starting on his own house, Günther made a trip back to Edmonton (20 hours by rail) to purchase necessary items such as tools and household goods, which they found to be much cheaper to buy in the city than in Spirit River. Among his purchases were a cookstove, tools, and some 3½ CWT of groceries, which he had to send up by freight train, calculated to arrive in Spirit River at nearly the same time as his return by passenger coach. It is interesting to note that homesteaders were allowed a special rate on their passenger fare. Instead of paying fourteen dollars for his trip to Edmonton and back he paid only seven. Smaller items he was able to claim as baggage, and included cooking pots, pails, pitchers, dishes, cutlery, lanterns, as well as mattress, blankets and pillows. He was proud of one particular bargain. He'd managed to get two spring-fitted army cots at an auction for $1.60!

The trip from Spirit River to the homestead, wagons loaded down with all the purchases, took two and a half days and was fraught with difficulty. Several times they got stuck in mudholes, had to unload so the horses could pull the wagon through, then reload. Günther had purchased a horse from a Spirit River farmer for eighty dollars, and it was with a feeling of pride that he rode his very own horse home. He was often thankful that he had this, his only mode of transportation. Nig (apparently so named because he was jet black) was, in spite of his spirited temperament, a quiet

Günther's first Horse "Nig"

docile animal. When not needed, he was tethered, and with a bell around his neck for easy spotting, fended for himself. Unfortunately, on only the second day at the homestead, he ran a twig into his eye, turning it blind.

Günther was quite taken with his first spring on the homestead, the fresh

Günther Clearing his first Land

green buds and leaves, the wild spring flowers, and surrounded by delightful birdsong. Lots of wildlife crossed his land and came to drink at the creek. He was particularly impressed with the powerful moose with its magnificent antlers. He had brought back with him from the city, two young Germans whom he hired to clear brush. The goal was to clear enough land to hire a tractor to break it, and then harvest the first crop in the fall of 1930. Clearing the land proved to be hard tedious work and took much longer than they at first thought. In addition to hewing the standing trees, there was a lot of windfall, rotting logs and roots which were not readily visible on their first rudimentary inspection. By the end of June some twenty-four acres were cleared.

House building proceeded with the help of his neighbours, Meier, Wulf and Egge. The roof and floor were delayed because the sawmill, only five miles away, was out of lumber. In describing his house, Günther writes: "It's constructed of raw logs and is six by seven meters in size. Later this will be the barn. When I bring my wife home, she should find something much better." Five men lived in this partially completed house, and one of Günther's concerns was feeding them. Preparing meals for five hard-working men, cooked on a wood-stove, with meagre rations, was no small feat. In his letters, he sometimes requested recipes (with directions, please) and menu ideas. These bachelors lived and worked together harmoniously and became friends. Two of them took up neighbouring homesteads of their own. They were amazed at the long, warm summer evenings when darkness did not come until eleven. They sat together by the house, singing folk songs, playing mouth organ, or just talking. In spite of the hard work, the unfinished house, the primitive conditions, Günther never seemed to lose his optimism, his sheer pride and joy at having his own place. He often raved about the beauty of the landscape.

This enthusiasm was not lost on the loving recipient of his letters. In July

Else wrote him a letter which left him speechless and overjoyed. Why, she wondered, could she not come over in the spring of '30, instead of waiting for Günther to get her at Christmas '30 as originally planned? They could save the cost of his ocean voyage, the cost of an elaborate wedding, and use that money more wisely on the fledgling homestead. It all made sense! But would her parents allow it? This whole thing was hardest on them. All the possibilities were considered and plans put into motion. Work proceeded with even greater incentive.

By July 20th, Hans Delfs with his tractor and breaking plow, had turned over thirty-two acres of new land. Because it was his very first field, this was an exciting event and Günther describes his feelings:

> These were strenuous and exhausting days for me that lasted from three-thirty in the morning until eleven thirty at night. I just felt I had to be there every minute! The plow tore out huge willow and spruce roots. Had I done this breaking with horses, many of these would have remained stuck in the ground, and I would have needed dynamite to blow them out. What a labor-saving machine, this tractor, and it never gets tired! It stood still only four or five hours out of twenty-four, when it was too dark. As soon as it's at all possible, I want to get one. (It is ironic and sad to note here that our father Günther never did own a tractor.) It's bad though when there's a breakdown. The nearest place to get repairs is Spirit River, and a day is lost. Three times we had trouble here, and Nig was pressed into service to take one of us to town for parts. It was a nerve-wracking time, but I couldn't get enough of watching as the big plow turned over furrow upon furrow of **my** land.

There were times when Günther worried about his young bride coming into this wilderness. Was it fair to expect this of her? He always tried to paint a very realistic picture when he wrote, so that she would not have unrealistic expectations. He felt sure that coming to a German settlement would make it considerably easier for her, and often told something about the neighbours they would have:

> My favorites of the Germans here are the Holsteiner Delfs brothers and their brother-in-law Toerper. Hans Delfs, forty, owns the tractor that worked for me. His brother Otto, thirty-five, a locksmith, is married and has two darling children. Otto Toerper, thirty-two, is newly wed. For the time being they're all living together. When I visited there on a Sunday, in their cosy log house, I felt quite at home. Also living with them are Hans Becker and Harry Schack. My nearest neighbour is Herman Wulf, his wife and four children. She bakes bread for us and does our laundry. We also get milk, butter and cheese from her.

So you can see that we have a nice German community here, neighbours living just a few miles from each other. All together, there are more than thirty German settlers in our area now. I want you to be able to imagine what your new home will be like.

A shadow was cast in this small settlement when the first death occured, one which affected Günther personally:

I have lost my Nig. Two weeks ago he drowned, together with our friend Fritz Friedrichs, as he tried to cross the flood-swollen river. It was incomprehensible folly to try to cross that rushing torrent. Horse and rider were caught, thrown over, and carried away by the current. Sellin was the only eye-witness, and brought us the bad news. We searched a long time for the bodies and found Nig three days later, five kilometers downstream. Fritz's body was found much later. These were not happy days, and we came home at night, solemn and shaken. We were fond of this man, and of Nig too, our good faithful horse.

With the future of his bride always in mind, Günther deemed it quite important that she should learn as much as possible to prepare her for life on the homestead. He suggested she should divide the time she had left in the homeland very carefully. She should learn such homemaking skills as bread baking, butter making, butchering, and sewing. Poultry raising would also be her domain. Perhaps she should work for a while in a hospital so she could deal with medical emergencies and child care! Also, she should take lessons from her gardener father so they could establish a vegetable garden and a beautiful flower garden on the homestead. All this in a matter of a few months!

Having children was very much a part of the hopes and dreams they had for their future. They prayed that they would be spared the complications and heart-break experienced by both brothers, Werner and Hansi.

Burning Brush Piles

Work continued on the new land, with more breaking, root-picking and burning. For a few days Günther had eight men to cook for, and they all slept in his little house. In the midst of all this he had an unexpected visit from a Baron von Eberstein, a student of agriculture, who was travelling through the United States and Canada on a student educational tour; a nice fellow who had been sent by Günther's former professor. He certainly got a first-hand look at the life of a beginning homesteader in Canada's west! He also got to witness the building of a particularly difficult stretch of road which eight men worked feverishly to complete before leaving to go south for the harvest.

It was while Günther too, was preparing to go threshing that the shocking news came. The sad drowning death of his friend was followed by news of a greater loss. An ocean away from his family, on his homestead in the Canadian wilderness, the young man, only twenty-five years old, held a telegram in his trembling hand: "Mother died August 12." Deeply shaken, he couldn't force himself to believe that she was gone.

> *It just won't enter my head that my Mütterlein is no longer alive, that her tender mother-hand will never again stroke my hair. But one must try to accept. For me it is a good thing that I have so much work and little time to brood.*

Now, even though he had brothers and sisters in Germany, with his mother gone, he had no real home to which he could return. The need to establish a home of his own over here became more pressing.

The first priority now was to earn some money, which had been sorely depleted by all the work on the land. He travelled to Edmonton, and before searching for a job, took in a special "Germany Day" celebration which happened to be on in the city. Quite unexpectedly he met von Eberstein again, and the two spent the day together. This time their roles were reversed, Günther was the guest, he the host. They attended all the festivities, including a banquet being held in honor of the German consul. These pleasant impressions were further heightened when news came of the Zeppelin's successful landing in Tokyo. All in all, he described these two days as a terrific experience which renewed his pride in his nationality.

Günther's Log House on the Homestead

In early September, Günther, after several attempts, was able to find employment with a threshing machine operator in Lacombe. Together with Karl Stein, one of his neighbors, he drove a team of horses, pitching bundles, moving from farm to farm. Crops in Alberta were poor that year due to drought, so wages were low — three dollars a day, whereas last year at Evans' in Oyen he had been paid four to six dollars. The meals at the farms were excellent, and he quite enjoyed this aspect, after his own cooking all summer. The Lacombe threshing job lasted until the early part of October, when Günther and Karl went back to the city, each with seventy-five dollars in his pocket.

Some of this was spent on food supplies to last the coming winter, and on the tenth of October Günther was back on the homestead. What a great feeling it was to come **home**, to his land, to his house! His friends Stein and Meier would live with him for the winter, while they worked at building their own houses on nearby quarters. There was so much to be done, now that the arrival of his bride was imminent:

> We are busy getting the house ready for winter. Tomorrow we'll finish crack-filling so that the wind can find no access. Next the cellar will be dug so that potatoes and other provisions are safe from frost. Then I'll lay the floor. Hopefully the snow and frost will stay away for a long time yet because I'd like to pick the roots and rocks off the breaking, so the work doesn't pile up so badly in the spring. What a wonderful feeling it is to work for our future. Especially the building and the finishing touches are so much fun! It's downright homey now in the evening, to sit beside the stove, the tea kettle humming, while the fall winds whistle outside.

Horst Solty, Günther Pankow, Hein Meier,
Horst Anders, Karl Stein.

Two more country men would join the threesome to live in the house that winter. Horst Solty, an East Prussian, had just recently claimed a nearby homestead and had no house yet. Also, Horst Anders, brother-in-law of Anneliese, Günther's sister, arrived from Tilsit in October. He had so much to tell Günther about family and friends "back home," and was able to bring along a number of household items. The five men took turns doing the household tasks — cooking, baking bread, washing dishes, and cleaning. Meier, Stein and Solty went each day to work on their own places, while Günther and Horst worked at home.

In December, Stein shot a moose, so for a couple of months they didn't have to worry about their meat supply. But it was a hard struggle to bring it in, lugging it out on their backs, through the dense snow-covered forest. Upon reaching the road, their burden was shifted to the backs of their horses.

The colder weather, and the slowdown of outside work, the enchanting white snowy landscape surrounding them, all helped the Christmas spirit to set in. This festive season was to be so different from the last one, when he spent it alone in an Edmonton hotel room. It's essence can best be captured by this descriptive excerpt from a December 27, 1929 letter:

Bringing Home the Moose. Günther on Horse

> On the day of Christmas Eve we five spent all day scrubbing, cleaning, cooking, baking, like real homemakers. Just before darkness came, Hans Delfs and Heinz Muehrer dropped by on their return from hunting. Stein wound up his gramophone, and as darkness fell, I lit the candles on our tree, a large beautiful spruce grown on my land. From the record player came the beautiful clear sound of bells, then "Stille Nacht, Heilige Nacht." Every one of us became solemn and still. With eyes reflected in the glow of the candle-lit tree, thoughts went out to loved ones so very far away. When Delfs and Muehrer left, we unpacked our parcels. Horst had two, I had four — from Werner, Annie, Tante Anna, and from you, my dear girl. Christmas Eve passed quickly, with conversation, reading, munching. On Christmas morning, Stein, who's turn it was to be on duty, awakened us with music, playing "O Du Fröhliche" on his gramaphone; and he had prepared a breakfast fit for a king. At dinnertime our first guest arrived. It was Willie Gottschalk. He is home alone right now because his wife is in Grande Prairie awaiting the arrival of their first child. In the afternoon the Wulf family arrived, six in all, also Fred Egge and Erich Kummitz, all German neighbours. So there were fourteen of us, and my house was like a beehive. The children, especially, were excited and enjoyed the tree and some little gifts I had given them. Just Egge stayed and had supper with us.

Naturally, as in old German tradition, we celebrated the second day of Christmas as well. Horst Solty and I visited Delfs, but found only the women at home. The men were on their way to our place! So we stayed

Standing: H. Becker, K. Stein, G. Pankow. Seated center: F. Egge, E. Kummitz, A. Sellin, H. Delfs, O. Delfs, O. Toerper. Front: H. Solty, H. Meier, H. Anders.

just a short time, and returned home to find a housefull. Fourteen men had gathered, and it turned out to be a most enjoyable "stag party." I was on kitchen duty and was I ever thankful that, on the day before, I had made a huge potato salad; so the "feeding" went quite well! We sang, made music, talked , and laughed heartily as someone would come up with a good story or joke. The "band" of Sellin on the mandolin, Kummitz on the fiddle, and Gottschalk on the flute did an excellent job of making music, and the rest of us sang lustily -- Christmas carols, folk and army songs. At times things got a bit crude and not fit for feminine ears, but that's to be expected when this many fellows get together. This was a most enjoyable evening, and it was almost one o'clock before we broke up. That was Christmas '29 -- such a nice true-German celebration that one would hardly know we were in Canada.

On January 8 Günther turned twenty-six years old. He was quite moved when the fellows, his house-mates, surprised him at breakfast with music, cake, and a garland placed around his spot at the table. This meant a lot to him, since such little touches usually come from a feminine presence. Later that day, he and Stein went off into the snowy woods to cut birch for support beams. Hardwood was very scarce in the area, but Stein had discovered a few birch trees during his hunting trips through the bush. In this way they were able to save a considerable amount of money. In February, the settlers again found a reason to have a party:

Saturday night we were all over at my neighbour Herman Wulf's to celebrate the completion of the new floor in his house. More than twenty neighbors attended, with delicious food, pleasant conversation, music, song and dance. It was four o'clock before we finally "hit the sack." It was a nice party! Oh, we know how to celebrate the German way. I know you will like it here.

Günther had no horses yet, but he did own a sleigh which he often lent out to neighbours in return for the use of their horses. In this way he was able to bring home seed oats from Spirit River, and lumber from Fredrickson's sawmill. The borrowed horses broke in the new barn, which he and Horst had built that winter. This kind of sharing was common and essential, so typical of the close-knit pioneer settlement.

Günther and Horst Anders Building the Barn

The next few weeks, a time of happy anticipation, were spent in working on the inside of the house, and the theme of several letters dealt with such things as room division, furnishings, wall finishes, window measurements, curtains — in short — interior decorating. Decisions had to be made about what Else should bring over with her. Or would it be more feasible to buy them here? How should things be packed for shipping? Instructions were sent, in some detail, about traveling, tickets, visas, baggage and freight, the hazards of young ladies traveling alone; transfers from boat to train; contacts in case of emergency. He thought of everything! Detailed planning was difficult because it all had to be done long-distance, by letter, and the mail travel time always had to be taken into consideration.

In March, 1930, just a short time before his bride was to arrive, and in the middle of feverish preparations, Günther found time to write a birthday letter to Tante Anna. This is somewhat indicative of the love, gratitude and respect that he had for this woman, and what an important place she held in his life.

In all sincerity and devotion, I send you birthday greetings and best wishes for the coming year. Stay healthy and cheerful, and enjoy life. And for us Pankow siblings, may you remain for a long time, our dear and wise Tante Anna, on whom we lean even more heavily now that our mother is gone.

Indeed, with the death of his mother, Günther shared his joys and sorrows even more with this aunt who had always been there for her brother's family. Now in the late winter of 1930, he was especially happy and optimistic as he shared his great anticipation:

Team of Grey Horses

*I'm doing well and am truly happy. I have every reason to be. Within a month, God willing, Else will be my wife. And I will be able to take her to my **own** house that I built on my **own** land! Now I can even talk about a farm yard, because the barn has been completed, also built out of logs cut on my land. It has a loft for three or four loads of hay. Right now my seed and feed oats is stored there. It's actually starting to look like a farm around here! Just two years ago I would have thought it impossible that in such a relatively short time, I would be a land owner, with house and barn. The fact that these were self-built without a builder or carpenter, gives me a great deal of satisfaction and self-confidence, and it was fun!*

Next week my horses will be moving in. On March 1st I bought two greys — a three-year-old mare and a four-year-old gelding from George Brownlee, a Bridgeview farmer. They cost two hundred and forty-five dollars with harness. That's a lot of money, but they're good horses; they're young and will pay off. They're still a bit wild and capricious and it takes calm and patience to handle them. But you know that I'm capable of both. I'll hitch them up daily to gradually get them used to the hard spring work which lies ahead.

Günther's last letter   (Number 112) could hardly contain the joyous anticipation of being united with his beloved:

God willing, this will be the last time that I have to communicate with you by letter. After this it'll be in person! You can't imagine how overjoyed and thankful I am that we have nearly reached our long-awaited goal. Hopefully all will go well in Bremen, and your wire from the "Berliner" will tell me that you are on your way towards your waiting boy. I'm glad to hear that you will have lots of well-wishers to see you off at port — Werner, Tante Anna, Mieze, and maybe Lena. They will show you a good time in Bremen on your birthday. It was just two years ago that I stood there, ready to board my ship. At that time I wasn't at all sure that you would be able to follow me so soon. But now it's a reality!

You will be spending Easter on that long five-day train ride across Canada. If you start feeling lonely and miserable, just think of the tall blonde German fellow waiting for you in Edmonton.

So Günther's days as a bachelor were numbered. Last minute jobs were completed around the homestead cabin, to make it as inviting as possible for the young woman who would set foot in it for the first time. Soon he would board the train to meet her.

Editor's Note: Here end the excerpts taken from the many letters which Günther Pankow wrote to Else Gesien during their two-year long-distance engagement in 1928 and 1929. In these missives, exchanged by two people obviously very much in love, many "terms of endearment" had to be indulged to get to the information of general interest to others! The other half of this letter exchange — that is, Else's letters to Günther, are not available.

In mid-April, 1930, Günther Pankow made his way on a slow-moving coach of the Northern Alberta Railway to Edmonton. He was on a very important mission. He was going there to welcome his bride, Else Gesien, the recipient of his many love letters.

It is time, then, to learn something about this young woman and her family. We have already met her parents briefly, as Günther visited their Cranz home to ask for their daughter's hand in marriage.

The Gesien family originates from a long line of German trades-people. Grandfather was a gardener and nursery owner, as was his father before him. Ancestry also shows such trades as tailor, blacksmith, coachman, plumber and chainmaker.

Maria (Schulz) Gesien at 93

Ernst Wilhelm Gesien was born on October 13, 1865 in Kapsitten, East Prussia, to Friedrich and Maria (Schulz) Gesien. Agathe Elise Müller was born on December 17, 1870, in Cranz, East Prussia, to Friedrich Wilhelm and Christlieb (Kecker) Müller.

On April 4, 1892, Ernst Gesien and Elise Müller, who would become our grandparents, were married in Cranz, a Baltic Sea resort. This small town was situated on what was affectionately known as "East Prussia's amber coast." Many children knew the thrill of finding a piece of "bernstein"

Cranz, Baltic Sea Resort

(amber) as they walked along the seashore and explored the dunes. Exquisite pieces of jewellery — necklaces, pins, rings — were fashioned from the amber and can be found in gift shops around the world.

Situated just a half hour drive from the city of Königsberg, Cranz was touted as the largest sea resort in East Prussia, featuring beautiful wide beaches of white sand, hiking trails on the dunes, seaside boardwalks (Ufer Promenade) and powerful breakers. The health resort was noted not only for its public swimming off the beaches, but for its baths: radium, moor, medicinal, and hot springs.

Dunes on the Baltic near Cranz

During the hot summer months, the town's population of 5100 would swell with the arrival of as many as 13,000 spa visitors. Being a tourist resort, the many guests were entertained with spa concerts, fireworks by the seaside, children's festivals, local open-air theater, lively dance evenings, arts and crafts displays and other social events. For the sports minded, there were playing fields, tennis courts, small-calibre shooting range, gymnastic courses, fishing and canoe regattas, pleasure boating, riding stables, glider pilot school — all within easily accessible distance.

The "Kurisches Haff," a long lagoon or arm of the Baltic Sea, which was separated by a 100 kilometer strip of land (Die Kurische Nehrung) contained some of the world's highest hiking dunes and areas of beautiful forest. In the winter, the "haff" froze over and thus provided many

Ice Sailing on the "Haff"

excellent opportunities for skiing, skating, and ice-sailing. Several competitive ice-sailing regattas were annual events, attracting local as well as neighbouring participants.

Fishing was a thriving cottage industry in the area, and Cranz tourists enjoyed the delicious, fat, freshly-smoked flounder, peddled by "fisher-women" at the market and from kiosks near the beach.

Hotel Königsberg and Schloss am Meer were among the hotels which accomodated the many summer visitors, and numerous smaller private "pensions" vied to make a little extra income from the tourists by renting out rooms. Soon the "Pension Villa Kornblume" owned and operated by the Gesien family, would become one of these.

Fisher Women with Flounder

It was in this bustling resort town that Ernst and Elise Gesien started with a small gardening and nursery business. The property was rural enough that they had small fields, kept a horse, wagon and sleigh. Their nursery plantings included fruit trees, berries, ornamental shrubs, annual and perennial flowers, as well as vegetables. Besides the garden, a flower shop was added, where seeds, bulbs, and potted plants were sold, in addition to

Gesien Greenhouses

fresh and dried flowers. In spring, large quantities of bedding plants were germinated in the greenhouses. During cold weather these were heated with coke briquettes and stoking had to be done two or three times a night.

All this was extremely labor intensive. Hired help was not easy to come by and retain. The business income could not justify the desired wage. One or several trainees were usually on hand, learning the business from the proprietor himself, then writing exams. Some stayed on as employees, others sought new positions elsewhere. Extra family members were pressed into service on exceptionally busy days.

Ironically, the Gesien's livelihood depended, at least in part, on the misfortunes of others. Their most brisk business occured when there were funerals in Cranz, on "Totensonntag" when people remembered their departed loved ones, and on "Volkstrauertag" which is probably the same as our Remembrance Day. On these occasions large numbers of wreaths had to be prepared, under time constraint, sometimes forcing work through the night. Ivy was used extensively and had to be wired to wreath forms. Adorning the wreaths, wide silk ribbons and banners were in vogue. Printing these was part of the florist's job. Christmas, Advent, Mother's Day and other gift-giving occasions were also busy days.

Another source of income was from kiosks set up at the market place in Königsberg, or at a local market on the tourist-laden beaches of Cranz. This, too, involved hours of picking, preparing, arranging, transporting and selling. The latter tasks usually fell to the young men, Ernst and Werner.

During the thirties there were times when the Gesiens had as many as seven business competitors in Cranz. But through years of hard work, honest and fair trade practices, as well as loyalty to customers, they grew into a successful and respected business. On November 1, 1942, they celebrated the golden anniversary of:

The Gesien family owned a large three-story house which was known as Villa Kornblume. Every summer rooms or suites were rented out to the many visitors who frequented the beautiful Baltic Sea beaches on the town's waterfront. Some renters were permanent year-round guests. This rental business was a good source of income, but also added considerably to the family's workload, to say nothing of the anger and frustrations often faced by landlords. This business too, was highly dependent on the weather for its success. Lengthy periods of cold, windy, grey

Pension & Gesien Home, Villa
Kornblume

days would cause sunbathers to move and look elsewhere. During times of depression or financial lows in the nation, people could not afford to take beach holidays, and some rooms would stand empty. During the winter months there was a constant round of cleaning, painting, wallpapering, repairing, renovating, all to make rooms ready for the summer tenants.

Each summer the family moved out of the spacious main floor quarters, which could be profitably rented out, into a convenient adjacent "Canada House," (so called because the now Canadian Pankows could live in it when they returned to visit

Gesien's Canada House

Germany). In the fall, the move would be made back to the big house. This seasonal move was made for many years, and became quite burdensome for Omama as she got older. Both businesses, with employees and renters, were hard on her, both physically and emotionally. At one point she was led to write:

> I wish we could just be alone, without constantly having strangers among us.

Ernst and Elise Gesien were the parents of nine children. Two of these, Kurt and Käthe, died at birth, leaving seven to live and grow up in Villa Kornblume, in the sea resort of Cranz. All except Else took their elementary schooling in Königsberg.

Walter, the first child, was born in 1893. He enlisted in the military during World War I and achieved the rank of lieutenant. He

Standing l to r: Lotte, Walter, Herta
Seated: Opapa Ernst, Else, Mieze, Omama Elise
Front: Ernst and Werner

was killed in action in 1918, at the age of twenty-five.

Lotte, the second child, was born in 1894. As a young adult, she spent many years working in her parents' business, being the mainstay of the

flowershop. In 1928, at the age of thirty-four, Lotte married Max Herrndorf. They struggled to make a living on a small rural acreage at Wickiau, near Cranz, growing fruit and vegetables, raising poultry, angora rabbits, and keeping a milk cow. The Herrndorfs had two children, Lieselotte (Lilo) and Hansmartin (Hansi) who spent a lot of time with their grandparents.

World War II caused incredible hardship to this family. Max died in 1947, and Lotte and her two children fled to West Germany. As a young woman, Lilo was institutionalized

Walter Gesien, killed in Action World War I

Lotte and Max Herrndorf

with mental illness. Hansi emigrated to Canada with the help of his Tante Else, and was able to start a new life. He worked for his electrician's papers in Grande Prairie, and later moved to California. Here his mother Lotte visited him, and on that same trip she came to Canada to visit her sister Else, nieces and nephew, who fell in love with the sprightly little lady. Hansmartin married Bertha Yany, and they had three daughters, Aldona, Annemarie and Charlotte. The youngest, Lottchen, died of a brain tumor at the age of eight. Tante Lotte (Gesien) Herrndorf died in Oldenburg in 1986 at age ninety-two.

Lieselotte and Hansmartin Herrndorf with their Parents

Herta, the third child, was born in Cranz in 1897. She married Fritz Steputat, a teacher, and they first lived in Königsberg, later Itzehoe. Herta had tendencies to nerve problems, high blood pressure and fainting

Herta and Fritz Steputat

Anneliese Steputat

spells; and by her own admission, was not a letter-writer. The Steputats had two children, Martin and Anneliese. Martin, sadly, was missing in action in World War II, at a very young age. Anneliese married Edwin Jost and they had two sons. After Fritz died, Herta moved to Traben-Trarbach on the Mosel, where daughter Anneliese had made her home after being widowed. Tante Herta (Gesien) Steputat died in 1979 at the age of 82.

Maria, (called Mieze) the fourth child, was born in Cranz in 1906. For most of her adult life, she was a bank employee. Being closest in age to Else, the two girls spent a lot of time together, had common interests and mutual friends. She wrote most faithfully to her Canadian sister. Mieze never married, but had a circle of friends with whom she played bridge and rummy, attended the theater, went skiing, sleighriding and hiking. She played the piano, sang in a choir, was a member of the Gymnastics Club and the Fire Brigade. Because of her bank experience she was often elected to the position of treasurer for various organizations. She frequently suffered from bad headaches, anemia and nervous stomach. She enjoyed spending time with her nieces and nephews and often lamented the fact that she couldn't do that with those in Canada. She made

Martin Steputat
Died 1943

Maria (Mieze) Gesien

up for it as best she could by sending gifts. Mieze suffered cruelly after the war and died of malnutrition in Cranz on April 9th, 1947.

Else was the fifth child, born April 5, 1908. She was to become our mother, and her life will be covered in greater detail.

Ernst Gesien

Ernst, a boy after four girls in a row, was born in Cranz in the year 1910. He graduated from high school in 1929 and went on to take teacher training. Ernst liked skiing and motorboat outings. He played violin and took part in drama and sang in musical productions. In the summer he worked at a photo studio and became quite adept at photography and film development. In the thirties he and Werner got involved with the "Deutschnationalen," (German Nationals) party which mocked and

Else Gesien

ridiculed Hitler. This caused him some difficulty in getting a job after he had secured his teacher certification in 1933. He loved children, and was

Peter, Grandmother Schaak, Ernst, Barbara, Rolf, Kate Gesien

able, in Cranz, to pick up short-term and substitute work, also supervision of a library, and tutoring some of the renters at Villa Kornblume. But his first real teaching position came in 1936 at Korschen. In October 1937 Ernst married Kate Schaak, also a teacher. They had four children: Barbara, Ernst, Rolf and Peter. Ernst joined the military in World War II and was killed in action in 1945. His widow Käte and his daughter Barbara make their home together in Breese,

Werner Gesien

Werner, the youngest of the Gesiens, was born April 21, 1914. It was his lot to follow in his father's footsteps and he had planned to take over the family business. He worked very hard at all facets – greenhouse maintenance care and heating, in the garden, in the flower-shop, buying and deliveries, at the Kiosk markets in Königsberg and on the

Werner Gesien, 16

beaches. These long days of hard work were sometimes done under frustrating conditions. As a young man, he wanted to expand, to institute newer more up-to-date methods, to take more chances, take bank loans. But his father, of the old school, and still needing to feel "in charge," often "put the brakes on." This, and also the constant lack of money, caused frequent clashes, with Omama as the "go-between." Werner was a trainee under his father, also went twice a week to vocational school for parts of the year, so studying for exams added to his workload. He had to earn his "Gartenmeister" if he ever wished to have trainees work under him.

In the little spare time that he had, Werner enjoyed puttering with his aquarium, also had some garden patches of his own. He was a member of the church choir and the gymnastics club. His real passion was for the "Young Glider-Pilot Club," where he became a keen competitor, attending meets in the surrounding area. He also joined the "Jung Stahlhelm," (Cadets) taking an active part in their meetings, practices and exercises. At times, young Prince Friedrich Wilhelm, a student in Königsberg, practiced with Werner's

Ida, Werner, Marliess Gesien

group. Of course, Omama Gesien sometimes had to scold because his mind was on all these other things instead of on his work. In 1935, Werner entered into his one-year compulsory military service, with the motorized division of the army information service. He enjoyed this hiatus from the gruelling

Werner, Mieze, Else, Lotte, Ernst with parents Elise and Ernst Gesien

schedule at the big nursery, but he returned home at the end of his stint, with plans for expansion and renewal.

But the war changed everything. Werner was drafted into the military and came home from the battlefield a survivor. He married Ida Hortian who had a daughter Marliess. Their toddler-aged son, Lutz Werner died of starvation in 1947 in the aftermath of the Russian invasion. Werner never really overcame the terrible trauma of the war and its resulting chaos. The Cranz nursery which was to become his, lay in ruins. He and Ida live in their apartment in Augsburg, where, for years they enjoyed their little "Schräber Garten" and summerhouse.

Because of the war, Omama and Opapa Gesien were never granted the opportunity to enjoy their "golden years" when life could have been easier for them. Nor could their fondest wish come true, that of seeing their five Canadian grandchildren.

Else Gesien 1928

With a family this large, and two businesses on the premises, there was always a lot of activity. The town, too, being a resort, was often teeming with holiday visitors. What a great adjustment it must have been for the young woman from this background in Germany, to come to a log cabin in the Canadian North! Yet, in February 1928, a young man, though with some trepidation, had asked her to do just that.

Else Gertrud, the fifth child of Ernst and Elise Gesien, was born on April 5th, 1908 and grew up in Villa Kornblume. Instead of travelling daily by train to school in Königsberg as her siblings had done, Else took all her elementary education in Cranz, at the private school of Charlotte Ewald. The reason for this is not clear, unless it was the fact that Else was, already as a young girl, very handy and capable at helping her mother in the large household and rental property, as well as in the flowershop; this way she was available for more hours a day. This working at home became a way of life until she was nineteen years of age.

Long walking tours on the beaches and dunes, in the company of siblings and her friends, was a favourite pastime. They would search for amber, sing and play the guitar, and go bathing in the sea. Gymnastics fests often included a large bonfire on the beaches, with singing, playing and folk dancing around it. In the winter months skiing, tobogganning and ice-sailing took over. Else was a member of the Gymnastics Club and would attend meets and special events in this capacity. She and her sister Mieze were part of a close group of girls who did many things together. At the age of nineteen, Else found the courage to tell her parents that she needed some life experiences other than those she found at the family business. They understood, though they missed her quick agile hands. She took a job as dental assistant at the practice of Doctor Werner Pankow. One week-end in January, 1928, the doctor's younger brother Günther came to have some work done on his teeth. And the rest, as the saying goes, is history!

Else Gesien (2nd from left, front) at Gymnastics Fest. Mieze 2nd from right (x)

During the next few weeks, the plans for Else's future took a sudden and drastic turn. She became engaged; her fiancé sailed off to Canada to prepare a nest; and two long years of waiting and longing, of preparing and letter-writing had begun.

Understandably, the thought of having their young daughter go across the ocean to the Canadian wilderness was very difficult for her parents. They wanted to be very certain that this was the right decision for her. Although it was already known to both families, Günther was most anxious that the engagement should be made known by public announcement, as was traditional. His letters from Canada frequently urged that this step be taken. Ernst and Elise Gesien's reply to one of these letters indicates a certain wariness:

> *Now, dear Günther, as to your ardent wish regarding the engagement announcement. To us, you are a dear, upright, good person and we trust that, if you remain healthy, and the good Lord gives you his blessing, you will succeed. And should God really have brought you two together, we parents do not want to stand in your way. Rather, we would give you our dear child, even though it has to be so very, very far away. We truly hope that Else will find, in you, a pillar and support for life, and that she will be a faithful life's companion for you. But now comes the hard part, which depresses us, and is the main reason for our long hesitation in answering. As you know, and as we already told you when you asked for Else's hand in marriage — We have no money! Else would require a dowry and ship's passage. For Lotte's recent marriage, we took a bank loan and have to pay high interest. The business doesn't bring in enough to pay it off. If we could, with God's help, secure a loan for Else, too, perhaps we could manage. So, dear Günther, consider all this in quiet deliberation, and be*

Engagement Announcement Designed by Anna Pankow

certain before you take the big step. There is still time. "Act in haste, repent at leisure." In these hard times, finances play such a large part, even when "Heart finds Heart." We are especially concerned because of our experience with our son-in-law Fritz. To this day, this has not been satisfactorily resolved, and is a constant source of hard feelings. But if you are satisfied with what we can offer you at this time, then do as your heart dictates. You can be sure that God's blessing, and ours, will be with you.

There was concern as to how Else should divide her remaining time in Germany to the best advantage, in preparing herself to become a housewife on a Canadian homestead. Here academia and the theoretical, as personified by the Pankow family, versus vocational and the practical, as personified by the Gesien family, becomes quite evident. Günther, Tante Anna, and Werner Pankow felt strongly that Else should enrol in the highly rated Rendsburg School of Agriculture for women, even sending her the school's prospectus and curriculum guide. Tante Anna offered to assist financially. This plan was not well-received by the Gesiens, and was made quite plain in a letter to Günther:

> *We could not, nor did we wish to fulfill your desire to send Else to Rendsburg. Firstly, because of the cost involved, and secondly, it would all be theoretical learning like in the schools everywhere. We would prefer to see her go to a small country estate where she could learn the dairy and poultry business, hands on. After that she could learn some sewing and cooking on her own.*

For several weeks after finishing at the dental practice, Else worked for her father at the flowershop because they were having difficulty finding hired help. But in the spring of 1929 she began work at the Head Forestry Station

Else's Farewell Party at the Gesien Home

at Wilhelmsbruck, her first time away from home for any length of time. It was a strenuous job with long hours, but also interesting and educational. Each day she was up at five a.m. and was responsible for the cooking, serving, cleaning and the laundry for the large household of thirteen. The large poultry operation on the premises raised chickens, ducks, geese and turkeys. Spring, with the hundreds of downy babies, was the busiest season.

After gaining experience and knowledge at this farming operation, Else switched jobs and spent several months working at a hospital in Königsberg. This experience served her well, later on the homestead, when she was often the one to be called in case of sickness or accident, but especially when childbirth was imminent.

Soon it was time for serious preparations for the big ocean voyage. The Gesiens had provided a dowry consisting of clothing, linens and household

Else Gesien in Bremen

Ready to Board Ship

Omama Elise Gesien

effects, as well as paying for her ship's passage. The days were filled with sewing, wrapping, packing and crating, and many decisions had to be made — what to take and what to leave behind.

A farewell party, doubling as a "Polterabend" (shivaree) was held at Villa Kornblume in early April, attended by a large crowd of well wishers, family and friends. It was a bit unusual in that the groom was not in attendance (they sent him a letter with many signatures) and the wedding did not take place the following day. It was a combined birthday party and send-off for the bride, for on April fifth, 1930, on her twenty-second birthday, Else began her long adventure.

Just two years earlier her fiancé, Günther, had taken this same trip to Bremen. Now, Werner Pankow and his wife Lena, as well as Else's sister Mieze, waved their good-byes from that same harbour, as Else boarded the "Berlin" and sailed off to meet her beloved. What an unknown but exciting future lay before her!

Once Else was settled in Canada, the only way of communicating with family and friends in the homeland was by letter, many letters.

Elise Gesien (Omama's) letters seem to indicate that she was a religious person, often quoting from scripture and leaving everything in "God's guiding hand." When her letters are read all at once, they sound like a litany of complaints — her ulcerated foot not healing for years, the problems with renters, the laziness of employees, the financial straits and the decaying moral codes in society, come up with great regularity. On the other hand, just when one gets a picture of a negative, complaining and joyless person, one reads of her great love, concern and compassion for her children and grandchildren. The possibility of accident or sickness, the childbirths in far off Canada were very scary for her. One of her greatest sorrows was never getting to know her Canadian grandchildren.

The changing and deteriorating mores of society and youth (seventy years ago!) upset her. As she keeps Else up to date on the "news" from Cranz she writes:

> *Eva Radke has a baby girl. Her parents are still very angry. This sin is especially prevalent now — six young single girls pregnant this summer. It's very sad. Today's youth!!*

Omama would have a difficult time accepting some of the changes that have taken place in our society today.

Ernst Gesien (Opapa) was it seems, a quiet man, obstinate at times and set in his ways. Like many of his generation, he was often slow to see the advantages of change and progress. This sometimes resulted in discord

Opapa Ernst Gesien

when his son Werner, the planned successor, tried to introduce newer methods and business practices into the nursery. Opapa too, was prone to worry — about taxes, debts, customers — and was easily discouraged and grouchy. But he also had a good sense of humour and enjoyed a little drink of cognac with friends and visitors. In his sixties he occasionally got dizzy spells, that were supposedly caused by arteriosclerosis, and often suffered from rheumatism. Later, inflammation of the veins sometimes forced him to take to his bed with great reluctance and impatience. At the age of seventy-two he suffered a slight stroke but recovered.

Opapa Gesien's work and career had much in common with that of his son-in-law Günther. In his work as the owner and operator of a nursery, he too was dependent on the weather, the soil and the resulting plant growth. It was seasonal and relied on the labour of his own hands. Therefore Opapa was deeply and personally interested in the Canadian homestead, not only because his beloved child made her home there. He often begged to hear more, but of course Günther had so little time for letter writing. Opapa didn't do much better himself, usually having just an "addendum"on Omama's or Mieze's letters. He shows his dry sense of humour as he makes excuses:

> Dear Günther, forgive me for not writing sooner, but the ink is frozen and I lost my pen! Now it's started thawing, and spring will soon be here.

He tried to make it easier for Günther to write, by asking direct questions:

> Do you have rabbits, martens, polecats and foxes? What about sparrows, swallows, crows, eagles? What do you do for firewood? Have you a large stockpile? What is the soil like? How do you feed your horses? Won't the mice destroy your unthreshed oats?On your last picture I see your Tante Meier (biffy). Isn't it rather far away from the house, especially when there's deep snow?

> May God give you strength in your work, now on your own land. How will it all turn out, especially how much will it cost, all this land preparation — the clearing, breaking and root removal? It will take a long time to get several acres under cultivation. If it weren't so far, I'd come and help you with my white and grey!! (horses.) If you have a little time, write me a few words and answer these questions.

Opapa occasionally sent seeds and bulbs, and was helpful with gardening advice — what and when to plant, cultural methods, followed by detailed instructions on how to build a hot-bed and greenhouse. It is quite evident that he would dearly have loved to come over and pitch right in.

The war brought an end to letters and parcels from Cranz. Omama and Opapa's fondest dream, that of seeing their Canadian grandchildren, would never come true.

Ostsee- u. Moorbad CRANZ Ostpreußen Bernsteinküste

Haff und Düne

Chapter 9   A Simple Wedding

Somewhere between Woking and Edmonton, the swaying railroad car made its way past miles and miles of bush and muskeg. The tall broad-shouldered young man found himself restlessly pacing up and down its aisles. He should have been very tired, nearly exhausted. For the last week of long days had been spent putting many finishing touches on his log cabin. This first home in Canada had to be made as inviting as possible for the coming of its first feminine occupant. It is understandable that this impending event was constantly on his mind, and though physically spent, Günther was much too keyed up to sleep.

He tried to put himself in her place. What a lot of impressions my little bride will have to absorb, he thought. First the trip from her home in Cranz to the seaport at Bremen; days and nights aboard ship on the long ocean voyage; the tedious train ride across Canada.   Then the wedding, under such unusual circumstances, and the new challenges and duties of a housewife on a Canadian homestead. What must she be thinking, as she, too, sat on a train, hers coming from Halifax to Edmonton?

It was a proud feeling, Günther wrote to Tante Anna, that he as a man, would have the privilege of guiding, helping and protecting this young woman who had been willing to put her life and future into his hands. He knew that, in this foreign country, he would have to take the place of parents, siblings and friends, and her home. That was a tall order, but Günther felt confident. Had he not faced and overcome many difficulties and challenges since he arrived in Canada two years ago? He had grown, not only in manly physical stature, but also in experience, competency, patience and confidence. In this positive frame of mind, he watched the lights of Edmonton come into view.

The next day, on the evening of April 24,1930, Günther stood expectantly at trackside, his heart pounding. As the train slid into the station, he spied his beloved! The long months of longing and waiting came to an end in one long loving embrace. The so often dreamed-of reunion had become a reality!

By previous arrangement, a German acquaintance, Erwin Deimling had come to the station with his car. This man had an insurance business in Edmonton, and had been a helpful facilitator to many German immigrants upon their arrival in the city. Now he took the two happy young people to his spacious home and introduced them to his wife. Else was tucked into a cozy bedroom for some much-needed rest, and Günther tried, without too much success, to get a little sleep on a make-shift sofa in an adjoining room. Only later, over a late breakfast, could they fully believe that they truly were here in Canada together!

That afternoon the Deimlings took them to the Department of Vital Statistics to get a marriage license. Later that same day, April 25, 1930, they stood before Pastor K.W. Freitag in a German Lutheran Church in Strathcona. He solemnly declared: "I pronounce you, Günther John Pankow, and you, Else

Certificate of Marriage

Gertrud Gesien, man and wife." His words echoed in the large empty church, for the only others present were Erwin and Margarethe Deimling, who served as witnesses. It was a strange wedding, in this respect, but these circumstances were unavoidable. They were strangers in Edmonton and thousands of miles separated them from their families. But they had each other, and at this point that was all that mattered. For a few days they were guests of the Deimlings, who took them shopping at Eatons and showed them the city.

Soon they were aboard the northbound train which carried them in the direction of the Peace River Country and home. To Else, it must have seemed like an interminable distance, with nothing but miles and miles of bush. She would have had good reason to ask herself: "Where is Günther taking me?"

Finally, the train pulled to a stop in Spirit River.This address she had so often written on her letters. For the first time in many days, Else saw a familiar face, for there, greeting them warmly at the station, was Horst Anders. He had come with a team and wagon to pick them up. Soon, settled among boxes, trunks, crates and suitcases, the threesome began the wagon trip — the last leg of Else's long journey. The first several miles went quite smoothly (though that may be an exaggeration) but as they neared the notorious mud-hole near McArthur's, they could see that more horses had come to meet them. Fred Egge and Herman Wulf hitched on their animals for extra horse-power to drag the heavily loaded wagons through the quagmire. Again, Else must have wondered! But with the many new impressions, the excitement and wonder, her own fatigue was forgotten.

Finally, in late afternoon, as the last rays of sunshine peeked through the trees, Günther pointed to the south: "There it is — our home, our land!" And Else gazed in wonder at the log cabin nestled in the trees. It is hard to imagine the gamut of feelings that must have overwhelmed her as the tired steaming horses stopped at the cabin door. The entrance had been decked with a frame of evergreen boughs, topped with a large hand-printed placard which read "Herzlich Villkommen" (Hearty Welcome). Some twenty neighbours had gathered, including the three women resident in the area at the time, and each one of them gave the young bride a warm welcome. She experienced the true hospitality of a German pioneer settlement, as they visited, made music and sang folk songs, and enjoyed cake and coffee. The young couple could not have imagined a warmer or more delightful reception deep in the Canadian wilderness.

Many hours later they waved good-bye to their neighbours as the wagons rumbled away on the bush trails. The lovely scent of wood smoke filled the air. The fire crackled as a dim soft glow emanated from the coal-oil lamp. At length there was just the dark, and the warmth and the quiet, with the music of the wind in the treetops.

The Welcoming Party
Standing l. to r: Horst Anders, Elise Delfs, Freda Wulf, Eilert Pleis, Margarethe Oltmanns,__?__Otto Toerper, Johann Oltmanns, Fred Egge, Alfred Sellin, Hans Becker, Herman Wulf, Carl Heinz Muehrer, Hans Delfs. Front : Four Wulf Children, and seated: Else and Günther Pankow.

This Marriage Announcement Appeared in a Königsberger Paper

Chapter 10   Homestead Honeymoon

Ten years from this momentous spring of Else's arrival, Günther was to write in his journal: "What a wonderful once-in-a-lifetime period it is when two young people who are in love begin their journey through life together. They are filled with ideals and dreams, and are not yet aware of the many difficulties, hardships and disappointments that life has in store for them. How different the whole world looks when you're newly wed, and how your whole outlook on life changes! It is no longer "I" but "we", and it affects everything we do."

Newly wed Else and Günther Pankow 1930

Indeed, that spring of 1930 was a wonderful idyllic time. The beginning of a new life together coincided with nature's spring awakening. The stream near the house babbled in its ice-freed bed. The swollen buds on the trees soon burst into fresh green leaves. Birdsong could be heard from every direction and new green grass poked through the brown earth. The sun's rays got warmer each day. Beautiful unspoiled nature was awakening all around the rustic log house.

Inside, too, a transformation had taken place, one that only a woman's touch could accomplish. The many boxes and trunks which had accompanied the young bride from Germany, were now unpacked. Curtains had appeared at the windows, bedspreads covered the bed, cloth draped the tables, and pictures hung on the walls. A simple log house had become a cozy, comfortable home, and for the young Pankows, it was a home blossoming with love.

But the reality also had to be faced, that spring was the season of hard work. The gardener's daughter, full of optimism, struggled to make a small piece of raw bushland into a friable garden. Günther was getting his own piece of land ready for its very first seeding. He worked together with his neighbour, Fred Egge, so that horses and machinery could be shared. The German neighbours in the settlement helped each other a lot in those early days, with field work, erecting buildings, as well as road and bridge construction.

When the seeding of field and garden was completed, there was fencing, clearing and breaking new land, and the many tasks inherent in making a homestead into a farm. Especially during that first year, the work did not seem burdensome, but was tackled with so much enthusiasm, such optimism and pride in working on their very own land. There was truly a "Joie de vivre." It seems that only after years of setbacks, misfortunes and disappointments, did this joy and optimism begin to falter.

1930, this "honeymoon" year can best be understood by taking excerpts from a letter which Else wrote to Germany in August:

> *The time just races by. When you receive this letter, I'll have already been married for four months, and away from home for five. We don't even realize it, with all our working and striving. Can you imagine, Anni, that I am really happy!*
>
> *What fun it is to milk Lilly, and to make golden yellow butter out of the rich cream. We bought a little four-liter butter churn for five dollars, and every two or three days I churn two or more pounds. Once in a while the bachelors come and get some. The Swede, (Ernie Gabrielson) is a steady customer.*
>
> *The baby chicks are doing well, but the hawk got seven of them. That's something we have to put up with when we're surrounded by bush.*

Even though our first year isn't turning out as we had hoped, we are by no means disheartened or depressed. One simply hopes for next year. (Ed. How long have farmers been doing this?) *It's the same for everyone, not just for us. We have to take into consideration that the soil is still raw and virgin, and its tilth will improve. The weather was bad, with too much rain in June, then drought later on. The garden suffered in the same way as the fields. Every beginning is hard, and the first years are learning years. However, we're always in good spirits and enjoy good times, by ourselves or together with neighbours.*

Milking Lilly

Fred Egge lives about a half mile from us, and right now he has five bachelors living there, just like Günther had last winter. They're a jolly bunch, and often one or the other comes to visit us. Then we make an exception and take a coffee break, or they join us for supper. Each week I bake six loaves of bread for these men.

Yesterday we took another nice horseback ride. We'd like to do this more often, but don't always get away, because on Sundays we usually have company. We're glad though, that people visit us and feel at home here. The first Sunday of every month a picnic is held in the river flats. People from near and far, not just Germans, get together. We had planned to drop in there later, but wanted to do a little exploring first.

On the way, we stopped in at Egge's bachelor haven. They promptly brewed us a cup of coffee, which we enjoyed with the cake I had brought along, all seated on wobbly benches of plank and wood blocks. Tafelmusik was provided by the jolly Saxon, Brünning, on his violin. I was rather out-numbered — one woman among eight men!

We were soon back in the saddle and rode in the direction of the (Burnt) river, through thick bush and wind-fall, down steep inclines. We so enjoyed exploring in this scenic valley, that we decided to forget about going to the picnic. This was completely new territory to both of us. We had a close call when Günther's horse, Ella, in the lead, suddenly sank up to her belly into a quicksand-like bog. I, riding behind on Toni, carefully turned back, just in time. After a desperate struggle, the frightened animal was able to get her feet back on solid ground. (Ed. This is most likely the same spot where our black horse got stuck many years later.)

After this rather unnerving experience, we turned back, on an old worn path which led to a long-abandoned trapper shack. Then we crossed the river on a trail that had, at one time, been used by ranchers in the Burnt River valley as they drove their cattle to Grande Prairie before the railroad was built. We continued our ride, uphill and down along this beautiful wooded valley, and finally ended up at Witte's where we were refreshed with cake and coffee.

On the way home, we met the young Wittes, Lieselotte and Georg who were returning from the picnic. They told us that in two weeks there will be a dance at Bulhofner's house (German Canadians) with everyone welcome. Maybe we'll ride over, although there will probably be many English people, and I can't converse with them.

Again, it was a nice Sunday, and we're glad that our "adventure" was not more serious. Today Günther is helping Sellin with hay-making, in return for hay. That's nice for us because we have no river flats, and Lilly could use the feed.

Else and Günther Pankow 1930

Recently Horst Solty shot a young moose. It's wonderful meat. Since it doesn't keep long, it was shared all around, so everyone would have some. We got a shoulder, which I divided up and made into aspic, a nice roast, and twelve pints canned.

In our barn we have a pair of chipmunks. The little critters are comical to watch, as with their characteristic squeak, they dart away at lightning speed. Prinz goes wild, barking for hours, chasing after them, in vain, of course.

In the evening we often see nighthawks and swallows. During rainy weather we've seen gulls. Woodpeckers find nourishment in dead trees, and their hammering sometimes gets quite loud. There are lots of prairie chickens, and soon we'll be able to shoot some young ones for dinner. We often meet them when we go riding. They suddenly fly up out of the grass and spook the horses.

The mosquitoes are not quite as bad now. In June and July they were unbearable. We do have a screen door and I nailed screens on two windows, so on hot days we can open them to get a through-draft without suffering afterwards.

You would love the wildflowers here, growing everywhere among the grass. There are hedge roses, goatsbeard, larkspur, fireweed, wild sunflowers, lilies, asters and goldenrod. It looks very pretty. Vetch grows everywhere and is excellent cattle feed. I have picked wild strawberries for a delicious dessert with cream, but they're very slow picking. Then there's a very tasty red berry that looks something like a blackberry, and creeps along the ground. Unfortunately, they are very scarce. (Ed. This is probably the dewberry.) I've seen blueberry, gooseberry, raspberry, and currant bushes too, but they've yielded no berries, at least not this year. For the first few years we'll have very little fresh fruit, but hopefully that will change.

And Günther's letter to Tante Anna that same year, though looking more at economic viability and financial realities, indicates that happiness, harmony and optimism reigned in the little log house.

Our life is simply splendid! Else has adjusted so nicely and naturally that it is a real pleasure. Our home is remarkably cozy and comfortable. What changes can be wrought by a woman's touch! As much as we are enjoying our house, outside things have not looked so promising. For four weeks this month, we have, with few exceptions, had rain every day. The result is that, in the garden, the vegetable seeds and potatoes rotted, and in many parts of the field, the oats did likewise. I could not even seed some parts. Where the grain did come up, it is not progressing because of the cold and too much moisture. Unless the weather changes, we cannot count on it ripening in time. Well, there is nothing we can do about it. Taking chances goes with farming. We'll get by.

Just to be safe, I wrote to Hellmut (brother-in-law and executor of Mother Else Pankow's estate) and asked for an advance of $350 from my part of the inheritance (minus interest for Hansi.) Furthermore, I hope, in July, to find several weeks of work in road construction, and then with some log-hauling in winter, to earn some cash. I'm not going to get grey hair over it yet. The bad thing is, as in agriculture everywhere, the turn-over is so

Time to Sharpen the Axe

slow. For example, money invested now in clearing and breaking cannot yield any returns until next fall.

The agricultural scene does not look rosy, and there is a lot of uncertainty in the world grain market. In spite of all that, we two farm people here in Northmark are happy and feel fortunate to be free, and working on our own piece of land. Our farmstead now consists of house, barn, outhouse, yard and garden, all situated in a lovely natural setting. On two sides of us there are greening fields, on one side there's bush, and on the fourth side the murmuring stream flows in its deep wooded ravine. To the north we have a nice view of a range of hills that reminds me so much of the Tautobergen, even though it's not as high. There is such lovely peace and silence here. The only sounds to be heard are the creek, the twittering of the birds, the peeping of our thirty chicks, and an occasional nicker from the peacefully grazing horses nearby. Hopefully we'll also soon hear the lowing of a milk cow.

The summer days are very long. It is still light at eleven o'clock, and it's easy to work too late, then suffer from lack of sleep. We really enjoy this freedom. We can divide our time and our life as we wish.

In the midst of all this optimism and hopefulness, some hints of hard reality began to appear. Their first crop proved to be a disappointment, much smaller than hoped for, because of adverse weather. As much as possible was salvaged for feed. But Günther was forced, with his team and hayrack, to join a threshing crew near Spirit River, in order to earn some money. For the first time, Else was left alone on the homestead for several weeks. It was not an easy time for either one. During rainy periods, when threshing was not possible, Günther, along with four German neighbours, would sometimes ride home. This was not a pleasure for horse or rider, travelling some twenty-five miles in the rain. Other times, when it didn't seem worthwhile to ride home, the seven-man crew languished in a damp, drafty tent, waiting for the weather to clear. But at the end of the threshing season, Günther was glad to return to wife and home with eighty dollars in his pocket. (Five dollars a day with team and rack.)

As winter set in, the young couple enjoyed their warm, cozy little home, as this snippet from Günther's letter to Tante Anna shows:

> We have been sitting all day, writing Christmas letters, in our cozy living room, and we have the real Christmas spirit already. There's a beautiful snowy winter landscape outside, and in here there's an advent wreath hanging from the ceiling, and we're nibbling on gingerbread.
>
> Tomorrow morning I have to get up at 3:30 to feed the horses, because I'm leaving for Spirit River at 5:30. Travelling is so much better with the sleigh than with the big rumbling wagon. And I continue to enjoy my two greys — faithful and quiet animals, but still with plenty of spirit. They're very fast and mighty strong. They've never left me stuck.
>
> Yesterday conditions were perfect for sleighing, so I hitched up my team and went to pick up our neighbours, Johann Oltmanns, his wife Margaret, her brother Eilert Pleis, and two young children. (Ed. Probably Hans and Helga Delfs whose mother was in Spirit River for the birth of her third child, Klaus.) We like these friends, and celebrated first advent together. In the evening we drove them back home because they have no horses yet. Else was delighted with the speedy moonlight ride.
>
> On Christmas Eve there was a get-together at Wulf's house. The pastor, in his car, had already arrived at our place in the morning and had dinner with us. Then he spent a little time going over his sermon, until we went over to Wulf's together. It was a pleasant afternoon, with some twenty-five Germans in attendance, and we sang all the beautiful old Christmas carols. A collection had been taken before hand, so the children each received small bags of treats.

We went home at 6:30 and enjoyed a quiet intimate Christmas Eve. None of the parcels had arrived in time, but we had a lot of letters, which we read by the light of our candle-lit tree. We sang, too, nibbled on goodies, and drank home-made raspberry juice. Our thoughts were with all of you in Germany. If there was a touch of home-sickness, no one knew. The next two days we had visitors who came in the afternoon and stayed until late into the night. With singing and visiting, a little schnapps, we had such an enjoyable time that you might have thought we were back in Germany. Several days after Christmas, the parcels came and amid excited unwrapping, we had a little celebration all over again. We were overwhelmed by all your generosity and love. The joy is always tinged with a bit of sadness, because we always wonder: How can we ever reciprocate?

The rest of that winter, there was enough to live on, and enough feed for two horses and a cow, so Günther stayed home. Probably never again would this relatively care-free time of two-someness, of communion with unspoiled nature, of true neighbourly and community spirit, be as prevalent as during that "homestead honeymoon" year.

Chapter 11   A Decade of Babies

"A baby is God's opinion that the world should go on." .... Carl Sandburg.

The homestead honeymoon for two was soon to be shared, for within the next ten years, Günther and Else became the parents of five children. The little log house would nearly burst at the seams and the already heavy workload would increase. Making ends meet, never mind developing and expanding the farm, was very very difficult during that depression era.

In November 1930, Omama Gesien wrote a letter to her daughter, which was similar to several others she would write in the future:

> *My dear child, did we understand this right? Your wish list includes material for diapers. Could it be, or is it for the young neighbour lady? We presume it's for you. What a surprise! We had hoped that this nice carefree and happy time of two-someness would be granted to you a little longer. But that's the way it is. It was the same with me. A true German mother is glad and waits in happy anticipation. Why didn't you tell us right away and we could have included some things in our parcel. Be sensible and careful when lifting and carrying. Don't stretch or bend over quickly. Always remember, you are carrying a God-given life, so put yourself completely in His care.*

The first child was on the way. The pregnancy went without problems. In case the doctor ever had to be fetched, a used buggy had been purchased at an auction sale and was over-hauled during the winter. It stood in readiness. But since this was the first baby, it was deemed wiser to go to Spirit River ahead of time, and have the baby delivered there. In mid May, Günther drove his expecting wife to town, where

Else and Günther Pankow with Baby Dieter

she was able to stay with the George Pring family. They spoke not a word of German, but were friendly, empathetic people. Günther headed back home to pressing spring work. Else found the next five days of waiting very long in a home where she could not communicate. She did a lot of walking, until she became quite familiar with every street in the small village. Then on Pentecost Sunday, things began to happen. In retrospect, on June 3rd, Else described the details in a letter to Tante Anna:

> *Since this will likely be my last day at Pring's in Spirit River, and I won't have this much time again, I want to write you a short note. I just can't wait to get home to our cozy little house. Never before have I been this homesick. It's so nice that our little Dietrich Fritz arrived on Sunday when his father was here with us. After a restless Saturday night, I was able to say with certainty that the time had come. Dr. Reavely and the mid-wife were summoned, and within eight hours, which is not bad for a first birth, our son had arrived. I think he'll look like his father–he's so long. Oh, Tante, you can't imagine **how** happy and deeply moved Günther is over this little mortal, and even more so because it is a **son** and heir.*

To share the joy, a telegram was immediately sent to Germany. At times like this the family was sorely missed. Under the care of Mrs. Pring, Else convalesced, while Günther went home to work. Ten days later he walked the twenty-one miles to Spirit River, as he had decided to hire a car to bring mother and baby home. Though still a strenuous trip, it was easier and faster than a buggy ride would have been. That homecoming to her humble log home, surrounded by burgeoning green trees and soft, warm spring air, a new baby in her arms, was one of the happiest days of the young mother's life. And the young father glowed with pride and gratitude.

Dietrich Fritz Pankow 1931

With the separation of thousands of miles, joyous occasions, as well as sad, had to be shared by letter — a rather poor substitute for a hug and a kiss or a heart-felt handshake. The time-lapse of the postal delivery didn't help. But, when Omama Gesien received the telegram on May 24th, she sat down the very next day and wrote:

To the happy parents: We send you our hearty congratulations and blessings on the birth of your son and heir! Praise and thanks be to God! May He keep your child healthy, bless him in body and spirit so that he may thrive for your and all our pleasure.

You, dear new mother, look after yourself. Don't lift anything heavy, and lie down when you feel tired. Now there's more work for a mother, but how gladly one does it all! I hope it will be a quiet, contented child. Do raise him by the newest method — nothing to eat during the night, even if, at the beginning, you have to let him cry. He will get used to it right from the start. Will you be able to breast-feed? Always wash your breast before and after feeding, and strengthen the nipples with rum-soaked cloths. Lotte can write you about her method.

Last Friday I worried about you all day, and we were so thankful and overjoyed to find the telegram in the mailbox. Doctor (Werner Pankow) is going to put a birth announcement in the paper.

Uncle Werner Pankow did indeed, put the good news in the paper. He was so happy for his brother, and so proud that an heir to the Pankow name had arrived. Mixed with this elation was sadness and heavy-heartedness, at the many failures to achieve this in his own marriage. Indeed, Lena, a few months later, was pregnant again, and house-bound with orders for complete bed rest. Hope had crept into their hearts once more, only to be shattered. Lena Pankow died in childbirth June 24,1932.

Meanwhile, on the Canadian homestead, a second child was on the way. On September 26, a dry autumn day in 1932, Ursula Anna was born, at home in the log cabin. Preparatory plans had been made, so that when the time came, a relay system of riders on fast horses made it possible to get to Spirit River in three hours. In this way Doctor Reavely was notified and was able, due to the dryness of the season, to drive his car all the way to the homestead. Labor pains had started at five in the morning and the doctor was there by nine. But this baby gave her mother a hard time and was not born until five o'clock in the afternoon.

Four days later, Else wrote to Tante Anna:

> *On the 26th of September we became the parents of little Urselchen. I think she wanted to play a trick on her mother who still had a lot of work planned when she arrived ten days early. But she is healthy and alert, weighs six pounds and sleeps all the time. We're so happy that the boy has a little sister; he loves babies. I'm so glad that I stayed home for the birth this time. Now we only have the doctor bill of fifteen dollars, and that will have to wait too. These are such difficult times. There is so much to do that Günther can't stay inside with us. Tante Lisi (Mrs. Egge,) our neighbour, has been a big help. Dieter, at one and a half, still has to be watched constantly, and is not toilet trained yet.*

Omama Gesien responded to the second Canadian grandchild:

> *My sincere congratulations! Dear parents, I'm sure you are enjoying your little daughter, but at the same time, there will be more worries and expenses. It's not so good that she came so soon after Dieterchen, but that happens. I hope it won't be the same with you as with us — so many children cause a host of small worries, and later big worries. Now you'll have so much work and stress. May God grant both of you good health and strength. Maybe you'll just have the two. It's nice that it was a little sister. May she thrive and become her mother's helper.*

Ursula Anna Pankow 1932

97

It was while Günther delighted in the birth of his second child, that he wrote a letter to his older brother, Werner. That man was suffering in sadness after his wife Lena's death in childbirth in June. That Günther was a very compassionate, caring human being is shown clearly again in these excerpts:

> For you poor lonely man, the joy of having a new little niece will have been tempered with sadness as you think of your dear Lena, and how your high hopes of having your own little "sunshine" were repeatedly shattered. But I know that in spite of that, you will share our happiness at the arrival of our little girl.

> I wrote to the Gesiens, in more detail, about how it all went, so I won't repeat it all here, as you'll get to read that letter. You know, it again became very clear to me, how much Lena must have suffered each time, physically but even more, emotionally. What a woman and mother must endure! First the burden of the long pregnancy, and then the great pain of giving birth. I witnessed it for the second time now, and this time not as onlooker only. I had various tasks to do for the doctor, even had to administer chloroform.

> When it was all over and Else awoke from a long, healthy, refreshing sleep, all the discomforts of the last nine months, and the pain of the birth itself, were forgotten. Little Urselchen lay peacefully sleeping in her carriage. But when this reward for all the hard hours is not there, when it is all for naught, when the mother has no little one to hold in her arms, as was so often the case with Lena, then the mind and the spirit must be grievously wounded.

On May 10, 1936, Gerta Helene, the third child was born at the Egge house, neighbouring the Pankow homestead. Else had moved to her friend's home for her maternity stay because her own house was in disarray during the process of a major renovation, that of interior plastering. Günther was renting the Menckens land right across from Egge's so was working close at hand. He was later to record the details of Gerta's birth in his journal:

> I was working at Mencken's during the week before May 10 and had made arrangements with Mother that she hoist a white flag at our house if she needed me. I would be able to see this with field glasses from Egge's barn. I climbed up that barn roof several times a day! However, when the time came it was at night and I was home. Quickly I hitched one horse to the buggy, tied two harnessed horses behind, and headed for Egge's. Again, arrangements had been made, to use the relay system on the way to Spirit River, but this time, because of the wet springtime road conditions, the doctor had to be brought out by team and democrat. While Egge had started off to town, Menckens, with the buggy, raced over to pick up Leni

Witte. She, a nurse, was there within an hour, and just in time. Gerta was in a hurry and Mother was not in labor for long. When the doctor arrived at seven in the morning, it was all over and he did not have to stay long. With a fresh team of horses, we took him back to Spirit River at a more leisurely pace.

After ten days I brought Mother home, and when she had regained her strength, the plastering in our house was completed, and later the painting as well. How mother managed all this in her condition and still kept up her spirits is almost unbelievable. However, our house now was cozy --- warm in winter, cool in summer, and above all, free of bed bugs! In it live

Gerta Helene Pankow (1936)
With her Mother, Ursula and Dieter

two very happy parents with three children. Dieter and Ursel are proud of their little sister and old enough to play with her."

Omama Gesien responds to another grandchild:

Yesterday we received news of the birth of your little Gerta. What a surprise! I had just remarked to Mrs. Kublum how nice it was that all my children have one girl and one boy. But it's good this way too. You, dear mother, need lots of helpers. We share your happiness, and wish God's blessing on the child. Each child brings more work and worry, but the heavenly Father will continue to help, and will give you all that you need. For the parents, we wish you good health, strength, patience and lots of love. The little ones will be overjoyed with the baby. Urselchen will have a real live doll to play with.

Two years later, on June 19, 1938, Heidrun Maria, the fourth Pankow child was born. She was welcomed as a strong healthy baby, with only a momentary disappointment that it wasn't a boy. She, too, was born in Egge's house, as the whole family had moved there for the summer. Egges were away for a visit to Germany and Günther had rented their land. Dr.

Reavely, who was close to eighty years old now, was brought out by Ewald Jacobs, the store-keeper. His car could make it to within four miles, where he was met by team and democrat. Before the doctor arrived, Hermi Delfs had come to be with the waiting mother. It was a long difficult labor but there were no complications. Next day the three other children, who had been staying at Solty's, came home to see their new little sister. During the mother's confinement Günther looked after house and family. Good neighbours Martha Janssen and Ursula Solty, having no small children of their own, came often to lend a hand. And the reaction from Germany came in a letter from the Gesien home:

We parents send our congratulations and best wishes on the birth of your little Heidrun. With God's help, may she thrive in body and spirit. Dieterchen, I feel sorry for you, that you didn't get a little brother, but sisters are nice too.

Gerta's Baptism
Elise Pankow (standing), Hedy Schack with Barbara, Elise Egge holding Gerta, Leni Witte, Children in front: Dieter, Ursula, Jochen Witte

Tante Mieze adds her greetings and congratulations and wonders:

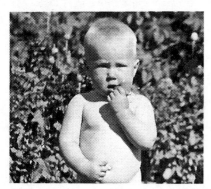

Heidrun Maria Pankow 1938

How did you ever come up with these names? Are they old Germanic?

Uncle Ernst and Tante Käthe write:

Congratulations! We drink a toast to the Canadians, especially to little Heidrun. By the way, it's a pretty name.

Whatever relatives may have thought of the name, it was Heidrun on paper only, and the little one was henceforth called Heidi.

On May 15, 1940, the world was already at war, but peace still reigned in the backwoods of Northmark when Irmgard Lotte arrived at the Pankow log cabin. Doctor Reavely, pioneer doctor who had helped so many in the homesteading country around Spirit River, had died. No replacement had been found. An experienced nurse had promised to come if she was summoned, but when Ewald Jacob's car drove in, it was without the nurse. She was tied up with other cases.

What to do? Panic was not the answer, though the pregnant mother was already in advanced labor. Tante Lisi (Egge) was totally rattled (as was her wont). But Günther remained calm and cool (as was his wont) and managed everything well. Actually, he had been witness to and assisted with the births of the other four children, so was not totally uninitiated. All the while, the brave patient herself gave running instructions, and little Irmgard arrived safely. Some time later, the nurse did arrive and gave her approval that all was well.

Irmgard Lotte Pankow 1940 (Held by Sister Ursula)

Since spring seeding had been completed, Günther looked after his wife, the four other children, and the household. Proudly he bathed and changed the tiny infant, cradling her gently in his large work-worn farmer hands. He enjoyed this period of domesticity and the happy harmonious family togetherness. Its like was not soon to come again. Brushing, breaking and myriad other homestead tasks were always waiting.

Certainly the families in Germany would have reacted and sent their congratulations on the birth of Irmgard, their fifth Canadian grandchild. But unfortunately no letters from that time period were available, so no excerpts could be translated here. This inability to communicate with the family in Germany was just one of the many hardships brought about by the war.

1940
Family Photo to Send to Father in Camp.
Taken during a Visit at the Otto Delfs Home.
Shown back: Ursula and Dieter.
Front: Heidi, Mother with Irma, Gerta and Prinz.

Chapter 12   The Depression Years

There is no medicine like hope, no incentive so great, and no tonic so powerful as the expectation of something better tomorrow. ... O. S. Marden.

It seemed that nothing could mar or blemish the love and harmony that reigned that first year in the little log house.   In its idyllic setting, surrounded by unspoiled nature, it seemed far removed from the hard economic realities of the outside world.

The settlers in this remote community were still filled with hope and optimism engendered by the past twenty years of growth and progress in Western Canada. Each had come with an opportunity to start a new life, with an iron determination to build a new home with the raw materials at hand. Each had 160 acres of free land which was to form the basis for his family's future.

Alas, this optimistic spirit was short lived. When the depression struck in late 1929, its effect was felt by all. It was characterized by a devastating drop in commodity prices and a rapid drop in consumer demand. This led to a depressingly high number of unemployed. There no longer prevailed any "upward mobility." People were forced to stay on their farms and homesteads, for lack of opportunity elsewhere, and live off the land on spare, sometimes harsh subsistence levels.[2]

The new Burnt River settlers, including the young Pankows, just struggling to get established, found this a time of hardship and discouragement. Some abandoned their homesteads in despair. Men tried to find jobs on farms in the surrounding more established areas, or in sawmills. If they were successful, they were forced to accept very low wages. All that the homesteaders could hope to do during the depression was to maintain a status quo, thankful to keep their families fed and sheltered. Günther and Else Pankow, too, found themselves in this position. The years that followed the "homestead honeymoon" were much more difficult.

But at this point they were by no means discouraged or without hope. In a letter of September 12, 1930, Father writes to Tante Anna, giving her an inventory of his pioneer operation, to console her, and perhaps to reassure himself:

Don't think that we are hanging our heads – you know us better than that. To reassure you, I'll give you a little overview of our situation, which I think will interest you. Our inventory includes one wagon, one sleigh, and a disc. My neighbour, Fred Egge the son of a veterinarian from Mecklenburg, has a seed drill, binder and plow. This way we help each other out with the machinery and won't have to make any immediate purchases. During seeding and harvest, we share horses as well. I have two horses and he intends to buy two in spring when he returns from Germany, hopefully with a wife. Besides my two very good horses, we have two productive milk cows. To make good use of the skim milk, we have three pigs, two for butchering and one for breeding; also twenty-three chickens that will, hopefully, lay lots of eggs this winter.

We have our warm comfortable house, a good barn with a large loft, a garden and 52 acres of land under cultivation. So you see, dear Tante, that although I have put considerable money into this, there is something positive to show for it – and all this within one and a half years, built and achieved by my own two hands. Again and again, particularly this gives me so much satisfaction. I have no intention of letting our first year's crop failure get me down. We have enough to live on and you need not worry. Our cost of living has become less since we got the cows, and since a woman has been managing the household.

They were indeed proud of their progress, and made the best of what they had. The house and barn were built of logs with dovetailed corners, and the house had cedar shingles. The inside walls were lined with varnished lumber. This provided an attractive background for the few pictures they had brought along. In the summer of 1931 a verandah was built on to the south side of the house, so that one would not "fall in with the door," as Father put it. Not as much dirt would be tracked in, and the snow would not drift right in front of the door.

There was very little real furniture, except the odd piece skillfully constructed by Horst Anders. The steamer trunks and packing crates brought over on the sea voyage, now served as storage units. Apple boxes were used in a variety of ways — as cupboards, drawers, end and night tables or stools, and were dressed up with bright paint or gingham curtains. (Apples used to come in large family size wooden boxes.) The spring-fitted army cots which had been purchased at an auction sale served as their first couch and extra bed. The kitchen, most important to the housewife, was described by Mother:

The stove in the kitchen is not large, but burns well, even though it's old. At the top of the back wall there is a warming oven which is very practical. To bake, I just need to pull up a lever and the firebox heats the oven. It gives off a cozy heat as well, and we often eat in the kitchen. Blue and white checkered linoleum covers the table in the dining corner. (I remember later, that for warmth and coziness, Mother fashioned a wall hanging for the area behind the table. It was made of brown cotton material, the top edged in a multi-coloured border made of scraps in a patch-work pattern. The little ones especially, loved it and would run their hands along the border as they climbed on chairs around the table.)

The floors were made of planed one by six boards, at first lye-scrubbed white, later painted or varnished. After washing them, a final rinse of skim milk mixed with water was applied to produce a shine.

Dieter, Ursula and Father Bringing in Firewood

A box for firewood stood beside the stove, as in every pioneer kitchen, and a large pile of wood would be found in the yard. Perhaps at the beginning of winter this would be in the form of long tree lengths that had been limbed and hauled out of the bush with sleigh and horses. Later there would be a large pile of blocks, because the neighbours had come for a wood-sawing bee. Splitting these blocks into smaller pieces for use in heater and cookstove was an ever-present chore.

So many times Father's letters told of crop failures — due to too much or too little rain, late springs, newness and lack of tilth in field and garden soil, and most often, early killing frosts. It makes me wonder how they could possibly, following year after year of this, have the will, the perseverance and optimism to continue. Perhaps it was the "next year" syndrome, so commonly held by farmers to this day. And occasionally it happened. Then the letter sounded so optimistic!

Day before yesterday I cut my wheat with the binder, so now, through the kitchen window I see a field of stooks. Tomorrow I'll cut the rye, then the oats. On the whole, we expect an average crop, certainly a lot better than last year. This time at least we'll have enough for feed and seed, and hopefully the burden of having to buy grain will end.

We're very satisfied with the garden too. Especially the newly broken piece in the creek flat, with its sandy humus, turned out very well. The garden by the house is much better too, as the soil develops better tilth. Since early summer we've had radishes, lettuce, and all kinds of vegetables. But we'll have no beans. An early frost got them. By covering, we saved the cucumbers, tomatoes and pumpkins. As a result, we had cucumber salad for dinner today!

In the too-short summer season, it was always a struggle, and very long hours of hard work were necessary to make progress.

We didn't finish seeding until the middle of June. The last field was for green-feed and then the land breaking began.My neighbour Egge (who had just returned from

**Father and Egge Breaking Land.
Dieter Learning How**

Germany with his wife) and I bought a big breaking plow in partnership. We hitched our teams up together, so with eight horses,we broke land until early August. We not only broke land, but also broke a lot of harnesses! Now we have it down to a system, and next year things will go better. It was slow going. July was hot, so for the sake of the horses, we worked from three in the morning until ten in the morning, and then again from five in the afternoon until ten-thirty in the evening, to avoid the greatest heat. We lost a lot of time with the frequent harnessing and then unharnessing, and searching for the horses, who, between work times, had to be allowed to feed in the pasture. I'm sure that neither man nor horse gained a pound this summer.

Fencing, a time consuming job, had to be worked in somewhere as well. In 1930 some eighty acres of land, mostly creek banks, were fenced in for pasture. And there was no break. All too quickly harvest time had arrived.

At threshing time I went to work for the same farmer as last year, near Spirit River, to earn some cash. And hopefully in the winter there'll be relief road work available. The government has to do something to give the many poor homesteaders an opportunity to work and earn their bread. The outlook here is not good. Grain and cattle prices are so ridiculously low that we can't even cover expenses. For example, last year I got seventeen dollars for a 200-pound pig and this year I have to be satisfied with seventeen dollars for three of them. But when we have to buy something, especially machinery repairs, the prices have not gone down. I wonder how long this can last. But these conditions prevail all over the world, probably worst of all in Germany. I got out just in time to come here. To make a beginning here now would be almost impossible.

In spite of these depressing conditions, the young Pankows were not depressed. In spite of all the hard work and seemingly little reward, they continued to be optimistic:

> *Here we live so peacefully secluded. Admittedly, our work, which often does not allow early quitting time, often no Sundays, can be exhausting and overwhelming. But we are content. And this year we can see some results from all our work. Above all, we are doing this for us and for the first young Pankow heir. Our little boy is thriving because his mother still has milk for him. He smiles now and nods his head. We are so happy and thankful for this precious little sunshine. Dieter was baptized the last Sunday in July during a church service at Wulf's house.*

(It is comforting to know that at least this part of Father's dreams and ambitions, that of working for his son, became a reality. His hard work, his foresight and perseverance, did indeed ensure an easier and better life for his son and future generations.)   Ed.

The son and heir, understandably, brought great happiness and pride, especially because he was the first-born. I'm sure all we other children were as dearly loved, but the newness, the primal position of the first child can, it seems, never quite be replicated. Furthermore, the depression was worsening, and with each child the time became ever more scarce, the detailed letters became fewer. Therefore, excerpts such as those that follow will not often be found again. In January 1933 Father wrote to Tante Anna:

Mother and Dieter

> *This year we couldn't set the beautifully carved figures of your gift creche under the Christmas tree. Dieter would have claimed each piece as*

undisputedly his own, and would have been anything but gentle in handling them. But what happiness that little rascal brings us! From week to week we can see his progress, and always he's discovering something new. He can't talk yet, but understands nearly everything. Upon request, he without hesitation, points to his own or his parents' body parts, or he brings his father whatever he asks – slippers, socks, shoes, cap and mittens. And you should hear him laugh! Especially when the cat and dog tear playfully around the house, then he holds his stomach in laughter. But he can be cranky and stubborn often enough too. His little sister is progressing splendidly too. She's a little round ball, laughs and flirts happily. I'm afraid that her father will spoil this sweet little lady! As soon as the weather is half-ways decent we want to take pictures so that little Urselchen can finally introduce herself to all of you in Germany.

These were the many precious moments in their home, that kept away feelings of hopelessness and depression when the dirty thirties were conducive to just that. Again Father shares his lot as he writes to his beloved Tante Anna, in whom he finds a true confidante:

It's nice to have wife and children all in good health in our happy home. In spite of the bad times, we've always had enough to eat. We really have to tighten our belts, we live in a foreign country far from home and loved ones, but in spite of all this we are not dissatisfied. But during these difficult times, without family, without the work and striving on our very own land, life here would hardly be worth living. Family happiness is an inexhaustible source of health and strength; my good wife and the children never fail me. This winter especially has been the worst one for me since I came to Canada.

Urselchen is a sweet little fat noodle, calm and quiet, always in the mood for laughing and playing. I'm afraid she will become her father's spoiled child. Already in the six months of her life she has robbed me of several valuable work hours. I just can't get away from this little girl, always giving in to a few more minutes of playtime. Who does she look like? Her figure is her mother's, her ears are mine, her face is yours.

And Dieter? — a real boy who discovers something new every

**Dieter Asserting his Authority
Over the Pig**

108

day, is cheeky and wants his own way, so that more than once he's had a spank on the popo. But he's very cute, sometimes a real clown, so that we have to burst out laughing. He runs around quick as a weasel, and feels that he is the master over not only the cat and dog, but also horse, sow and cow. He scolds loudly when they don't get out of his way, or when they curiously sniff at him. He has no fear and always wants to go outside. Whenever possible, I do take him along on short sleigh rides.

He can hardly talk at all, but seems to understand everything. Sometimes we're baffled. For example, when I casually mention to Else that I'm going to feed the pigs, he immediately gets the pig pail and wants to come along. If only spring would come so that he could be outside more, and he wouldn't whine so much.

The winter of '33 was one of the most difficult because of feed shortage, brought about by a very poor crop and an exceptionally cold and early winter.

In order to get together enough feed this winter I traveled roughly a thousand kilometers, one step at a time with my sleigh, hayrack and two horses, sometimes in snow storms and temperatures as low as –45 Fahrenheit. The night before one of these trips we would go to bed early, because at three in the morning I'd have to feed the horses. The first night would be spent on some farm in La Glace, and the following night, if I was lucky, I'd arrive back home with my load of straw. I certainly didn't get fat, and my poor horses are thinner than ever before. There were a total of fifteen trips, at thirty to forty miles each, taking two days, sometimes three. At times it took real careful driving. On the "road" there is only one packed track, with three feet of loose snow on either side. Even more

The Pioneer Log Church on Site of the Present Cemetery

109

difficulties arose when a strong wind had drifted in the track. If we got even six inches off the beaten track, an upset was the likely result. Meeting another loaded sleigh became quite tricky, but we helped each other, and I managed to upset my load only three times!

At least I gained something "culturally speaking" on these long hauls. How? You ask. When it wasn't too extremely cold, I took along reading material, finishing a book on nearly every trip. So the time passed more quickly, and when I got back to our comfortable little house, Mother and I would "review and discuss." She had read many of the same books, often while she was nursing the babies. So we got in some reading while we worked, the only time we had. I'm so glad that we were able to do this. That's all we have for intellectual stimulation.

It was also in this winter of '32 – '33 that the settlers got together and built the little Lutheran log church on the river bank. Now services no longer had to be conducted in the homes. Father helped during the log hauling and building bees. Mother was part of the organizing committee, along with Fred Egge, Harry Schack, Mrs. Querengesser (the pastor's wife) for a Christmas program in 1935.

In spite of cold temperatures and occasional drifting snow, winter was the season of preference for traveling, especially freighting. Grain, straw, hay, livestock, lumber and firewood were all much easier and faster to move with a smooth running sleigh over snow-covered, frozen hard ground, as opposed to the big rumbling wagon over rough roads and sometimes near impassable mud holes. It was easier for horses and passengers too. Occasionally, in winters of little snow, the steep hills on the poor ungraded roads became very icy, and the horses, though well shod, struggled to keep their footing.

In 1933 it was with mixed emotions that Father applied for his citizenship papers:

I must apply for my citizenship as this is a requirement before I can secure title to my homestead. There are mixed feelings connected with this but certainly I am fair-minded enough to acknowledge gratefully, that Canada has given me my very own piece of land. So becoming a loyal Canadian citizen is a price I am willing to pay. Last week two other Germans and I appeared before the high court in Grande Prairie. The whole procedure took less than half an hour, the judge presiding in his robes, the policemen (RCMP) in their smart scarlet dress uniforms standing guard. Now the papers will go to Ottawa for final approval and Canada will have three new citizens.

Pring's Sawmill 1934

The financial situation in 1934 was not good. Crops had been poor and job opportunities were few and far between. So, when offered a job at a sawmill some fifteen kilometers from home, Father decided to take it. On January ninth the big move took place. The whole family, necessary household goods, two cows and two horses all went to Pring's sawmill. Uncle Horst Anders stayed to look after the remaining livestock at home. Mother could earn money here too, by cooking for the boss at seventy-five cents a day, and they were able to sell fresh milk. Father had a logging contract, so his horses were earning too. Altogether they could average three dollars a day. That sounded really good, but the catch was — these dollars were not in cash but in wood! They were paid in lumber. This was not readily marketable but it did make a good barter medium. In this way Father hoped to acquire some of the machinery still needed on his homestead.

At Pring's Sawmill: Men Left to R. Otto Delfs, Gunther Pankow,
Hans Delfs, Hans Becker, Charlie Muehrer, Georg Witte, Horst Solty.
Front – Else Pankow holding Dieter, Leni Witte holding Ursula

111

In some ways they enjoyed that winter at the mill. In a large bunk house they had a roomy kitchen and a bedroom. Above them lived a number of hardy lumberjacks. Beside them the boss, George Pring, had his room and office. The youngsters, Dieter and Ursula, often stood by the window and watched the busy operation of the mill close by, and being the only children there, were quite spoiled by all. It was nice too, that several Germans worked here. Six bachelors lived in one bunkhouse, and new residents were the young newly-wed Wittes. Leni had just come from Germany in December and was a good friend and neighbour for mother. The mill workers visited from door to door, played Skat and enjoyed German gramaphone music. But ten o'clock was curfew hour — this was camp law, and for good reason. Mother had to have the boss's breakfast ready at six-thirty and work started at seven.

It was not an easy life. For six days they worked from dawn to dusk, then on Sunday they'd take a load of lumber home and bring back feed for horses and cows. They realized even more the value of having a home of their own, and waited anxiously to get back to it in April. They also realized the value of good health, as for the first time in fourteen years, Father was seriously ill and bedridden for two weeks with a throat infection. That

Hauling Home the Lumber

winter was not like the cozy family life they had become accustomed to, but the family could stay together and a reasonable income was realized. During those depression times, many had to put up with less than ideal circumstances.

After putting aside lumber that would be needed for building projects on his own place, Father thought he would have enough left to deal on a used

The Pankow Homestead Buildings in 1934

binder. New, these machines cost an unaffordable three hundred dollars. Bartering was quite difficult for him. Whereas some reveled in this dealing, it was not part of his nature. But how else was he to acquire the machinery which was still needed? The building plans at home had suffered a setback in time due to the mill work, but had gained in lumber. By July '34 Father was able to report that there now were five buildings on the farmstead — house, barn, combination workshop/granary, smokehouse and toilet! Mother enjoyed the new verandah on the south side of the house and made the most of it. Pansies and nasturtiums bloomed profusely in her planter boxes and brightly enameled tin pails. Trailing hops had begun to surround this attractive little retreat. Some progress was also made on the picket fence around the garden to protect it from the scratching hens.

In those difficult early years, another task that had to be worked into the busy schedule was road building. During the first year of settlement all the young homesteaders got together on Saturdays to build or improve roads — voluntarily, without pay. Gradually, as the population increased, the government took over road building, and the locals were hired at a fair wage, completing some miles every year. First, the stretch from Chinook Valley towards Spirit River, including the steel bridge over the Burnt, was completed (graded), then from Northmark corner to the store, and eventually west to the end of settlement. This included a good crossing through the creek at the Hans Delfs farmstead, south of the location of the present church, which had always been a trouble spot.

Father took a road building job in the fall of '33, which took him to the very west end of the settlement on the north side of the river. He rode six miles to work, leaving in the dark, then cut brush and grubbed stumps for ten hours before riding home, again in the dark. It was a very strenuous job, but he did not have to move away from home and was given the opportunity to earn some much- needed cash.

When the road on the north side was completed, the settlers on the south side of the river started pressuring for a road on their side. More than once, Father rode around seeking signatures on a petition of request. This finally brought results when a government bridge crew with pile drivers was brought in. Wooden bridges were built to span the creeks at Dale's, Pleis', Oltmanns' and Egge's, the local men doing all the earth-moving with their horses. Teams of four were hitched to a large fresno (a large shovel) with which innumerable cubic meters of heavy clay were moved from high to low spots and to bridge approaches. All this was finally finished in 1938. Now the settlers on the south side had a direct access road to Woking. No longer did they have to cross the Burnt River twice as they detoured via Northmark Store when hauling grain to the elevator. By today's standards the roads were still terrible. The grading had provided ditches for better drainage. It was possible to travel by car in dry weather, and even in wet conditions, the mud holes were not quite as bad. Winter travel was still

Mother and Dieter on the "Bridge" over the Creek

preferred. When temperatures dropped far below zero drivers sometimes walked behind their horse-drawn grain boxes in order to keep from freezing. Lighter sleighs, called cutters were used for passenger travel and some people had built on an enclosed box with a heater inside.

Families were concerned not only with their own, but also with the welfare of others. On December 1, 1933, while doing his Christmas mail, Father writes:

I am home alone with the children this afternoon because Else went to our neighbour Dick Moll's house. She wanted to clean and tidy the house up a bit so it would be nicer for Mrs. Moll when she comes home from Spirit River with her new baby. Dick has been batching, and Egges, who have none of their own, kept the two older Moll children.

Our two little darlings are doing fine. While I'm writing, Dieter is sitting on my knee and following my every move most intently. He says quite a few words now, although only we can understand some of them. The rascal is quite smart! As Else was leaving, I mentioned to her that I was going to write letters. Promptly he came with the bottle of ink "Here Papa." He can tell all our horses, cows and calves apart, even when they are inter-mingling outside. And Urselchen? She is taking her first careful steps without hanging on, all the while grinning from ear to ear. She's plump and chubby and always has a good appetite. That's not always the case with Dieter and he's quite thin. But all four of us are happy and healthy.

Dieter and Ursula by the Flower Beds

In July of that same year, after telling Tante Anna something of his pride and enjoyment in the growing numbers of livestock in his operation, he continues:

But my greatest happiness is in my family. With his sister, Dieter is definitely the boss, but at the same time he can be quite cavalier – without fear and beyond reproach. Now he quite often brings my lunch to the field or bush. If it's not too far he brings his little sister along. The lunch pail clutched in one hand, his sister's wrist in the other, the two come trudging towards me. It just looks too comical! At noon or in the evening when I'm unhitching, he comes to meet me and has to ride along. He'll be a real farmer! His speech is coming along now too. He's coming out with new words almost daily, first coyly with care, then with confident pride. One can't possibly write it all. Every day we experience our children in their innocence, their moods, their learning and their sweetness.

Following the moves back and forth from Pring's sawmill in '34, unwelcome guests had infested the Pankow log home as well as many others in the settlement. Bed bugs had become a real unpleasant nuisance. So the decision was made to do a major renovation. The attractive boards lining the inside walls were all removed and replaced with lathes (edgings from the sawmill). One of the neighbours, George Baschawerk, a Hungarian German plasterer was hired. Under his direction, Father mixed the plaster which consisted of sandy loam, straw and water, stirred to just the right consistency. Then George, with his trowel, deftly filled the cracks between the edgings and left a hard evenly finished wall. When all the surfaces were done, they had to dry for four weeks, at which time a finishing layer of thinner plaster, using chaff instead of straw, was applied. Finally, the smooth hard walls were painted with bright pastel colored kalsomine, a powder that was mixed with water. What a change! Now the house was bright, cool in summer, warm in winter, due to the insulating properties of the plaster, and above all, the bed bug situation was greatly improved.

A harmonious home and family life saw us through many difficult times. Most winter months were not quite so hectic, even though there was feed and grain hauling to do, firewood to cut, harness to repair, and the many livestock chores — a daily commitment. The long winter evenings could be quite cozy, the children all tucked in, the coal oil lamp casting a dim glow, the fire crackling in the heater. Occasionally a loud crack sounded as the deep frost permeated the log walls. Mother had an endless supply of sewing and mending, these chores increasing with each child. Her deft fingers darned many a sock, altered many an item of clothing to make it fit and fashioned many a new dress for four girls to wear to the Christmas concert. Especially if the family planned to go visiting or expected company the

Dieter and Ursula at Bedtime

following Sunday, which happened quite frequently, Mother often worked very late. Her patient washing, mending, and last minute ironing with the heavy unwieldy iron, had us all looking our best.

Father often made these long work evenings more enjoyable for his wife by reading aloud, so that she too could enjoy the book he happened to be reading. In this respect, perhaps Father was "ahead of his time." Today young husbands and fathers actively paricipate in daily housework chores and childcare. Not so in the early 1900s. Father helped in the house whenever he could. Especially during Mother's pregnancies he washed the floor, helped with the laundry, or whatever needed doing. Wood and water supply was always his job, later helped by the children. He took on bath night and quite enjoyed this Saturday night ritual in which one youngster after the other would be scrubbed down in the square galvanized tub, then allowed to romp in fresh clean nighties.

Hair care was all "in home." None of us went to a hairdresser. I can't recall having shampoo, until sometime in the fifties. We used bar soap, and for a little extra shine, a few drops of vinegar were added to the rinse water. Mother was the barber and did all the hair cutting. For the girls this was not a frequent chore because we all wore "pigtails" until we were well into our teens. For special occasions, our long braids were sometimes wound around our heads, or crescent-like, pinned over our ears. With three younger sisters, "doing their hair" was often my job and I became quite practiced at braiding, making sure the parts were perfectly straight and centered. Then there came a phase when I learned to create curls instead. Hair was wound around strips of cloth (rag curlers we called them) with the resulting head full of "ringlets." Toni home-permanent kits became popular, and neighbours "did hair" for each other. Each strand was rolled onto metal rods, snapped into rubber vices, then soaked with nose-tingling, ammonia smelling setting lotion. For a newer look , we graduated from metal rollers and wave clips to "pin curls" twisted around the finger, and fastened flat to the head with bobby pins. The pin-curled head was often covered with a triangular bandana tied at the top.

Managing a household with no electricity, no running water and indoor plumbing, no central gas heating, was so much more difficult, so much more labor intensive. Washing clothes took a whole day of hard physical labor, starting with heating the water in a large boiler on the wood-stove. Then each article was rubbed with soap on a corrugated glass or metal wash board, then agitated by hand, then rinsed and wrung out. In the summer the rinsing was done down at the creek by kneeling on a

**The Board Crossing over the Creek
Dieter, Gerta, Ursula**

board crossing the water. When diapers were part of the laundry, as was the case for most of the thirties, the workload increased. During these depression years when there was such a dire shortage of cash, Mother made soap by boiling together lard (home-rendered on butchering day) and lye, letting the mixture cool and set, then cutting it into squares. We had no bleach so whites were boiled, or in the winter, spread out on the snow on a sunshiny day for a dazzling whiteness. There was another unusual task on wash day. Used sanitary napkins were not discarded, but washed and reused. Mother made them from used underwear or other porous material, sewing several layers together. The used ones were stored in a paper bag, then soaked in several changes of water, scrubbed with soap, dried, ready for use again. This may have been done purely for financial reasons, or perhaps because these personal hygiene items just were not readily available. Again, Mother's trusty old treadle sewing machine served a useful purpose. Ironing day should follow washday, but was worked in wherever possible. With sad irons and hot-coal irons, it was necessary to have a hot stove, so ironing was often combined with bread baking. Never-press and easy-care had not even been dreamed about. Cottons were starched, sprinkled, then ironed – tedious hard work.

Feeding the family in the thirties, in a pioneer kitchen, with little or no money to spend, required ingenuity and imagination – perhaps wizardry. Mother must have possessed a little of each. She could produce a tasty meal from the most humble ingredients. We as children were not aware that we were poor, and I don't ever remember feeling deprived. We knew no other lifestyle and our neighbours were all in the same position. Our garden provided vegetables, our fields, grain for flour, our livestock produced meat, milk, cream, butter and cheese. These were there for us regardless of the economic climate, and we were fortunate indeed that we had a mother who made maximum use of these resources.

Butchering day and the sausage making which followed remains as an unpleasant memory of a messy kitchen, steamy odours, greasy utensils and short tempers. I must have been about twelve years old when I was cranking the handle on the meat grinder, stuffing in piece after piece of raw meat. Alas, in a moment of day dreaming, my finger pressed too deeply into the cutting mouth of the grinder. I drew back, shrieking, as my blood enriched the sausage mix with a touch of extra protein. Mother was not sympathetic. She seemed to think it was a ploy to get out of work, as all she said was "Verschwind!!" motioning towards the stairway. I crept away, nursing my

The Creek Flat Garden

injured finger and my wounded pride. After all the work was finished, including the stuffing with a community-owned sausage machine, a supply of liver sausage, lung and blood sausage, and the most popular, mettwurst, lay on the large table, ready for the smoke house.

Baking with a temperamental wood stove was a skill that had to be learned, but Mother soon mastered it. We always had home made bread and buns. At times during a given year there may have been a shortage of butter. As a substitute, we used rendered lard with bits of onion and apple mixed in. Favourite dishes that I remember as part of my childhood were Königsberger Klopse, (meatballs in mustard sauce), fresh pea soup, cream of beet soup with miniature meatballs in it, potato pancakes, rote grütze (pudding made with berry juice), floating island (chocolate or vanilla flavoured milk soup with dollops of stiffly beaten egg white floating in it). A special rare treat was zucker ei (egg yolks beaten with sugar until thick and pale). Eating raw eggs seemed to hold no fear of contacting salmonella poisoning.

A bacteria-free home would have been much more difficult to maintain, given that there was no running water, no indoor plumbing, and none of the numerous cleaning and disinfecting products on the market today. But basic soap and water cleanliness was the rule and proved effective. One daily task was that of keeping the cream separator impeccably clean. The Germans called it the "centrifuge" because that was the principle by which it operated. The warm milk was strained into the large vat on top, then we cranked and cranked the handle until the speed was just right. Then the tap was opened, sending thick cream through one spout and skim milk through the other. That part was almost fun. It was the daily dismantling to wash and scald, then reassembling the several parts, including twenty thin metal discs in just the right order, that was the tedious part.

But it was worth it all. We drank whole milk, which was taken out before separating. When Heidi and Irma were toddlers, they stood with their cups ready, when the milkers came in. They loved "neue" (new) milk while it was still warm from the cow, and got their calcium at least twice a day. And the delicious thick cream! We used it on everything — porridge, pudding and other desserts, berries, fruit, coffee, and a special treat —homemade cottage cheese with cream and sugar. It seems everyone did enough hard physical work to burn up all those calories, and no one ever talked about cholesterol.

At times we had enough cream to "ship". We took it to the train in Woking in large metal three or five gallon cans, to be taken to the Northern Alberta Dairy Pool in Grande Prairie. We were always pleased when we got No. 1, for excellent taste, freshness and consistency, and the resulting top price. We kept enough cream to make butter in our earthenware churn with the wooden paddles which were repeatedly plunged up and down. The length of time it took for the butter to "come" depended on the temperature and consistency of the cream. Butter making was a tedious task, but we could read while doing it. After the buttermilk was saved, the butter was washed and squeezed in several changes of cold water. If it was to be sold at the local store, it was pressed into one-pound wooden forms, then wrapped in parchment paper especially sized for a pound of butter.

During the hard times Mother made marmalade out of carrots, adding just a

Sunday Morning Breakfast

touch of lemon or orange zest to enhance the flavour. Our creek flat garden had a long row of rhubarb. This had been raised from seed supplied by Opapa Gesien, then small transplants set out in the garden. Rhubarb became a staple of most pioneer kitchens for preserving, making jam and juice. Nature also provided. After a rain, lovely brown capped mushrooms or the white champignons popped up all over the pasture, and our fingers turned black from picking and cleaning them. In the spring, Mother sometimes put gloves in our lunch pail so we could pick stinging nettles on the way home from school. There was a good patch beside our trail, and we knew we'd have nettle greens, boiled potatoes and scrambled eggs for supper that night. We often picked berries. Wild strawberries grew along the creek banks, and their delicious flavour, especially with cream, made a very special dessert. To the northwest, along the school trail, there were several good patches of the tasty low-bush blueberries, which we harvested with homemade pickers, then "winnowed" them clean in a gentle wind.

Sometimes we picked raspberries near Oilund's mill, perhaps four miles south into the hills. We left in the morning, on horseback, following a trail that bore faint traces of an old winter lumber-haul road. The terrain was rugged, covered with bush and high grass, and crossed by small creeks. The rusty remains of an old steam-engine and some sawdust piles were all that remained of a once active lumber industry. We were a bit wary, knowing that there was always the possibility of coming face to face with a bear, enjoying the same berries. We picked until late afternoon, stopping only for a quick sandwich. Then, our pails of juicy berries strapped to the saddle, or held in front of us, we rode home, tired and stiff, but pleased with "the fruit of our labours." We also picked saskatoons, but had to go farther afield for them. I remember on at least one occasion, that Toerpers took us along in their truck, to a site along Emerson Trail, where these berries grew in large , juicy purple clusters.

Even though the heavy workload and short summer season often necessitated working on Sunday, Mother and Father always tried to make Sunday morning breakfast special. In the summer it was served in the southside verandah, a bright cloth covering the rough table and often there were rolls fresh from the oven. This became a traditional time for conversation and seldom-granted relaxation.

Harvest time in the life of a farmer should be the highlight of the year, the reward for all his hard work, the time to reap what he had sown. Unfortunately, during those first years, then the depression era, it was often a time of disappointment and let down. The first small fields were cut with a binder, stooked, then hauled to the farmsteads and layered in stacks. Pring's threshing machine was the only one in a large area, and he could not risk coming until the ground was frozen. It could not have been a profitable business

Cutting the Crop with a Binder

with the few small stacks scattered here and there.

As the fields got bigger and the roads improved, more threshing machines came into the area, and the sheaves no longer had to be hauled into stacks. With their horses and hayracks, the crew of men, armed with pitch forks, quickly dismantled each stook in the field, feeding the sheaves directly into the machine's hungry maw. Each farmer took his turn on the crew, in order to pay his own threshing bill. I remember Otto Toerper had a threshing outfit, with Lloyd Mack as separator man, and on the south side it was Hans Delfs Sr. who moved his machine from farm to farm, with Johann Oltmanns as the separator man.

Hans Delfs' Threshing Outfit

Threshing day on our farm was a time of excitement. Mother could be heard in the kitchen very early in the morning, starting a hot fire in the cookstove. Bread, buns, cakes and pies had to be baked. Feeding the threshers was a matter of some pride, and reputations were at

Pitching Bundles into the Thresher

stake. To serve cornflakes (with no staying power) for breakfast, as one lady did, was not acceptable. One farmer, not known for his generosity, told his wife to serve the wings, necks, and lesser parts of the chicken to the toiling crew, so that his own family could savor the breasts and drumsticks. The bundle pitchers were not sure what to make of an "onion pie," quite strange to them, served by the new Swiss woman in the west. It was probably a delicious quiche! Mother took pride in serving her flaky-crusted lemon meringue pies for dessert. At any rate, the hard workers were given sustenance and strengthened several times a day by the best efforts of the womenfolk.

I remember the putt-putt of Delfs' John Deere tractor as its long belt powered the rattling separator; the rumbling of the wagons and racks, the occasional snort of a horse. Throats became dry and voices raspy as dust and chaff filled the air; the straw pile grew steadily wider and higher. My excitement changed to anxiety when it was my turn to climb into our log granary to wield the grain shovel, in order to keep the incoming grain spout clear. My panic level rose as the pile got higher and higher, and my space got ever smaller and dustier. Mercifully, someone would come to change me off.

Being the farthest away, the Westmark farmers were often the last ones to "get threshed." The machines were very busy, sometimes bad weather interfered, and with winter on the doorstep, everyone wanted to be first. Given all this, and the fact that this was their very livelihood, there were bound to be hard feelings and frustrations, even some behaviors bordering on the unethical. After a long day of pitching bundles, Father came home one evening, bone weary and discouraged, but, shaking his head, his only comment about a neighbour's conduct was "Kleiner Mann" (little man.) He was not referring to physical stature.

In the end everyone usually got his grain in the bin, and there would be the good feeling that another harvest was finished. Regrettably, this euphoria soon waned. When all the bills and debts were paid, the realization came, that there was not much left to live on for a whole year.

Father had been keeping his eyes open for more land, especially for hay making. So in 1936 our family got caught up in a bit of the excitement so prevalent in Western Canada in earlier days during the land rush. A homestead on the Burnt River had been owned by a German count, von Berlepsch. He gave it up and returned to Germany, making this land again eligible for homesteading. Father was informed of its availability, but the timing was rather crucial. Father had gone to Spirit River to attend the celebrations for the coronation of King George VI, going as a representative of the German settlers in Northmark, pledging their allegiance. When he got home after midnight, there was a letter from the Land Titles office. Seven hours remained before

Unloading Hay

123

this land would be open for homestead application in Grande Prairie, fifty miles away. Knowing that others were interested as well, they had to act quickly. The children were left in the care of Uncle Horst, and Mother and Father jumped into the buggy and headed for Northmark Store. Ewald Jacobs, the storekeeper, was awakened and coaxed into driving them to Grande Prairie. They arrived one hour before the office was to open and waited at the door as the official came with his key. Mother filled out a form, they paid the ten dollar application fee, and twelve dollars for the small cabin situated on the land. Now Mother was the proud owner of 160 acres of bushland, well cut up by the river and small creeks. They deemed their nocturnal rush trip a success.

Certainly this new acquisition brought with it even more work. True, they could grow more feed – hay and greenfeed in the river flats, and thus sell more of their grain. But first there was an incredible amount of work. The flats had little bush, but windfall, driftwood and stumps had to be removed before hay could be cut. Access was fraught with difficulties. Roads and river crossings had to be built through terrain that was anything but level, and encroached on the property of others because of the difficult location of the legal road allowance.

I remember this river quarter with mixed feelings. The landscape was beautiful; the dips in the river, the horseback rides through its valleys — these were enjoyable. But the haymaking was not easy. It meant maneuvering the horse drawn mower, then the rake, into many a difficult corner, on many a treacherous slope. Long, hot, sweaty days were spent

Memories of a Wood Sawing Bee

making haycocks, then pitching them high up on the rack. The ride home through rocky river crossings, up and down steep hills, was not for the faint-hearted. Sometimes the big load, with the kids perched on top, listed rather precariously as Father carefully guided the straining horses. We were always glad when we got to the level road on the home stretch, and snuggled into the hay for a short siesta before the unloading began. This too, was hard work, with its pitching, pushing and stuffing, to utilize every last corner of the hay loft. I can still feel the hot, dusty, itchy, muscle-aching sensations of that task. When the loft was full, hay stacks had to be built. This took skill and practice, placing each forkful just right in consecutive layers, to make a straight- sided, rain impenetrable and stable stack.

Forest fires were a mixed blessing to the homesteaders. They helped in land clearing by burning up acres and acres of bush, but could also be dangerous. In the summer of '37 the Saddle Hills to the south were on fire and for days the sky was dark, the sun a red orb, and the acrid smoke stung eyes and nostrils. On several occasions settlers were called together quickly to save someone's house or barn as flames raged too close. For Uncle, help arrived too late, and his home was burned to the ground. Serious ground fires were also an aftermath of forest fires, sometimes smoldering for months, and burning up valuable topsoil.

In spite of the Spartan existence of the thirties, or perhaps because of it, the community spirit was alive and well. Everyone was in the same position — had the same problems to deal with, the same small victories to celebrate. Working together, helping your neighbour, was a necessity and a way of life. In addition to the many "random acts of kindness" there were threshing, woodcutting and building bees.

For fun and entertainment, to break the monotony of the long hard workdays, the settlers made their own good times. Of necessity, these had to be within horse-traveling distance. A moonlight sleigh ride could become a party in itself, a load of revelers tucked into the sleigh box, with the happy sounds of song and harmonica to accompany the crunch of horse's hoof on snow. Visiting, mostly on Sunday afternoons, was a very common outing. Especially the bachelors sought the company and home cooking of a family home. Women were sometimes left alone for weeks while their men worked away from home to "keep the wolf from the door," and visitors were a welcome sight. Father writes, in 1931:

> *My neighbour Egge did finally become engaged and the wedding is on March 30. On May 2 the young couple sets sail for Canada. We are so glad that another young German woman is coming here. It'll be especially nice for Else, as Egges are our close neighbours. Hopefully the young women will get along as well as we men have for a long time.*

The following winter, an enjoyable outing together with that same young couple was undertaken:

Two weeks before Christmas we took a nice sleigh ride outing together with Egges, to visit two German families who live in La Glace, some thirty kilometers south of us. It was a cool −20 but we had fur coats and warm blankets. All you could see of Dieter was the tip of his nose. In order to make the trip go faster, we hitched up "four long" — quite royally! The four horses fairly flew along, so that it was pure enjoyment for all. The winter scenery was beautiful too, as we sped through miles and miles of hoar-frost covered bush and forest. Especially for the women, a trip like this is a welcome change because they don't get out often. We didn't leave until afternoon, but in three hours we had reached our destination. Molls are Mecklenburgers. Dick had already visited us before, and now we got to know his wife Else and their little daughter Ingrid. After an evening of lively conversation, it was time to think about sleeping arrangements. The three women occupied bed and mattresses downstairs, and we three men bedded down on the floor in the attic. Next day we visited another German family, then in late afternoon we hurried home again.

In 1932, Mrs. Baker, wife of Northmark's storekeeper and post-master, organized a type of ladies club in the area. The idea was to provide a bit of entertainment and change of pace for the local women. They met twice a month and one of their mandates was to help the new immigrants with the English language. Mrs. Baker, as well as another homesteader's wife, had formerly been teachers so were well equipped for this task. Mother rode horseback to these meetings while Father was the baby-sitter. That also became his job on several Sundays before Christmas. A holiday celebration was being planned for all the Northmark families, and the Germans were to

River Flat Picnic

perform a number of folk dances. Mother took part. Joe Hitzlberger and Charlie Kolmus are remembered for their spirited performance of the "Schuhplattler." Practices were held every Sunday, usually at Egge's, because they had the largest house.

That same winter was described as particularly early, cold and harsh. Knee-deep snow and heavy frosts began in early November, prompting Mother to write:

> Close to the stove it's quite nice and warm, but we can't spend much time in the far corners. I hope it won't be this cold on Sunday, because we had hoped that Urselchen would be baptized, and it's quite a ways to the church.

New Year's Eve saw a lively gathering with a costume party at Wulf's house, to see in the year 1934. That summer the settlers hosted a big picnic in July:

> For next Sunday we have organized a German fest to be held on a nice meadow by the Burnt River, with all kinds of amusements — sack racing, tug-o-war, pole vaulting, target shooting, folk dancing, stab-the-ring,(a horseman's game originating in Holstein,) and more. In the evening there'll be an outdoor dance. It could be quite a nice affair.

For some time these picnics were held regularly in the summer and became quite popular with all the settlers, not just the Germans. It was fun to be a part of the development of the little pioneer settlement. Since Father arrived in 1929, five of the bachelors had married. The addition of five young women made a huge difference to the social life of the bushland. Houses were becoming more numerous, the fields were getting larger. Where five years ago there was a wilderness without path or road, rarely trod by human foot, now there was a blossoming settlement.

For recreational and cultural development, the Deutscher Bund (Canadian Society for German Culture) was established in Northmark. This society was registered with the Canadian government and was a cultural organization which did not participate in party politics, and respected the laws of Canada. These "bunds" existed in German settlements throughout Canada. Their mandate was to further German culture — language, art, literature and music, by supplying the membership with appropriate materials, such as books, films, gramaphone records, song books, theater production materials, speaker and discussion subjects. Members paid a small membership fee and were expected to contribute to the growth and welfare of the local group, come to the aid of the needy, to respect the flag and the laws of Canada. The goal was to maintain goodwill and friendly relations with Canada, even while keeping German culture alive.

Outdoor Dance Following the Picnic

Much of the social life of the Germans then centered around this organization. Father was the president of this society, a fact he would live to regret. Mother was always very active in helping with the entertainment aspects — drama, choir, folk dancing, shadow and puppet shows, for their social evenings. This involved much planning, brain wracking, hard work, and sometimes frustration. But when things turned out well and people enjoyed, then it was all worthwhile. People had to resolutely take time to do these things, or they would never escape from the yoke of work that shackled them daily from dawn to dusk.

The families often got together for birthdays, an excuse for a party with singing, friendly visiting, and the standard wiener and potato salad supper. We children sometimes had birthday parties, but they were a far cry from today's loot bag, go to MacDonald's affair. I remember one gift in particular and can still see Willie Janssen walking up the hill on the west side of our house, carrying a doll bed he had crafted for me — a thirteen year old building a gift for a six year old girl! And on a later birthday I received a bright green barette for my hair from Clesta and Elma Dale. I felt special, and in no way disparaged. Our values and our expectations were so different.

The year 1938 marked a very important milestone in the life of the pioneer settlement and our family was also involved. When it was established that the required number of children now lived in the area, steps were taken to open a school. At a meeting held during the winter of '37 – '38 a school board was formed, with Günther Pankow as chairman, Clara Oltmanns as

Westmark School Under Construction

secretary, and Harry Sloat, Fred Janssen and Johann Oltmanns, trustees. Father circulated a petition of request signed by the electors residing in the proposed school district. After some controversy, and finally a vote regarding the location of the school house, construction began in the spring of 1938. Nearly everyone participated in some phase: yard clearing, log hauling, building, furnishing, fencing and outbuildings. School building and improvements could be done in lieu of taxes, a big help to the cash-strapped settlers.

In September 1938, the doors of the school opened for the first time, and the district would henceforth be called Westmark. Children from seven families attended, Dieter and I among them. Many of us spoke no English, and several pupils were older than six when they enrolled in Grade one. The contribution of the rural pioneer teachers cannot be too strongly commended. With dauntless spirit and determination, they did their best under adverse conditions. In addition to the three Rs, each in his own way, gave something of himself to enrich the lives of these home-steader children. The annual Christmas concert, now held at the schoolhouse, added a new dimension to the social life of the community.

In the fall of '38 another devastating disappointment struck the small settlement. Hopes had been high and again there was a lot of optimism. The crops had grown well and matured nicely. Even the usual August frost had stayed away. Alas, in early September a snowstorm flattened all the grain. This in itself could be managed and many bought pick-up guards and fastened them to the binder knife, planning to cut from only one side instead of going round and round the field. But now the waiting began, for the soft, wet fields to dry enough to carry the binder. This waiting and hoping continued until mid-November — a most nerve-wracking time — during which rain fell frequently, and the fields became even more impassable. When winter really set in, they knew that another crop was lost. Father wrote:

Our plans and dreams were shattered once more, because we had yet another disaster. We don't even like to write to you any more about all the failures and setbacks, most of which are not of our making. Up to now they've always been caused by the forces of nature, but they are nevertheless very real. But once the bitter truth has been faced, we find ourselves slipping back into our thick skin, something we absolutely need here. Again we will hope for next year, and have decided to stay for a while.

A happy harmonious family life is the foundation that makes it possible to bear it here and to be happy, and children add so much. Dieter is a bright lad, small but strong and healthy, very good-natured and not as whiny as he used to be. Ursel, in spite of the one and a half years age difference, is just as tall, but stockier and heavier, and thus more awkward, not nearly as agile and quick. She loves dolls, is quite affectionate and a bit smug. She loves "mothering" her little sister. Gertachen is a real sweet angel. I could play with her for hours. She's just starting to talk and understands everything.

Right now I'm home alone with the children for a few days. During the night before last our neighbour Johann Oltmanns came to get Else. His wife's first baby was arriving a week earlier than expected. For eighteen hours the poor woman was in labour, before her big boy finally arrived. The eighty-four year old doctor had arrived from Spirit River, in spite of thirty below with an east wind. He was able to travel most of the way with his car — in February, in northern Canada! That happens only once in ten years. We have very little snow. At first Doctor Reavely was not home when they tried to get him, so Doctor Goldberg, a Prussian Jew who has been in Canada for ten years, was supposed to come. But he refused (the third such incident) because it was too cold, and he'd have to see the money first. The worst of it is that, legally, there is no way to get at this wretched person. Fortunately Doctor Reavely soon arrived back in Spirit River, and was immediately prepared to come out to Oltmanns. He is a man of rare magnanimity always ready to help, and so often he sees no financial return. Unfortunately he's getting so old and shaky.

Else will stay at Oltmanns for two more days, until Clara's mother can come. In this respect, she's more fortunate than most of the German women here, because her relatives live close by and are readily available in such cases. This is Oltmanns' second wife. His first died three years ago of a lung ailment. He has been through a lot and we were all happy when,

130

last spring he married a nice young German girl, born in Canada. Now he has his son and heir. In his first marriage, two children died at a very young age. Yes, there are many cruel twists of fate. This is much more noticeable here, where only a few people live. Everyone knows everyone else and there is a greater sharing of joys and sorrows. In Northmark alone, an author could write a wonderful and valuable homesteader novel. Too bad I can't do that. It would probably be an easier and surer way to make a living! But life is good. We are and remain optimists.

An optimistic outlook was imperative in order to continue. A decade had passed since Father set foot on Canadian soil, and a large part of this time could be described as "depression years." It was inevitable that some doubts would begin to creep in. He was asking himself many questions.

Dieter, Gerta, Ursula

Chapter 13   What A Difference A Year Makes

The nationalistic fervour and the optimism on the economic and employment scene, were on the rise in Germany. But Father was dubious. Is it real? Will it last? Is Hitler a true statesman? He was skeptical about all this. Many of the Germans in Canada during these depression years were quite enthusiastic about Hitler and his dictatorship. They felt sure that now things would improve quickly in the homeland, and they spoke of regrets at coming to Canada. At this point Father didn't share their sentiments. He'd have to stay here, considering all the time, work and money he'd invested. But under these depressed conditions it would be difficult to make any progress.

There were certainly a number of things that were better in Germany, especially culturally and educationally speaking, Father always thought. Perhaps now the economic climate was better too. But there were some societal behaviors and affectations that he did not miss in the least. He tells Tante Anna about it in a letter of July 1, 1934:

> Here it is, the first of July. How the time flies! How slowly the days, weeks and months used to creep by when I was still in Germany, working as a trainee. I wouldn't want to trade places now. In the six years that I've been in Canada, my whole way of thinking, my whole attitude has fundamentally changed. So many of the things we did (or had to do) as employees over there seem utterly trivial, almost laughable to me now. There was this whole thing about "supervision of the workers," the constant feeling of never being able to make decisions without asking the boss, always being the servant, never the master over your time. Further to that — the formalities, the doff of the hat, the hand-kissing, these ridiculous terms of address — Honorable sir or madam!

> Even in matters that have nothing to do with any of my previous places of employment, I think differently now. It is almost frightening how cool and objectively I take note of the present political developments in Germany. In the past, I would surely have been very excited by the impressive rise of nationalism. Today it leaves me cold. One is just too far removed from the action to fully empathize. One is more inclined to find fault and see the weaknesses, which, of course, are present in every regime. Case in point — the outrageous and shameful condemnation of Father Gesien.

> I now think of the concept "Fatherland" in more generous terms. Ultimately it's the people who make a homeland, especially the people whom we hold dear — our own immediate family, our relatives and friends. We, Else and I, have all of you over there, we know our beautiful Germany. We will never give up hope of seeing you and Germany again. This longing will always remain with us. But our children?   They will

know their parents' homeland only from our accounts and through pictures. (We display every page of the beautiful calendars.) They will speak German with a Canadian accent! They will know no one over there. So where is their Fatherland? They will not be aware of this as an enigma. For us as parents, in spite of all efforts at open-minded objectivity, this question of national consciousness, world citizenship, and homeland, is somewhat problematic. In just three years Dieter will have to attend an English school.

Nevertheless, it's nice here, and we certainly don't feel without a homeland. We have our own family, in our own house, on our own land. We are surrounded by German neighbours, with whom we have cordial interactions. I have written you about all the good times we have together.

Meanwhile, in Europe, Hitler's aggressive moves — the breaking of the Treaty of Versailles and subsequent reoccupation of the Rhineland; also the alliance with Austria, were not viewed favourably by the English and the French. But in the fall of 1938, it was the German occupation of Sudetenland in Czechoslovakia that brought Europe to the brink of war. Only through Chamberlain's timely meeting with Hitler at the Munich Conference was appeasement reached and war avoided. The world breathed a collective sigh of relief, not least in the German homes of Northmark. Father writes:

What a blessing that war was avoided. Here too, we lived in great suspense and apprehension as we waited anxiously for every bit of radio news. At that time I had to go to the Post Office every mail day (twice a week) because for some time we had been trying to get a teacher for our new school. So I always brought the latest news.

Repercussions of the incidents in Europe were felt in Canada. In the fall of '38 there was a subtle but very real change in the attitude towards those of German descent. Although they were Canadian law-abiding citizens who had contributed substantially and positively to the growth of their settlement, the Germans began to receive hostile treatment. There arose a climate of suspicion and hate mongering. This grew even stronger after the events of September, 1938.

Following a report by an anonymous informer, Father, in his capacity as chairman of the Society of German Canadians, had to go to the police station in Spirit River to answer to complaints. The society had been accused of holding secret meetings and practices, and of sending money to Hitler! How ridiculous those accusations were! These people didn't have the money to feed their own children. However, this incident was an indication of the presence of anti-German sentiment.

Perhaps this, together with yet another crop failure, yet another drop in commodity prices, all added fuel to the fire already smoldering in Father's heart. In December, 1938, he sat down and penned a long heart-felt letter to his siblings:

The price of wheat fell by half and with it all other agricultural products. Last year we got between ninety cents and a dollar per bushel of wheat, and this fall we got forty-five to forty-nine cents. The treatment of farmers is fraudulent and deceptive. They are offered prices below their cost of production, yet everything they have to buy remains outrageously expensive — machinery, repair parts, everyday farm necessities, even flour and groceries. It must be something similar to Germany after the inflation.

One becomes embittered and reluctant, and it really rankles that again we worked a whole year for nothing. I threshed 400 bushels of wheat, 277 of barley, and 230 of oats. In spite of our poor crop, at last year's prices there would have been enough to pay the bills and make the most necessary purchases. We would have been able to hang on without going into debt. But now ? All the grain is sold and the money is gone. There are no jobs to be had. There was not even road work available this fall. So what choice do we have, but to cut back drastically again and live on credit until the next harvest.

These are not happy prospects for the future, so it is no wonder that many questions come to mind. Now .... You will be surprised. For the first time in my eleven years in Canada, I am seriously considering a return to Germany. My faith in a reasonably secure future for my family in Canada has been shattered. So I want to end this while I am still young. At thirty-five I trust that I have the strength to make a new beginning in Germany. Of course a decision of this magnitude cannot be made overnight, and requires careful thought. The fact that I am writing this will assure you that I am very serious. This is not something done in the heat of the moment. Since the end of September I have carried this problem with me, and weighed the pros and cons, together with Else and many a German neighbour. I must discuss this in greater detail with you too, so that you can give an opinion.

There is a real curse and a tragedy in this. We have such a nice place here, which, in ten years of hard work, we have built up from next to nothing. Yet we have only our bare existence, caused not so much by unfavourable climatic conditions (that's a risk every farmer anywhere has to take), but by the fact that the wretched and muddled economic situation in Canada is so uncertain. There is no assurance whatever, that honest hard work, such as was done in Northmark during the past ten years, in exemplary fashion, will have any rewards or guarantees. In future, will we, and later our children, be able to live a carefree life on our farms? There may be just enough to live on, but should an unfortunate stroke of fate come along, then we would be ruined. With a few dollars of relief the government would make sure that we don't actually starve, but could vegetate and drag on.

In our own family, the (possible) returns from the next harvest would not be enough to bring our health up to standard. Mother's teeth, her bladder problems; my teeth and eyes (lately I've had nausea and sore eyes again, and only a good doctor would be able to find out what's really wrong); Ursel should have glasses because she's cross-eyed; and Dieter's teeth are already bad. We've had to neglect our health for so long because we were always hoping for next year.

If we are to have only the minimum standard of living, why live and slave under such unfavourable conditions, here in an anti-German foreign country? It would be different if we could afford even a few small luxuries — a short-wave radio, an old rattle-trap of a car to provide wife and children with an occasional break. Sometimes I feel so sorry for my brave, hard-working little wife — nothing but cooking, baking, cleaning, mending day after day, week after week, year after year. We have not become insensitive enough yet, we're still too young, still have too much energy, to let this become our destiny. I have finally allowed sober rationality to speak, to decide our future, independent of all the maybes, ifs and buts. And the decision is — Germany!

Something else to consider — What would become of our children here? Now that the two oldest ones are going to the English school, it becomes crystal clear: 'You and your family belong in Germany. What opportunities do the children have here?' Even when the parents have money, the career choices are very limited. The education is not thorough – so superficial. In comparison, how well schooled and educated the young people in Germany are today.

Carrying out this decision, to return to Germany, will naturally be very hard for us. We are quite attached to this, our piece of land. Here I am my own boss. We enjoy the legendary Canadian freedom, and we have our circle of German friends. Especially bitter is the realization: What would this property be worth in Germany?! If one could just take it along and continue over there! But these are moot observations. The sober reality remains that it is highly unlikely that I would, in the next ten or twenty years, improve my financial situation here. And the sooner I sacrifice my livelihood here, the better. Without a doubt it is a sacrifice. One would practically have to give away the inventory, and the farm would be hard to sell, even at a rock bottom price. Perhaps, with any luck, a person could get six hundred to seven hundred dollars for the farm, and one hundred and fifty to two hundred for everything else on it. That means I'd have to be satisfied, if with next fall's harvest, and a sale, I'd be able to pay for the ship's voyage, and land in Hamburg with five or six hundred dollars in my pocket.

That is not a rosy outlook, especially when I have a family with four children, and I have to be quite aware that it'll be the end of the wonderful freedom and independence. I imagine that I'll have to change careers. Even the smallest settler would require some capital and that just isn't there. On the other hand, I don't want to return to my position as agricultural employee. After eleven years in Canada I'd be no good for that. It should be possible to get on with some small enterprise, and in Germany there are classes available for people who wish to make a career change. I know that I am a person who can adjust, and when you've got eleven years in Canada behind you, you can do anything. My goal is a lofty one: absolute security for my family, and that in our beloved Germany! That's worth a sacrifice. And Germany needs people, especially families with healthy children.

Some Northmarkers have already returned and very few have regretted it. Some are in the Heinkel factories in Rostock, one is with Osram in Berlin. Tomorrow another one, Harald Glimm is going back. Yesterday we had a farewell party for them at the Club. He too, has four children and will land in Hamburg with no money worth mentioning. Mind you, he has a brother with a government job in Berlin, so through him, he'll probably soon have a job. He also retained his German citizenship. In a few months Harald is going to write and give me a detailed report on his experience. Then if I could get an opinion from each one of you, my idea can assume a more concrete form.

I am sure that, after the unbelievably nice high lights of the trip home, then the reunion with all of you, the serious realities of finding work will hit me. There will be moments when we will long for our nice farm in Northmark. But if it's true that, in Germany everyone who wants work will find work then I'm not afraid. And there are other values found only there. I picture Else and I attending performances in music, film and theater; or visiting relatives in the beautiful German countryside. When I think of all this, it becomes abundantly clear just how much we have been missing.

Two years ago when Horst Solty returned from over there and told me about Germany, I would have considered this move as impossible. But at that time the price of wheat was a dollar – now it's forty-five cents, and there are no jobs to be had, to earn the shortfall. These are the conditions in Canada. And in Germany? People are needed, the economy is thriving, and the Reich is stronger than ever before. Is it any wonder then, that I want to return home?

But I will never regret the eleven years in Canada. I am going of my own free will, and not without making a fairly large sacrifice. In spite of everything, this past phase of our lives has been good, we were always happy and satisfied. But the basis for this was primarily our harmonious family life. And this, my most valuable and precious asset I'm bringing with me. So what can go wrong?

I've given you a lot to think about. I would ask that each of you write me your opinion. Possibly it will be necessary for you to destroy some illusions; perhaps some of you will advise against my plan. Nothing can be done until next fall, or even the fall after that; soon enough then to work out details. There is one more serious problem: Upon the death of Tante Anna, I will owe each of my siblings two hundred and fifty dollars. During the first years of my new beginning in Germany, it will surely be very difficult for me to pay off these debts. Will it be possible for you to be generous and patient? Discuss all this amongst yourselves. After all, this concerns a member of the Pankow clan and his family.

Father's ears must have been ringing during the weeks that followed the arrival of his "bombshell" letter. Although other replies are not available, it would seem that the majority approved of his decision to return — but not Tante Anna! He had great respect for his aunt and her opinion. She was a great judge of character and had a lifetime of knowledge. He was not about to take her opinion lightly, so he wrote again, trying to reassure her:

Your letter saddened us greatly, and we couldn't get over the fact that we caused you sleepless nights. So you cannot come to terms with the idea that we want to return to Germany? No, no one talked us into it. Quite sober and rational, the realization came, that in spite of all our hard work, we would get bogged down here. Conditions in Canada are becoming ever more hopeless, similar to those in Germany when I came here.

I know you do not agree or approve of all that's happening in the Third Reich, but why do you think it would be even worse for us in Germany? I don't think so. After all, we are not going to lie around, but, after a short happy reunion with all of you, we will immediately begin working to establish a new livelihood. I still trust myself to accomplish this. Tantchen, you should and must not worry about us. Why would Werner, Hansi, Hellmut, and even Uncle Fred say, without reservation, Come Home!? They are not blind and have good sense. We have no grand illusions and are not painting a rosy picture of this new beginning, but it can't be worse than it is here right now. The will to work, all ambition deteriorates here because of the constant failures and setbacks. Furthermore, it's impossible to keep our health up to par. Good health is worth a large sacrifice.

So, dear Tantchen, don't be sad, but rather be happy and look forward to seeing us again. It's clear that not everything will suit us over there, but there are unpleasant aspects here too. We wish you rest and peace for your twilight years, and please anticipate our coming without bitterness."

All the pros and cons, all the opinions and judgements became irrelevant. Father had the decision taken out of his hands. Hitler had built up the German economy to an unbelievable level; unemployment had been nearly eradicated; nationalistic pride reached a fever pitch, as "Der Führer" became a heroic figure. Perhaps all commendable to this point?

Alas, Hitler did not know his limitations, did not know when to stop. He became power hungry, fanatical and irrational in his quest for more territory for his country. In September 1939, he ordered his troops to invade Poland. He had gone too far — his actions were challenged, and on September 3, Britain and France declared war on Germany.

Now there were no more plans or even thoughts of returning to Germany. There were no more letters or parcels, and the future path of our family was drastically and forever changed. (It is interesting to speculate where we would be today, had our parents returned to Germany in '39. Perhaps we would not "be" at all. Ed.)

The difficult decision had been made, following many serious discussions with family, friends and neighbours. The Pankow family would give up their hard earned Canadian homestead and return to their German homeland.

However, fate intervened before this decision could be translated into action. In the summer of 1939 the Northmark homesteaders had been listening anxiously around the few battery radios which existed in the pioneer settlement, trying to hear the latest news. Hans H. Delfs remembers September first, 1939 very clearly. He was fourteen years old. After hearing the news, he hurried out to his father who was stooking in the fields. "Dad, I just heard it on the radio. Germany has invaded Poland!" His father, a calm, reserved man, answered quietly "Don't worry, son. It probably won't amount to anything." But Otto Delfs was wrong. The move of Hitler's armies into Poland did indeed amount to something — the second World War. England and France declared war on Germany on September third, 1939. The number of lives that were changed, indeed lost, by that war cannot ever be comprehended. The consequences would be felt around the world, immediately and for decades to come, in our family and families everywhere.

The declaration of war created an uneasy situation for the people who had been born on German soil, including many of the Northmark settlers. There was an escalation of the already existing anti-German sentiment. The Mackenzie King government got caught up in war hysteria which created a climate of suspicion and mistrust amongst the people. All German-born residents over fifteen years of age, naturalized or not, were treated as enemy aliens. They had to report to their local R.C.M.P. detachments for finger printing, were asked to give up their firearms and to report to the police on a regular basis. The loss of firearms was a very real hardship because in the pioneer settlement there was a heavy reliance on wild meat for the year's food supply. Regrettably, firearms were not returned until the end of the war, some never. [2]

War changed the once harmonious little community. The ethnic song, dance and drama staged by the German Canadian Society, once mutually enjoyed by all nationalities, were now viewed with suspicion. Activities to further the cultural heritage of a homeland are usually considered highly commendable, and are widely supported. But now these very activities to uphold German culture became suspect.

Individuals reacted in different ways. Some became over-zealous in their "patriotism" and reported every remotely suspicious movement by the German-born settlers. When Hans Delfs built a larger than average hip roof on his barn, it was reported "the Germans in Westmark are building an aircraft hangar." And Otto Delfs was to be watched carefully because he was once part of a submarine crew in Germany, and is bound to have German U-boat information. These were totally ridiculous accusations, but nevertheless real. There were those who chose to deny their heritage. This kind of cowardice could not command respect from either side.

As the war dragged on, the Canadian government introduced military conscription which called upon all physically fit males over eighteen for military service. Ironically this included men who had previously lost the right to possess personal firearms. There was a sad irony in receiving a conscription order in the mail one day, and a letter edged in black the next, announcing the death of a brother, killed in action on the other side. Uncle Horst Anders was a case in point. While his brother Hellmut fought in the German army, he enlisted in the Canadian counterpart.

Membership Registration

German Canadian Societies became objects of suspicion. Local groups such as the one in Northmark, had no desire to provoke authorities, so they simply went into limbo, ceasing all activities during the war. Local leaders, however, were singled out to serve as an example, taken into custody and interned in concentration camps.

One of these leaders was our Father. On August 11, 1940, he had intended to go to the river quarter to cut hay, but decided instead to help other neighbours with manse renovations at the pastor's place. Unfortunately, his generous volunteerism was interrupted by a visit from Corporal Watts of the Spirit River R.C.M.P. detachment. "I'm sorry Mr. Pankow, but my orders are to take you in for interrogation" said the corporal. I don't know that this was a complete surprise to Father. Several of his fellow "Bund" leaders had met the same fate several months earlier.

Father packed a few things, changed his clothes and said his good-byes to the family. All the while, the policeman, wishing to grant them privacy, went to the woodpile and split block after block of fire-wood, until a large pile lay on the ground. Corporal Watts was a decent and compassionate man who knew in his heart that he was taking in an innocent man. But he had to follow orders. As Father embraced his wife and three little girls, the corporal said "Would you two like to ride along for a bit?" Dieter and I hopped excitedly into the back seat. A car ride was a rare experience. We drove north along the narrow winding road that followed the creek bank through our, then Sloat's land. When we reached the main road, Dieter and I hopped out and waved goodbye. How could we know that we would not see our father for two and a half years? What thoughts would crowd the mind of seven and eight year old youngsters as they trudged home on the hot dusty road? What would be their conversation? Why did the policeman come and take their father away?

Two men from the little settlement were summoned for interrogation that day. One puled and groveled, declaring that he had just married his young wife. And although he had a large Nazi swastika painted on the wall of his farm shed, this man went free. The other responded in quiet dignity. The man with five young children was taken away to be interned.

Thus began two and a half lonely difficult years for Mother and her five children who were too young to understand. Adding to the stress, the government implemented rationing of essential goods and some food products. Sugar, butter, meat and coffee required ration coupon books. Farm families did not suffer as much from this,

Pankow Family 1941
Dieter Holding Gerta, Mother Holding
Irma, Ursula Holding Heidi

141

except for the sugar and coffee. Many people got their own hives of bees and honey was widely used to replace sugar. I can remember Mother roasting barley, then grinding it with a bit of chicory, for a coffee substitute. Tooth paste and shaving cream could be purchased only if the empty tube was returned. We brushed our teeth with salt water! For Mother these material deprivations were not nearly as onerous as the mental anguish, the loneliness, the absence of companion, bread winner and father.

Neighbours were very helpful — out of genuine concern and kindness, and a sense of duty. There was probably also a bit of "there but for the grace of God go I." Any one of them could have been in Father's position. Mother wrote:

> The helpfulness of the neighbours is most gratifying. They're saying "Günther's internment is not a reflection on him personally. He is the least dangerous of any. But he is serving time for all of us."

This feeling seemed to exist not only in the immediate community, but in other surrounding German settlements as well. Individuals were moved to try and help in some way and would enclose five, ten or fifteen dollars in their letters of encouragement to mother. These included Fred Paschatag of Clairmont, Scribas and Rozinskis of Heart Valley and Erich Andersens of Wembley.

A group of local friends and neighbours (Hans Delfs, Pastor Krisch, Alfred Sellin, Otto Toerper, Reinhold Witte) got together to be guarantors in case Mother ever defaulted on her grocery payments. Gus Nagel requested not to be overlooked if it came to taking a collection. She hoped fervently that it would never come to this — that these measures were only put in place in case of dire emergency. Certainly the goodwill of these people was evident and commendable. It was not easy, however, for Mother, self-sufficient and independent, to accept these acts of generosity, even under these unusual circumstances.

The neighbours, who were also family friends, took their sense of responsibility and friendship very seriously. Fred (Fieten) Egge and Horst Solty were true stalwarts. Otto Toerper looked after the north side of the river quarter because he had easier access from his side, and Mother didn't have to worry about that part. In nearly every letter Mother told of the helpfulness of some one in the community:

> One day last week Hein (Schuett) and Horst (Solty) came to fix the roof. Today Helmuth (Glimm), Fieten (Egge) and Papa Witte helped with the stooking. Horst was on his way to our place to fix the granary floor when he met Frank (Schulz) on the road. So Frank came and helped too.

Helmuth, Pastor Krisch, and Mr. Maltzan worked hard today to help us haul the rabbit-ravaged haystacks home from the river quarter. Last week Orm Bryan from Chinook Valley came to castrate the colts. Dick (Moll) helped haul our wheat bundles into stacks. Last week he took our calf to the stockyard and had to use four horses because the roads were so muddy. Hans Delfs offered to thresh our grain for the price of the gas and oil, and the bundle haulers volunteered their work. Karl (Stein) was one of the first to come forward.

You know those old pieces of saddle that were always hanging around in the barn? One day they disappeared. Horst (Solty) had taken them, fixed the saddle and made it usable again. This was my birthday present. You know how he is a man of few words, but always quietly helpful.

For obvious reasons, Sellin seemed to feel more duty bound and obligated to Mother than many others did, and sometimes brought little gifts, like Easter eggs for the children. The war, with its belt-tightening on the home front, made local self-sufficiency seem even more imperative. Mother became quite adept at mending not only the family clothing, but also horse collars and harnesses and binder canvasses. Hein Schuett had a mechanism for making twine into rope, and other settlers brought him jobs. He also had an artistic bent, and made colorful wooden puppets which were used for presentations at social functions. Hans Delfs had a grain crusher and did custom work. Loads of grain were hauled to his machine to make chop for feed. He also did land breaking with his John Deere steel-wheeled tractor and plow. Otto Delfs and Jacob Knoblauch were blacksmiths and were kept busy sharpening plow shares and making repairs. Johann Oltmanns was "the man" when it came time to butcher or make sausage. Fred Neiser had a wood sawing outfit with which he travelled around to cut the neighbours yearly supply of firewood. Local men helped each other by making up the crew. Egges owned a sausage-making machine, which was, it seemed, used by every family in the community at some time. Eilert Pleis was handy with clippers and scissors and served as barber for many a neighbour.

Ewald Jacobs, operator of the Northmark General Store, and Edmund Krisch, pastor of the Lutheran Church were two of the few owners of a motor vehicle so were often in demand for taxi service. One had to reserve a ride ahead of time, unless it was an emergency. Visiting the doctor or dentist, getting machinery repairs and reporting to the police, were reasons for a trip to town. In April Mother wrote:

We're so sad that our young pastor is leaving. I can understand that he would be fed up as a pastor here and I certainly don't begrudge him a better parish. I believe part of the reason (for him leaving) is his wife. She never really wanted to be here.

Edmund Krisch had been a true benefactor in the community. It is hard to imagine anyone more helpful, more unselfish and generous. Medical emergencies were rushed to the hospital in his car, at all hours, in any kind of weather, over all kinds of roads or non-roads. Under these conditions he served both the Northmark and Heart Valley parishes. This was an example of one of his trips:

Last Thursday (it was in March) we went to the dentist in Grande Prairie and for now our teeth are OK. But what a trip it was! In the morning as we travelled on frost, we had no trouble, but it was very rough. But on the way back — Dieter and I, along with Helga Delfs, were pastor's passengers. We eyed each oncoming vehicle with apprehension, because turning off the track was very difficult. Nevertheless, our dauntless driver got us safely to just before Ralph Otto's. There a culvert that had been newly filled in last fall was our undoing. We got badly stuck. It took two hours before we finally got out. After that we had to drive our waiting horses home from the manse and finally arrived home at one in the morning.

Back: Pastor Edmund and Mrs. Krisch with son Teddy, F.W. Egge, Else Pankow with Heidi, Friedrich and Martha Janssen. Front: Elise Egge, and Egge and Pankow Children

Another time the pastor drove to Scriba's in Heart Valley for the baptism of their baby, Fritz, and got hopelessly stuck on the muddy road near Prestville. After spending a cold night in his car, he managed to get a farmer with his horses to pull him out, and arrived home at noon. Is it any wonder that his wife was not deliriously happy about living in this parish under these primitive conditions? How many times was she awake at night, sick with worry because her husband had not come home?

Some of his final duties as pastor in this community were the baptism of our little Irma, Hans Egge and Sieglind Solty, at Egge's house, and the confirmation of Otto and Emil Hessler, William and Alvina Knoblauch at the church. In early May Pastor Lütkehölter from Edmonton came to a meeting at the church to see what could be done with this isolated congregation. On May 25 a service was held to bid farewell to Pastor Krisch and to install the new pastor. The church was full and Mother described the new Pastor Grober as "a tall strong man with dark hair and eyes, and a little black moustache." His wife Esther, "a tall blonde with a stately bearing" is the daughter of Pastor Wahl. When Mother visited at the manse, she found him to be friendly and kind, very talkative, perhaps too much so. His twenty-three year old wife had plans to start a choir and liked to have young people around her.

In the summer holidays Dieter and I attended Saturday school at the church. We learned prayers and the catechism, and came home singing "Weil ich Jesu Schäflein Bin." I remember that it always took us a long time to walk home. There was so much to explore along the river and around the sloughs. We discovered robins and red-winged blackbirds' nests, garter snakes and tiger lilies. Nature study was more exciting than church school.

Father had been active in getting Westmark School District # 4799 established in the settlement, and was chairman of the local board when he was taken away. On October 27, 1940 Mother kept him informed:

> Yesterday a meeting was held to elect a new Westmark School trustee, to fill your spot. Very few people attended and Fieten Egge got stuck with it. They had to go and pick up Mrs. Schulz and Mrs. Janssen to provide a quorum. Clarence Dale was the only non-German to attend. He is pressing for Grade nine to be offered at our school. Twila is that age now, he said, and next year there'll be Willie Janssen and Hans Delfs. They agreed that an application would be made to get grade nine.

The local board met again on January fifth in the new year. Mother describes that meeting:

Just imagine, this meeting lasted all night, from seven p.m. until seven a.m.! True, there's a lot to discuss regarding the takeover by the Department of Education, but certainly most would not have taken that long. It takes an eternity for Schulz to think, then speak; for Egge to think, then forget; and for Dale to figure out and fill out forms! At least in this respect you can be glad that you aren't here.

In 1941 for the first time, all school supplies were sent out to the schools from the Department of Education, and families did not have to purchase their own. Mother happened to be at the store when a large shipment arrived, and she was able to deliver a load of scribblers, pencils, erasers, chalk, and more to the school.

In the fall of '42, Mother told of the new teacher:

> *Now school has started and a young student teacher is here. The children love him. He is German — Weisgerber — nineteen years old, still speaks the language, and ended up having to stay at Egge's in the upstairs bedroom.*

Teacher Pat Weisgerber

In the Grande Prairie School District that fall, twenty-four schools could not open because they had no teachers — certainly an effect of the war. Weisgerber, too, did not stay the full term, in spite of local meetings and efforts to keep him. When he enlisted in the army, local resident Mary Rowe became Westmark's teacher for some years.

These years were not easy for many families. Women were often left alone while their husbands found off-farm jobs. The building of the Alaska Highway, with its military supply depots and airports, created jobs for many, including local men. Otto Delfs, for example, worked for the U.S. army at Muscwa Airport near Fort Nelson, B.C. Bridge timbers and lumber were required in large quantities in the building of this new highway, so these products were in high demand at area sawmills. Homesteaders had no trouble getting jobs, but wages in '41 were still low. In February '41 Mother writes:

Dick Moll went to work at Sedore's mill for thirty-five cents an hour. Although he had lots of time to prepare, Egges and I are frequently getting letters from Mrs. Moll, via the children. She needs milk, potatoes, butter, chicken feed, oats, chop. I feel sorry for her.

Mother's situation was quite different. Father could not come home on weekends or even once a year. He did not have a job and was not in a position to support his family. He was sitting idle and helpless in the internment camp. This was the most difficult part of his confinement.

Moll and Pankow Children:
Back – Ingrid, Ursula, Margaret, Dieter.
Front – Maria, Gerta, Jürgen.

The regular reporting by all German-born settlers became a real chore and inconvenience, especially during busy seasons:

On Monday we three women, Frieda Witte, Lisi Egge and I went to Spirit River to report. Papa Witte took us to the store. We waited for two hours but no Jacobs appeared. We were about to leave when Ivan Higginson came along. Seeing our predicament, he promptly took us to Spirit River in his old car. On the way in, the roads were good, but on our return trip it had poured at Bridgeview and the road was very slippery. Corporal Watts was very friendly.

Being alone with the children meant many adjustments for Mother. She had to make trips and attend to business matters usually undertaken by the men. In spite of her short stature and small build, she soon became quite adept at harnessing and unharnessing, hitching up and unhitching the horses — her sole mode of travel. On January seventh '41, Mother undertook a "day trip." She got up very early, in time to do the chores, then hitched up the horses and took the two oldest children to school. Gerta and Baby Irmchen were dropped off at Egges. Heidi couldn't stay there because she and Erika couldn't get along. Their constant scrapping made it too hard for Tante Lisi. Mother, with three-year-old Heidi headed west, then north through the Burnt River at Witte's crossing, to Otto Iseles. Olga, the young mother, had just lost her new-born baby Albert and Mother administered what consolation and encouragement she could.

The next stop for mother and child was the Hans Delfs home, at that time in

Northmark, opposite the present church. She needed to discuss the stock water tank "rotation." There was a water shortage that winter, and not enough snow to melt for livestock. Delfs had a large tank which fit on a sleigh and he lent it to neighbours who took turns hauling water from the river for their animals.

Northmark Store was the next stop, where the very talkative Peter Frank, brother of Christine Jacobs, was looking after the store while the owners were in Grande Prairie. It was evening by the time Mother arrived back home, after picking up the children, and having made many a mile with horse and sleigh, over cold, snowy roads. This part was always difficult:

> *It had turned very cold and we were glad to be home. It's at times like this that I feel especially vulnerable, lonely and deserted. We arrive home shivering and tired, to a cold dark house. Quickly I carry the little ones, all bundled up, inside and make a fire in the heater, and light the lamp. Then I unhitch the horses, let the cows in, and do the chores.*

Our father loved little children and had often written about his own to his relatives in Germany, describing, in some detail, our growth and development, our behaviors and antics. Now he was missing out on these precious years in the lives of his little ones. This was one of the most painful aspects of his confinement. Mother was very aware of this, and now she took it upon herself to keep him posted — it was her turn to write about the children.

Even Dieter and I, eight and nine, would not have understood the full significance of Father's absence from our home and family, and the responsibility and difficulty this created for our mother. All discipline, all comforting in time of sickness or trouble, she now bore alone. Even seemingly small problems had to be dealt with. In September a pack rat had moved in upstairs and made a terrible racket, so that every night Gerta cried and couldn't go to sleep. We hoped it would soon be caught in our trap.

During the first months of Father's absence we children got to take turns sitting in "Vater's Platz" around the table at meal time. At first the little ones did ask a lot of questions. Heidi often called for father. When Prinz barked at night, she would come running, "Vater kommt! Vater kommt!" Mother would have to tell her "No, Prinz is just being silly." Then, thoughtfully she'd say " Father far away. Father no comes home. Just Nummi here."

Dieter and I grew up fast, I think, during that time. We had to assume responsibilities that were beyond our years. When Mother had the flu and was bedridden, I had to stay home from school and look after three little sisters, one of them a wee baby. I was eight years old! A trip to the dentist was planned, so a spot had to be reserved in Jacobs' "taxi." Dieter drove the team, with a sleigh full of girls,

Heidi, Irma, Gerta in "dress-up" Hats.

including two of Molls, to Northmark Store to make the appointment. No adults accompanied us, and at ten, Dieter was the oldest!

Mother seemed to have confidence, and placed a great deal of trust in us. But sometimes we were not so confident ourselves, felt abandoned, and needed reassurance:

> *Two weeks ago, on Friday, I went to Solty's to help with sausage making. I left Gerta and Heidi at Moll's, where Ursel and Dieter would pick them up after school. I took Irmchen with me on Moritz. When I returned before noon the next day, as we rode out of the bush, I glimpsed a red dress flitting into the house. Immediately all three came running to meet us. Dieter was in the bush where Uncle was cutting firewood. The girls had cleaned the house and Ursel was washing dishes. That night at bedtime they all crawled into the big bed — needing a greater feeling of "togetherness" and security.*

In September, Mother praised our work:

> *Finally, with great difficulty, our wheat is cut. The children and I did all the stooking . Even if they can't do a lot, the little ones are not so alone and I don't have to worry about them. Yesterday the children did the milking alone while I finished setting up the last bundles. Now Uncle has gone threshing in La Glace and we are managing well by ourselves. The children are helping so nicely. Sometimes I don't have to do the milking at all, and now we are digging potatoes.*

At Andersens, Wembley
Vera & Oscar Thiel, Dieter & Ursula Pankow
Front – Karen and Erika Andersen

When Mother plowed the summerfallow field, Dieter and I took turns staying home from school. We looked after the household and the little ones, helped water the horses, and dragged manure out of the barn.

During the summer holidays Dieter and I had been invited to the Erich Andersen's at Wembley. We spent a week there, together with two Thiel children from Elmworth. We were impressed with Andersen's extensive chicken operation, and their large garden which included many long rows of strawberries. We had never seen or eaten that many tasty berries! These friendly people were most generous and empathetic towards our family's situation.

Mother had missed her two big helpers, and although she was very glad to have us exposed to these new experiences, she was happy to have us back home. Following our visit, Helga Andersen wrote a letter to Mother:

Back – Dieter, Mother, Ursula
Front – Gerta, Irma, Heidi

> *What a lucky mother you are to have such dear good children. It was with a heavy heart that I saw them drive away today.*

This prompted Mother to share with Father:

> *The children — how we love and cherish them. To live for them, to provide for them, to nurture and protect them, is our sacred duty. That they may go forward to face a brighter future is my constant prayer.*

The first Christmas of separation was difficult, especially for Father. Mother had the children, and was too busy to spend time brooding. Her pre-holiday schedule was crowded:

We will start our Christmas Eve early, around four or five, so that Irmchen will not be such a disturbance – the evening is always her restless time. The children are so excited! The two little girls will each get a small doll. I got these from the pastor. The two big ones will get school supplies—a scribbler, a pencil and a cheap fountain pen. Dieter will get a plain bookbag because he has lots of homework now to keep up in Grade four. Uncle was in La Glace with Solty so he probably picked up some little things. I have new underwear for him. So everyone has a little something.

And you were remembered too. Hopefully the censor won't cause too much delay. The large parcel from Tante Minna is intended especially for the bachelors and the orphan boys. You see, many are thinking of you and your fellow internees.

The school concert is on the twentieth. The children are busy learning their parts. Uncle has to make a wooden gun for Dieter's part, and Ursel has a long recitation which she already knows well. All they think about these days is Christmas. Heidi sings "Alle Jahre Wieder" all day long. She still calls you every day and then scolds "Bad war!"

Dieter and I had picked out the Christmas tree that year. It had to be tall and thin to fit into a corner of our crowded little house. We proudly came home with one we had found on the creek bank beside our school trail.

The second Christmas, Father could still not be home with us. We hoped and prayed that it would not happen again. Mother had sent him a little package

My dear children!
I wish you a happy Christmas, which this year you will experience without your father. Hopefully my parcel will have arrived, and I'm sure the Weihnachtsman will remember you. Always be good, obey and help your Mother, and look after the little ones.
Your Father.

of homemade goodies and a cushion cover she had fashioned. Once more, she worked hard to make a nice Christmas for her children, in spite of their father's absence:

On Sunday we want to do some baking. You will remember that there's no use doing it too soon. Nothing lasts long around here and I can really notice that the children are getting bigger, and that there are five. Egges

151

butchered yesterday, so I got some meat and lard on loan until we butcher.
So we'll have pork roast for the holidays, and try to make things festive.
The radio will help entertain us with good music.

My latest game with the children on Sundays is a card lottery with beans
and marbles. What fun that is! It reminds me so much of my own
childhood when mother played it with us. And I think, just as I have these
memories, our children will later have them too. I want to contribute as
much as possible towards making happy memories for them, even when
their dear father is not here. How we miss you! What we wouldn't give to
see you, to speak to you! But life is hard for so many during these difficult
times.

On Boxing Day Mother's letter became a "Thank-you" for Father had sent a
Christmas parcel containing simple wooden treasures which he himself or
his camp friends had made:

You wouldn't believe how happy the children were over the little barn.
Even the big ones left everything else to put Moritz, Suzie and Blackie into
their stalls. The little pigs are especially cute, and the big dog turned out
well for you. My tears fell hot and unbidden on its black head.

Everything arrived safely. The sewing box is splendid! Dieter doesn't
believe that you made it. I find the egg cups particularly nice. Did you do
the painting on them? You see, now I too, am doubting your artistic skills!
And the barn — the way you did the logs — it's ours in miniature isn't
it? Gerta is fascinated with the see-through windows.

The belt buckle is just right for Dieter. Ursel's little heart with the forget-
me-nots is charming and Heidi wailed loudly because she didn't get one.
The sewing box came filled with German materials — probably gifts?
Uncle Dick did a wonderful job on the wooden salad sets. Thank him
kindly for us. You must have had a real craft workshop going at camp
during the last few weeks.

In winter when the roads were frozen, Larson's General Store in La Glace
was a popular place to shop, and was the same distance away as Spirit River.
One person or family would make the trip, and the Larsons must have been
happy to see them, for they carried "store lists" from several neighbours, as
well as their own. The Sieberts and Metzingers, La Glace Mennonite families,
often welcomed these Northmark shoppers to rest a while and feed their
horses.

Everyone had an Eaton's catalogue and mail order was a popular way of
shopping. Household goods, furniture, gifts and clothing would arrive from
Winnipeg, either by mail or by rail freight. It was always an exciting day

when an "Eaton parcel" came. Such enthusiasm reigned at the Toerper house one day in 1940 when Mother was visiting there. Tante Minna, with great pride, (as was her wont) showed off her new washing machine and radio, as Mother returned home to her tub and scrub board.

But she was never one to wallow in self-pity, and knew others also had a "hard row to hoe." Thinking of them, she brought some records over to Mrs. Moll, and later had to report to Father:

> *You had asked for some records. I picked these out from the ones I gave to Molls. Unfortunately they broke the one from the Bund, with the beautiful lieder. I should not have given them to Mutti, but these were not being used, so I thought some one may as well get some enjoyment from them, especially since she's home alone so much.*

Mother kept up her progress reports to camp, even though she was often physically and emotionally drained by the end of her long workday:

> *The little girls love to play with the toy tea set. Yesterday, with Erika and Elke, the kitchen was drenched from all their dish washing. It is quite touching to watch Heidi play with her little doll Dora, which is carefully put to bed in a shoe box. She is quite proud that she has two pigtails now, and declares that they should be very long when her father comes home. Better not! They're all quite enthusiastic about the tiddly wink game that you sent. Gerta's eyes just sparkle when she gets a button in the pot.*

> *Our Irmchen is everyone's darling. She sits by herself in the carriage now and I'll soon have to tie her in. She is small but her little body is plump and firm. Now she eats potatoes, carrots and grated apples. When her big brother plays with her, she laughs so hard she can't stop. That boy is often so full of nonsense, always teasing and annoying his sisters. In spite of myself, I am pleased at his boyish ways. He has so much female influence around him.*

Ursula and Dieter behind Gerta, Irma, Heidi

When it warms up I'll have to take some pictures of the children. We especially want to show you our little Irmchen. She is such a cute little bundle — a real ray of sunshine. I am so happy and thankful to have her.

Much as the little ones provided pleasure and enjoyment, there were times when five children under the age of nine, in a crowded small house, made for stress and commotion. What a to-do there was one afternoon as Pastor Krisch and his son Teddy came to the door. Heidi was howling uproariously because she had been scolded for biting the tip off the large nipple, and Irma cried even louder because she was hungry. Pastor promptly grabbed the little one in his arms, trying in vain to console her, until Mother could assemble another bottle. Following the clamorous beginning, the adults were able to have a pleasant visit over coffee, and were joined by Fieten Egge who had just come for milk. With the fourteenth coming, the older children had been occupied, painstakingly tracing, cutting and colouring hearts in all sizes for Valentine's day. Gerta was getting very excited, because as a pre-schooler, she would be allowed to go to school for the party.

In March Mother writes another "progress report":

Did I tell you that I got some "relief" clothing for the children? It's mostly underwear — good quality things. The children are happy that they can be outside again. Gerta and Heidi always go in search of eggs, but the old hens are eating many of the eggs again. All five kids have really grown, I can tell by their clothes. I said to Heidi "Your father won't know you!"

One of Many Letters Written by Dieter and Ursula to their Father in Camp

Close to tears, she replied "Yes, Father know me. I know Father too. He a man, a big man."

As a result of their immigration to Canada, one of the fears that our parents had, was that their children would be educationally and culturally deprived. These amenities were unsurpassed in their homeland, and could not possibly be replicated in a small one-room country school in the Canadian wilderness. Mother tried to reassure father that it was not completely hopeless, especially with our musical ability:

*Irmchen is a dear little rascal. In her white crib, she bounces up and down on her little bum, especially when she hears music. She bounces with me when I hold her in my arms and twirl to the rhythmic beat. Maybe **she** will have inherited more from your dear mother, as I have hoped with each child. But they're not that unmusical. They would learn a lot if they had singing lessons available to them, like in Germany. Nevertheless, in this too, Mrs. Coogan is quite good. Every morning now they sing previously learned songs. Ursel enthusiastically performed Silent Night and it was pretty well right. Gerta followed with "Alle Jahre Wieder." Now I'm singing spring songs with them, and we're learning "All the Birds are Here Again."*

The gramophone is a fair substitute for a radio, and I'm so thankful to Glimms for the nice records. Gerta can recognize the records by the outside labels, and together with the big kids, they have a lot of fun playing guessing games. The first few beats are sufficient for them to recognize each piece. Even Heidi knows quite a few. So you see, they're not totally lacking in musical ability, and I'm glad about that.

Mother had ordered a hand wagon from Christine Jacobs' catalogue, and

The Children with the new Wagon

Helmuth Glimm, who happened to be at the store, brought it out for us. Uncle helped assemble it and we were all excited about this new addition. It would come in handy for many chores as well as games. Perhaps Irma benefitted most as everyone was happy to oblige when she wanted a ride.

Irmchen is happy in her little red wagon. She has two teeth now and is crawling around everywhere. The cupboards are her favourite places and she clears everything out of them. I have to carefully guard the medicine shelf. She is sometimes quite cranky, goes into a tantrum, throwing herself on the floor, blue in the face and screaming. On the other hand, she can be so happy and endearing. Tomorrow it will be one year since I brought her home from the hospital after her terrible illness. She has grown so nicely, is healthy and plump, runs around so nimble and quick, climbs onto the couch by herself. She's still a bit lazy with her speech though, managing only "Mama" and "Acka" (Uncle) and her own babbling. She is everyone's darling, but Heidi is often very jealous. If I dance around playfully with baby, Heidi comes running for attention. She hits too, when Irmchen won't give up something that she wants.

Heidi and Gerta often play house. Apple boxes are arranged in different corners — by the bookshelf, behind the rocking chair, or by Dieter's bed. Once when one was visiting the other, I heard Heidi say "My father is in camp. He always has to camp." One wonders what goes on in that little head.

When the weather was nice, playing house was done outside, on the sheltered east side of the house. Here a collection of boxes, pails, pots and pans made up a farm kitchen. Dieter had built them a real clothes line so occasionally they had a big wash day. After an evening of this playing, Mother was at the barn milking, when Heidi came running, brokenheartedly weeping "I can't find my Dora and she'll be out in the cold all night!" Mother took her by the hand and started the search. The missing doll was soon recovered, tucked carefully into a shoebox and pushed under the couch so that Irma couldn't find it.

For her own mental health, Mother tried to find a little quality time for herself. When possible, she tried to have even just fifteen minutes of quiet contemplation in the evening before going to bed. Sometimes she played the beautiful "Adagio" by Brahms or some other classic, and read a little. Usually she was so tired that she'd soon be nodding off. Sometimes she read aloud to the children at their bedtime, a chapter each evening, of "Biene Maja", a beautiful story which Mother remembered from her childhood.

Mother also tried her best to continue another family tradition — the annual "signs of spring" walk-about. First stop was at the hotbed to see the emerging seedlings; then a look beside the pig fence to see if the nettle was coming up; down the hill to see the rushing ice-freed creek; and in the nearby garden, a search for the first fresh red shoots of rhubarb. The return route would take us up the hill path to the south, circling back to the house. During this outing too, Father was sadly missed.

They granted themselves few luxuries, but in 1941 Uncle scraped together his money to buy a radio, and set it up in our kitchen. Mother describes the reaction:

> *The radio has arrived, and it's wonderful! We play it nearly all day long, but we'll have to stop that soon, to save the battery. I'm afraid this first one won't last long! But we've waited a long time for this. The children listen to their "Uncle Tom" and Dieter even writes the song lyrics into a scribbler. The continuing dramas are highly exciting too. There are the western stories with lots of neighing and galloping horses, barking dogs and yelling people. I'm not impressed with the ghost stories on "The Mystery Club' and just now there were tears again when I shut it off. Most importantly, we can get news from Germany once a week. I built a little stand for the radio out of three apple boxes.*

Keeping clothing in order for five growing children, considering water and laundry facilities, lack of money and shopping places, was always a daunting task. We were fortunate that Mother was so capable with her old sewing machine and needle and thread. She cut one letter short by saying "It's getting late and I still have things to do. The boy tore his last pair of pants while coasting down the hill today, so that nice green pair from Uncle Werner is finished."

We always came to the Christmas concert performances proudly when Mother had fashioned our costumes, whether it was a fancy cheese-cloth dress for a star drill, or a ragged outfit for Dieter's role as a tramp. And we girls always had special dresses for the concert, whether new, or altered by Mother as she sat stitching by the dim light of the coal-oil lamp.

She was good at "making over" clothes, and was so happy when some article turned out well and she'd saved money:

> *Imagine, I've fixed up Lena's fur coat! You know, the one with great grandmother's pelt? With the collar from an old "relief" coat it turned out quite nice, and I'm so happy. For fifty cents I bought some trim for the old coat, mended, brushed and pressed it, and it looks quite decent too.*

Mother was generous in letting others use her trusty sewing machine, and in assisting those with less experience. Ursula Solty came over more than once for a day or two of sewing. During this time of war, and during Father's absence, Mother was not too proud to dress her children in used clothing, and gratefully accepted gifts from Lutheran Relief, the Red Cross, or from her American friends, the Rampoldts. Nothing was wasted. Clothing no longer fit to wear or outgrown, were bundled up and sent to a mill to be made into blankets.

Garden with Sunflowers

Spring was always the time of new hope and new beginnings. After the little "spring exploration" walk with the children, planting the garden soon followed. And Mother wrote "Again I planted many sunflowers especially for you. Hopefully this time they won't stop blooming before you see them." During the first spring, and then harvest, of Father's absence, Uncle managed, in spite of his tedious ways, and with the help of neighbours, to get the crop planted and harvested. But Mother soon realized that trying to work together was impossible, and the neighbours couldn't be expected to help every year. They had enough work of their own. So for the year '42 Mother rented our land to Uncle, thinking this would give him more incentive. He was very proud of this arrangement, as he told the neighbours, and at first made a great effort. But nothing changed — he could not get things done. Mother had the same worries and responsibilities, saying "He can't help how he is."

Otto Toerper and Horst Solty had agreed to make hay, on shares, at the river quarter. Mother would get one third, and was pleased with the exceptionally good yield:

> *The haymaking is finished. Imagine, fifty-nine loads! It has been an exceptionally good year for hay. Unfortunately, at the end there was an ugly scene. For two weeks our "friendly neighbour" had always allowed Horst Solty to drive through with his loads of hay. But then he'd had a fight with Fieten Egge again regarding some fence. Having to vent his*

rage on someone, Stein promptly barricaded the gates. When Horst came along with his load of hay, he opened them to get through as he had always done. Like a madman, out of the blue, Stein grabbed the horses' reins and yanked them around. Then it came to bloody blows. A blow from an iron rod resulted in a hole on Horst's head, and a very swollen black eye. The frightened horses, now without a driver, ran back down the road , where Toerper was able to bring them to a stop at the lower gate. He had been raking hay in the nearby flat.

Horst went to the police, who suggested he should lay charges against his assailant. Tommy (Crawshaw) was in Spirit River for eight days, as replacement for the chief.

"My friends have advised me to hire a lawyer," said Stein. Although Oltmanns supposedly drove around with him, no one would lend him any money; not Shofner or Bryan, or whoever else he asked — just Oltmanns' ten dollars! The police probably expected that they'd be keeping Stein there right away, but the judge was lenient, considering the war and the shortage of personnel. Stein received a warning that next time he wouldn't get off so easy and had to pay twelve dollars in costs. The judge said that as long as he didn't have his fences in the right place, others could drive through. Walter Lawrence had testified that neither gate was on Stein's property. For now he has been dealt with.

The weather, as in farming everywhere, again played a crucial part, and harvesting was fraught with difficulty that fall of '42:

The children and I are busy stooking. Unfortunately, rain is coming at the wrong time again. Yesterday we made only four rounds. Gerta and Heidi ride the binder-pulling horses; they're the "whips." Yesterday they were soaking wet when a shower came very suddenly. I was down in the garden, and with Irmchen on my back, I just barely made it up the hill before the rain came. The two big ones are a big help in the garden. (I remember weed pulling as our least favourite job. Those long rows

Stooks of Oat Bundles

in the creek flat garden seemed endless to us. Digging potatoes and hauling them up the big hill was not quite as bad Ed.) *They help water the horses and bring them out of the barn — otherwise Uncle wouldn't get going until evening!*

The knotter on the binder is not working right again, but I told Uncle not to stop on that account. It's so cold, we fear snow is coming. I carry a big pile of binder twine by my side and tie up the loose bundles. At first my finger was blistered, but now the skin is tough.

Threshing was always an exciting and hectic time, also a time when feelings ran high. No wonder — livelihoods were at stake! In September 1942, Mother wrote, telling some of the "complexities" of threshing time in Northmark and Westmark:

This year Otto Toerper threshed for us. Unfortunately, he threshed a lot of grain into the straw. I noticed it the next day as I was cleaning up around the strawpile. I immediately sent a note over to Egge's where he was threshing , to alert him of the situation. Better that I tell him, than having someone else make fun of it, especially Oltmanns. Otto had already noticed the problem and corrected it. Of course I won't talk about it.

You can't imagine how hectic this "race for the dollar" is by these threshing outfit owners! Earlier they always thought "oh those people on the south side can wait. They won't run away." This year three outfits were here! Egges and Soltys had ordered Toerper from the beginning. Hans Delfs had indicated, that anyone who didn't thresh with him wouldn't get their feed grain ground. Under this threat, Wittes switched back to Delfs. He was out west, threshing feed grain, but when it wasn't dry enough, moved out again, to Mitchells, leaving Wittes high and dry. So then Joe Murray moved his machine from the north side, and threshed the whole west. What a performance! You wouldn't believe it!

Mother on the Plow

In September, Uncle went threshing in La Glace. At other times, too, when he would leave in anger or frustration, unhappy with his own inefficiency or after a "difference" with Mother, there would be an air of relief and calm around our farm, even if there was more work. We children seemed to help more willingly when

Water Barrel

Mother was alone. And she took pride in little "accomplishments" like backing the wagon up perfectly to the hog barn door to unload the chop. She even borrowed Egge's sulky plow, and with three horses she plowed the summer fallow. Frieda Witte always does it. Why can't I? she reasoned. And Mutti Moll admired her newly plowed field with its straight furrows.

Before winter set in, we all did a major cleanup around the yard. We cleaned the chicken house and put fresh straw on the floor; we picked up and hauled away scrap wood and garbage; we cleaned up the workshop and tool shed; we cleaned the barn and hauled the manure to the garden. Last of all we hauled two large barrels of water. Although we were very tired, we felt pride and satisfaction at this family effort.

Our entertainment was simple and we demanded little. Perhaps this was because everyone was in the same boat, and we knew nothing else. Cowboy song records, serial radio programs, the "funnies" with "King of the Royal Mounted" and "Blondie" once a week in the Free Press, Mother's reading to us — these were all simple enjoyments.

In June when Dieter was eleven years old, he wrote to his father:

> *Yesterday most of the kids from Westmark School walked over to Northmark School to play ball. Northmark won 55 to 9. On the way over there we found two birds' nests, a prairie chicken's and a graybird's. On the way back we had to stop at school to pick up our lunch pails. When we got home we ate Heidi's birthday cake.*

Picnics, Christmas concerts, birthday parties with simple home-made or no gifts, these were attended by all and cost very little. Any outing, no matter how short or simple, was a treat. One day Mother put the three little girls on the back of Uncle's bay mare and led her east along the bush and across to Tante Hermi's. That was great fun for the girls and they got to play with Christa and Hella.

Father could never get enough of hearing about his children, especially the baby he didn't know. And Mother complied:

Irma is quite a little rascal and is mimicking a lot now. When she gets scolded, she goes to the other children for sympathy and protection. She loves Dieter most of all, which makes the big boy proud and he plays and jokes with her.

Ursula Solty's Birthday Party, July 2 '41
Back: H. Solty, R. Moll holding Jürgen, H. Glimm holding Peter, R. Witte
Middle: U.Solty, E. Moll, M. Toerper, O with Otto, F. Egge with Erika
Seated: E. Egge holding Hans, E. Pankow holding Irmgard, F. Witte holding Siegi Solty,
Trudy Glimm holding Ulrich
Children in front: Geesche Glimm. Heidi and Gerta Pankow. Elke Egge

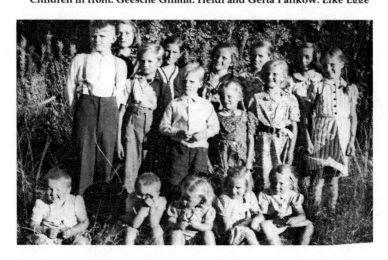

Ursula's 10th Birthday Party
Back: Clesta Dale, Ingrid Moll, Margaret Moll, Ursula Panko, Elma Dale
Middle: Klaus Delfs, Dieter Pankow, Victor Delfs, Gerta Pankow, Maria Moll
Ursula Delfs. Front: Elke Egge, Erika Egge, Irmgard Pankow, Christa Delfs, Heidi
Pankow

It's good that the snow isn't deep. Heidi packs one or two layers of kitchen stove wood into the wagon and hauls it into the porch. She does this all alone until she has a large pile, and then she's very proud. She's a real little schmoozer, the first to get up in the morning, the first to go to bed at seven at night. Heidi is a strapping, strong little girl. She can be very sweet to Irmchen, but usually there's war. She wants to be first in every situation, especially with Gerta. They're very competitive when it comes to gathering eggs, each wants to carry the most or be the first to announce how many there were. Heidi's tears flow very easily these days. It's comical to see how she hides her things — hat, mittens, doll — just to keep them safe from Irma. Her favourite song is Wilf Carter's "Back to the Bible" which they hear on the radio, and she sings it with gusto, to her own tune.

Gerta recognizes a lot of songs. The little ones have an advantage over Dieter and Ursel, because they've had a lot more exposure to records and radio. Gerta, as the middle child, feels that she belongs to "the big ones," especially when the Moll children are around. As they walk home, she accompanies them a ways — up to "Dick's foot." That's her sign, near the south gate to where the dog dragged the old horse's foot. She's getting quite good at hopscotch and wants to be prepared in a lot of ways when she starts school. The two girls follow Uncle everywhere, and are a patient audience when he extolls the virtues and condemns the vices of the horses and cows.

Ursel is quite sensible for her age, even when it's not always easy to be the "big sister," and to have a brother who wants to be boss. They have quite a bit of homework now. Dieter is starting to read fairly big books, mostly cowboy and mountie stories. He wants to be a policeman but worries that he won't be tall enough. Sometimes he takes down the guitar and pretends to be Wilf Carter, singing and yodeling.

It was good to have the big ones back after their week in Wembley. They help quite a lot — you don't realize it until they're gone — with so many little jobs that I had to do myself. Now they take the cows out to pasture, and bring them back in the evening. They do most of the milking. Even Irmchen brings her little syrup pail and has to be allowed to squeeze out a few drops.

That little one is a real sweety and has the other children wrapped around her little finger. I think she has the cheekiness and clowning of your brother Hansi. She has to see and examine everything, running around saying "Let me see!" At bedtime when it's time to say prayers, she calls "Mama, Amen."

I feel so sad for you, that you can't enjoy these precious years with your youngest. When she sits on Uncle's knee and they laugh and play together, a feeling of sadness and bitterness comes over me.

Heidi is still a real egoist, always has to be first, have the biggest and best of everything. Gerta usually gives in, just to keep the peace. Heidi always wants to speak English now, and was very proud when Mrs. Hague in Woking understood what she said. Gerta is really looking forward to school, but the prospects of finding a teacher are not very good. Dieter is complaining that the holidays are too long. He's rather moody and reluctant these days, complaining about every task. He, most of all, needs his good father. Ursel is very ambitious about learning, and though it doesn't come as easy to her as to Dieter, she's ahead of him in Catechism. She helps in the kitchen too. Today she had to make dinner — sauerampfer suppe — while I patched overalls. Then she's quite pleased.

During those "camp" years, letters were the all-important link, the ties that bound, the bright spot in the week. For Father it was relatively simple to time his mailings to arrive regularly for the Friday mail day. Mother wrote faithfully every week, but for her to get letters mailed was an ongoing problem, and opportunities had to be actively sought.

Egge was going to Woking to haul a load of wheat to the elevator, or Mother had to go to Spirit River for binder repairs, Janssen was going to Woking to ship pigs, or the pastor was taking  Mrs. Witte and Mrs. Delfs to Spirit River to "report." Dieter or I could ride Lucie to Northmark Store; the truck driver who hauls lumber from the mill would mail a letter. All these were opportunities to make sure Father got his letter. Sometimes it was more difficult. During busy harvest season, no one could take the time. Sometimes after a chinook the roads were so icy that one could not travel with unshod horses.

Even church services presented possibilities for getting the mail away:

On Sunday Ursel and Gerta rode to church to take the mail to the pastor. But they missed him. Apparently he had gone back home because the parishoners were all too busy with these terrible harvest conditions to attend a service. So the two girls rode on, all the way to the manse. You can imagine how proud Gerta was!

Mailings at Northmark had to be timed so that Jack Ranch, the local mail hauler, would not be missed as he took the mail to the train in Woking.

Mail to and from Germany came to an almost complete standstill during the war. While interned, Father could receive 25-word post cards from Germany, and could in turn let Mother know any news about her family. The International Red Cross also served as an intermediary for short messages. Before the U.S. entered the war, American relatives received letters from Germany, then sent them on to Canada. Else Moll's Aunt Kate Rover in Seattle, and Elise Delfs' sister Martha in San Fransisco kindly served as "mail forwarders" for several Northmark families.

Since Father was allowed to send cards to Germany from camp, Mother admonished him:

> *When you write to Germany again, please do send a card to my family in Cranz, with congratulations and best wishes for my parents' golden wedding anniversary which is on May fourth — if Mother and Father are still alive. How I had always hoped, that under any circumstances, I would be home with them for that occasion. I have to try somehow to get greetings to them.*

All mail in and out of camp had to pass through the censor and his little red stamp could be seen somewhere on each letter. Father cautioned Mother never to write anything that could possibly incriminate her or arouse any suspicion. The length of his letters was limited to twenty-four lines and could not be sealed. Given the rural postal system, Mother never knew how many curious people had read Father's letters before they finally arrived in her hands. Pastor Grober alleviated some of this by picking up Mother's mail and delivering it personally. The Northmark post mistress was one of those "over-zealous" patriots who was rumored to examine all mail to and from Germany in a "more than careful" manner.

One day when we visited Witte's, Mrs. Janssen had just brought over a letter from Georg, which they shared with Mother. They knew that Father was in camp, and Leni had immediately written to Königsberg although Mother didn't know how she knew the address. Georg was active in the western campaign in Germany where Harald Glimm, H.von Berlepsch and Gottschalk are all proud military men.

During that same time, Gertrud Glimm had been notified by the Red Cross that her only brother, younger, just twenty-one years old, died during an air battle. And Karl Stein's brother, the captain of the Lloyd, is supposed to be in a Canadian prison. They nabbed him near Java.

Mother knew how much our father missed his children, and again she wrote:

> *You will be reminiscing a lot about the past, because the present holds so little for you now, and who knows what the future will bring? If only the war were soon over! The waiting is so hard, the yearning so strong. But I mustn't complain, and should instead, think of you and your comrades, whose freedom has been taken away, and of all the misery caused by war all over the world.*

> *Sometimes when I am so tired, I have to force myself to write, but my thoughts are with you always — daily and hourly. No writer could keep up with all the letters I compose in my head. And sometimes, so unlike you, I break down and the tears come unbidden. But in spite of all, the children love their mother, and the little ones come and stroke my hand and wipe away my tears, so that a forced smile reappears. Oh, I should not have written today, in this mood, but the children are going to church school in the morning and can take my letter for the pastor to mail.*

Mother was curious and asked Father if a Pastor Harder had ended up in camp. Apparently he had preached in Chinook Valley School a number of times, and said that England's downfall had been predicted in the Bible! Thornton and company immediately reported him. Tommy (Crawshaw) burned or took away all the Bible study materials. She also wondered if a Pastor Wulf had recently become an internee. Apparently he was also a "sacrificial lamb" like Father. And Wolfram, does he hold services for you in camp? she wondered.

George O'Hara, the elevator man, had once hunted in the mountains, and told Mother that Kananaskis is the most beautiful place in Canada. But beauty was a small consolation for having to kill time there.

The homesteaders in Northmark noticed little of the war. Everyone was pleased with the good livestock prices! The economy was on the rise. Shortages, however, were becoming evident. The many customers who shopped at Larson's in La Glace — Delfs, Nagels, Molls, Egges, Wittes, Soltys, Toerpers — used to buy in large quantities to make the long trip worthwhile. Now they were lucky if they got half as much. At Jacobs' store they could buy only the bare essentials because he could not afford to buy large stocks. Eaton's mail order goods were "war quality" and only a portion of each order would arrive. For those with money, opportunity beckoned and competition thrived. When a whole business block , with four stores, burned down in Rycroft, Mrs. Dodge in Spirit River was not properly sympathetic. Probably envisioning future business, she commented "What's that in comparison to the sufferings of war?"

Mother was not impressed with the comments of another woman in the community:

> At the Woking Store, Mrs. Hague, that old bag, is always sweetness personified. But she has spread unbelievable rumors about you. And now she pretends to feel sorry for me, and purrs "He was always such a nice man." What a fake.

Another sign of war was evident as Mother and the children stood on the station platform in Woking, waiting for the N.A.R. to take them to the dentist in Grande Prairie. As its whistle sounded loudly, a long military train whizzed by, each car filled with grinning and waving black American soldiers. Apparently it was the second of its kind that day — probably headed towards the Alaska Highway.

One day in July, '41 while Mother was working in the garden, she heard a very loud roar. Seven planes flew overhead, heading north on the old postal route. Three had often been seen, but now these seven gave them a small glimpse of what war is like. The first one was flying very low and could easily be identified as a bomber. "Are they going to bomb us?" asked Gerta in a frightened voice.

The effects of conscription began to show and local men went off to the military. The young teacher, Pat Weisgerber, would enlist in the new year; next Willie Janssen and Hans Delfs would be old enough. Clarence Rye joined the R.C.A.F., Norman Rowe, the MacDonalds and Tommy Crawshaw joined the army. Freddy Mitchell, because of his large farming operation, was excused from duty. He had just married Dixie Gray, the young Chinook Valley teacher. And there were indeed many mixed emotions when our Uncle Horst Anders got his call!

In a letter of encouragement, Mother tells Father to keep his spirits up, and reminds him of his experiences when he was first taken in:

> We just shook our heads at the idea that you would ever have to be in handcuffs in this "land of the free." If it weren't so serious, you could laugh yourself to death at the thought — Günther Pankow in handcuffs! Really you should be quite proud that they consider you so dangerous! But that's war. And as Tante Anna always said of any questionable situation "Who knows what it's good for?"

In an effort to gain freedom, the prisoners of war and their families sometimes requested a hearing to have their case reviewed. These hearings, if granted, were held with the prisoner at one end, and the family and home community on the other. Mother knew that their request had been granted, when on November 21, 1942, she received a telegram. Later, noticeably

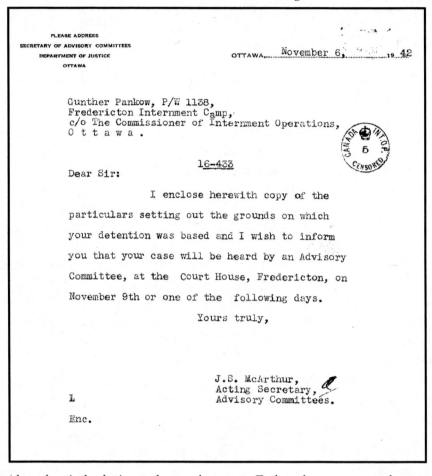

PLEASE ADDRESS
SECRETARY OF ADVISORY COMMITTEES
DEPARTMENT OF JUSTICE
OTTAWA

OTTAWA, November 6, 19 42

Gunther Pankow, P/W 1138,
Fredericton Internment Camp,
c/o The Commissioner of Internment Operations,
O t t a w a .

16-433

Dear Sir:

     I enclose herewith copy of the particulars setting out the grounds on which your detention was based and I wish to inform you that your case will be heard by an Advisory Committee, at the Court House, Fredericton, on November 9th or one of the following days.

     Yours truly,

     J.S. McArthur,
     Acting Secretary,
     Advisory Committees.

L

Enc.

excited, and quietly daring to hope, she wrote Father the sequence of events:

I want to start out by telling you that our impression is one of hope, and we think that from Ottawa's viewpoint, you are already destined to be freed. But here, we're not sure. Because the telegram came via the post office, our opposition knew about the hearing. They have had time to plan and were working very hard.

On Friday the 21st there was a meeting at the school, which I attended. We wanted so much to keep our young teacher (Pat Weisgerber) a little longer and this was up for discussion. Afterwards the men of the U.F.A. had their farmer's meeting. Sloat's children called to me "Mrs. Pankow, there is a telegram for you. We put it on the table at Egges because no one was home." Naturally, I rushed right down there and read the good news. I was just going back to the school when I met the police. They were looking for Dale and found him at the meeting. Harvey had disappeared from the army training camp. Poor Dale became very agitated, and everyone immediately thought of the other brother, Harold. But it turned out that Harvey was perfectly O.K. and just didn't want to be sent overseas. So Dale calmed down and was able to turn his attention to my problem. He promised to be in Spirit River on Tuesday for the hearing.

On Monday, Fieten rode around trying to recruit. I was very discouraged with his report. Many were backing out. On Tuesday I got up early in order to get going on time. Uncle agreed to look after the children. The roads were icy, but at the store I was very happy to see "my delegation." We were in Spirit River much too early, because the train carrying the dignitaries was, again, late. I had taken along some knitting, and from my seat in the hotel lobby I could see out to the street. "The others" were whispering and scheming with the fox and the post mistress. Corporal Watts' presence had thrown a monkey wrench into their plans. He is stationed in Manitoba and wasn't expected to appear.

The "opposing" group consisted of Frank and Maude Rowe, Marie Eyres, Don MacDonald, Fred and Lloyd Mitchell, all brain-washed by Rowe. My group appeared first, and consisted of Hans Delfs, George Shofner, Orm Bryan, Clarence Dale, Joe Murray and Don LaPointe. Others had agreed to come but were afraid to openly support you, fearing to appear pro-German and suffer retribution.

The biggest help for us was the appearance of Corporal Watts. Judge Miller was a humane gentleman with a sense of humor. One of the observers was Doctor Levy, the eye specialist, who recognized me right away and spoke to me in German. The other observer spoke German too, and was quite friendly. I couldn't place him but felt I'd seen him somewhere before. They looked a bit surprised when they saw me and smilingly asked "How did you manage to harness the horses? Did you have to climb on the mangers? You're not very big!"

The judge asked me "Can you promise me that you will look after him and see that he never again spreads propaganda?" Promptly George Shofner spoke up "I will accept full responsibility for that." All the men who came along with me knew that "the old fox from the west" was the ring leader. The good part for us was that they all thoroughly disliked him, and this was an opportunity to stand up to him publicly. And the postmistress has a reputation for dubious behavior.

But Watts was the greatest help as he said "Yes, I know all of you better than anyone else." The judge commented "I can see that Pankow is the honest one in the settlement, but what is his opinion of the Third Reich? I think the concentration camp will have cured him."

While the opposition prepared for its appearance, I just remained sitting in the lobby, much to the consternation of the ladies. They had unexpectedly met Mrs. Poirier from Chinook Valley as they were coming in, so she was cajoled into coming along. She kept whispering nervously "But Mrs. Eyres, you have to tell me what to say. I don't know anything." I'm sure she doesn't know you. It was nauseating to watch. They kept leaning over the table, stretching their necks, trying to hear what was being said in the next room. So these are our proud and loyal Canadians! It's this underhanded skulking manner that our men so detest.

During the interrogation, they said that they had nothing against Pankow personally, but certainly moral would suffer if a man who was once found guilty and dangerous, were now allowed to go free. I'm sure they will, in the fastest way possible, send fat letters to Ottawa. We'll have to be patient until some answer comes.

I have completely lost my peace of mind, that which I had so painstakingly tried to achieve in the past few months. I keep thinking there's more I should have said, things I could have done better. But it was such a nerve-wracking experience. After the fact it's always easy to think of what one should have said.

The first half of December came and went. No answer, no indication had come. Mother feared that her Christmas letter wouldn't arrive at camp in time. She had put it off as long as possible, secretly hoping that it would not have to be written. We were all hoping so strongly that Father would be home for Christmas. But that was wrong, and we all sent our greetings and best wishes for his third Christmas away from home. Our parcel to him was rather "war like" with sugar rationing and all, but it was prepared with love. Dieter had to be admired for his self-control and did only a little "taste testing." Karl Toerper had come over for the address. So Tante Minna must have packed a little parcel too.

Mother's mood and peace of mind were not conducive to writing a happy Christmas letter, but she did not want to disappoint him:

My dear, this will not be a decent letter. I have so little time, so little peace. Last night I finished costumes for Dieter and Ursel. Then the chop was all gone, and Solty couldn't come. So I had to go to Hans Delfs again to get the grain crushed. Daisy had a big healthy bull calf and she's turned into a nice quiet milk cow. Water was getting scarce again, but the recent chinook cured that.

Now a little about the children. Dare we hope that you will soon see them? They're very busy learning their parts for the concert. Remember just a few years ago they were the beginners. Now they're the big ones. The young teacher is very conscientious. Even Gerta has a recitation. I told the children I'd rather stay home, have peace, and keep the house warm. You should have heard the protests! Dieter said "Why am I learning all this if Mother isn't coming?" So maybe I can make a deal with Dick Moll. I'll offer him our big sleigh, so he can take us all along, and I won't have to see to the horses.

Gerta is managing school just fine and likes it. The big ones are often impatient because she dresses so slowly, can't find her things ..... Heidi and Irmchen start in the morning, playing with the barn and the animals. All old building blocks are gathered together to build a fence. The living room is always one big playroom. Dieter thinks it's terrible when he comes home and finds everything in a mess. It's the same on wash day when the table is piled with wet clothes. "Ja, der Herr Sohn!"

The children are suddenly big, the house too small, the sleeping arrangements insufficient. Irmchen is looking forward to seeing her father, and Heidi says knowingly " Father will come. Mother went to the police."

Yesterday a car drove west on the main road, and Hans Delfs thought the police had brought you home. He was all excited. But probably the big law men won't have time to review your case before Christmas. So we have to be patient. Our minds will search you out on the twenty-fourth.

Else Pankow 1942

Father's hearing at the Court House in Fredricton, and the presentation by Mother and her supporters at the hearing in Spirit River were not in vain. By the end of December, Father was released!

Excitement ran high in the little house on the homestead. Mother made hurried preparations. She had always dreamed about meeting Father "when he got out." Now arrangements had to be made so that she could be absent from house and livestock for a few days. We children would stay at Solty's. I can remember so clearly the day Mother left the Solty house to go to Edmonton on the train. She had skillfully "fixed up" a hand me down dress from the states, and it now fit her perfectly. We children thought she looked beautiful — so slim in the blue outfit with subtle rose and gold patterns. Her face glowed with happiness and anticipation.

A few days later, our parents came home — **together**. The long-awaited homecoming was, no doubt, a happy joyous occasion, but it was very subdued. The little girls smiled shyly at this man, and Irmchen peeked cautiously around the corner. We had to become reacquainted with our father, who had become a stranger. It did not take long, and he was so happy to be home. Father's sister Anneliese in Germany learned the happy news from a camp friend, and would let other relatives know.

Fredricton, N.B.
December 25, 1942

Dear Mrs. Anders

I can give you good news that your brother Günther Pankow was released from here and has gone home to his farm. Although he won't be able to correspond with you from there, I would be happy to serve as an intermediary.

With best wishes,
Manfred Ropp.

The war was not over, and the results, it seemed would not be as Father had anticipated. There was no possibility and no desire now to return to Germany. He returned to his family and to his homestead, happy to be in Canada. (For Mother it must have been quite a change, and a relief that she didn't have to write a letter every week. But how fortunate we are that she was such a faithful letter writer, and that she preserved them all. Otherwise the many excerpts used here would not have been possible.)

A Family Reunited 1943

Mr Barrier
Kananaskis.

Chapter 15   Impressions Of An Internee

During Father's two and a half years as a civilian prisoner of war, he found himself with a great deal of time on his hands — time to think, to brood, to contemplate. He felt a need to share these thoughts, and it helped to pass the time. The twenty-four line censored and unsealed letters that he was allowed to write, severely cramped his style, so he wrote two journals. One was intended for his children, and included family history as well as experiences during the first years in Canada and on the homestead. Information from this journal has been incorporated in several chapters.

The other journal was intended for his wife, our mother, and was directed to her. This diary contains a great deal in the way of information and philosophy, as well as everyday camp happenings. It also reveals something of its author's personality. So it was deemed appropriate to include here the translated account as he had written it. These impressions were written during internment in Kananaskis, Alberta; Petawawa, Ontario; and Fredricton, New Brunswick; in 1940, 1941, and 1942 .

KANANASKIS, Alberta

3. 2. 1941 Today, with six months of confinement behind me, I feel the need, and above all, have found the inner peace of mind, to put to paper the many thoughts and impressions that have been going around in my head. I consider this quiet morning to be a cozy visit with you and feel a very strong emotional bond. That, of course, is always the case, on a   daily, almost hourly basis. I miss not being able to visit undisturbed. What can one write in twenty-four paltry lines? And then always under the eyes of the censor, and since it is an open letter, the occasional curious but unauthorized eye of some Northmarker? In order to avoid this state of affairs, I'll write some of my thoughts down, and you can read them when I'm back home. That will save me a lot of telling, and provide incentive to write more. And something else — very seldom, the thought occurs to me that I may not see you again. One could be unlucky, and through an accident, either in felling trees, or by driving on these treacherous mountain roads, be suddenly called home. In such a scenario, it would be nice for you to have a few written mementos from your husband, telling you of his life in prison. For the very first time in our marriage, he was separated from you and the children, for a lengthy period of time.

It was not until I was here, that I came to the full realization of just how much, with every shred of my being I am attached to you and the children. In conversations here in the barracks, one hears so much about other marriages, about family life, and there is so much smut, unfaithfulness on both sides, meanness, misunderstanding, and many other evils. Then I ask myself how you and I have been so fortunate — what did we do to deserve this? Because I think we enjoyed, as the term goes, "a happy marriage." We never said so in so many words, but inwardly we both sensed it. And remember how, during the first eleven months of the war, we were so glad that I could be home with the family?

I remember vividly the 11th of August, and am still glad that on Sunday, instead of going to the river quarter to cut hay as I had originally planned, we slept in, and I had to rush, grabbing breakfast on the run, to race over to the Pastor's, to help with the manse renovations there — or rather to receive my summons to appear for interrogation. You will have heard through Alfred Sellin how things went in Spirit River. Was he ever lucky! And at that time he made speeches and promises about protesting, hiring lawyers etc. There are rich people sitting here who have already spent hundreds and thousands of dollars on lawyers, only to remain confined behind barbwire. And Otto Delfs was lucky too, because as Corporal Watts and I drove by the Delfs farm, he expressed the opinion that Otto would be the next one he would have to pick up — because of ridiculous reports that he possessed German U-boat information.

As Alfred was released and I remained in the cell I did feel rather alone and abandoned. In the following days and weeks so many impressions engulfed me, that gloomy thoughts were temporarily subdued. I thoroughly enjoyed the sixty mile an hour trip to Peace River in a brand new car.

But it was a terrible feeling that evening as the door of the basement solitary cell in the Peace River prison closed behind me. Especially since no one knew, or wanted to know, what was to become of me. In this manner, Saturday, Sunday, Monday and part of Tuesday passed by. Only for the three meals a day was I let out of my cell into a small lobby. Here I ate without much appetite, together with six or seven fellow prisoners, mostly young natives.

On Tuesday afternoon, after I had been photographed from every angle, "my" mountie took me, by car, to the station and we boarded the train to Edmonton. At nine o'clock in the evening we had supper at the hotel in MacLennan, and of course people stared at me. I saw the school inspector there, but under the circumstances, I refrained from greeting him.

For the night we made ourselves comfortable on the train. That is to say, the mountie, a conceited, unpleasant official, locked my right hand to his left. He commented dryly that this way we could both get a good night's sleep. I got quite a fright when we arrived in Edmonton early in the morning. The car seemed to be heading in the direction of Fort Saskatchewan where the big penitentiary is located. To spend the rest of the war there would not be a rosy prospect. Luckily, we did eventually turn off at the somewhat outlying police prison, and it was here that I finally found out that I was to be sent to Kananaskis. In Edmonton it was more bearable than it was in Peace River. Only from seven in the evening to seven in the morning were we locked (two to a room) into the small cells. During the day we could spend our time in the large, bright, high - ceilinged waiting room, pacing up and down, reading, playing cards and visiting. I soon met a Schwab and a Berliner who were also destined for Kananaskis. Day and night there was a constant "coming and going" in the prison and that was quite interesting. One could see and converse with all kinds of law-breaker types.

I had a feeling of horror that people are forced to spend years in prison, especially if, due to unfortunate circumstances and less through their own will, were forced into a criminal act. I know today that ten out of the 670 men here, have their wives in the prison in Kingston, Ontario, and only because they are German, and some scoundrel reported them to the police. Just imagine, the husband here, the wife in Kingston prison, and where there are children, these farmed out in some institution! I feel an especially deep compassion for these comrades. Our room elder, Prof. Dr. Bürzle of Munich, had his wife there until Christmas, and suffered greatly as a result. But they have no children and now she is living in Winnipeg again. So compared to many others, to whom fate has, through this war, dealt much harder blows, we must not complain. If only I could let you know that you must be even more careful in your letters and avoid any hint of criticism. One can trust no one, least of all our censor, and we must give no one the slightest reason with which they could possibly incriminate you, the wife of "the dangerous P.W. No.572." But I know that you have the good sense to write very little politics in your letter.

But back to Edmonton. On Friday morning we got ready for our trip to Seebe, after an awful night with terrible diarrhea amongst all the prisoners. A variety of sounds and odors, plus the constant clatter of the chamber-pail covers in the cells continued all night long.

In the morning, we three Germans, pale from the previous night's experience but in good spirits at being out of prison, were taken to the railroad station by a pleasant Mountie. A beautiful new train brought us to Calgary. Our "bodyguard" treated us like gentlemen, even invited us for lunch in the dining car. Naturally we enjoyed this last bit of freedom. We spent from two in the afternoon 'til midnight in the prison in Calgary, then boarded a very crowded Continental Express for the two-hour ride to Seebe. As we were leaving the train our good Mountie had to hand-cuff us together, as these were apparently his orders, and the three "criminals" had to walk single-file through the long crowded car to exit. At the station, similar to Woking, a military truck was waiting, we were released from our hand-cuffs, and a half-hour drive through the dark cold night took us to our camp. Lit up like a city, it lay in deep sleep, except for the patroling guards, side-arms ready. I recognized the double fences and the watch towers from pictures I had seen in the newspaper.

Our Mountie handed us over to officers of the military police who were on duty inside the camp, unarmed except for night sticks in their pockets. We were temporarily accommodated in an empty barracks and soon fell asleep. Next morning there were many new impressions. Through the barbwire-covered windows we could see the camp, the mountains and several P.W.s who had on their backs a large bright red circle, and on their right pant leg a wide red stripe. So this is what prisoners of war look like!

A good substantial breakfast was brought to us in our locked barracks, and after two hours we were led to the Quartermaster store to be clothed. We turned in our civilian clothing and received the blue denims with the red markings, underwear, shirt (with a red circle called the target ring), shoes, socks, razor, toothbrush — practically everything, and in good quality. Then we were designated our places in the mess hall as well as our beds in another hut. For dinner that day we appeared for the first time among the others.

7. 2. 41 The "new" ones were stared at curiously and appraised, but especially were plied with questions about the current events. "What do you think — how long will the war last?" being a common query. The comrades from the bund (Society of German Canadians), whom I knew only through correspondence but not personally, soon got wind that Pankow finally landed here too. They had not been able to understand how come I had not been interned right from the start. Naturally there were many conversations back and forth and it was a good feeling of security that one was not here alone among strangers, but had found colleagues with whom I had been connected for several years through work with the Bund.

I soon became accustomed to camp life. Our barracks which held only two men when the three of us arrived from Edmonton, soon filled up with new internees and reached its full capacity of twelve men. They wanted me to take the responsibility of "room elder," but with wise foresight I declined. Dr. Bürzle, although only thirty-four years of age, was professor of German language in Winnipeg, and he took the position. On the whole we are satisfied with our room. There is relatively little quarreling and friction, and with few exceptions the roommates are pleasant and likeable. Of course everyone has his foibles but in time we got used to each other. We arranged our room to make it "homey," but I and many others didn't take this too seriously, because we thought in a few short weeks, at the most months, the war would be over. To spend the whole winter here was a thought I refused to accept. But this is how it was with every newcomer here. Even the first winter of the war, the prisoners here thought it would last, at the most, until spring. And that is how it was with us who came in the fall. At the beginning one reckoned time from room-duty to room-duty; you ask yourself "will your turn, twelve days from now, still come around?" And then with each haircut, that it would be the last one in camp. Then we no longer did this, and now one doesn't think at all anymore.

To blame for raising these false hopes were the rumor mills which daily circulated some momentous happening in the war. Many times there was to have been a major invasion of England, in which according to Kananaskis rumors, huge numbers of enemy ships were sunk, so that England could endure for only a short time more. The same thing with air raids and so on. At one time it was even rumored that Spain had definitely also declared war on England and that Gibraltar had fallen! On that particular evening — it was the end of November — we found ourselves in a real crazy, wildly optimistic mood because it seemed certain that we would be home for Christmas after all. But the cruel awakening and disillusionment came the following morning when we found out that none of the rumors were true. From that day on I was cured and am now immune to any so-called news. I no longer let things get to me. On rare occasions I am very excited when a dependable and true report tells of a successful German maneuver and I must fight to keep my emotions under control.

So life goes on at a fairly monotonous and uniform pace. Practically from the beginning I've been with forestry — that is road building with pick and shovel until freeze-up, then in winter cutting trees in a burned-out mountain forest. Of course, with the wonderful salary of twenty cents a day, no one kills himself working! This annoys Stan the foreman but there's not much he can do about it. He can't be everywhere at once and as soon as he is out of sight, very little work was done. In summer one sat in the ditch, stripped to the waist to tan, and watched if and when Stan would re-appear. Actually the guards said little and made life easy for themselves too. Often they would chat with us for hours. Only when a car with officers appeared they quickly placed their rifles on their shoulders and assumed a grim expression. Usually they are elderly good-natured fellows — very unmilitaristic. They regard the whole thing as a good job opportunity, as many of them had been unemployed and on "relief" for years. Rarely is there a mean or spiteful fellow among them. When they feel secure that no one is watching they curse the capitalist system and their superiors, but with no hint of German partisanship. As a P.W. one became quite accustomed to these fellows. At the beginning it was a strange feeling to be accompanied step for step by soldiers with loaded and safetied rifles and to be under constant surveillance. During our drive to work the officer with the six or seven rifles belonging to his soldiers sits in front, and the unarmed guards sit with and amongst us in the back. The whole thing seems almost comical at times!

Three times now we have had a break in the monotony of camp life when two inmates escaped. During the five o'clock evening muster when we are counted and have to show our numbered tags, two men were missing. All the barracks were locked at six, everything was recounted and double checked; the officers and soldiers were very nervous. In the following days, until the escapees were pursued and caught, there was no work outside of the camp. For the forestry this meant a holiday. All the jobs inside the barbwire confines — kitchen, carpentry, wood cutting and hauling, laundry — were also done by inmates, and these tasks went on uninterrupted. This was a hard time for the soldiers because they were on duty day and night. Together with the military and the police from Calgary, all passes and roads in a wide radius were occupied. By this method all past escapees had been captured in a short time. It is virtually   impossible to get out of here. It's not without good reason that this camp was located in this rugged terrain.

Correspondence from a German Battlefield to a Canadian Internment Camp

26 . 2 . 1941 With every escape attempt it would be said that we would lose some of our privileges, for example, the canteen would be closed, there would be no more film presentations, newspapers would be withdrawn, etc., but nothing much became of this. Two months ago when the last two

escaped, there was considerable unrest. Without prior announcement, the siren sounded at six p.m. ordering us to the barracks. But no one obeyed, and everywhere prisoners stood around in groups. In the large square in the middle of the camp, some seventy prisoners, in two formations, marched up and down, singing army songs. In about half an hour our "spokesman" appeared with the threatening command from the prison commander that within five minutes everyone must be inside barracks. The response: cat calls, shouting and whistling. Shortly after that, soldiers spaced only a few meters apart, marched between the two rows of eight–foot high wire fences, rifles cocked, and formed a "front" against the camp. Renewed, increased whistling, laughing and shouting ensued. Eventually the prison commander himself appeared, accompanied by his adjutant and some unarmed military police. Through persuasion and reasoning rather than by harsh commands, he managed to disperse the crowd of prisoners. Some rash unthinking guys wanted to jump him, but thankfully level-headedness prevailed among the P.W.s, and common sense kept the upper hand. Otherwise there would have been dire consequences, because we are powerless unarmed prisoners, and the others have rifles and machine guns. Many hate the old guy, and in truth he is miserable and petty and appears to have little feeling of compassion towards us. But I try to view the situation objectively. Of course I sometimes complain along with the rest of them, but I don't think I am capable of feeling a deep hatred. One has to try to adapt to conditions that are beyond our ability to change, and here in my confinement I must make the best of it.

I am more a victim of my various mood swings than I would like to be. I'm afraid a rather gloomy face is often visible, even though inwardly things are not always that bad. But you know and so do I, how hard it is for me to "come out of myself" and that I don't talk much. But my thoughts are all the more occupied and wander too frequently to Northmark in search of you and the children — most of all while travelling back and forth to work in the mountains, and then before falling asleep. I often feel a terrible longing for all of you. How I yearn to be near you, to play with the children, especially to hold Heidi on my knee, to admire little Irmchen, to hug her, to feed her. But it can only happen in my dreams and then there is the cruel awakening. But I must not, we must not complain. Many are already here for one and a half years and I for eleven months less. And what courage our brothers in the German homeland are showing. They are sacrificing their worldly goods, their blood and life itself. And yet, how I would like to be over there, a part of it all. At least one would know what one was good for, and wouldn't have to lead a totally useless drone-like existence in Kananaskis. This reality besieges me often but cannot be changed.

I do not think too often of what we will do with our lives when the war is over. First I have to be back home with you and we can decide together.

Many plans for the future are formulated here, but mostly in a rather abstract form. Many believe in fantastic compensation payments that will be made to them for their time of imprisonment. I too am hoping for some modest compensation because there was such a thing after the last war. But I certainly won't depend on it. A terrible amount of nonsense is spoken and fabricated here, especially when the Kananaskis strategists and politicians are at work. I very seldom take part in such debates. I try to view things objectively, to reflect and reason.

There are all sorts of characters assembled here. Many (about thirty) can't speak a word of German; they are communists and technocrats, mostly of Ukrainian descent, who believe in Russia. Then there are about fifty Italians. Most of them have been in Canada for decades, and have only a very loose connection with Facist Italy. Many of them are rich, successful business men, mostly from B.C. When the Italian troops in Albania and Africa had some failed missions, which the newspapers hailed as huge victories for the British, there were some German prisoners in camp who turned up their noses and made disparaging remarks at the "inefficiency" of their confederate allies. Our room-elder and his father are guys like that, and that evoked some heated debate in me. I often have to disagree with him.

By far the majority of prisoners are Germans. The youngest is sixteen, and the oldest seventy years old. Unbelievable, such old people — many over sixty — that they would still be interned. In many cases father and son are here. There are many citizens who have been in this country for thirty or forty years. Others really don't belong here at all because they have little or nothing to do with the "new Germany." The starkest contrast to these are the fanatical Nazis and noisemakers. In short, it is an assembly of men who have been thrown together, and it is no wonder that quarrels and friction arise. With the exception of the really calm and lethargic, everyone is somewhat edgy and nervous. Regrettable is the lack of discipline. There is precious little self-discipline in evidence, and militarily speaking, the three daily "musters" resemble hog runs! There is no direction in the ranks, chattering, smoking, and childish behavior. Naturally, one could only expect perfection in this regard from the military prisoners (that is P.W. No. 1). One would see military polish there! But with us it's really a "Hommelherde" with no dignity. Of course the positive element in camp try to improve this state of affairs but it's very difficult.

It is hard to believe the number of egoists, misers, complainers, know-it-alls and slobs that can be found here. Theft is common and some go around begging and manage to collect a dollar or two when in reality they are not needy. Some have such petty and suspicious natures, such low self-esteem, that they cannot trust themselves, much less their fellow inmates. You know

Northmark is a paradise and the people there angels compared with what can be seen and heard here. Sometimes one can lose faith in humanity, but that's because the noisemakers and louts are the most conspicuous, pushing aside the good and sensible.

Doubtless there are also many fine and valuable people here, but naturally, with 650 inmates one cannot become aquainted with them all. It is a great pleasure to me that I got to know and appreciate Dick, a.k.a. Eckhard Kastendieck. I get along very well with him and unless I deceive myself, he is a real friend, in the truest sense of the word. I have written you before about the many things that he and I have in common. He was also a leader of the Bund but achieved more than I did. We agree on many things and especially enjoy chatting about our families. We have the same viewpoint about wives and children, the same respect and love. His year and a half of separation from his family have been very difficult for him. His nature is one of basic good sense and honesty.

Since October Dick and I have been working together. We are flunkies, for forty to fifty men at the forestry work site. So we have many opportunities for conversation. Child rearing, religion, work, life experiences all come up for discussion and we found these chances to share something of ourselves to be very valuable.

2 . 3 . 41 Just a short time ago something happened which affected and disturbed me very deeply. The postman brought me a card from my sister Erika. Finally the first mail had come from Germany! They are all in good health, they know since the 28th of December that I have been interned and are thinking of us all in the true spirit of family unity. That part is a good feeling. The part that so disturbed me and moved me deeply was the fact that my two brothers and also your two are in a position to help, even to take part in battle. Hans Jürgen has been a soldier since September '40 and is stationed in the West. On the day of my birthday Werner left, after his holidays, to return to his troops. And I? You know how much I enjoyed those three months when I was a soldier in Allenstein, and what a burning desire I have, to be one again now when it really counts. That is truly no empty phrase, nor is it inconsiderate thinking with regards to the family. But of what use are these impotent thoughts? I sit here behind barbwire and others over there can be a part of it all! Sometimes it is not easy to quietly accept all these things. And in the coming months there will be a number of happenings, when without a doubt the German military force will have great and decisive victories. Today, for example, it was learned from a reliable source, that German troops had occupied Bulgaria — without any resistance. It will be an arduous task to remain prudent and not take it for granted that the war will be over in a few months. That will probably take

until the middle of the summer.

I find it very hard to just sit and wait while history is being made in the outside world. Sometimes I think of it this way: Through my internment, you and I will at least notice and remember something about the war. Later, we too can join in the conversation and feel some pride.

But on to another subject, that of our "flunky business." After a forty-minute drive through the beautiful, majestic mountain forest we arrive at our worksite. While some forty fellow internees travel further up the mountain to cut trees, Dick and I immediately start work in the tent. We have two and a half hours to make meal preparations. In less than half an hour officers as well as P.W.s working nearby, with their guards and truck drivers who haul the wood away, drop in for a cup of tea. Sometimes it's almost like a restaurant business! We are on good terms with most of the guards and also with the officers, chatting amiably on a wide variety of topics. We rib them when they forget their rifles in the tent or when they suddenly put on their "duty face" when a superior appears. Most of the time we two tall, strong men have as our body guard a fellow who is anything but a powerful soldier and either one of us could practically blow him over. It is all so laughable! Swearing is the strong suit of these fellows. It's unbelievable! But we get along just fine with them. One has to know just how to take them. At eleven-thirty forty hungry workers arrive for their lunch of soup, sandwiches and tea. Once or twice a week we (mostly Dick) treat the men to pancakes, potato pancakes or doughnuts. On these days we really have to rush, while on other days we have plenty of time.

Another lively subject is the camp's requisition system (or lack thereof) especially when it concerns clothing. At first these seemed to be in short supply but since November everything was available in generous quantities. It is hard to understand that the quartermaster store would dole out clothing to internees with an absolute minimum of control. Never in my life have I had so many shoes and so many items of clothing. They would last me for many years. Many made no effort to look after their things. Barely worn shoes, socks, underwear found their way into the stove, it was so easy to get a new requisition. There is an unbelievable sloppiness and mismanagement on the part of some military authorities and it would seem that through their totally unacceptable bookkeeping methods they were able to cover up many improprieties of their own. Such is democracy! But thousands "outside" run around in rags and are unable to purchase even the bare essentials. In the last twelve years we ourselves belonged to that class! I can only shake my head at this senseless waste.

The same holds true for the camp food. How much garbage is produced by

650 P.W.s and 150 military men? And nothing is recycled. The waste is unbelievable. Now why should I care? Perhaps such ideas would not even come to me if we hadn't, all these years on the homestead, skimped and saved, making do on our meagre income. The incredible waste I see here then comes into ever sharper focus.

In this context I am involuntarily reminded of several other facets, brought about by the crass sudden change in my way of life and my human habitat. Before my internment, our whole world actually revolved, more or less, around Northmark, and we knew only a limited circle of always the same people, who lived under circumstances very similar to our family. Here I have become aware, even if only through conversations, of the fortunes and careers of others, that there are many things in the world besides Northmark settlers. Perhaps for me this is a pretty good period of transition and preparation for Germany. One learns to use a different measuring stick for some things. Today, for example, I can't begin to understand why we, in spite of our most difficult financial situation, did not get a radio, or a washing machine. That I didn't more often keep Sundays and stop work in the evenings; that you have to this day, never seen the Peace River. And then too where cleanliness is concerned: here it goes without saying that I shower twice weekly, shave daily and brush my teeth twice a day. Unfortunately it was very different at home and it was quite a concession on your part to put up with me and my prickly beard! Now in this respect the camp has succeeded where you were unable to. Of course personal hygiene is so much easier and more convenient here with showers and running water. However, I hope I will not fall back into my bad habits when I'm back home again. In the final analysis, what were the reasons for us at home, that we cared less about outward appearances, that we allowed ourselves so little, that we never took the time? One lived under the delusion that this life-style would result in progress. In itself a commendable goal to strive for, and certainly better than having to feel reproach for laziness and indifference. But now that is all for naught. With renewed hope and courage we will make a new start in Germany. I believe that I have the necessary strength, both mentally and physically. I am so glad that, on the whole, I am quite healthy, robust and strong. Sometimes we have wrestling matches in our barracks and so far I am undefeated.

7. 5. 1941 Now almost two months have passed since I last wrote anything down. So time goes on and the war is still in progress. One can be truly satisfied with the progress of the Germans lately. These are unbelievable achievements. As a result the mood in camp is one of optimism and it is firmly believed, that in a matter of weeks, at the most months, England will be defeated. Some English and U.S. newspapers have already admitted to this. But even in me, the optimist, there is always a shadow of doubt — too

often we have hoped in vain. And so I am careful in what I say. It is a miracle that England has been able to withstand the massive air raids and the major defeats in the Balkans and Africa. And now if there is the possibility of the U.S.A. becoming active in the war, who knows how long it could drag on, especially for us here in Canada. There are some days when everything becomes totally repugnant to me and I become utterly depressed, a feeling I have never known before. At times like that I get the horrible feeling that the war could possibly last for months, maybe even another winter. Luckily these depressions never last long with me, I'm able to shake them off and soon be myself again. You know my attitude: one has to come to terms with facts and reality; also with the fact that spring is here and we are still separated. How often I would like to hold you in my arms! And that I can't work in the fields now and seed the crops — this bothers me very much. This tells me that perhaps I am, at least partially, a farmer, and any possible conversion to an urban career would probably be quite difficult for me. After different conversations with fairly knowledgeable people here, I do have an inner hope that we could find a rural settlement over there where we could make a living. Hopefully Germany won't treat us Canadian-Germans any different from her native sons out of the Baltics, Bessarabia, etc. A massive resettling will occur, and under these circumstances our farm in Northmark could have considerable value. With regard to the resettling of the Baltic people, Ropp just had good news from his brother. If it turns out as well for us, I see a rosy future for the Pankow family. For you as a woman, life would be no harder over there than in Northmark, perhaps somewhat easier, because a mother with five children would qualify for the help of a B.D.M. girl. But these are probably just pipe dreams and we must wait and see.

I'd better tell you some more about camp life instead. You probably read in the paper about the escape of twenty-eight prisoners from a camp in the east. You can imagine how empathetically we participated in the event. In honor of the four men who were shot to death, we rose to our feet at the barrack leaders meeting. Through a guard we learned further details about the escape and the ensuing pursuit. This guard had returned the last two escapees, who had fled as far as Medicine Hat (1400 miles) before being captured. He had a lot of respect for these two young pilots — quiet, educated men who spoke both English and French fluently. During the many nights these men had dug a long tunnel underground and carried the dirt out in their pant pockets. That camp was situated in a wilderness of sand and pine forest. The discipline there is outstanding — the prisoners administrate it themselves. They decorated the graves of their slain comrades with flowers and wreaths and were busy chiseling grave stones.

Sometimes we can get all kinds of information from individual guards. Of course this event was highly interesting to us. Since this mass escape, our camp, too, has tightened regulations. Now there are unexpected middle of the night inspections, to make sure that no one is digging! During the day, mattresses and blankets must be rolled up in such a way that two - thirds of the bed-springs are visible. Maybe somebody could be hiding tools under there! It is laughable!

I want to say a few words about our national holidays — January 30, April 20 and May 1, the celebration of which has been prohibited. As a result we had to resort to trickery. At the last possible moment, the time and place of the meeting is made known by word of mouth and everyone congregates at the hall. The orchestra, seated on the decorated stage, plays a march, then short "to the point" speeches, our national anthem, Horst Wessel lied, and a closing march. Before the police can or want to do anything (they have a habit of trying to avoid trouble) everything is over.

I feel the need to communicate with you again today, because emotionally there is so much for me to assimilate. Yesterday the news struck like a bomb that Russia is now also at war with Germany. Now it will be another tremendously difficult task and a lot of sacrifice before peace can even be contemplated. To think that we little, insignificant Kananaskis inhabitants had already imagined that in a matter of weeks, possibly months, England would break down and there would be peace. But this huge war truly consists of many wholly unexpected actions. Now one has to adjust one's whole thought process. At first we were totally naive and saw the whole thing only from the narrow perspective of our camp: bury your hopes once more and sit here a little longer. But human nature is really quite tough and tenacious, and we are inclined to look for the good and the hopeful rather than the evil and undesirable in any situation. So after only a few hours, the numbing silence was replaced by lively debate, the consensus being that peace will still be achieved this year. And the end result of this war would, now that Germany will acquire a lot of land in the east, be of special significance to us German land seekers. But the waiting is so very, very hard.

My homecoming will be so wonderful that it's beyond imagination. There will be a return to some privacy in my life. The presence of so many people is really getting to me, the worried and unhappy faces, the barely controlled and thinly disguised nervous tension. Any humor is forced and is expressed in the form of dirty jokes and crude stories. How I long to sit around the cozy family table in our little house at home after a lovingly prepared home-cooked meal; a clean white bed; in the morning I would play with the children. But we have to continue to be patient.

In camp today I had an interesting change of pace. As a fill-in I worked in the officers' quarters. Three times I washed huge quantities of dishes; swept, washed and waxed floors, dusted the furniture, etc. I wanted to become acquainted with the operation of a Canadian officers casino. These fellows have it pretty good and on average their work and their capabilities are less than that of a German officer — the same is true for the soldiers. The kitchen is very well organized and practical. I just hope that some day I will be able to arrange one as comfortable and work saving for you.

Recently another small sensation was created in our camp. The police discovered a tunnel under the building, which a number of inmates had built in order to attempt an escape on some dark night. The tunnel started under the addition to the new kitchen and was nearly half completed when it was, quite by accident, discovered. The poor guys had a rather rude interruption to their plans, and for several days hung their heads in disappointment. The commandant breathed a sigh of relief because the thing was discovered in time. Had the escape of twenty or thirty men succeeded, he likely would have been fired. Now of course more stringent security measures were instituted. All the barracks which were nearest to the eight foot fences had walkways made around them so that during the night the guards could shine their lights and listen to make sure no one was digging. That's how dangerous they consider us!

You know what is going to happen now? The whole camp is going to be disassembled, but not because we are going to be released, but to be transported to two other camps in the east. Today we know only that we're going east and that the "Reichsdeutschen" and the Canadian citizens will be in separate camps. Without the Communists and the Italians there are only about fifty of us German Canadians, so we will probably be put in an international camp at Petawawa near Ottawa, Ontario. The other five hundred will likely go even further east to New Brunswick on the Atlantic coast. On Monday the twenty - first of July we will start the long journey — three to four days. Under other circumstances a trip like this would be a welcome change. But as prisoners under military surveillance it will not be a pleasure. At least for the present time our thoughts are occupied with this large-scale move, and for a little while you forget this wretched existence. Everyone is packing and by way of the stove untold valuables are going up in smoke and flame. It is a disgrace, the amount of little or never used clothing and shoes that are being destroyed, simply because one cannot or does not want to take too much baggage. What mismanagement! And millions, even in Canada, are unable to buy themselves even the most essential clothes.

This evening the band played for the last time and there was a festive yet solemn atmosphere as we sang the old army songs. We will lose some

187

comrades who had become friends, like Ropp, who will be going to a different camp. But my closer circle of friends, like Kastendieck, Tobber, Jaske, Mayer and others will be staying together. That is worth a lot.

PETAWAWA, Ontario   25. 7. 1941

We arrived in Ontario! I must tell you a little about this huge relocation because we are allowed to write so little in those paltry censored letters. On Saturday the nineteenth of July all large baggage was inspected, some meticulously, some just superficially, then taken to the railroad station. There were huge amounts because in the course of time every one had, through "requisitions" and souveniers, accumulated a lot of things. The suitcases which we ourselves had constructed now came in handy. Sunday was rest day and we were asked to turn in our blankets. Each man was promised two new blankets for his use on the last night and then for the trip on the train. In reality, these "new" blankets were taken from the pile which had just been turned in that morning. This was a highly unhygienic situation. Among this many men there are always a number who are not clean and chances were you could end up with their blankets. Of course a storm of outrage followed and the furious official in charge had to order all blankets to be turned in again! New blankets were ordered from Calgary but these did not arrive until we were on the train. Consequently our last night in Kananaskis we slept without blankets. Again and again we met with unbelievable mismanagement, waste and abuse of public revenue. For example: the quartermaster exercised no control in assuring that the original number of blankets, mattresses and pillows were turned in. Dozens and dozens of these went up in smoke.

On Monday, the first group, those destined for New Brunswick, stepped forward. In their blue "uniforms" with the bright red circles and carrying canvas bags, they marched in goose-step through the gate, being counted many times in the process. The rest of us stood like a guard of honor and called our last farewells. At noon the rest of us followed the same procedure and were all loaded onto trucks. A whole motorized column, some thirty-five trucks and motorcycles, which had arrived during the night, then brought us to Seebe. Here we were loaded onto the waiting train. So we got a chance to see a part of the Canadian army in action — outfitted in military fashion, complete with steel helmets, machine guns, and gas masks. What a procedure, all for civilian internees!

We traveled first-class, on green plush upholstery! Walking canes and jack knives had to be turned in and windows could not be opened more than four inches. There were three unarmed soldiers in each coach and two armed ones at each outer door. During station stops these soldiers took up their rifles and stood guard all around the train. Civilians were not allowed within thirty meters of the train. For our three meals, five men at a time from each coach marched to the kitchen and picked up their very meagre meals, and ate them at folding tables. Four internees then washed the dishes in the coach washroom. Hot soapy water was procured from the kitchen. The dishes remained in a cupboard in each coach. It was all very practically arranged, especially the kitchen. But was it hot!

On the morning of July twenty-fourth we arrived at the railroad station in Petawawa. The military reception here was huge. Between each truckload of P.W.s there was a truck manned by six fully-outfitted soldiers, and on each P.W. truck there were two unarmed soldiers. The whole convoy disappeared in a huge cloud of dust and we could not even wave good-bye to our comrades travelling on to New Brunswick. After a half - hour drive we arrived at the camp and again found ourselves behind barbwire. To start with we don't like it here at all. There are only about 120 Germans here, 50 Frenchmen, and 400 Italians, so a real international situation, and hence a spirit of good comradeship is lacking. There are no flunkies to serve us as they did in Kananaskis; instead everyone picks up his own food, then bolts it down at any non-designated, none-to-clean table in the mess hall. We live in large well-built barracks with sixty men and the beds are bunk style. So again we are surrounded by many people, — no coziness, no privacy, no peace and quiet. The sports program is poorly organized too and if we want

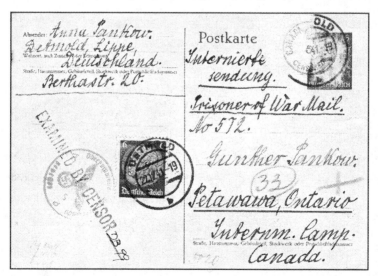

Card from Tante Anna

any improvements we'll have to fight for them. If we stay here, that is. There are constant reports which will not be stilled, that we Canadian citizens are due to have a court-hearing, after which we would either be released or transferred on to the camp at New Brunswick. The commandant told us in a welcoming speech, that Petawawa was only a transitionary camp. In contrast to Watson, this First Lieutenant treats us like human beings, at least appears to. He blathers a bit too much and it remains to be seen whether or not they're just empty words.

10. 8. 1941   The beginning stages of our life in the new camp are now behind us and we all agree that it was considerably better in Kananaskis. Perhaps it is because the confinement has worn us down and we are emotionally preparing ourselves, with horror, for the reality that winter will find us still here. Yesterday the newspaper carried the story of the annihilating battle of Smolensk, which awakened a ray of hope that it may soon be over in Russia. Then there is still England and they certainly won't give up. It is so terrible that nations cannot reach an understanding by peaceful means, that millions have to die, as in Russia now. I so often think of your and my two brothers who must surely be in the midst of it. And I? Always when great critical incidents are happening, I find this confinement especially difficult and sometimes want to argue with fate. But who knows what fate has in store for us. At times I feel such an unrest, as if Werner and Hans Jürgen will not come home from the war and I would be the only one left of the three brothers.

What misery war brings to millions of innocent people! In comparison, imprisonment is a lesser evil in that there is no physical harm. But the mental and emotional strain is great. Even with my quiet, even temperament, I find it hard because we have such a firm conviction and so honestly believe that we are innocent, and would never consider taking any kind of action against Canada.

Your last letter worried me when you wrote you were not well and had to see a doctor. If only you would soon get better! That is another of the cruelties of war. They lock me up to punish me and you become the victim instead. And I can't even write you a tender and sympathizing long letter. Oh, if only this whole misery would soon be over, and people everywhere, not just here, could heave a sigh of relief. But here I am complaining again. Later when you read this at one sitting, it will probably seem like a long litany of complaints. It isn't quite that bad and I'm always thankful for my naturally calm disposition. I try not to let things get me down and one can't always read my mood from the somber expression on my face.

23. 8. 1941 You dear good soul! Today I got your letter with many beautiful photos. How the children have grown, especially Ursel — what a big girl she has become. The little ones are so sweet, but you look so serious and so tired and seem to have lost weight. This separation is so cruel! It is hard to believe that an adult thinking man would often suffer from severe homesickness.

Strangely, as a young man when I was first away from my loving parental home for a lengthy period of time, I never knew homesickness. Yet now, as the father of a family I feel it so deeply. Perhaps that is natural.

We have so much time here, to think about many different things. One of the difficult problems which I had often discussed with Dick, Tobber, and especially Ropp in Kananaskis, was the subject of God, religion and Christianity. On the whole we are pretty well in agreement; even Ropp who has read many philosophical works, and who looks at many human problems with an air of mockery and self-irony. He believes in God as a higher being who guides the world and the insignificant little humans in it. We also came to the conclusion that in Christianity and it's writings in the Bible, there are many lofty ideals and values......brotherly love, loyalty,

Camp Friends left to right: Hans Mayer, Wuth, Kaiser, Eckart Kastendieck, Tangemann, G. Romanus, Günther Pankow

faithfulness, and a rock-solid belief in a concept that cannot be grasped by human understanding; so there is a surrender to fate. But one thing we just could not follow: the concept of sin and divine grace. Everything else can be brought into harmony with nature, but not this. You are familiar with my point of view in this area.

I believe that every time one of our children was, rather reluctantly, brought to baptism, we talked briefly about it without ever coming to a satisfactory solution. Now the children are getting older and no doubt asking questions concerning God and religion. Through many conversations here, and by attentive reading of good books, I think I have learned a lot, and will be able to handle pedagogic problems fairly confidently when I get home. It is very important to never lose control in the presence of children; to always be aware that children should see, in their parents, a role model worthy of emulating; never put a child in a position where he has to tell a lie.

Regarding questions related to religion, be clear and deliberate, referring to the events of nature, which God created in infinite beauty and inconceivable attention to detail. About church and Christianity, one could explain it this way: People don't know how everything correlates but they have their own theories.   And the various churches consider it their right to be a collaborator between man and God. Some people need this liaison, others manage without the clergy and church — and these are definitely not the worst ones. It comes down to inner cleanliness or wholesomeness; a conscious striving for all things noble, good and uplifting, and with that a fight against all that we feel, with a healthy instinct, to be inferior, dishonorable or degrading. May we as parents, succeed in teaching our children these concepts.

It may sound arrogant or conceited, but I imagine myself to be a half-decent and not sinful person. For many years I have not prayed, that is, talked to God or trusted Him with my innermost thoughts. Yet I believe that the last few years have, with you and through you, become the best and richest years of my life, and that I was not a bad person. I also believe that my quality as a person did not change, decline or improve, as a result of no prayer. However recently my thoughts have turned to God and I have asked Him to stand by me. Hidden somewhere within me is this feeling of discomfort, that it was an emergency that prompted me to take this step. It's the worry, the fear that you or the children could get sick and would be unable to cope with a difficult situation. Now at night before going to sleep, these thoughts do not torment me, but instead they find a place of rest and peace up there with God. And like a good child in the last war, I pray that this war will soon end, that our brothers will return home safely, and that I may soon be home with you. Now as an adult thinking person, I find that a large part of prayer is egotism. Every man prays, first of all, for the well being of his own. At this point I feel a strong inner stability, and I pray that it may be the same for you, so that in this way your cruel fate may be somewhat lightened.

I doubt if I would have been able to express some of these thoughts to you in person. It seems somewhat easier to put it on paper. That is true for many things I have written here. But this need for some kind of communication with you shows me how very much I miss you, not only as my beloved, but in so many things that have contributed to our rich and happy marriage. If only we could be together again, happy and healthy! If fate decrees otherwise, and something should happen to me, hopefully this little book will arrive in your hands, to testify once again how very much I am attached to you and the children. For their sake you would probably have to return to Germany. With time grass grows over all sorrows and even under the seemingly most hopeless circumstances, there is always a way out. In the event of my death it would be my sincere wish that you might find a man who is good to you and who would love you even half as much as I do. I think that would be enough, because perhaps I loved you too much. It is useless to discuss here, how you would have to continue life without me. You have proven, during the last year as "grass-widow" that you can cope with life. Your job remains the same, being the mother of our five children, and financially, a way would be found. Should something happen to me as a P.W. you would probably receive substantial financial compensation, and the farm is a valuable asset too.

But enough of that today. I felt it had to be written, but God grant that it be unnecessary, and that very soon we will have each other back. A kiss for you, and give one to each of my five. The two big ones look so sensible and mature; and the three little girls are adorable.

Father's Five at the Hein Schuett Home

Now another month has passed, and at least in the forseeable future there seems to be no hope that this war will end. The English seem to be hanging in there, and with some resignation we will have to accept the fact that we will be here another winter. It is so hard, the insanity of having to sit here for no reason at all. And you have to work so hard at home, even stook the grain, in bad harvest weather. Often I feel a powerless rage in the pit of my stomach, sometimes even a real hatred. But here there is no one on whom I can vent such feelings. The soldiers are harmless and good-natured; the officers leave us alone and do their duty. Oh how I envy our brothers! You know how I enjoyed being a soldier, and now more than ever I'd like to be one. But these thoughts are useless and lead to nothing. One always arrives at the same result: that one will sit on the bed for a while, brooding, like a heap of misfortune. Then one pulls oneself together, shakes it all off and tries to look forward to a rosy future. I hope you are able to do this too, although you don't have the time for melancholia. You are a person who is usually cheerful, plucky and optimistic and I hope our long separation will bring no basic change to your nature. At least you have the children, and I can imagine they bring you a lot of joy, in spite of all the hard work and, I'm sure, some aggravations. Especially little Irma is so cute and sweet at this age. I imagine the little ones are getting quite used to Uncle Horst. Well, I will win them back! You feel the absence of only me, and I presume mostly as a man and a father for the children, to help with their upbringing, to look after the farm and business matters, all those things that have now become your responsibility. I miss so much more, not only you as my beloved, but my good little mother, my life's companion, someone who endured with me through thick and thin for eleven long years, a confidant in whom I always found understanding. And how terribly I miss the children! You know how attached I am to them and how I always spent time with them. I long for the farm and all the work connected with it. Do you remember how proud and happy we always were (with the exception of last year, when we made the decision to return to Germany) to be working all year long on our very own piece of land? And how, in spite of all the slavery, we always looked forward to Monday? Wouldn't it be nice if we could continue this way in Germany? It's a good thing that here in camp we don't see or hear about all those good things I mentioned. Were they visible, yet we couldn't partake, it would be that much more difficult to bear. The long cross-country trip on the train was an all-too-clear example of this.

Soldiers endure many of the same experiences, but in addition they put their lives on the line. But they live or die for a high ideal; their entire living and fighting has a purpose. We surely can't say that about our existence at the present time. The soldier is also separated from his family, longs for his wife and child, but for him, as opposed to the prisoner, there is the possibility that he may never see them again. And yet, how gladly I would trade! What is an individual little human in the world perspective? Naturally a war like this is gruesome and when one gives it some sober thought, it appears like insanity. How much sorrow and misery will be caused again. Who knows, death may already have struck our family and taken a vibrant young life. There will be immeasurable pain for millions of women, mothers and brides, not just in Germany and now in Russia, but in many other countries. A quick heroic death may ease the pain a little for the relatives. On the other hand there will be, as in the last war, the dreadful army of poor unfortunates who are crippled.

And how many marriage rifts will be caused, as many a young girl goes astray. It is easy to understand, human nature being what it is, that a young man, or even a faithful family man, who has been lovingly cared for by a young nurse in a lazarette or elsewhere, could fall in love and start an affair. After the terror-filled experiences on the front every man would probably yearn for the sight of a woman, and some would be unable to wait until they got home to their wives. Conversely some women will not wait until their husbands come home. What misery the war causes in this respect as well.

11. 2. 1942 After a three week absence of mail I received two loving letters

Rear: Ursula, Dieter, Gerta
Front: Heidi and Irmgard

from you, with a number of photos of our life together. It became clear to me once more, what a wonderful time we have spent together in spite of all the hard work and many failures. The most fortunate part is that we loved each other, and that five healthy, happy children were born of this love. Although we found it hard and undesirable at times when a new life had begun so quickly again, this mood soon passed. Through experience and more maturity, and especially through our long separation, we can now recognize God's hand in this. How thankful and proud we are of our five!

The older one gets, and the more time one has to think about all these correlations, the clearer the inconceivable wisdom of the Almighty becomes. If our seemingly long, cruel and hard separation will have achieved this: that you and I have made a conscious return to God, then it has deep and significant value. If we have recognized these things, it will be easier to guide our children in the right direction and to give them a valuable base to face life's challenges. It is good that parents have had to go through all the stages of development, and in that way have an understanding of what is happening in the life of a child and later the young adult. Then they can provide a solid moral basis for the children, who in turn can use it in their own lives. I think back to my own boyhood. When I was the age that Dieter is now, I no longer had a father. That was a grievous loss, especially for a boy, and I realize that even more now that I am the father of a son that age. I can't remember being influenced or affected by any religious training that we had in school. We had nothing but pranks and nonsense in our heads during these classes. I know that in my last school year religion was no longer a compulsory subject and I was excused from those classes. However, in my confirmation classes I was somewhat more deeply moved. But this effect did not last long. What did stick with me was the admonition to always strive for the good, and the will to do that was a step in the right direction. We hope that the nature of our children will have more of the good than the bad, and that a strong will in them will prevent downsliding. You and I have managed that fairly well.

5. 3. 1942 I am very dissatisfied with myself at the present time. For a long time now I have not had a lesson book in my hand. I just have no energy or desire to learn anything. Even with my book of memories I am making no progress. Especially in the chapter on Northmark, the one of most importance to the children, I have only finished up to the year 1931. I just can't force myself to get at it. At least I still enjoy reading and have learned to play chess. But I feel such unrest. Is it spring which hangs in the air, bringing with it the powerful events awakening on all fronts? Will it be the last summer of war? Or does the British Empire, in spite of the monstrous earth-shaking events in East Asia, still stand too solid? It is very hard, in the face of such powerful world events, to be just a silent and idle bystander. Werner has been wounded twice and has received awards of distinction, and Hans Jürgen and your brothers are in the midst of it too.

Although I suppose I would have the same feelings if I had not been interned and were at home with you where I could relieve you of so much of your workload. On the one hand, I certainly belong at home to support you and make it easier for you. But I also know that, financially speaking, I would be hard pressed to have ten dollars in grocery money each month, as is available from the government now. But it would probably be no worse than our fight for existence has been in the last ten years. And yet we would be asking ourselves, had I not been interned, how we deserved to barely feel the effects of this terrible war, when it is having such a decisive effect on our loved ones in Germany. I think you will often have the same thoughts. When you find it particularly difficult to cope alone with all your problems and responsibilities, you must often think of your sisters-in-law and all the other German women whose husbands are not only far away, but also whose lives are in constant danger. I have no doubt that you will continue to accept your fate with courage and understanding, and I know you would not expect me to go against my conscience to gain freedom. Often during the newly revived hearings against P.W.s, the judges ask outrageous questions. For example: Do you hope that Germany will win the war? In case of an invasion, would you be prepared to fight for Canada? And so on. In the interest of diplomacy regarding such questions, one can go as far as a certain boundary, but not an inch farther than your conscience as a German would allow you to go. Should I be granted a third hearing, I will experience these things myself. And should I be released without having to make impossible promises, I would jump for joy. I had given up any hope of coming home before the end of the war. But since a few weeks ago we have dared to rekindle some hope. The fact is, intensive discussions regarding internees are taking place in Ottawa. The indefensibility and unfairness of our imprisonment was brought forward, and in actuality, six or seven men are released daily, although to this point they have been mostly Italians. Will our turn as Germans come too? But the last to be released, if at all, will probably be those of us from the Bund. There is also a rumor in circulation that we may be moved to a different camp. This eternal uncertainty is terrible.

I think when we finally get out of here, for a while we'll feel funny and disoriented in the outside world. This world of men behind barbwire, living in such close proximity, and with so many side effects, is a very unnatural environment. One of our comrades recently came to this realization when he had a visit from his wife. For several months now the P.W.s have "generously" been allowed visits from relatives once a month and to carry on a half-hour conversation, in English, in the presence of an officer. Had we still been in Kananaskis, I would have made you aware of this and you could have decided whether or not you wanted to come. The cost would have been twenty or thirty dollars and somehow we would have found a way. In spite of the short time period — many of the officers are generous and tactful and allow German conversation — with our ever-lengthening separation, we would have found this half hour very precious. We could have embraced and gazed into each others eyes, to discover that we are still attracted to and love each other and nothing could come between us. You could bring the two youngest with you. I could see them and you would not be so lonely on the return trip. In addition to seeing each other, the trip would be a pleasant change for you. This is the image that I always create for myself when the cars of visitors from the east arrive for the P.W.s. But for us from the west this is out of the question. There are 2500 miles between you and me, and it's financially impossible. That's why I've never written you about this. It would just make you more painfully conscious of the vast distance that separates us. For me and for many others from the west, it is always a bitter experience when the others get visitors and we are left empty handed.

17.7. 1942 Our days in Petawawa are numbered. Within the next few days the whole camp will be moved. We do not know to where. Nevertheless, this gives me the push I needed to finally get something written down again. One had become reasonably accustomed to this place. Since three months ago it had become fairly crowded in camp. A portion had been divided off by a special barbwire fence, and here two hundred Japanese had been interned. Now the international composition was complete. Through the wire we had the opportunity to observe these charming Asiatics, and to even speak a few words with those who knew English. The commandant has a lot of difficulties and headaches with the Japanese. They will put up with nothing, have staged a hunger strike and avoid work. One night one of the volunteer workers was beat up. There was mass confusion, and not until machine guns were fired from the watch tower towards the offending barracks, was order restored.

Apart from that, every day is just about the same. The past two days in forestry have been nice. With deep awareness we observed and enjoyed the greening of the forest in May. It was beautiful in the woods even though the mosquitoes were sometimes a nuisance. At the end of June, Dick and I unexpectedly got back our old job as cooks for the twenty men in our work crew. But here we had to prepare full noon meals, not just soup and sandwiches like in Kananaskis. I was not at all enthusiastic about this cooking, but soon got used to it and was trying out my culinary skills at gravies, white sauces and other dishes that I had learned from you. The afternoon made up for all the rushing and sweating that we did in the forenoon. Our little cookhouse was situated about half a mile from a small lake. Right after dinner and dish washing we marched down to the lake, under the pretense of fetching water. In reality this was only an excuse to make our actions more plausible. With delighted abandon we removed our clothes, winked at the uneasy and confused guard on the shoreline, and went swimming for fifteen minutes. In this manner we were able to enjoy at least ten afternoons of swimming and reveled in our own cheeky impudence. It was especially amusing how each individual guard reacted to the situation. Most of the guards are A okay. Many of them were Frenchmen, some of whom can hardly speak English, and hate the British. They admit this quite freely and claim to have joined the military for the money only. They earn between one hundred and one hundred and fifty dollars a month, plus a family bonus, and including room and board. This is more than they had earned before the war. There are many nice, likeable fellows among them and they tell us, with love and respect, about their large families and their farms. We respect their guard duty as having the same authority as their officers. They must not be caught talking to P.W.s as though they were equals. During conversations like these, the insanity of war and our internment again comes into sharp focus.

9.19.42   Now we are ready for departure. Tomorrow, exactly a year after our departure from Kananaskis, the entire camp, unfortunately not just the Germans, will move to Fredericton. Apparently this camp has to be freed for German P.W.s No. 1. So the same hectic rush prevailed in camp as it had a year ago in Kananaskis. Feverish packing was in evidence everywhere and one heavily loaded truck after another rolled, far into the night, towards the railroad station. And tomorrow, we the "living cargo" will follow, probably again under heavy military surveillance. We'll be another 800 miles farther away from you, and distance wise it's almost like a Siberian exile. I have now covered half the distance to Germany. If you were over there already, I would be getting closer to you. If only that were so! During these last days, besides the moving, the monotony was broken by some other events. On the 16th Martin Bodenschein escaped. For a long time he slept in the bunk above me and I had a congenial relationship with him. A pastor's son, a bachelor homesteader, very quiet and prone to despondency, he probably could no longer endure this existence. One afternoon he disappeared into the bush. He had eaten dinner with the rest of us at the forestry job, when all of a sudden he was gone. There was a lot of excitement among the soldiers, road blocks and search commandos were set up, but to this day they never found him. Maybe he will manage to find freedom for a while longer than the past escapee. It's a hopeless situation and an unenviable life, to be pursued like a hunted animal in the woods. But the escape attempt is made over and over again, especially by young German soldiers. Family men usually don't even consider it. The sensational news of Martin's escape had just subsided when a report came that a death (the first in camp) had occured. A black man of the Netherlands marines, who had been ill in hospital for some time, did not wake up yesterday morning. Twice his Hollandic ship, which sailed for England, had been torpedoed but he escaped with his life. However, he was never quite the same again, and when he refused to continue sailing for the English, he was locked up. Many seamen from other nations suffered the same consequences. At noon the hearse came and picked up our Negro. Now we have no black men left, except for the occasional one among the soldiers. What a mix of nations here!

FREDERICTON, N.B. 3. 8. 1942

We are here three weeks now and I must record some of my impressions before they become blurred. One is not nearly as open to new impressions as at the beginning. So the move to here held few new experiences — we knew it all from last year, leaving the train in a column of heavily guarded trucks, every other one manned by eight soldiers with machine guns. We had

Fredericton POW Camp

noticed in the train, that we were not as heavily guarded, had more freedom of movement and were not as crowded. This time we had only twenty-eight hours of travel time ahead of us and spent most of that enjoying the scenery. This time no one was allowed to sleep in the overhead baggage compartments at night. Apparently a short time before, during the transport of German war prisoners, a young soldier had cut out a piece of the roof and was able to escape. Hardly a month goes by without someone, from some camp, attempting an escape. In spite of the complete hopelessness — especially now that the U.S.A. is at war too —many young single fellows keep trying it. Besides a certain spirit of adventure, it's probably a strong desire and pressure to take any kind of action which would interrupt the monotony of imprisonment. The day before yesterday two men escaped from here. While outside the military instigated a great search for the two, the rest of us sat around without any work, until they had been captured.

Back to our arrival here. Our reception was not as warm and spontaneous as in the past when new men came into camp. With time and repetition, things became so mundane. The fact that only one quarter of the increase in population consisted of Germans and the rest of Italians, French and Dutch, contributed to the apathy. This camp can accomodate only six hundred instead of nine hundred. For the kitchen, this creates a greatly increased and unwelcome burden, to say nothing of the three hundred men who are forced to camp in tents. In spite of this, I like it much better here. One just feels a lot more comfortable in a camp that is under German leadership and design. Of course there is unpleasantness here too, quarreling and arguing, but it is best not to pay any attention. Above all there are the fanatical Nazis who consider themselves superior to other good Germans. These people get especially upset when someone takes steps to try and get released. They come here with such "proper" ideas about German honor and integrity, and forget that a family man would be much more useful to his family and his country if he were at home, rather than sitting here idly in camp. Usually these minority types are ignorant and narrow minded, creating a bad image for other Germans.

Also to be found here are bachelors, who, for the duration of the war, have a better life here in camp than they would have on the outside, where they might be homeless or unemployed. Or, there's the family man whose marriage and family is in discord so he is quite content to live here.

I don't let all this affect me any more. During the last two years of maturing, I have on several occasions, had to compromise my pride as a German. I have reached the point where I will make an even more intensive effort to get out of here and to go home where I belong, with you and the children. Whether or not I will succeed is another question. First of all, I'm going to request that another hearing be arranged. Even then it will be very difficult to pass the Commission. At least I will have exhausted every possibility. Who knows how long the war will last. The fall of '42, on which I had pinned such high hopes, is moving considerably closer, and not even Russia has been conquered. Even if this should happen, will England surrender? Judging from past experiences, this is highly doubtful. If the war drags on into winter, then it will likely continue on into summer. One does gradually become, if not exactly pessimistic, but very serious, and tries more and more to face the bare facts. How is it possible, even though they have won no major victories, that the Allies can still hold on? But I better stop talking rubbish. I try not to think this way too often because it is of no avail. Patience is everything!

Yesterday we saw the German film "Heimat" (Homeland), which this commandant, as opposed to the last one, readily allowed us to see. What a wonderful experience it was, for the first time in fifteen years, to see and hear a German work of art, and to let its performance deeply move you. I realized then how much we had missed during our fourteen years in Canada. Hopefully we can soon make up for a lot of it. We as Germans just can't comprehend the American attitudes towards film and culture in general. How painful it would be for us as parents if our children were to take a liking to this shallow philosophy of life. That's something that would be unavoidable if we stayed here. And yet, these years in Canada were so nice! When we have started our new life in Germany, we will have so much to talk about when we are finally together again.

I am always so glad to get your letters and am so glad that you are deriving some pleasure from the farm and outside work. If only there were not that bitter pill concerning Uncle. I fear that his constant presence is more nerve wracking to you than anything else. And there is nothing I can do to change it. It's a dreadful situation that depresses me greatly. We certainly have a cross to bear with these "relatives by marriage."

You wouldn't believe who I met here: a brother of aunt Ella Sürth, Uncle Fred's wife. This Walter Knabe was a boatman on a ship's crew. Known as a globe-trotting bum, he does not have a good reputation around camp. Apparently he has picked up a "bug"— that's the camp term for "barbwire disease." He is happy he has found some one with whom he can share his ideas in endless verbosity. I hope this will ease off. At first it was kind of nice to chat with him about Königsberg, Uncle Fred and Aunt Ella's wedding etc. He is fabulously skilled and has built wonderful models of sailing ships of all kinds. But at least this "Uncle" is not a burden to you, as Uncle Horst is. In our eyes, an exchange between Horst and myself would be an ideal solution, and he would be quite content here. But in the context of world history we are not asked for answers.

4. 10. 1942.   Today my separation has hit me particularly hard. I miss you in every respect, as my beloved, as the mother of my children, as my truest and only companion. It is a beautiful autumn Sunday afternoon and lovely tunes are sounding from the loudspeaker. There is a great unrest in me, I can't seem to undertake anything useful, and this yearning for you, the children and my home has become overwhelming. These feelings come to the forefront all the more because conditions in camp are becoming more unpleasant. Given my good health, strong nerves and calm temperament, I am seldom plagued by pettiness, lack of enthusiasm, irritability, rage, or unhealthy cravings. For many this is a permanent condition, and almost daily there is a minor "explosion" somewhere. This doesn't often get physical, but there is a lot of shouting and insulting. Some old-timers who were already imprisoned in the First World War, tell us that this kind of behavior is a typical phenomenon of internment camps and prisons. I've read about it in books too.

The thing is, this is a most ridiculous and unnatural environment -- some nine hundred men locked up together in a space the size of three or four acres. The little bit of labour that is expected from the work crews at twenty cents a day is a farce. It occupies time but can hardly be classified as work. The daily task is to solve this problem: how to make time pass as pleasantly and quickly as possible. It's good that everyone's taste is different. Many different careers are represented here, and as a result, there are various activities going on, representative of each occupation. Where handicrafts are concerned, this activity is classified as "making souvenirs." At least something positive results from this, even if it's often not practical or useful. Intellectual endeavours are also more or less productive. Various courses are available in camp, many study privately, many a good book is read and reviewed, and deep discussions take place about a wide variety of subjects. A significant number of men find satisfaction in playing cards day after day, even "Patience" or "Solitaire." Some do nothing at all except an unbelievable amount of "bullshitting." One cannot condemn even this type of "occupation." For each is trying, in his own way, to kill time and make his imprisonment as bearable as possible. Truth is, for most the time passes fairly quickly, in spite of the monotony. It is a drone-like existence. Although we do nothing in return, three times a day the state gives us excellent meals, such as many could not afford in private life. There are good warm accommodations, beds with down mattresses, plenty of blankets, and good lighting. We have an abundant supply of good quality clothing such as the average man on "the outside" would not have. Furthermore, we have free medical and dental treatment, film presentations, library, and opportunities to participate in sports. In addition, one can earn twenty cents a day for two or three hours of work. There can be absolutely no complaints about our treatment. The soldiers and officers just do their duty and are almost courteous in their manner. One can almost say the commandant is popular with us. Why is it, that in spite of all these seemingly favourable conditions, one should be so sullen and dissatisfied? What's missing, of course, is freedom, and a man's dignity to carry out his solemn duty of providing for his family.

Then there is the incredible contrast. You sit at home, are forced to do a man's work and don't know how you'll get it all done. Most families of P.W.s are in the same boat. And the men, well nourished, healthy and strong are condemned to sit here in idleness. All over the world people are working to the absolute limit of their capacity to help their country to win the war. Only in prison camps all this able-bodied manpower is wasted. This becomes quite obvious here right now during the construction of new barracks. Youngsters, mere children, and unfit old men struggle labouriously as the strong able P.W.s stand, hands in pockets, watching them. Again, I can only shake my head at the insanity of this world.

(Father's camp journal ends here. He was released from the Fredericton, N.B. camp at the end of December, 1942. When Germany lost the war, his homeland, East Prussia, became part of Russia and Poland. Many relatives lost their lives during the war or while trying to flee to West Germany. There was no possibility, no desire, now to return to the land of his birth. Father went back to his homestead and family, thankful to be in Canada.)

Chapter 16   All Was Not Well

The first wealth is health. .... Ralph Waldo Emerson.

Illness in the family is always cause for great concern. It was even more so in pioneer days. We couldn't call 911. In our valley there were no telephones, no ambulances. Few people had cars, and at times the roads were impassable. The nearest doctor and hospital were hours away. What a helpless feeling it must have been when illness or accident struck.

My first memory of this goes back to when I was eight years old and our father was away in internment camp. The baby sister whom we all loved so dearly was gravely ill. She had failed to gain weight, and now this condition was worsened when she developed vomiting and diarrhea and could keep nothing in her stomach. I will always remember looking up at mother seated in the saddle, on the back of our long-legged old Dick, the tiny child cuddled in her arms. The sadness on mother's face reflected the gravity of the situation as she rode away that evening, to the home of Mrs. Schuett three and a half miles to the west. Dieter and I sobbed quietly as we helped Uncle tend to the little girls who did not yet understand.

Mrs. Schuett was nursing her Bernie at the time. She put the baby to her breast, and promised through tear-filled eyes "I'll help you if I can, even if the little one stays with me for three weeks." For a brief time the two young mothers dared hope, as the breast milk seemed to help. But soon the symptoms returned. Mother again mounted her horse with Baby Irma and rode to Egge's. Fieten summoned the pastor and his car; mother and the deathly ill infant were driven to Grande Prairie where the child was admitted to hospital.

With a heavy heart, mother returned home to be with her other children. Every day at 5 o'clock we listened for messages on Radio C.F.G.P. Announcements were made to people who could pick their patients up at the hospital. Or, "It is with regret that we announce the death of ......", and this message would always be preceded by Dvorák's plaintive "Going Home." Whenever I hear this music even now, I associate it with a death in the community. These announcements were not aired on Sundays.

As we worked with mother in the creek flat garden that weekend digging potatoes, she did not know if her baby was dead or alive. She worked mechanically, forcing herself to keep occupied. Tears fell on the dark soil, and we children did not know, in our own sorrow, how to comfort her. Then on Monday, after what seemed like an eternity of waiting, the message came: "Mrs. Pankow, you may take your baby home from the hospital." What great relief and rejoicing filled our humble little farm house! Irma thrived after that and became a beautiful healthy child.

In her next letter, Mother had good news:

> First of all I must tell you that last week we brought our little Irmchen home. She still looks quite pale, but milk agrees with her now and I hope she'll gradually gain weight. Doctor Little's fee was five dollars and the hospital charged three dollars. The children were very happy, especially Dieter and Ursel, because they were allowed to come along to Grande Prairie. Mind you, they had to use this opportunity to visit the dentist. Dieter was lucky, but Ursel had to have two teeth pulled.
>
> Imagine, Pastor Krisch refuses to take any payment for our trips. Twice he took us to Grande Prairie and once to Spirit River. Hopefully I won't soon have to impose on his generosity again. These trips are quite a strain. In order to arrive at the pastor's by nine, I have to get up very early to get the children ready and the chores done. I brought the little ones to Egge's, and was at Otto Delfs' place right on time. Here Mrs. Solty was waiting to come along for her doctor's appointment.

In March, Mother was sorry to report the troubles of the Schuett family —the lady who wanted so much to help little Irma at the time of her grave illness. Now her own little Bernie, ten weeks younger than Irma, had developed a weakness in the chest and bronchia. Twice he was rushed to hospital with life-threatening illness. Then he was to receive shots for asthma. His mother stayed with him at the hospital constantly. It would be very expensive, to say nothing of the worry and anguish over their only long-awaited child. Now they lived under constant fear and worry because the child was not to catch a cold. The news got worse. Mother's letter in January was one of great sadness:

**Helga, Ilse and Klaus Delfs
Ursula, Gerta and Dieter Pankow**

Helga Delfs came to our place to borrow a hot-water bottle for her little five-year-old sister Ilse, who was sick in bed. I was going to visit Delfs that afternoon to see how the little girl was doing, and take along a fever thermometer. But Horst Solty told me he had met the pastor with Otto Delfs, and what looked like bedding in the car. So we knew they were on their way to the doctor. That same evening Fieten Egge brought us the alarming news. Ilse had died of appendicitis. The operation was too late to help. You can imagine how we are all grieving with them. It came on so suddenly, and there was no severe pain, otherwise they would have gone to the doctor sooner. But this winter there is so much sickness that one does not always expect the worst.

Today at three o'clock I went to the funeral. Oltmanns brought the little white coffin which he had lovingly constructed, and the immediate family, then the Hans Delfs and Toerper families, formed a sad procession behind it. There was a large attendance, both German and English were spoken at the service. While Egge helped cover the grave, I went along and stayed a while with the grief-stricken family. It will take a long time for this mother to overcome her grief. It was with this child that she spent so much time, while the others were in school.

After the death of the little Delfs girl, everyone became more careful, almost paranoid. Since then there were five surgeries that spring, and there was even talk of a virus. The hospital in Grande Prairie was full of appendicitis cases, including a MacDonald girl, Mrs. Kolmus and Frank's granddaughter from Chinook Valley, and Mrs. Jacobs. In March a Neiser boy had his appendix out, and little Victor Delfs was taken to hospital with ominous symptoms. All of this gave Mother pause for thought:

As so often before, and again now, I am so sad that I don't have more skill and knowledge. They often come to me for advice in such cases, and during childbirth . I wish I could be, for this community, that which I'd like to be. You and I have talked about this. But I do what I can. Thursday I'm going to take the expectant mothers, Gertrud Glimm and Lisi Egge to Doctor Gamey in Sexsmith.

One evening Mother had just settled down to write a letter to camp, when there was a knock at the door. At this late hour, there stood Olga Isele who was cooking at Joe Dahl's mill. She had badly scalded her hand, and came to Mother for something to soothe the pain and heal the burn. Mother did what she could and invited Olga to stay overnight.

In April, Mother was again called upon to help:

My dear, last Friday was our wedding anniversary and I had planned to bake a nice cake and take it easy. But things turned out differently. At five o'clock in the morning, Johann Oltmanns knocked on the window, and I had to ride quickly to Gertrud Glimm. Although her water had broken at four, I got there in time and at seven-thirty a big boy (nearly ten pounds) was born — quite a feat for that little woman. All went well. I was all alone with her. Helmuth had gone outside momentarily to see to the other children. I had soon looked after mother and baby Ulrich, laundry and house, and we spent a pleasant afternoon together. Helmuth took me home in the evening.

The Schulz family too, had a new baby, but all did not go well. With the help of Doctor Law, Hildegard came into the world by way of a very difficult delivery. The mother had a troublesome and slow recovery. At one stage, Mother was summoned:

On Monday, Tante Lisi came to get me. Mrs. Schulz was very ill, with heavy bleeding. I drove over immediately and stayed there overnight. Next morning we made a bed on our democrat and set out to try and get Mrs. Schulz to Spirit River. The river was in flood, the roads were extremely muddy, and rain was falling. Thankfully, Jacobs was waiting at Kollmus's, we shifted the patient into his truck, and made it safely to the hospital. Apparently, during her difficult labor, something had been injured, and she would probably require a D and C.

Ursula Solty was probably short-changed, because she had come to our place to sew for two days. Instead she looked after house and children in my absence. But, more importantly, the mother of the four Schulz children was spared.

As Mother finished writing about all these troubles, she concluded by saying that Mrs. Otto Delfs had been bedridden for two weeks with a dislocated foot. She fell on the ice. Hans and Helga had to take turns staying home from school. And how Mother hoped that her family would stay healthy! Irma tried to do something about that one day in March:

Irmchen was sitting beside me as I worked at the sewing machine. She was playing with Dieter's eraser. I noticed that she was rubbing her eyes, which were already filled with tears. When I noticed blood-tinged mucus by her nose, I knew that something wasn't right. With great difficulty, I was able to remove a bean-sized piece of eraser from each tiny nostril. Luckily, that problem was solved.

Then on Sunday Heidichen had a bad fall from the rocking chair, and landed most unfortunately on the sharp edge of a coffee tin. She got a nasty cut on her thumb. As I bandaged it, she sobbed "Father will see my sick thumb too." Then he'd have to come home very soon!

Some more cheerful news. The population of our settlement is increasing. Harry Schack has his son and heir. Everyone in the store that day got a cigar. Just as the threshing machine was at their place, Olga Isele gave birth to twins, Hans and Helga. Lena Backer was quickly fetched to lend a hand. That same evening when Lena had returned home, she gave birth to her eleventh child, all alone. Also, Mrs. Sloat had her eleventh child, and Mrs. Dale, finally after all those girls, had another boy.

Keeping the family happy and healthy was a daunting task for Mother. Fruit and vegetables, though some were canned or stored in the cellar, were not available fresh. Apples, though usually available, were expensive, but the children loved them:

Now again you're sending us your carefully saved pennies. The children were so happy, and will add a little more from their bank. Then we'll go and see if Jacobs has apples. They're so expensive now, four dollars a box — so I haven't had any for a while. But the children just love them, especially Irmchen. I just need to go near the cellar and she cries "Appa, appa," and lies on her stomach, the better to look down. The canned crabapples are gone, so she munches on the marrow pickles, which the others don't like. You will have heard that sugar is rationed now — three-quarters of a pound per person. Who would've thought this could happen in Canada? There certainly won't be any more rhubarb!

Our sausage is disappearing quickly. Irmchen is a firm believer that "In der Not schmeckt die Wurst auch ohne Brot," and holds her empty slice of bread out for more sausage!

In spring the earliest nettles were picked for a delicious and nutritious feed of greens, until the spinach in the garden was ready. The fresh lettuce, served with rich cream was so good that it replaced dessert, which sugar rationing did not allow. Fortunately we children were quite fond of canned tomatoes, and Mother bought them when she could. Mother saw to it that we took cod liver oil as well:

Recently a salesman was here and I bought some cod liver oil with the money that Helga Andersen had sent. This oil is red and tastes better so they like to take it. Right now they're all doing quite well. Just Ursel has another boil in her ear — that's the third one since this fall. During these cold days Uncle drives them to school.

Gerta always wants to come along to do the chores. She is so thin. The little ones are not good eaters, neither eats porridge. At least now they'll be able to have eggs. Ursel is big, but unfortunately she has poor posture — drawn up shoulders. I'm going to order a shoulder brace for her. Maybe it'll help. Dieter is quite lively, but occasionally his eyes hurt. The difficult

*road to school is a strain on the children and they often suffer from groin
and leg pains.*

In June Mother took Gerta to see Doctor Law. He pulled a back molar that
had been giving her so much pain, and also a baby tooth because the
permanent one was already growing in behind it. The doctor told Mother
she should take her to a dentist in order to fit correctional braces. Who can
afford that, Mother thought. Gerta was also measured and weighed, and
found to be only two pounds under the average weight for her age. At forty-
two pounds, she was exactly the same weight as Heidi. So it was decided to
send her to school in the fall after all.

When Dieter was taking part in a pillow fight at the Northmark picnic, he
fell and hurt his arm. It was quite painful and the doctor determined that a
small bone in the forearm was cracked. The boy was to take care and wear a
sling for three weeks.

In July of that same year, a mobile medical school clinic, with two doctors
and three nurses, came to Saddle Mountain School. Mother loaded her five
children into the democrat and drove them the twelve miles to the clinic.
From there, she scribbled a quick note to Father :

> *Greetings from our outing. We just finished with all the examinations. All
> the children were vaccinated. Gerta couldn't get her tooth pulled because
> she was crying so hard. Dieter is supposed to have his tonsils out, but I
> think we'll wait. I want to hitch up the horses now and head back home.*

Father, understandably, often thought and worried about the safety of his
family so far away. The danger of fire, especially with wood heating, was
always there, and no matter how carefully one dealt with it, occasionally
accidents did happen. Mother sought to reassure him:

> *When I go to the barn or somewhere outside, I light just the hanging lamp.
> The large lamp standing on the round table once tipped over, table and all,
> when Heidi leaned on it. Thank God we escaped with only a bad fright.*

> *You know how the matches always hung on the wall on the right side of
> the stove? Well, I had to move them to the other side. Irmchen often
> climbed to look out of the window, and could reach the match box. She
> would chew the tips off the matches. This time the result was not good.
> The match ignited and started to burn. Howling with fright, she threw it
> away. Luckily I was right there. With children, a person just can't be
> careful enough. But you must not worry. These things could happen even
> if you were home. I always knock the soot out of the stove pipes, and this*

winter we have not required real high heat. At times we've even been able to sleep with a window open.

There were the more common less dangerous illnesses which were treated by various home remedies. Mother had occasional bouts of kidney and bladder related problems. Father had a tendency towards migraine headaches, which were sometimes accompanied by nausea, and at times became so severe that he was forced to take to his bed.

Gerta would have been about three years old when she became so ill that diphtheria was suspected. She was rushed to Spirit River, where mother and child were able to stay with the Otto Delfs family until she was sufficiently recovered. Gerta seemed to be most seriously affected when a whooping cough epidemic made the rounds. I remember holding one hand on her tummy, the other supporting her head, as the wracking cough shook her thin little body. I always seemed to feel particularly protective towards this sister, who appeared more vulnerable, her ribbed brown stockings always wrinkled because her thin legs failed to fill them out.

When Heidi was just a toddler, she was seriously scalded when a pot of hot coffee spilled on her back. I can still see the blistered back of the suffering little tyke, as she lay on her stomach on the couch, her back bared to help the healing. A scarred "map" on her body remained for a long time as a reminder of this mishap.

One winter when chinook weather had turned the fields and roads into glare ice, Dieter became very ill with laryngitis and threatened pneumonia. He sat on the edge of the bed, fighting for breath, a sheet draped over his head to contain steam from the kettle. Mother said to me "You must catch the horses. We have to take Dieter to Pastor's so he can drive him to the doctor." Her manner implied great urgency as she urged me to hurry. I think mother was afraid to leave him. Gale force winds blew as I hastened to the barn for halters and oats. I struggled to stay on my feet as I ran towards Bill and Rex, shaking my pail of grain. They could not hear my lure and ran from me, their hooves slipping and sliding on the ice. Again and again I fell as I willed them to stop. The picture of Dieter under the sheet would not leave me. In my child's mind I was sure that my brother would die if I did not catch the horses. Finally they stopped for me and I was able to lead them to the barn. My knees were bleeding, my throat burned in pain, and I sobbed uncontrollably as mother drove off down the slippery road with Dieter. Fortunately he was soon well again.

I had an unfortunate, and probably quite unnecessary incident happen to me the year we walked to Northmark School. On the rough uneven school

211

grounds, I was running a race with my constant rival, Klara Schulz, the spectators cheering us on. Suddenly my foot struck a hole and I went down heavily. Excruciating pain shot through my shoulder. Somehow I got through the last hour of classes. We began to realize that something was quite wrong when I had difficulty walking the three miles home, and Dieter had to help me crawl through the barbwire fences which we had to cross. By the time we got home my shoulder was black and blue and so hugely swollen that mother had to cut my dress before she could remove it. My arm was completely immobilized. The next morning I had to catch a ride to Grande Prairie with Mr. Jacobs. In hospital there, Dr. O'Brien anesthetized me with ether in order to work my arm back into its socket. I had to wear a sling and move carefully for some time, and thereby was excused from milking, feeding and cleaning the barn. But I couldn't play ball either!

The following autumn I spent a few days in Spirit River Hospital with "binder-twine poisoning." After several days of stooking, one finger became very sore and badly infected. Again I was put under ether as Dr.Law lanced and drained the swollen hand.

When I was ten years old, mother took me to eye specialist Doctor Levy who came from Edmonton to Grande Prairie for a few days. We had to drive with horses to Jacobs' store to get a ride to town with his truck. Helga Delfs also had to get her eyes examined so we picked her up. It was in spring, during break-up. The river was so deep at Delfs' crossing that the brown swirling water rushed over the box of our democrat. I remember pulling my feet up on the seat and hanging on for dear life. After a rough ride over the old highway and "suicide hill" we found ourselves in a dimly lit stuffy basement at the hospital. Here we sat for hours, our eyes

Ursula and Dieter with their new Glasses

blurred from the drops, our heads down on our laps to combat nausea. The doctor finally came, and I can remember even then I felt bad for mother when he said, rather brusquely "If you had brought this child to me eight years ago, I could have done something for her." How would this city doctor even begin to understand? At any rate, a week or two later, Helga, Dieter and I appeared at school bespectacled in round steel-rimmed glasses. I don't think I even realized, when I was a little girl, that I was quite cross-eyed. It was not until the jeering and finger pointing at school later, that I became painfully aware. My self-esteem went downhill. I avoided looking anyone right in the eye and developed a "head pulled in" posture. Now these glasses! Would they draw even more attention?

When I was seventeen, something was to be done about this "affliction." Perhaps the widow's allowance partially paid for such an operation - I'm not sure. I just know that one summer day I was on the train to Edmonton, and was soon settled in a room in the University Hospital. Dr. Levy told me something about the impending surgery. The eyeball would be lifted from its socket and before being replaced, a muscle would be shortened. It would be of cosmetic value only and would not improve my vision. He reiterated his earlier statement that this should have been done when I was very young. Mother found it hard to like or trust this man who would operate on her daughter and part of the reason was because he was Jewish. I was more concerned because he was so old and frail!

The following morning the nauseating smell of ether again assailed my senses as I "went under." For several days after the operation my eyes were bandaged and I got a first-hand impression of what it would be like to be blind. On the third day, the nurses gave me a kind word of warning as they removed the bandaging. "Don't be alarmed when you first look in the mirror. This is normal." But how could I not be frightened? My eye was like one huge blood clot, and no white could be seen. This took some weeks to clear and although I still had vision in only my left eye, the right one now looks straight ahead!

When I left the University Hospital I boarded a Greyhound bus to Hillmond, Saskatchewan. I don't know why this trip to Kastendiecks was planned for me. Though "Uncle Dick" was a good friend of my father and a fellow internee, there were no girls my age in the family. I think there was a little hopeful matchmaking going on here. But Herman was either painfully shy or scared off by my red eye. He spent the full time fencing in the pasture and showed up only for meals!

In the year '48 an unseemly amount of misfortune struck our family. It started early in the new year when Heidi, at the age of nine years, began to have appendicitis attacks. The whole community was especially sensitive, almost paranoid about this particular illness. Understandably so, as earlier a ruptured appendix and failure to reach a doctor in time, had taken the life of beloved five-year-old Ilse Delfs, Hans' youngest sister. Now in the middle of the night when Heidi showed the symptoms, our neighbour Johann Oltmanns was summoned, and in his car, Father and Heidi started for Grande Prairie. The roads were extremely icy after a chinook and before even reaching Woking, the car skidded into a ditch and tipped on its side. Fortunately no one was injured. The doctor suggested that Heidi should have an appendectomy, as this was not her first attack.

About the same time, Dieter developed a baffling illness. He would bruise at the slightest impact and be covered with large areas of blue discoloration, apparently caused by a weakness in the blood vessels. And Mother's chronic kidney condition worsened. So towards the end of January, Father took his three patients to the railroad station in Woking. Mother and Heidi boarded the Grande Prairie bound train for their hour and a half ride. Dieter waited for the next train going in the opposite direction for his sixteen-hour trip to the University Hospital in Edmonton. It must have been with a heavy heart that Father drove his team back home, where only Gerta and Irmchen were left to greet him.

Heidi underwent her appendectomy and was hospitalized for ten days. Being young, strong and healthy, she rebounded quickly and was soon her exuberant cheerful self. Mother spent four days in Grande Prairie Hospital undergoing X-rays and tests. These indicated that Mother's left kidney was dead, and that she should be seen by a specialist immediately. On February 20th Mother boarded the train to Edmonton, where she would be admitted to the same hospital in which Dieter lay. He was hospitalized for several weeks for tests and observation by specialists.

Mother's doctor determined that her non-functioning kidney must be removed. This would be major surgery so Mother deemed it imperative to have Father nearby. A message was dispatched over Radio C.F.G.P. in Grande Prairie: "Please come immediately. Surgery to proceed." Faced with this grave situation, he took an unprecedented step. Instead of taking the slow train, he decided to fly from the Grande Prairie airport - one and a half hours instead of sixteen - and the first flight of his life. A neighbour girl was recruited to stay at the homestead with the little girls. Upon Father's arrival at the University Hospital, he was able to meet with Dr. Elliot, who instilled confidence and gave him assurance. The operation was performed on Tuesday morning and would require a two to three week convalescence in hospital. Between his visits to Mother, Father was able to make a long-time dream come true. Before leaving Grande Prairie, he had wired his good friend Eckart Kastendieck in Saskatchewan to suggest that this might be an opportunity to meet. Sure enough, Uncle Dick arrived in Edmonton and the two ex-internees spent many happy hours together, also looking up other camp friends. Thursday at five, Dick boarded the Greyhound back to Hillmond, and Father took the train back to Woking, both so glad that unfortunate circumstances had at least allowed this happy reunion.

Although Dieter had, all this time, been in the same building, on the third floor, he was able to see his Dad only once, and could communicate with his Mother only through notes. A diphtheria outbreak had forced his section of the hospital into quarantine. When consulting Dieter's doctors, Father had learned that although many remedies had been tried, the fragile blood vessels continued to burst at the slightest impact. The specialists made the decision to remove the spleen. This was major surgery and Dieter was forced to endure considerable pain and discomfort. Mother, herself convalescing and still in a somewhat fragile state, really did not deserve to watch her son go through this ordeal. And there must have been a nagging doubt: "Will spleen removal really cure this unusual condition?" With this thought in mind, she sadly bade Dieter good-bye at the hospital and started the long train journey back home. On Good Friday she returned to her waiting family. Some post-operative care was required at the Grande Prairie Hospital, but gradually Mother recovered, regaining her strength. Dieter soon returned home as well, and being young, his recovery happened more quickly. It would remain to be seen whether or not a permanent cure had been affected. Now in April all the patients were back home and fervently hoped that they would see no more doctors or hospitals for some time. Spring was just around the corner, and before the seeding season would start, Father felt that a letter to the relatives in Germany was long overdue. On April 19, 1948, he sat at the kitchen table and penned a long letter — the last he would ever write. After describing the family illnesses he wrote:

> The little girls were truly remarkable during Mother's and Dieter's absence. Gerta (11) and Irmgard (7) did washing and cleaning, even baked bread. Heidi (9) helped me with the feeding and milking, and they didn't even miss much school. I'm sure our quota of illnesses has been more than met. How thankful we would be if Mother and Dieter regain their health as quickly as Heidi did. But we must not be impatient and expect that everything will be back to normal in a few weeks or even months. The financial part of all this will not be easy either and will probably cost about a thousand dollars altogether. We'll have to take a couple of years to pay, but will manage if we get a good crop or two. It's just so painful that a number of urgently needed purchases for farm and house will have to be put on hold. The same goes for a number of care packages to Germany. With last year's frozen crop and the debts incurred in clearing our new land, we are in pretty deep. And right now it's pretty hard to look optimistically towards next year's crop. We just got another ten inches of snow and it's -10F.

This letter spoke of hardships and misfortune, yet had a spirit of optimism for the future. Father sent it to me in the States, to type several copies for him. This raises the question: Where was I during this fateful year when I would have been so desparately needed at home? Although there was nothing I could possibly have changed, I was often plagued with feelings of guilt.

Ready to go to the Railroad Station at Woking where Ursula Boarded the Train for Niles, Michigan

In the autumn of '47 when I was just fifteen years old, I travelled to Michigan to take my Grade X, and to "broaden my horizons." The family took me to the Woking railroad station with the team and democrat. It was a beautiful August day, but my spirits were not bright. A great unknown lay before me, and I was anything but confident. Although I'm sure we loved each other dearly, our family was not one to express feelings openly, especially in public. There were no hugs or kisses from Mother or siblings as we stood on the station platform. Perhaps it was somewhat surprising then, when my father, just before I boarded the train, took me in his strong arms. For a long moment we clung to each other tightly, almost desperately. Call it premonition or foreboding — there was something. I would never see my father again. Fate had not yet finished its dealings with our family in that year of '48.

(Ed. Certainly there were many more cases of illness and accident in the settlement, but could not possibly all be covered here in detail. Therefore, only those that had a connection to our family, or involved Mother's assistance, are included here.)

Chapter 17 Homestead Animals

Our perfect companions never have fewer than four feet. … Colette.

"Our Jutta had a beautiful colt today. The little stallion is roan with a white blaze on his face. The children love him. Tinka has a strong new bull calf and she gives us a full pail of rich creamy milk at each milking. That will be good for shipping cream. I think we will have to butcher our big Emma because the last trip to the boar was unsuccessful again."

These were typical "news items" found in Mother's letters to Father in camp during the early forties. Animals were such an integral part of our childhood on the homestead that I think we could not have survived without them. Some were, at times, cause for anger and aggravation; others became almost like faithful friends and were given names as part of the farm family.

Ursula and Dieter Learning to Ride

During Father's internment, so many decisions regarding crops and livestock now had to be made by Mother. Her letters indicate that sometimes this weighed heavily upon her. Will we have enough feed? How many sows can we feed through the winter? How many do we have to sell? Then there were sickness and accident cases. Some horse was lame, another had collar sores, one got into the grain and became stiff, and another had a dislocated hip. The newly castrated colt became infected. Who will shoe the horses for icy roads?

Getting the cows bred was always a problem because we had no bull. Fortunately, Mr. and Mrs. Maltzan and their daughter Beata, for years kept a bull which serviced many of the cows in the growing cattle herds. This was a big help to Mother:

> *Daisy was in heat while Uncle was away with the horses, taking wheat to the mill. So I had to take her on foot. She leads well, so even though it was getting late, Gerta and I set off with Daisy in tow. Gerta stayed at Egges to play with the girls, and I went on to Maltzan's with Daisy. We were back home by ten.*

When our mares had to be bred, we took them over to Dick Moll's or to Ernie Gabrielson's stallion. In later years, Mr.O'Neil from Silverwood rode around with his stallion and also served as veterinarian on occasion.

There was a time when the cows would not get pregnant because bovine vaginal catarrh was going around. This was serious because no one wanted to be without milk, and many relied on cream shipping and selling butter at twenty-five cents a pound, for extra income. The cows had to be treated, and the question arose "Could the bull possibly be infecting them?" Understandably, Wittes were reluctant to have their bull breed any animals that had been exposed.

Regrettably one of our best cows developed lump jaw. Mother wrote to a veterinarian for advice, and he prescribed a remedy, which Mother ordered. Alfred Sloat brought it from the post office one day. Otto (Isele) and Horst (Solty) tried on several occasions to treat her. But it was all in vain. The lump got ever larger, and finally burst. So we had to "euthanize" Blackie. We had hoped that the meat could be used, but the doctor said no — the carcass was to be burned immediately.

Keeping the cows in the fence was often a problem, and they were forced to wear wooden collars, which prevented them from going through the wire. I always felt so sorry for them with this awkward contraption around their necks. One day our good milk cow Minka somehow got her collar stuck in a rail fence. In trying to extricate herself, she jammed a large nail into her eye.

Only in Spring the Creek Ran High

The poor frightened animal, swollen and bleeding, ran away into the bush. An injured animal seeks solitude. Mother searched for two days and finally found her. Her eye was much better, but had discharge for some time and became blind.

For less serious or more routine ailments — collar or saddle sores, cracked teats, or barbwire cuts, Rawleigh's carbolic ointment, often called "man and beast" salve, was the remedy of choice, and a staple item on every farm. To combat equine worms, our horses were given "sure shot." What seemed to us children like a **huge** capsule was "shot" down their throats, with a trigger-like mechanism. Our baby pigs were given an iron supplement. Each wriggling, squealing little porker had its mouth held open so that a bit of grey powder could be deposited on its tiny tongue. As they got older, brown tankage was added to the feed chop.

Water for the livestock was often a problem especially in the winter. There were no dugouts and even the deepest holes in the creek ran dry. The horses were "trailed" to the spring at Ernie Gabrielson's, and snow was melted in a stock tank for the cows.

In August when Mother was bringing the cows home, she noticed that the creek was running! It had been dry for most of the summer. What a beautiful sight that was, and how thankful we were! "A miracle has happened. God has given us water!" we marveled, and the little ones jumped for joy. We presume that it came from a spring upstream.

Prinz with Irma

I remember our dog Prinz with special affection. He was a handsome black and white part-collie, intelligent and loyal. One winter day he was missing and we were worried. As we searched around the yard we heard a distant sound — a faint whimpering bark, like a plea for help, from somewhere to the north. The tone was somehow familiar. Dieter and I set out through the bush and snow-covered fields, following the sound. Suddenly as we came over a small knoll, there was our Prinz. He was so excited and happy to see us. Why then did he not run to meet us? Because his left front paw was caught in the steel jaws of a trap. We looked at each other in dismay, each knowing what the other was thinking. This was Karl Stein's trap and it was on his land.

219

Many youngsters were afraid of the rather gruff trapper who skinned animals and reportedly shot other people's dogs. But we knew that he was away and would not see us. We had watched him ride south into the bush on his daily trapline check, a big wicker basket strapped to his back. We wanted to act quickly, but alas, our small hands were not strong enough to release the trap. What now? We could not leave our Prinz here. We were able to undo the chain which tied the trap to the tree. With a sigh of relief we led our faithful pet, limping and hopping on three legs, the mile and a half home, where Uncle freed him. We all hoped he had learned not to stray from home again.

Mechanization was slow in reaching our pioneering valley so horses played

Father Using his Horses for Seeding

Uncle Breaking with Six Horses

a vital role in agriculture. They were used to pull farm machinery, to bring produce to stockyard and elevator, to haul feed, to build roads, and to provide transportation for the family. Around the farmyard, we had some "one horse" jobs, like pulling a little cultivator or V-shaped hiller up and

down between rows of potatoes. This required a quiet, patient animal. Hauling water up the big hill from the creek in a large barrel on a stoneboat, had to be done slowly and carefully to minimize spillage. And of course, horseback riding

Cultivating the Potatoes

was the primary way of getting from one place to another, accomplishing countless errands.

I especially remember Jutta, Lottie and Lucie the three bay mares who mothered colts, and were gentle hard working animals. There was Rex, the long - legged black gelding who grunted with each step, and Moritz who was pure white and had pink eyes. Bill and Sonny were roan colts foaled by Jutta and Lucie. Then there was Old Dick who succumbed to old age and had to be put down by Harry Sloat. (Our rifles had been confiscated during the war.)

Erika Egge, Gerta Pankow and Chris Andersen

Often the horses were difficult to catch in the pasture when we needed them. I guess they knew what was in store for them! Then we'd have to take a pail

The Pankow Family Ready to go Visiting

221

of oats as a lure, shaking it to entice them closer, then quickly pull on halter and bridle.

When Dieter and I were just toddlers, Mother took us, along with Mrs. Egge, in the cutter to visit the Witte's. Horses would often become quite frisky and high-spirited when they hadn't worked for some time in the winter. That must have been the case with this team. Suddenly we found ourselves

L to R: Uncle, Heidi, Gerta and Irma

fairly flying along the snowy road, quite wildly out of control, with Mother pulling desperately on the lines trying to slow them down. Before we knew it, we were rather unceremoniously dumped in the snow with our cutter upside down. Dieter and I (and probably

Ursula with Lucie

Tante Lisi) were terrified and howled uproariously as we picked ourselves up out of the ditch, the horses, now on their own, galloping far ahead. We'd had a real runaway! I often wondered how Mother, a fairly confident driver, ever explained this episode to Father and "Fieten"Egge.

Our white horse Moritz was a skittish nervous animal. If we had him hitched to the democrat when we drove to the store, I was sometimes a bit uneasy. Spying a seldom seen car approaching, I would quickly pull the team over as far as possible to the side of the road. Leaving Gerta to hold the lines, I would jump out of the wagon, hold Moritz's reins, stroking his head and speaking softly to him. He trembled and got a wild look in his eye as the strange noisy vehicle drove by him, but stood his ground.

Lucie was my favorite riding horse and I think our fastest one. We had an old delapidated English-style saddle, but as children we rode bareback. I think I was not a poor rider, but I always felt rather sheepish at my inability to mount easily. I had to lead my horse to a fence or other fixture and hop on from there, or get a "foot lift-up." I envied those who could just jump up from the ground. Especially when we were "racing" with the neighbour kids, we had to try everything to speed up our would-be thoroughbreds, our plodding work horses, and would vigorously prod their sides with our heels — a rather gentle substitute for spurs.

I was always saddened when I witnessed cruelty to animals in any form. Unfortunately, when a man worked as closely with them as the homesteaders did, there were bound to be times when tempers flared. Men who were not ordinarily cruel sometimes lost their cool. I particularly remember one neighbour, also Uncle, beating mercilessly on horses when they had apparently disobeyed in some way. The nearest object, anything from neck yoke, to lumber, to large hammer became weapons. I often broke into tears of sympathy for my beloved animals, but dared not intervene. It also used to bother me when another neighbour's skinny underfed horses were often bleeding at the mouth from the cruel bit, and windbroke from brutal whipping to get more speed out of them.

Rounding up Cattle in the River Flat

We used to keep some livestock in the pasture at the river quarter two miles away, and we'd have to ride over to check on them periodically. One day after school, Heidi and I undertook this task and rode down to the flats. Everything was in order, but Nigger was missing. This horse was relatively new to us. I think he was purchased at the

Troesch sale. As we searched the bush we heard an eerie groaning sound coming from the direction of the dreaded "quick sand" area. There was

Our Horses Beside the Woodpile

Nigger, only his head and neck exposed, hopelessly submerged in the mire.

We decided that help was needed quickly and hurried to the Walter Lawrence's, less than half a mile away. Mr. Lawrence, a tall gaunt elderly man and his gentle white-haired wife had always been truly good neighbours. When we told him of our predicament, he immediately hitched his team to a double-tree and followed us. He was able to edge out on a log to attach a chain to the entrapped horse; slowly and carefully he guided his team to pull our Nigger out. Gratefully we thanked this good Samaritan and began our ride home, leading the trauma victim. The poor animal was so weakened by his ordeal — who knows how long he may have been stuck — that we had to stop occasionally to let him rest as he staggered along, bumping into trees. We must have made an eerie sight as we rode home in the moonlight, the now dry-mud-caked animal clackety-clacking along behind us.

We never became as attached to cattle and swine as we did to dogs and horses. For some years cattle were allowed "free range" in the bush to the south where there were no fields. It was not always an easy task to find our cows and bring them home each evening. Then there was the milking, the feeding and watering, and the eternal manure removal. But the benefits, the nutritious milk, the delicious thick cream, butter and cheese were the rewards. Minka, Tinka, Daisy, Blackie and Susie were valuable members of our herd. For some reason, all male calves were always "Piefke," perhaps because they were not permanent residents, and ended up on the butchers block or at the stockyards.

Dieter, Gerta and Ursula Feeding Calves

As children, we always loved the baby animals best — even pink, silky-skinned piglets were adorable, and who could resist "feeling" the yellow fluff on the baby chicks? We couldn't help giggling as the awkward long-legged foals wobbled their first tentative steps, and the new calves frolicked in the pasture. Teaching the freshly-weaned calves to drink milk from a pail was always a challenge. Instinctively, they wanted to reach up to drink. We learned to let them suck our fingers, and when they had a firm grip, we'd lower our hands, along with their heads, into the milk pail. After some sputtering, they were soon swallowing hungrily.

Pigs, although the source of good ham, bacon, sausage and chops, were never favourites of mine. They still bring to mind lugging heavy five-gallon pails of chop and slop, the wire handles cutting into our hands. Whenever some had to be loaded for market, this became a true test of human patience and at least one family member, would end up in a rage at the "stubborn, grunting creatures." And we were not supposed to strike them because this would supposedly bruise the pork and lower the grade!

Our other livestock consisted of poultry. Baby chicks were raised by clucking hens. Gathering eggs was a pleasant chore and held an element of surprise and wonder for young children. Mother tried raising turkeys just once, only to have a dozen or more all disappear in one night, probably the victims of a coyote attack. We sometimes raised geese. I remember one big aggressive white gander who thought he ruled the farmstead and nipped and hissed shamelessly at every pig or dog or human that came too close. We had been fattening a goose for Christmas dinner one year. But the morning after Hallowe'en, her pen was empty and only human foot prints could be seen in the fresh snow. We learned later that Natalia had a number of young people in for a Sunday dinner of roast goose. I still feel sad and disillusioned when I think about it. Only people without conscience could have enjoyed a meal stolen from a widow and her children.

Exposure at the right time was imperative — the mare to the stallion, the cow to the bull, the sow to the boar, the rooster catching the hen. Livestock increase depended on it! These were simply facts of life to farm kids. It was sex education first hand. I don't know at what point we would have made

Our Log Barn

the connection between these happenings and human sexuality. The log barn was a safe warm shelter for our animals. The stalls on the west side were for the horses and colts; in the middle was an aisle, at the end of which stood a ladder going up to the hayloft and an oat bin with a chute attached. The east side had two long stalls for the cows and calves.

Except for times when some cow would kick or be uncooperative, I remember milking time as being rather pleasant, with the cats waiting around for that perfectly aimed squirt of warm milk. We sometimes sang together during this task, and the job would be done in no time. Again the axiom so often heard in our home: "Viele Hände machen schnell ein Ende" could be applied. During short winter days, the evening chores often had to be done by lantern light. We would trudge to the barn, our breath steamy in the crisp air, our boots crunching in the snow, milk pails in hand. The coal oil lantern cast a soft glow from its hook between the stalls, as we busied ourselves with feeding and milking.

To know that the animals were all safely sheltered in the warmth of the steamy barn on a cold and stormy night, bedded in clean straw, contentedly munching hay from the manger, was a feeling that cannot be known to one who has not experienced it. I have fond memories of our animals on the homestead and feel that our close contact with them, our communion with other living things, was something valuable in our "growing up" years.

Chapter 18 Post War Developments

It was a wonderful way for a new year to begin — that year of 1943. Our family was whole again. Our father had returned home after two and a half years of internment. There was a period of getting reacquainted and a time of adjustment. Mother was able to concentrate more on house and children as she helped Father ease into his old homesteader role. After the first few days our estrangement turned into warm affection and we truly had our father back.

For Father, the many adjustments had to be made not only in his family, but in the community as well. It was almost like a reassimilation and he took it slowly and cautiously. He felt it was prudent to "lie low" and was content to stay quite close to home. The Germans gave him a

Back: Dieter, Else, Günther, Ursula.
Front: Irmgard, Gerta, Heidi Pankow.

warm welcome home; some still a bit reluctant and afraid to openly show any pro-German sentiment. After all, the war was not over. To meet those who had conspired and testified against him sometimes created awkward situations, but could hardly be avoided in such a small community.

It was no longer necessary for Westmark residents to patronize the post office in Northmark. When Father came back home, he found that a cooperative mail delivery service had been organized by eighteen Westmark farm families. The reason was not entirely clear, except that the Northmark postmistress had gained a reputation for not being entirely trustworthy, especially with war-time mail. Now this new cooperative by-passed Northmark and got the mail directly from the Woking post office. The farmers took turns. Every Friday one family would be responsible, not only for picking up the district's mail, but also delivering it and posting out-going mail for all members of the co-op. Each family erected a mail-box by the main road. Friday became special because it was mail day, and there would be plans and discussions about who got to read the "funnies" first. For our parents it was the day they eagerly awaited mail from home – letters from Germany.

It was during Father's second winter after internment, in 1943. Given recent

227

experiences, our family chose to keep a low profile when dissension developed in the local congregation of the Lutheran Church. Differences peaked in December '43, and the congregation split in two. One faction decided to build a new church on the land belonging to the church in Northmark. For some years, services were conducted at two locations — the new church and Westmark School. Given the circumstances, perhaps building a new church was understandable. But coming like thieves in the night, and demolishing the original pioneer log chapel, then allowing the logs to rot on a creek bank, was not understandable. It was probably one of the most dastardly deeds ever committed in this community. In the minds of many, the names of the perpetrators would be forever tarnished.

Irmgard Brings Lunch to Creek Crossing Builders, Father and Uncle Horst Anders

There was a lot of catching up to do on the farm. During Father's absence, not even maintenance could be managed, and progress had come to a standstill. That first winter, Father did a lot of repairs around farm buildings and fences, harnesses and machinery in preparation for spring seeding.

In early summer, after the crop had been put in, work began on building an addition to the house, which had become much too small for the growing family. A structure made of strong straight logs was built on to the full-length north side of the existing house. The flat roof was covered with heavy tarred building paper, and a tall brick chimney was added to provide good draft for the kitchen stove. The interior walls and the ceiling were covered with lathes, and again the skilled plasterer, George Baschawerk, was hired to come and apply a professional finish. At this time he also plastered the sloping attic walls upstairs.

The large addition became our kitchen and dining room. With white kalsomined ceiling, two-tone pastel painted walls with enameled chair-rails, bright gingham curtains on windows and cupboards, it was a bright inviting room. A large all-purpose home-made table, used not only for eating, but as a work surface for many things — homework, letter-writing, games, sewing, baking, laundry, was the focal center for many daily activities.

Finishing a Meal in the Homestead Kitchen (1954)
L to r: Irma Pankow, Anneliese Witte, Ursula and Hans Delfs, Dieter Pankow
Front: Else Pankow and Elise Delfs

The old bedroom was transformed into a living room, with varnished floor, matching varnished valances with bright home-made curtains. The old kitchen became the master bedroom, and upstairs were two small sleeping places with low sloped ceilings. Dieter slept on the west side of the stairway and we girls had the east side; the "rooms" divided by the chimney and a short wall. Heat came up through a grill in the ceiling above the round airtight heater below.

East Side of the Pankow Log House

Father drove a bundle wagon with Hans Delfs'

229

threshing crew that first fall back, and was soon a part of it all again. In the winter that followed, there was severe water shortage, and I can remember "trailing" a long line of livestock, single file on a narrow path through the snowy bush to a spring south-east of our farm.

After spring work in 1944, a fairly major project was the construction of fences on the river quarter. Besides the hay flats, there was an area of hills and valleys covered with lush growth, ideal for cattle pasture. Importantly, the river was a dependable source of water for the livestock.

During those early forties, even though the war still raged in Europe, life on the farm in Westmark went on as usual, though in a more buoyant economy, and with more modern farming methods. The workload never diminished, with the quest for more land and larger cattle herds. Perhaps it was good that our parents were so busy, so tied up in making a living on their little farm. There was no time for brooding and worrying. In spite of that, their thoughts must often have travelled to the homeland and their loved ones, wondering sadly "Are they still alive? Will we ever see them again?"

Then in June, 1945, came D-Day. The allies had won the war. We went to school as usual, and were met by taunts and cheering from the small minority of non-German children. Understandably, they were celebrating, but probably knew little of the full significance of what had happened. They mocked us and we did not know how to respond. What do children know of war, its losses and victories? Were we not all Canadians?

The first news from Germany since the war came from Tante Anna, Tante Annaliese and Tante Herta in June, 1946. The long-awaited letters were opened with bated breath, and great fears for the worst. Father replied immediately, this one to Tante Anna:

> *We are just so thankful that we can write again. It was through Annaliese that we got the first family news.What misery and heartache! We had braced ourselves for the worst, but as long as there was uncertainty, a small ray of hope had remained. Now the dead have peace, and hopefully in the meantime the surviving relatives will have overcome some of the terrible pain of being left alone. We already knew of Hellmut's death, but then when we heard that Lotte, Helga and Hansi are no longer living, it was very hard for us too, even though we haven't seen any of them for eighteen years. Then from Herta came the sad news about Else's parents. They died on the terrible trek out of East Prussia, and Mieze didn't want to leave them. Lotte is still in Cranz, and Herta in Sachsen. Her son Martin was declared "missing in action" two years ago. There is no word regarding Else's brothers, Ernst and Werner.*

And why all this? It is a futile question. How did we seven Canadian Pankows deserve to be spared? By a mere hair's breadth we would have experienced the same fate as all of you. People say "Perhaps it was meant to be." In spite of our hard and never-ending work, we never forget how good we have it, compared to all of you. It was a kind fate that saved us from a similar lot. At that time in '39, did you have a premonition, when you kept advising us, until the very last, not to come to Germany?

But who knows what awaits us, even here in the bush? In the next war there will be no distances, and we in north-western Canada are not all that far away from the Russian border. What a world this is! And the whole thing is called "civilization." Who can comprehend it all?"

That summer Father gave Tante Anna a bit of an update, explaining how farming methods had progressed, making it easier to get ahead :

At least in the last five years the farmer has been getting better prices. As a result it is easier to make ends meet now, than before the war. During my absence we got behind, but now we are making progress. We have seventy acres under cultivation, and this summer I plan to break another twenty acres. Since last fall we don't have to brush by hand with the axe anymore. Now there are huge caterpillar tractors which have a V blade in front that cuts down the trees. The necessary money — ten dollars per acre — can be borrowed from the bank on a two-year loan. So now there are prospects of being able to break ten to twenty acres every year, to get ahead faster.

For a few years now, the government seems to be taking a greater interest in the farmer, and supports him through a number of programs. In this way, we were able, this summer, to have a large dug-out excavated — forty-five feet wide, one hundred and sixty feet long and twelve feet deep.

Brush Piler 1946

231

Hopefully next spring we will be able to catch enough run-off to fill it. The cost, after government subsidy, was one hundred and seventy dollars. We hope this will end the water shortage that has plagued us for the past few years. Our nice little creek that used to supply plenty of water for the animals, is getting drier each year.

Now in the spring of '46, we are taking some chances, are stretching our credit at the bank. We have to get more land under cultivation. Only cleared land, not bush, can produce profit and progress. So, just before Christmas we had another forty-five acres cleared with the big brush cutter. Next week another machine will come and push the brush into huge piles. Then we just have to burn them and break the land.

After breaking, the discing, root-harrowing, and especially the root and rock picking by hand, is an incredible amount of work. The whole family was out there helping. The cost of getting one acre of land under cultivation is twenty to twenty-five dollars, and this would be higher if the children didn't put in hours of labour.

Field work, and especially breaking, is easier now that Horst (Anders) has a powerful tractor, which is at our disposal at any time, just as our machinery and horses are to him. This working together is far from ideal, but we're more or less dependent upon each other. It is not easy to get along with Horst, but we have to make it work. Neither of us must lose sight of the end result — that of getting as much as possible out of our operation so that we can continue to send parcels to all of you in Germany. And perhaps in the next few years, we can have one or the other of you come to Canada. I have applied to have Gunthard (Anders) come over, but that was refused because he is still considered an enemy alien. But we hope that the hatred will diminish, and that Germans will again be allowed to immigrate.

There has been great progress in this little settlement after the war. Farmers are getting better prices for all their commodities. Isn't it absurd that all this came about as a result of war? We are certainly not as poor now as we were when we had planned to return home in 1939.

But to say that they were well off would have been an exaggeration. Farmers made every effort to improve their lot. In September 1946 there was a farmer's strike, organized by the Alberta Farmers Union. The purpose was to try to force the government to set higher minimum prices for farm commodities. The strike resembled a labour strike, with pickets at the grain elevators, signs (on binder twine) stretched across the road, and the odd strike breaker. In this community, commodities in question were grain, livestock and cream. Only pigs and cream would be adversely affected by the strike. A pig would grow over-weight, bringing about a price reduction, and cream would spoil. When strike action ended in early October, the roads to Woking were very busy with loads of grain, hogs and cattle. Elevator operator Howard Christie was amazed and commented that never before had he seen anything like it at the local rail outlet. Farmers' cash flow depended heavily on regular commodity sales. Apparently the strike did not

Field of Oats South of the Farmyard

result in any appreciable improvement. Post-strike discussions were on the agenda at the A.F.U. convention held in Edmonton in early January, 1947. For twelve days Mother looked after three little Sellin boys, one, three and four years old, while their parents attended this convention.

Father, as he had done for many years, still went out working at threshing time and in the winter to earn cash or lumber. The farmyard still needed a hog barn, a machine shed and a shelter for the calves, and he could not afford to buy the building materials. In January '47, he, with neighbours Hans Delfs and Hein Schuett felled trees in the bush and lived during the week in a crude shack, while "his five women" looked after things at home. It was an exceptionally cold winter, with deep snow, making bush work difficult. In January the temperatures were constantly between –30 and –50 degrees. It was the coldest winter since they came to Canada.

In spite of all the hard work, time was made for recreation. These homesteaders were still relatively young, and now the babies born in the thirties were teen-agers. The families enjoyed socializing and made their own good times. Westmark School was used for many social functions. I remember crowded dances, music supplied by local fiddlers for a nominal fee; the "stag line" taking up half the floor and the occasional floor-clearing brawl, probably brought on by too much beer.

When money was needed to purchase balls and bats, or for candy bags at Christmastime, then various socials — (box, pie, shadow) were staged as fund raisers. I remember the mothers helping to create nice fancy boxes, (fashioned into various shapes) using crepe paper, ribbon, and paint. Each young lady hoped to earn the highest bid, and to share her delicious lunch with the desired partner.

One of the last functions to be held in the old West Burnt Hall in Northmark, was a pie social and dance. Dieter and I really wanted to take this in, but our parents were not eager to go.

Back: Ursula and Dieter
Front: Gerta, Mother with Irma,Father with Heidi

So Uncle, always glad to make us happy, was persuaded to come along as chaperone. I recall the three of us riding horseback in the dark, through the deep river crossing at Witte's. I was on our long-legged black Rex, reins in one hand, a lemon meringue pie tied in a tea towel, clutched tightly in the other!

It was in 1947 that the only "shadow" social ever was held in Westmark School. I don't know whose idea it was or who organized it. A group of young women and teen-aged girls giggled nervously behind a back-lit bed-sheet curtain. Then one at a time they stood in silhouette, and the men and boys bid on each shadow, the highest bidder having the privelege of sharing her carefully prepared lunch box. Henry Sloat paid three dollars and fifty cents for my shadow, a lot of money for a young lad at that time, and one of the highest bids of the evening. I think he had earned a little money at Toerper's sawmill that winter!

In the late forties it was realized that the school building was too small. A meeting was held, an executive and a building committee was formed to plan the building of a community hall. This organization was named the Westmark Farmer's League and was duly registered as a society. After a great deal of volunteer labour, the new Westmark Hall was opened in 1950.

For a few years, before dance bands were readily available, a battery operated record player with amplifier provided music. Every country dance in those days included a square dance or two, a schottische, a heel and toe polka, perhaps a "bunny hop" in addition to the regular waltzes, two-steps and polkas, and the styles and movements came in varying degrees of grace, or lack thereof! A "floor manager" kept it all lively and moving. Coffee, brewed in a large boiler, and sandwiches were served at midnight after the "supper waltz" had been played and the gentlemen had chosen their lunch partner. There were no liquor licenses and drinking in the hall was against the law without one. So there was a considerable amount of "nipping and necking" in cars or dark corners. Given all this, it is understandable that our parents, accustomed to dance lessons, theater and musical performances in their youth, deeply regretted our lack of "cultural" opportunities.

Our parents were of the firm belief that all young people — boys and girls, should finish high school. This meant much decision making when we had completed grade nine, the last grade available in our local Westmark School. The high school of preference was in Grande Prairie, but it would cost approximately three hundred dollars a year for dormitory room and board. This would mean that an animal or two would have to be sold, something done with reluctance when trying to build a herd. However, it was made possible, and Dieter attended Grande Prairie High School in the '46 – '47 school year. For the following term, the rates were increased for those outside the Grande Prairie jurisdiction, so Dieter was enrolled in Spirit River High School for grade eleven. He stayed in the dormitory, and it was easier for him to come home on weekends.

In the meantime I had completed grade nine as well. Mother had been corresponding for some time with a friend in Michigan, U.S.A., Kate Rampoldt. That family invited me to come and stay with them, and attend high school in Michigan. Their daughter, my same age would enjoy the company, and I could surely benefit by getting out of the narrow confines of Westmark, the two mothers reasoned. The long train trip would be costly, but not as much as a whole year's dormitory fees. As a result, in mid-August, 1947 I travelled by train to Michigan and attended Niles High School for nine months. I was certainly exposed to many new experiences, socially, culturally and academically.

Piling Brush (1947)
Ursula, Gerta, Heidi, Father, Irma

That summer of 1947, before I left for the U.S., was filled with hard work for the whole family. Forty-five acres on the south-east part of our quarter had been brush-cut and then piled, and now it needed to be made clear and ready for the breaking plow. Father and I were working side by side, both sweaty and black from the burned brush. As we threw piece after piece of wood on the growing piles, he took this opportunity to "educate" me on some of the finer points of a young lady travelling alone — the dangers, the precautions, the evil of some lecherous men, what to do in case of problems. Never breaking stride, he patiently and quietly talked to his oldest daughter, she with eyes averted, feeling a little uncomfortable, but listening attentively, all the while piling more brush. It was always our father, not our mother, who did this kind of communicating.

In his Christmas letter to me in Michigan, it was also our Father who expressed some concern about my well-being:

> Have a nice Christmas, and don't let homesickness get you down. For the first time you will be spending Christmas far away from home, and just as we will be thinking of you, your thoughts will be with us. But you are not alone, rather in the friendly Rampoldt family circle. Our greatest hope is that you are happy there, and that you like and understand each other. Every person has his good and bad sides, and in life it's important that we cultivate the good in ourselves, and combat the bad. In those with whom we live, we should accept the good, and reject that which we consider undesirable. Now, my big girl, I don't want to preach a sermon here, but I think you understand what I mean. Be brave, and go your way straight and sure. That's not always real easy, but you will manage it. If you ever have a heavy heart or something is bothering you, then write us or Dieter and get it off your mind.

> I am just home on Sundays now and am writing this from our bush camp. Hans Delfs is busy preparing the soup for tomorrow. We are at the highest point in the hills, two miles west of Scotty (Maxwell) and can see the whole settlement. Our nearest neighbours are Toerpers and Lloyd Mack, with their mill crew, just a hundred paces away. We built a barn, jointly, and often visit each other in the evenings. The earnings are quite good – six to seven dollars a day. Hans Delfs, Hein Schuett and I purchased a power saw for three-hundred dollars, and we've got the price of that back already.

> All the pulpwood goes to the U.S.A. where they apparently make plastics and nylon out of it. We have the logs trucked to Woking, where there are mountains of logs at the siding. Everyone's getting into cutting pulpwood. In this way we can make up a little bit, for the frozen crops, although it's very hard work. I'm doing the skidding with Bill and Rex. Mother doesn't

have it easy at home either, with all the livestock. We're all looking
forward to the Christmas holidays, when we hope to have some rest.

While these decisions regarding our education, and how to make ends meet, were being made here, terrible unimaginable suffering, and decisions of life and death were taking place in Germany. Roles had been reversed. Now instead of receiving parcels from the homeland, the German settlers in

Tante Anneliese Anders (front) with Children (1949)

Canada, though relatively poor themselves, were sending food parcels to starving relatives in war-ravaged Germany. Mother knew so little of the post-war fate of her family in East Prussia, and it seemed so hopeless to find anything out. She wrote to several missing persons services, but to no avail, and thought hopelessly "My brothers are probably no longer alive, or they're in Siberia. How we would have loved to have Mieze here. Hopefully someone was able to give my parents a proper burial. For them it's better — preferably an end with terror, than terror without end." Mother eventually found out that her brother Werner had escaped to the west, and had found employment with a nursery in Augsburg.

The known dead were, perhaps, the fortunate ones. Our uncles — Hans Jürgen Pankow, Hellmut Anders, and Ernst Gesien were killed in action during the Russian invasion of East Prussia. Opapa and Omama Gesien and Tante Mieze died of starvation related illness, as did Uncle Fritz Seidler. Cousin Martin Steputat, eighteen, was reported missing in action. Cousin Lutz Gesien starved to death while just a toddler, and Cousin Helga Pankow died at the age of twelve.

For the survivors there was horrendous suffering. Tante Annaliese, now widowed, and her five children were forced out of their home in Tilsit. After a long harrowing trek, including weeks at a time in sordid refugee camps, they arrived in West Germany with only the clothes on their backs. They managed to find a place to live in Tiefenort, where, once some normalcy had been restored, Tante Anneliese was able to get a teaching position and raise her children. It seems that she showed amazing strength and grit in her difficult circumstances, as Father described in his letter to Tante Anna :

Apparently Anneliese is fighting her way through all this better than any of the others. In spite of all her physical and spiritual suffering, she has such confidence and such strong faith that I am simply amazed. Nora is facing her destiny with much more difficulty and bitterness, as is Erika.

Tante Erika (Pankow)
Seidler (1949)

Uncle Werner Pankow was an officer in the army during the war in Russia, was wounded twice, was awarded medals of honor, and taken prisoner. All the while, his wife Grete and their four daughters faced a fate similar to that of Tante Anneliese. They were forced to flee from their home in Cranz when the Russians came. Through many

Tante Grete Pankow and Daughters (1946)
Ingrid, Gisela, Karin, Gudrun

dangers, near starvation and emotional horrors, including six months of confinement in a refugee camp in Podibrad, they managed to make their way to Helstorf in West Germany. Here, under extremely Spartan conditions, they waited for five years for the return of husband and father from prison.

Uncle Werner, incarcerated in Russia, had a degree of good fortune amid the bad, in that he was not forced into hard labour, but was pressed into service practicing a rudimentary form of dentistry in prison. Father found himself empathizing, and hoped that his older brother would be treated as well as he had been as a prisoner of war in Canada. Father's internment experience remained only as a dream and a distant memory, and no longer evoked nightmares. Through the Red Cross in Moscow, Uncle Werner was able to send post cards with very short messages to Canada. Our parents, in turn, forwarded the news to Tante Grete in Germany. In 1950 he was released from prison, reunited with his family, and set up a dental practice in Helstorf.

As Mother went about her daily tasks on the homestead that summer after D-Day, her mind often wandered to her home in the beautiful Baltic Sea resort. She thought of her mother preparing rental rooms in Villa

Werner, Mieze, Elise, Ernst (Sr.), Ernst Gesien.

Kornblume, and her father toiling in the garden or the greenhouses. But that's not how it was anymore. She would have been shocked and deeply saddened if she could have seen her beloved Cranz in 1945. In a letter from her sister Herta in 1946, Mother learned the devastating truth about the death of her parents. It was not until 1952 that she found out the details, when a friend's aunt, Mrs. Sywietz, wrote her a letter:

> *As you may know, on February 4th, 1945, the Russians moved into our hometown, the beautiful Cranz. We spent the first fourteen terrifying days*

in Cranz, were forced to leave our homes and search for shelter elsewhere. Your parents got together with several friends and found temporary refuge in the Luther House. After two weeks we were forced to vacate Cranz entirely. Within a very short time only some four thousand people remained.

We were not allowed to take anything along, because we had to march on foot in the long trek. In the area of Insterburg a stop was made, and at this point the Russian guards left us. We found shelter in the villages from which the Germans had fled. On our way, during the trek, we had run into your dear parents, your sister-in-law (Werner's wife) with two little children, and were able to find over-night shelter. Every day the trek continued, until finally we were able to settle down for a greater length of time. We were a group of twenty persons whom a common crisis had brought together, and we lived in one house. Your parents were part of this group, and the name of the place was Hohenholzburg.

The strain and the many horrors were terrible, especially for your mother. It is impossible to describe in detail — especially the plight of the young girls and women, the nocturnal visits by the Russians. What little we had was robbed or vandalized. Your sister Mieze was there too. Due to poor and insufficient nourishment many people became ill and died. Your mother, too, became ill.

We spent a lot of time together. She told me her troubles and felt that her end was near. She spoke a lot about her children — they were so very dear to her heart. Two large spruce trees grew in front of her window, and one day as we were sitting together, she was lost in thought, and gazing out of the window, she murmured "Here under these evergreens I wish to be buried." And that's how it came about.. She kept getting worse — she had some kind of abdominal typhus. The last day before her passing, I was at her death-bed. She was in and out of consciousness, but her lips moved in prayer, and I could discern the soft words "Lord, not my will but thine be done." Next morning she peacefully slipped away.

My husband and several women dug the grave, and a little wooden cross was created. Our daughter Ruth burned the name and date on it, and so, with prayers and God's blessing, we buried your mother under the trees. It was particularly hard for your father. As he stood beside the plain board coffin, he quietly commented "I will soon follow mother." And he did soon follow.

He was able to return to Cranz with us and saw his property in ruins. He died and was buried in Cranz. Again my husband did the service as there were no clergy. Your sister Mieze had to work very hard for the Russians, until her strength too, was used up.I talked to her during her last days,

240

and supported her because she couldn't walk. She felt very lonely and abandoned.

It is believed by some, that Tante Mieze could have escaped to the West had she been on her own. But she refused to leave her parents and stayed with them to the end. Then it was too late. The resulting anguish and suffering can be felt in her letter to her friend Freda Masuhr:

We are always so happy to hear from the Reich, but that happens very rarely now. My dear friend, be glad that you are there. You cannot begin to imagine what it looks like here, and what my life is like. We are starving. At the present time I am very ill and can't go to work. I have no strength left. Who knows how long I have left to live? It's in God's hand. It's very cold and it's so difficult to get wood from the forest. For two months we've received no rubels, and live on oat gruel, if we can even buy that. I have sold everything I can possibly spare. But God has always helped, and His will be done.

We hope so much that we will be able to come west, but when will that be? So many people are dying here — their last strength leaves them and they just fade away. Life is really very hard. Who will survive? Please don't laugh at my writing paper. I have nothing, just "found" things. You would not recognize me. My face is swollen, my clothes are rags. We still have hope.

Tante Mieze's future, as well as that of other Gesien family members was graphically described in a poignant letter that Lilo Herrndorf, then eighteen years old, wrote to her Tante Else Pankow in Canada, on January 28, 1948. Excerpts follow :

Now we surviving East Prussians have arrived in Germany and we feel so alien. On November 16th last year we left Cranz. Even though it was so devastated and destroyed, and swarming with Russians, it was our home. Oh, we have lost everything! Russians from deepest Siberia are living on our acreage. When we heard of the impending Russian attack, and then when the bombing started, we lost contact with Oma and Opa in Cranz, and fled, along with the soldiers, to Neukuhren. Here we stayed for seven weeks, then on to Pahnicken, where the Russians didn't arrive until April 15th, '45. In Cranz they came February 3rd. So we were able to avoid the extermination trek. During a snowstorm, all Cranzers were driven, on foot, in the direction of Schlossberg. Oma was part of this trek when she died. She was buried in Hohenholzburg on Palm Sunday.

In May we returned to Cranz, and in June we were reunited with Tante Mieze, Opa, Tante Ida, Marlieschen and little Lutz, who had all returned. There was great rejoicing! Papa and Hansi slept at our house on the acreage, but Mutti and I went to Cranz to sleep, because there we had more protection by the presence of the commandant guards. Because of the nightly break-ins at Wiekien, it was not safe to stay there. At that time, little Lutz Werner was still alive, but he too, died of starvation in August, as did Opa. Dropsy and diarrhea dealt the final blow. I can still see Opa as he stood with tears streaming down his face, amid the devastation that was once his nursery, the destruction that was once his life's work. Opa and Lutz were buried in the Gesien family plot. Tante Mieze lived for some time in the big house.

Soon a deluge of Russian civilians arrived and moved right in. Instead of getting better, things got worse. Nothing was rebuilt, and thistles grew everywhere. We had been keeping ourselves barely fed. Armed with a big stick, we went to the old Roggenberge and flailed grain out of the sheaves. With the coffee grinder we ground up the kernels and cooked gruel. Many times the Russians came and stole it all and beat us. But that was not the worst ......

Perhaps 400 – 500 Cranzers had returned. The rest died or starved, were murdered or banished to Siberia. We four in our family were always together, except for six weeks when they took Papa away from us. When the civilian Russians came in we were forced off our acreage, and came to Cranz where we lived on Kirchenstrasse by the Catholic church. Now all Germans had to work for the Russians, because anyone who could not work or was sick, received no bread and had to starve. All old people and sick people died of starvation.. Tante Mieze worked for the health authorities, where most of the women worked — cutting wood, cleaning drains, demolishing houses, knocking down bricks, doing laundry — these were the typical jobs. Hansi got on with the electrical works. Men and boys had it easier than the women. I worked at the construction site of a sanatorium, as stone mason's helper.

Mutti was at home and went to the black market to pawn our last possessions so that we could buy our daily 500 grams of bread. Papa was standing guard as night watchman at the main supply depot. Then came the terrible cold winter of '46 – '47 when so many starved and froze to death. Papa died February 2nd 1947. Until morning he had stood his post, then while still on duty, he fell over dead. At –33 degrees Hansi and I tried to make a grave for him. But even with the help of a fire, we managed to dig only a shallow hole. But we were so glad that we didn't have to lay him in a mass grave. Eight such graves were used at the cemetery this winter. The hunger was so terrible that in some places there were rumours of cannibalism.

We were glad to find potato peelings, and on the stove top we baked them into "pancakes." Tante Mieze had to walk to work at Bledau, and she always took a "potato peel mash" along for lunch. She ate too much of this and developed dropsy. A Russian lady doctor told her the entire structure of the blood had disintegrated. Mutti couldn't stand to see Tante Mieze suffering, so she brought her to our place. We had nothing to eat, but at least we still had a little bit of heat. But nothing helped anymore. In the evening of April 9th, 1947, Tante Mieze died, like Papa, of weakness and exhaustion. We buried her beside Opa at the cemetery. This time it was not so hard because the ground had thawed out. Mutti was really run down too, but she took Papa's place and stood guard night after night in the cold. Hansi and I couldn't change her off because we had to work. Everyone had to try and work for "bread coupons" to keep from starving.

In spring and summer we could eat nettles and pigweed, and later berries. Occasionally there were fish available to buy. On the whole, conditions improved in the summer. The Russians were not quite as spiteful and nasty to us, and food at the black market was not quite as expensive. Life there would have been bearable now, if only we could have had more rubels, and a bit of clothing. But that's how it was. The Russian women were dolled up in our dresses and shoes, lived in our houses, and we stood ragged and tattered beside them. Now and then Mutti would take a plate or some other possession to the black market so that we could buy a few potatoes. We had only wooden shoes, no bedding, just a few ragged blankets.

And so we came here. All the time, during those three years in Russia, we thought about the west and longed to go there.

Alas, the long awaited move to the Reich turned out to be a big disappointment. Perhaps in the long run it was the wise thing to do, but initially they felt like strangers, unwanted in their own country. Lilo expresses her disillusionment :

Now we are here, but how disappointed we are. We ragged "resettlers" are disrespected and pushed around by our own countrymen. Then at times, in spite of everything, we almost preferred the Russians. When one sees the people here — how they live and laugh, talking about movies and theater; then after all the hardships and trauma we've been through, it all seems so insipid and trivial.

After seven weeks at the refugee camp near Kirchmöser, we were referred to Schönbeck, where we spent another two weeks in a camp, before finding a 3m x 4m subrental room. It was furnished with a sofa, a table, three chairs, and a toilet. After days of scrounging around, we managed to round up two bedsteads and straw, but no sacks to put it in. So now we are sleeping "on hay and on straw." Blankets are not available. It's all so dreadful. We have potato ration cards, but there are no potatoes to be had. The employees at the various offices hand us one little voucher after another, but no one really helps us. It's just the opposite — they just wish we'd go away.

Mutti is so nervous and exhausted because all the responsibility rests on her. We eat our 300 grams of bread and drink coffee, which is nearly gone. Right now we don't know how we can help ourselves. We don't have enough to wear for one change of clothing, and there's nothing available to buy. Uncle Fritz (Steputat) is going to try to get an apprentice electrician job for Hansi. I don't know what I'll do. Hopefully Mutti won't get really sick.

Then Lilo goes on to tell Mother about old friends and neighbours from Cranz. Several committed suicide when the Russians came in, many starved to death, some were able to escape to the west. She also told of the damage and destruction. Villa Kornblume had some bomb damage on a gable end but was standing. The large seaside hotel "Schloss am Meer" and the post office were burned. The once beautiful resort town was broken, dreary and desolate.

Her update of other Gesien relatives indicated that Tante Herta and Uncle Fritz Steputat had survived and visited the Herrndorfs at the refugee camp. Tante Kate Gesien too had come to see them there, and sent newspapers. Only Uncle Werner did not write. Lilo often thought about her five cousins, her aunt and uncle in Canada. These Canadians would have liked to help more. It was not until June 1946 that letter post began arriving, and Father answered :

Now that letters are going through, hopefully parcel post and money exchange will soon follow. Then at least we can do something concrete to help, and can occasionally send you something. Although no one has mentioned anything in letters, we know there is no doubt that everyone has had to severely "tighten the belt" when it comes to sustenance. Although we are certainly not rich, we never have to worry about getting enough to eat. When we sit down around our table for a meal, we often wish you all could come and join us. You can imagine how our thoughts are with you there in the old, now shattered and destroyed homeland — so much misery and hunger!

In September '46 the first chance to help in a substantial way, was made possible. Parcels were not allowed to be sent from Canada, but in New York there was an organization C.A.R.E. which was non-profit and genuinely interested in helping. Through this, Father ordered two parcels, thirty pounds each,filled with calorie-rich nutrients, one for Tante Grete and one for Tante Anna. Unfortunately, these parcels could not be sent to the Russian zone. But one-pound packages could be sent from the western zones to the

Russian. So Tante Anna "sub-divided" hers and sent little packages on to Tante Nora, Erika, and Anneliese. (Germany had been divided into zones — Russian, American and British.)

As of January '47, eleven-pound parcels could be sent directly to the Russian zone, and within the next few weeks many parcels left the Westmark homestead. I can remember Mother putting a great deal of time and work into the preparation of these food gifts. Several neighbours had, together, purchased a machine for sealing tin cans, so that canned meat and lard were often sent, as well as commercially canned meat, bacon, coffee, honey, and more. Mother spent hours packing, then sewing these items into cloth (from flour bags) coverings so they would withstand the long trip overseas.

After all this time, work and expense, there was always the worry "Would the parcels arrive safely at their destination?" It was said that a lot of thievery took place enroute. The rogues would make money by selling these lovingly packed gifts of food on the black market. It was hard to believe that it could come to this — that even the mail was not safe. It is hard to know just how many, but a large number of parcels went from our house to Germany during that post-war period, to many Pankow, Gesien and Anders relatives.

Kate Rampoldt and Irene DeWitt of Niles, Michigan wrote to Mother requesting names of German refugee families with children. Mother forwarded the names of Anneliese Anders and Grete Pankow, among others. These families subsequently received several parcels of good quality used clothing from these kind Americans. Kate Rampoldt wrote a letter to Tante Grete on February 3rd 1947, explaining the circumstances of how this all came about :

In 1937, through a friend and her husband (Leni and Georg Witte) who returned to Germany from Woking, Alberta, and visited me in Michigan enroute, I heard about your sister-in-law, Else Pankow. Since then I have carried on a friendly correspondence with Else, finding her to be a kindred spirit. Through her last letters, I learned of the terrible suffering of her relatives in Germany and her burning desire to help them in some way. I offered her my assistance, in that the need was for clothing, and I knew that some had accumulated from my own three children. I myself have a mother and sister, parents-in-law and sisters-in-law in Germany that I am trying, to the best of my ability, to support with food parcels. But in my own family there are no longer growing children, so no need for children's clothing.

So Else Pankow sent me the names and addresses of her relatives and told me briefly the fate of the individual families. I can't tell you how deeply your suffering has touched me, and I knew instantly that I would help as much as I possibly could. When I read the list of families, and the many children, I began earnestly to pray. How would I distribute my things, which were hardly enough for one family? Sure, I could have asked friends and acquaintances for their used clothing, and I probably would have got enough. But these parcels don't go overseas postage free! Unfortunately we don't belong to the small percentage of millionaires in America, but rather to the large masses of the working middle class. I could manage only one parcel a month in addition to the obligations to my own family.

But I am convinced that miracles still happen even today. I told my neighbour about my problem. Quite unexpectedly, she offered to approach her Bible study group, some fifteen or twenty young couples, to see if they would be interested in making this their project. She told me this group had, in the past few months collected clothing, but instead of donating them to some organization, they were more inclined to personally give to needy families. Since no one in the group had personal connections to anyone in Germany or other European nations, this list of names from Else Pankow would surely be welcome. Irene DeWitt is an exceptionally helpful and sharing person. Her heart is in the right place.

The next day she excitedly informed me that her Bible study group had accepted her suggestion and promptly gave her a big box of clothes for immediate packing. On January 20th seven packages were sent, two of them for you, dear Mrs. Pankow. Hopefully you'll find the most needed items for your four girls. Each couple will accept the financial responsibility for one parcel. So don't hesitate to say if there is something you especially need. These warm-hearted people take pleasure in giving.

I think that you will agree that this generosity towards former enemies is highly commendable. During the war these people heard only anti-German propaganda, and they had no personal connections with us or the Pankow family in Canada. Unfortunately there are too few people like this group, who believe in brotherly love and compassion. I dare say that if this principle, which represents the ideal of Christian teaching, could reign all over the world, we would not have to fear any more wars and their terrible consequences. Then my dear old homeland could hope for rehabilitation and a better, more promising future.

Would you be so kind as to notify this group, in care of Irene DeWitt, secretary, of the safe arrival of the parcels? These modest and certainly not rich people expect no thanks, but would like to know that their gifts arrived safely and will be useful.

There were also a lot of pipe dreams during that desperate difficult time:

Tante Anna, you could come here and spend your twilight years in peace and quiet. Werner could be dentist in Grande Prairie; Anneliese and Nora could be teachers in the area — there's a great shortage here. Erika could live with you in a little house on our land. But I'm building castles in the air......

And how I wish that some of the younger family members could come over here and make a new beginning after all the horror and suffering over there. We won't let this idea drop, and hope that in a few years, when the hatred has subsided, Germans will again be allowed into Canada.

Father was really letting his imagination run wild one day when he wrote to Tante Grete, while Uncle Werner was still a Russian prisoner of war:

Dentists will always be needed and Werner will probably want to start a new practice somewhere. If this is not possible in Germany, you should all come over here. In a few years, after he learned English and got his Canadian Dr. of Med. Dent., Werner could open a practice in some small town. These are only dreams, but the fact remains, that rather than vegetating miserably over there, you could begin a new life here. You could have a little house on our land, with a large garden, some small animals and poultry. It would mean an unbelievable adjustment for you, but nevertheless a possibility. A prerequisite, of course, would be permission to immigrate, which is not yet available.

Only in the case of cousin Hans Herrndorf did one of these dreams become a reality. When Canada allowed German immigration in 1953 he came, with financial assistance from Mother, and did indeed make a new beginning and a successful future.

In the local settlement, a number of young men had served in the military, the majority serving only on Canadian soil. When they returned home, they were able to benefit under the Veteran's Land Act legislation, making it easier to acquire land and machinery. Uncle Horst Anders was one of these veterans. He had been stationed at various locations in Canada, with the Royal Canadian Engineers. When he was discharged from the army in 1945, he obtained two quarter sections of land through the V.L.A. and was able to buy a tractor and breaking plow.

A young neighbour was not as fortunate, and on this side of the ocean, too, mothers grieved. Jay Sloat, who lived close to the Westmark school he had attended, did not return from the overseas battlefield. This friendly young lad had once come to shoot a pig for us on butchering day, when our guns had been confiscated. He and his sister Hazel joined the army, and now he had become one of the many innocent victims of war.

Over a period of many years, the spirit of the people, the economy and the culture of Germany was restored. The Pankow and Gesien families, as countless other families, had to overcome the great sorrow at the loss of loved ones, and go on with life. We Canadian Pankow children were forever prevented from getting to know our grandparents — a great deprivation. And people of every nationality, on both sides of the ocean, hoped fervently that the horror, the inhumanity, the barbarism, of another world war would never happen again.

Chapter 19   A House Of Sorrow

Father and our whole family had worked very hard during those five years since his release from internment camp. An addition had been built on the house; more land had been cleared and brought under cultivation; the cattle herd had grown. It had been made possible for Dieter and for me to attend high school. In addition to this, Mother and Father took from their own meager income and sent countless food parcels to starving relatives in post war Germany. There prevailed in our house, a feeling of gratitude and optimism. Had fate not spared us and given us the opportunity to strive anew, even to help others?

The winter of '48 had become a test of perseverance and was particularly challenging in terms of the family's well-being. Three surgeries — Heidi's appendectomy, Dieter's spleen removal, and Mother's kidney operation, all came within three months. Father, in his quiet confident manner, helped them all through it, and managed in spite of all the stress and growing

Günther Pankow 1948

medical bills, to keep an outlook of optimism. He tried hard to sustain this bright outlook as, during a still snowy mid April, he made preparations for spring seeding.

Three weeks later, spring had finally made its presence known, and Father was anxious to get on the land. On Sunday, May 9th after supper, he mounted Ellie, the new young filly from Troesch's sale which still needed some training before it would become a good family horse. He rode the one and a half miles to the river quarter to check out the flats. Near the hayfield close to Stein's boundary a small creek crossed the path. The young horse, his unfamiliar mount, refused to cross. Father dismounted to try to get the animal to cross over. In a flash, the horse's hoof lashed out and struck him full in the abdomen, knocking him to the ground. Stunned, he lay there for some time, realizing that no one would find him if it got dark. In terrible agony and by sheer power of the will, he managed to mount his horse and start for home. Karl Stein, who happened to be working outside, heard Father call. Quickly he hurried towards the sound, only to find his good neighbour suffering in terrible pain. He helped Father to his nearby bachelor home, and settled him on the couch. Then he galloped at full speed to tell Uncle, who came to tell the family what had happened. Dieter had already started out to look for his father.

Now they frantically hitched up the democrat and rushed over to pick up Father. As they started out for Woking, the pain became so intense that they stopped at Oltmanns to get a couch so the patient could travel in a reclining position. Oltmanns rode ahead to alert Jacobs, who immediately came to meet them with his truck and started out towards Spirit River. The roads during that late, wet spring were brutal and well-nigh impassable. It was six o:clock in the morning before the doctor was reached, in what had been an all-night ordeal, first on horseback, then by wagon, finally by truck, through

mud-holes, water and deep ruts. One cannot begin to imagine the horrendous physical pain of such an injury. But the mental anguish of knowing that there was probably little chance of coming through this, that he would be leaving his family alone, would be the worst suffering of all. Doctor Law operated immediately, but with little hope of success. The stomach and intestines had been ruptured in eight places.

On Tuesday, May 11, 1948, at six in the

morning, our father, Günther Pankow died at the Spirit River Hospital, at the age of forty-four years. Suddenly all the health problems of the past winter paled in comparison to this final cruel blow. Due to road conditions, no clergyman was able to come to the funeral, so local lay-minister Peter Frank conducted the service. On May 13th on a beautiful spring day, surrounded by family, friends and neighbours, Father was laid to rest at the little cemetery on the river bank.

In a state of shock and still in rather fragile health, Mother tried to cope with the cruel reality that had struck our family. Again, at times like this, the absence of extended family was so strongly felt. A warm embrace, a sympathetic handshake, offered generously by so many friends and neighbours, could only be communicated to the distant homeland by letter, as this one to Tante Anna on May 18, 1948:

> *Today I come to you and sit beside you on your little sofa, and hold your faithful withered hands in mine. You know how much sickness and worry we had during the past winter. But now the worst of all has befallen us. On May 13th we buried our dear devoted father, my beloved Günther. To all of us, to the whole settlement, it is like a bad dream. No one can believe it.*

> *It is so hard to accept that he was taken from us after he saw us through our illnesses this winter. How good and kind he always was, and he found so much pleasure in his work and his land, his home and his family. In every little detail, how terribly we miss him! How nice it would have been for father and son to work together. It will be especially hard for Ursel because she hasn't seen her father in almost a year.*

> *It is too soon to decide exactly what will happen in our future. I hope Dieter will mature into a strong young man. Since his operation he's had no more spots, but for his seventeen years he's physically small and immature. We hope to get our fields seeded in time, with the help of neighbours. It's such a late spring — it's late May and no wheat is seeded. The fields are so wet. Hopefully it'll all even out in the fall, and snow and frost won't strike too early. Another crop failure would be hard to bear. We have a very heavy debt load.*

> *My most fervent prayer is that I will remain healthy and gain my strength back, so that the children may have their mother for a while longer, and that they may become true Pankow children. In their father they had such a shining example and worthy mentor. The whole settlement is mourning our dear father, not just Germans, but Canadians too. God's ways are so very hard to understand.*

All the while, I was very far away from my family, in Niles, Michigan. Kate

Rampoldt received Mother's wire, and to her fell the formidable task of breaking the news to me, Father's sixteen-year old daughter. Excerpts from her condolence letter follow :

> *Probably never in my life had I been faced with a more difficult task, than the one that was required of me after I received your tragic news — that of telling Ursel about the appalling death of her father. Words are so empty and sound so cold. I just hope that, as I held the girl in my arms, she was able to feel some of the empathy and love in my heart. The shock, because it was so totally unexpected, was horrible. The incomprehensible naked truth stood suddenly, without warning, before her. I tried my best to ease her sorrow at the thought that she would not see her father again.*
>
> *Slowly we began to talk about it, and both of us wished desperately that we had wings and could fly to you, who are most in need of comfort, to give you our support. What can mere words say to you? What has happened is, for us pitiful little humans, simply too overwhelming. We can ram our heads against the wall, and cry in vain "Why?" There **must** exist a greater plan, one which we don't understand. "In my Father's house are many mansions; if it were not so, I would have told you." (John 14, 2.) has to be enough for us now.*
>
> *I have reverted to wordiness again. That's because I feel so helpless. If only there weren't this separation of hundreds of miles. For now, all I can do is send Ursel home to you. She will be a big help to you. She is physically and mentally strong, and will be ready to step in wherever help is needed. She is anxious to come home as soon as is humanly possible, and rightfully so. I will see to it that she gets her final report card, even though she won't be writing the exams. But her grades were very good all year. I will write or wire you when Ursel leaves here. We feel so terribly sorry that her happy year with us had to end in this very sad way. I can't grasp it.*

Friends and neighbours empathized with my plight, all alone so far from home, and in their own way, sought to help by writing letters, such as this one from Ursula Solty :

> *I see so much of your father in you, dear Ursel. Yesterday we buried him on a beautiful spring day. Your siblings were very brave and your mother showed great strength. I admired them.*
>
> *You will have overcome the first great shock now, and you will be brave too, I know, because you are the daughter of Günther Pankow who was the strongest, the most supportive, the most highly esteemed person in this settlement. Now you will soon be home. Mother really needs a grown-up daughter now. She has very difficult days behind her, and needs*

convalescence, diversion, and a little good cheer, which you will bring her,
in spite of all the hardship.

And Willie Janssen, the young lad who had once brought a doll bed for my sixth birthday, was now twenty-two and sent not only a letter, but a poem, so rich in meaning that it deserves a place here :

My deepest sympathy goes out to you in the loss of your father, who was
so well liked by all of us. Personally, I am deeply grieved that he was taken
from the district. I am confident, though, that you will stand up to the
strain, which I know must be almost too much to bear.

AN ETERNAL MESSAGE
I am your friend, and my love for you goes deep.
There is nothing I can give you which you have not got.
But there is much, very much, that while I cannot give it,
You can take.

No heaven can come to us unless our hearts
Find rest in today. Take heaven!
No peace lies in the future which is not hidden
In this present little instant.   Take peace!

The gloom of the world is but a shadow,
Behind it, yet within our reach, is joy.
There is radiance and glory in the darkness,
Could we but see, and to see, we have to look.
I beseech you to look.

Life is so generous a giver, but we
Judging its gifts by their covering,
Cast them away as ugly or heavy, or hard.
Remove the covering, and you will find beneath it
A living splendour, woven of love, by wisdom, with power.

Welcome it, grasp it, and you touch
The angel's hand that brings it to you.
Everything we call a trial, a sorrow or a duty
Believe me. That angel's hand is there,
And the wonder of an overshadowing Presence.

Our joys too, be not content with them as joys,
They, too, conceal diviner gifts.
Life is so full of meaning and purpose

So full of beauty — beneath its covering
That you will find earth but cloaks your heaven.

Courage then to claim it: that is all!
But courage you have, and the knowledge
That we are pilgrims together
Winding through unknown country, home.

And so, at this time,I greet you.
Not quite as the world sends greetings,
But with profound esteem and with the prayer
That for you, now and forever
The day breaks, and the shadows flee away.

Author Unknown

Kate Rampoldt stood at the Chicago station platform that day in late May, 1948. She waved a tearful goodbye to the somber-faced young girl who was homeward bound — back to the homestead in Woking. I remember nothing of that long weary train ride, and I don't know what was going on in my mind. For certain, there were no happy thoughts, even though I was going home, to my mother, to my siblings, but not my beloved father.

As the Northern Alberta Railways engine blew its whistle and slowed to a stop at the Woking station house, I could see our team, Bill and Rex, tied to the nearby hitching rail. The familiar sights brought a quiver of excitement in spite of my weariness and heavy-heartedness. Mother, Dieter and my three sisters greeted me as I came down the train steps. What a welcome sight! They smiled at me a bit distractedly (I had gained some thirty pounds due to a thyroid condition) and they were not quite sure how to react. But little eight-year-old Irma clutched my hand tightly and beamed with pleasure as we found our places on the seats of the democrat.

On the way home we stopped at the cemetery, and Mother slowly led her

254

grieving children to their father's last resting place. In front of me lay a mound of green spruce boughs covering a raw pile of brown earth and stone. The sun shone brightly and a gentle breeze wafted through the grass to break the silence. An involuntary shiver shook me through and through. I knew somehow, that I should be weeping, but I could not. This was a sorrow too deep for tears. My mind went back to that day in August, 1947, on the Woking station platform, when my father and I had clung to each other as we said goodbye. That's what I wanted to keep forever locked in my memory, not this lonely desolate grave.

Though I had just come from a suburban home with all the amenities – electricity, water, central heating – I was so very happy to come home to our primitive homestead house. There was an empty seat. The very heart of our home was gone. But somehow we all felt a strong need to rally around our mother, and to keep going. He would have wanted us to strive hard to continue that which he had, with so much work and sacrifice, achieved. Spring seeding was completed, with the generous help of many neighbours, and now we worked our way into a routine of hard work. Since a lot of land had been cleared, there were many, many acres of roots and rocks to be picked (by hand at that time); hay to be made for the growing cattle herd, and the endless every day farm chores. Gradually Mother's health, following her kidney operation, improved, and she showed remarkable strength.

I remember sitting with her one day while she worked at the living room table, surrounded by mail that waited to be answered. It was a difficult and emotionally draining task, this replying to letters of condolence. While we were talking about the kindness of so many people, in response to our fate, she broke down and sobbed bitterly. With tears streaming down her face, she lamented " I would live in any hovel if only I had him back!" She had mentioned to me once before that she felt very guilty about having complained at some time about no power, no water, no "nice" home. Certainly, after so many years of roughing it and countless crop disappointments, it was understandable that feelings of dissatisfaction would arise. But now in retrospect she was deeply regretful and was afraid she may have hurt Father. I was quite unaccustomed to seeing Mother in tears. She rarely broke down in our presence, and awkwardly I tried to console her.

Among those letters on the table, awaiting a reply, was one from Hein Krog, who had homesteaded Minna Toerper's place before going back to Germany in the thirties :

> *Through Otto Toerper I heard of the tragic misfortune that has befallen you and your children. Please accept my sincere and profound sympathy.*

Your dear Günther was one of the very best, and was not spared from the arduous task of trying to wring an existence from the land. But always remember that it was you, his loyal companion, who brought joy and sunshine into his life.

And our good friend, Ernie Gabrielson, the Swedish bachelor who lived west of us and often visited us, had also lost a friend. He wrote to Mother:

I have received some very sad news today – the loss of your beloved husband Günther Pankow, and my sympathy goes to you and your family. I remember when Pankow shook hands with me and neither one of us knew it was the last time. Günther was always so nice and kind to you, to his family, to me, to everybody. Indeed, I have lost a good friend.

In Germany, Tante Anneliese Anders herself had been widowed during the war, and was left alone with five young children. Now she lost her brother Günther, and attempts to console the sister-in-law with whom she now had so much in common :

As I try to write to you today, my pen is not willing to obey. God has indeed laid an oppressing heavy burden on you. I can't grasp the fact that I can no longer imagine Günther among you.

No matter how calm, how prepared we might be, how we think we can come to terms with this so changed situation, and have faith in the ability to master our tangible future, this deep, deep sorrow at the loss of our life's partner will not soon be silenced. It remains our companion on lonely evenings and long nights, and demands that, over and over again we must confront it. And one has to experience it all, weep and cry through all the soul's distress, again and again. Not that this is an indictment — that one reproachfully raises the usual superficial questions: Why him? He who bore more than his share of labour and responsibility; he whom the children loved; who was a comfort and a mentor to many; who was respected and loved for his plain straight-forward ways?

This is what's so especially tragic – that not only his family, but all humanity becomes poorer when such a man dies. How badly the world needs these strong unassuming and steadfast people, by whose dependable calm nature, many a difficulty is resolved, many a turmoil stilled. It becomes so clear to us women, why we moved so confidently into the arms of our strong protective men. You will be deeply thankful that you were granted this privilege once more after those long fearful war years alone. Even though it is only a memory now, you will look back on it as a special gift of grace. Was it not a preparation for this final separation, that you had to endure those two and a half years alone? The independence in managing the farm that you had to learn then, will stand you in good

256

stead now. You will stand fore-armed, confident and decisive, as you face these enormous problems.

Though life will be considerably more difficult now, inner strength grows with suffering. And slowly, gradually, one belongs to "Those faithful who know God." Is not life here on earth just one great opportunity to purify, reform and mature? Only through this kind of thinking is it at all possible to understand the early death of so many of the best people, and the long battle of existence in the discordant types. The latter basically need more time to come to terms with their situations while the others have already walked a little way towards a realization of their potential. Did Günther not demonstrate this in the exemplary way in which he dealt with all the problems last winter?

This same Tante Anneliese wrote to me in Michigan, and because I had travelled home, the letter was forwarded to Woking. Though surely well-intentioned, it was fairly heavy reading for a sixteen-year-old mourning the death of her father :

How very heavy and sad my heart became when I received the terrible news from your mother, of the death of your beloved father. What a cruel blow fate has dealt you, so far away from home and family.

Now when I think of all of you, of that little cluster of dear people in far, far away Canada, who are so precious to me and my children, I find it impossible to believe that the strong manly focal point, your good father, is no longer in their midst. Apart from the direct loss of breadwinner, who is indispensable and irreplaceable, you have been deprived of his love, his care and support, his wise, broadminded advice; his perceptive understanding of your problems.

It was just so natural that he was always there, the way he weathered last winter's worries and illnesses – Heidi's, Dieter's and Mother's surgeries. He was like an unshakable oak tree. By his quiet strength, he lightened everyone's load, and seemed like a calming influence amid a sea of worry and distress – until the tree itself was struck down. "For my thoughts are not your thoughts, neither are your ways my ways." (Isaiah 55, 8) Again these words become so clear, and in the midst of our deepest sorrow, we can only be still.

For the first time, death has come so suddenly into your young life, and as the eldest daughter, at sixteen, this puts you into a position of responsibility. Already, although we would have wished you and Dieter more worry-free years of youth, the young generation will have to take on the work and the responsibility of filling the void, and of supporting your still-vulnerable mother in the struggle to go on.

Tante Grete, wife of Uncle Werner the dentist, was also deeply shaken at the loss of her brother-in-law Günther, and wrote to Mother. Parts of her letter indicate a different philosophy about life and death than the previous excerpts have shown :

> We are totally stunned and still can't believe what has happened. Poor Else, how appalling and unexpected; how far from anything imaginable this shock is. And just after the hard experiences of last winter, you are bereft, alone. And none of us can come and help you. Not a day goes by that I don't work in some field or garden — for strangers, just so I can feed my children. How I would love to come and do this work for you! But it is futile to waste time thinking that way.

> When Günther wrote that last long letter to all of us over here, it almost seemed that he had a premonition. He felt an urgency to write a detailed account about his family and his farm. He'd had so many fears and worries about his family's health, and was so thankful and happy to have everyone back home for Easter. He was probably already formulating plans on how to fill all the gaps that had been eroded by medical expenses. It's just too cruel and inconceivable. Werner (in Russian prison) will find this bitterly hard to accept.

> You're right when you say "God's ways are hard to understand ." Yes, if one believes in a personal, loving and just God! I haven't been able to do that for a long time. One would be forced to feel wrath and resentment towards a God who would allow indescribable misfortune, misery and cruelty. One has to free oneself of the image of God as a human or superhuman being. In terms of the huge majestic universe, that would be too small-minded. Our human life is just as subject to accidental and coincidental happenings as an animal. When the worm is trampled, its life is snuffed out, without there being any underlying reason or purpose. That's how it is with us humans. But what differentiates us from the animal, is that we can experience in full awareness, elemental forces, godliness, as well as the unexplainable. We must consciously recognize the divine harmony that rules in nature, and we must try to instill that harmony in our lives as long as we live. After our death, this divine harmony comes to an end when our body dies. (I am not sure that this was a comforting thing to write in a letter of condolence! Ed.) I wish we could discuss these things. I have studied this subject in some detail.

In her Christmas letter to Tante Grete, Mother reacted to her sister-in-law's letter of condolence and outspoken philosophies:

> I too, would like to have the opportunity to discuss many of these things with you. I know that your perception of God is so different from the

258

Christian belief. But for me, the hope that somehow, after death, we could meet our loved ones again, provides comfort when the terrible longing overwhelms me. Yes, to achieve a godly harmony is a life-long task. For a person like Günther, who was blessed with a serene nature from birth, it was not difficult, and his calm, stable presence was transmitted to the rest of us.

Tante Grete concludes her letter with some down-to-earth advice and caring:

You will have to be very patient with your recovery. Above all avoid over-exertion. Ursel will be the hausfrau now that she's back home, and will be lovingly concerned with your care. Hopefully Dieter is better, so you don't have that worry. If your little ones were so brave and helpful during your illness, they'll be even more so now, and they will help to cheer you up. What riches we have in our children! One realizes this even more in hard times. Nourishing them is our sacred duty, and in spite of all hardships, this is what makes life worth living.

I know that all this will be little consolation to you, because you are inundated with problems, and the deep wound is still so fresh and painful. But keep the comforting assurance, that very slowly and gradually even the deepest wounds heal.

The news of Father's death was especially difficult for Tante Anna to accept. Her Günther had always been like a son, and more. On May 27th, in her beautiful script, she shares her sorrow :

I am still numb from this terrible news. You can imagine my horror. Günther no longer there? Gone, forever gone! And you all alone with the children, and again the whole burden on your shoulders. You proved before that you could carry it and you will again, but how hard it will be. Now there will be no letters to look forward to, as from the camp. And you always knew he was coming home. And now? Where is he? In our hearts, certainly, but no one, to our knowledge, has ever come back. We know nothing about death, except that it means the end here, and grieving and pining for those who remain.

Your daily work will ease the pain, and the children who have been entrusted to you will be a big help. I hope you will regain your strength and stay healthy.

I can't even begin to tell you what that boy meant to me — from his childhood in Königsberg, his training in Lippe, the agricultural school in Landsberg, then after your engagement, his preparations to go to Canada. And then his many letters from the homestead — how I looked forward to them! How glad he was that we could write letters again after those

desolate Hitler years. I remember being so afraid in 1939, that he might
fall for all those Hitler promises and bring you all back to Germany.

I just can't grasp the fact that I may no longer imagine you both happy
and content in your little Canadian home. I know what a sweetheart he
always had in you, and because of that he was happy and satisfied. For that
I thank you with my whole heart. For Werner this will be worse than war
and prison.

These samplings from many letters of condolence give just a small indication of how much our father, Günther Pankow was loved and respected, not only by his family, but also by friends and neighbours. Naturally, we his family missed him most of all. That empty place in our home loomed large, and only time would gradually diminish the pain. This was a pivotal turning point in our lives, but we had to carry on, with integrity, that which Father had worked so hard to bring into existence. He would have expected nothing less.

Bereaved Pankow Family July 1948
Ursula, Mother, Dieter
Gerta, Irma, Heidi

Chapter 20   The Ever Present Uncle

As Mother continued to try to come to terms with her bereavement, feelings of sadness and hopelessness did nothing to help her with the important decisions regarding the future of her children. Friends and neighbours were helpful and tried to advise her, but ultimately, the final resolution would rest with our family. And always wanting desperately to help, but only causing dissension and adding to the frustration, was our dear "Uncle" Horst Anders. Sometimes Mother needed to share her feelings on this subject, as in her December '48 letter to her sister-in-law Grete :

> *As helpful as Horst Anders tries to be, and I must be thankful to him for that, things just can't go on this way. We will both go to pieces. If he were a person who could be relied upon, he would be a big help to us. But he simply is the way he is, and it's extremely difficult. When even a person like Günther lost his cool with Horst, how could I possibly control myself? I know that part of the blame lies with me too. How often we have wished that he had never come to Canada. So much heart-ache and anger could have been avoided, on both sides. If at all possible, I want to spare Dieter a repetition of this kind of entanglement. The boy deserves better guidance and a strong mentor. How Günther would have enjoyed fullfilling this role!*

The subject of "relatives by marriage" such as Horst Anders, came up in letters occasionally. Although we children were quite fond of "Uncle," it would seem that he was indeed somewhat of a "thorn in the side" of our parents. I have tried to determine the circumstances of his immigration from Germany, without too much success.

Horst Richard Anders was born in Tilsit, East Prussia, on November 26, 1902, to Leo Anders and Emma (Schlick) Anders, the eighth of eleven children. His father was a lawyer in Tilsit, and owned a cottage on an acreage in Pogegen, where his large family often spent summer holidays. His mother, weighed down by heavy social obligations and many children, was frequently unbalanced, nervous and irritable. Three children died in infancy. The home did not provide a stable nurturing atmosphere. Four adult Anders offspring lost their lives through suicide and there was also a case of incest. In this type of home environment and under these influences, Horst Anders spent his childhood. As a young man he was undecided about a career, but leaned towards carpentry, and learned to construct and finish furniture. This, however, did not secure a sure livelihood in Germany.

Given this, and the less than favourable conditions at home, it was deemed a "solution" or an "opportunity" for Horst to emigrate to Canada. He now had a goal or destination in that far-off unknown, because he had become "related" to Günther Pankow, homesteader in northern Canada. Horst's brother Hellmut, lawyer, had married Günther's sister Anneliese, teacher near Königsberg. Thus, in October, 1929, Horst Anders set sail for Canada and brought with him, in addition to his own belongings, several packing crates of useful items which relatives had sent along for Günther's new homestead. He also brought a touch of the homeland with him, and the two young men had many things to talk about — the one bringing family news and greetings, the other beginning to orient the newcomer to the Canadian homestead.

Neither man could know or anticipate at this time, that Horst's coming to Canada would bring in its wake, certainly some advantages and positive results, but much more in the way of disharmony, burden, and great amounts of nervous tension.

As early as 1932, some evidence of this had appeared, as, in November, Father wrote a letter to his brother Werner:

> *Just a few words about Horst, to get it off my chest. In his whole unfortunate disposition, he's rather more burden and stress than help and support to us. Earlier, it was more bearable, when he had opportunities to go out working on other farms to earn some money — then he was only here in the winter. But now, when it's very difficult even for an efficient, competent person to find a job, he has developed a terrible apathy and a very thick skin. He hasn't a cent in his pocket, and hangs his head in*

Horst Anders and his Mare Lottie

> *discouragement. But who else here has it any better? Yet others have an altogether different energy and attitude towards life. He's not stupid, and in no way inferior — just the opposite — in many ways, especially in finicky, exacting tasks, he's quite skilled. But his whole ponderous nature*

makes everything so difficult for him, and for us who have to co-exist with him.

*But enough of this. It is an unpleasant subject, one which I could tell you about for hours, but won't waste time in a letter. In any case, he will be put out before Christmas. He'll **have** to move to his shack, even if he comes here to eat. Else and I are looking forward to the moment when we are finally alone. Our little house, now with two children, is pretty crowded.*

A strange family, the Anders. Very rarely do any of Horst's relatives write to him — once in a great while, Hellmut, otherwise no one. And in Hellmut's letters, even those to us, in spite of the many pages, there's little in them. — all well-intentioned, many high-sounding words of idealism, but little that's concrete and positive. I think I asked you this before. Is our Anneliese happy with Hellmut? Now for four consecutive years, in every year a child! That's too much for a woman.

Then during the war when Father was away in the internment camp, the situation sometimes became quite strained. Uncle Horst's efforts were accepted with mixed emotions. He had for years been "ever present," a hanger on in the Pankow family, an unfortunate soul, genetically challenged, who could never quite "get it together." With a heart of gold, he had always looked to Father, with his empathy and infinite patience, as a hero and a

Private Horst Anders with Heidi, Irma and Gerta Pankow

mentor. Now that support and example was many miles away. Uncle, in his own way, felt a strong sense of responsibility to help Günther's family through this difficult time. Though his intentions were always good, his ponderous and impractical ways of carrying them out nearly drove Mother to distraction.

His weaknesses were known in the settlement, but so were his strengths. He could fix just about anything and was often called upon to make repairs. In this way he earned the nickname "Der Doktor" or "Doc." But in terms of initiative, zeal, organizational skills and emotional strength, he did not cope well. As young children, we loved him and he loved us. In this respect he was a big help during Father's absence. In 1940, Mother writes to camp:

> *Uncle finally finished cutting the wheat. Sometimes I'm nearly at my wit's end watching him work, getting nothing done. Then I run to the blueberry patch, and fired by frustration, I fill the pail very quickly. You know from experience how it is, but he is good with the children. He is peeved when the neighbours come to help because he considers it a reflection on his integrity.*

Then in 1943, Uncle received his conscription order, and with mixed emotions, he became a member of the Canadian army. There is something incongruous about the fact that for Horst, his short time in the service was probably amongst the happiest times of his unfulfilled existence. He felt needed and useful for his mechanical and "fix-it" abilities, he had three good meals a day, a roof over his head and good clothes to wear — none of which he was able to achieve for himself as a civilian.

After Father's death in 1948, Uncle's life became even more like a ship without a rudder, and as we Pankow siblings became adults, he no longer felt needed, even by children. Hopelessness engulfed him, and in January 1954, Mother found herself writing a very difficult letter to Germany. She had to inform the relatives of Horst Anders of the tragic death of their brother. The recipients were brother Kurt and his wife Hanlyd, sister Lydie and her husband Hugo Preusshof, and sister Ursula Gerhard.

> *Hopefully the police department has not reached you before you receive this letter, because I promised them that I would accept the responsibility of notifying you. Your brother Horst is no longer among the living. I should have written immediately, but you will understand that this has been a very confusing time for me, and I had to regain a certain peace and stability. Just a short note would not have been appropriate, so today I will write in some detail.*
>
> *You may be aware, that for some months I had been away from home, in Calgary and Edmonton, attending the School for Nurse's Aides. At the beginning of November, I returned home to settle and arrange things, inside and out, at the farm. It was my intention to move to Spirit River for the winter, with Gerta, Heidi and Irmgard. They would attend High School and I hoped to work at the hospital. Why would I stay alone at the farm all winter, the roads drifted in, Dieter out working?*
>
> *Uncle knew all this but refused to let himself believe it would happen. It was the same last winter when I left for Calgary. You have probably heard,*

that he had irrevocably set his mind on marrying me. During his youth a fortune-teller had told him he would find his happiness with a widow and her children. In my absence, this idea, through anxiety and jealousy, was strengthened and became an obsession. All that he dared not express personally, was poured out in passionate, imploring letters, which seemed to give him a certain satisfaction. He dwelt on the subjects of women, friendship, marriage, and ultimately he held his mother responsible for his plight. In her stern unyielding manner and discipline during his youth, she had allowed no interaction with girls.

I felt so terribly sorry for him, but I could not help him. He just couldn't accept this, and lay for days on the sordid cot in his shack, brooding and asking himself what he had done to deserve this fate. It got progressively worse — the terrible scenes, often in the presence of the children, trembling, sobbing, dropping at my feet in tears; running away like a man possessed. Many a night, I did not dare close my eyes to sleep.

When he would not reappear for a few days, the children were afraid to go and check on him, and would ask neighbours to look in. We feared finding his body hanging from a beam or lying on the ground. He talked of regretting that he lacked the courage to end it all. He spoke of death and how he envied Günther. At first I tried to advise him and reason with him, never believing it would happen, because someone who often talks about suicide, seldom acts on it. He practically searched out accidents — driving like a madman with his tractor or the little old '27 model car that he had recently purchased for fifty dollars.

Then Christmas was approaching, and with it, Ursel's wedding, which we celebrated on December 28, 1953. There was much to do, but in spite of everything, we celebrated a nice Christmas Eve, even though we had to go and get Uncle from his shack, where he had disappeared while we were in church. It had been the custom all these many years, that he spent Christmas with our family. Again, he was very generous with his presents. Giving us gifts was his greatest pleasure – but was often very uncomfortable for us, because he spent nothing on himself. He seemed to believe, that with money he could buy that which was denied him. For example, last summer he bought Dieter a car radio for seventy-five dollars, with which he could have bought two for his house. Dieter felt he could not accept such a gift, and did not want to be indebted in any way. Enraged, Uncle charged down to the creek and threw the radio into the water. Now ruined, the expensive thing lies useless upstairs. These kinds of scenes occurred many times.

But our good uncle helped faithfully with the wedding preparations, especially since Dieter had come home from the lumber mill with an extremely sore back. Since Hans and Ursel both grew up in the community, it was really the first wedding in the second generation of us original pioneers. We had invited all the neighbours — sixty people, without children. We took out the wall between the kitchen and the living room so that we could set a large L shaped table to seat all the guests. With all this Uncle was most helpful. It was a happy celebration with wedding songs, verses and speeches, in true German fashion. Laughter and merriment reigned. Only Uncle couldn't get into it — he ate and drank nothing. At ten o'clock we all moved to Westmark Hall for the wedding dance, and here he did make an effort to join in. During the night, the happy newly-wed couple drove off. The rest of us returned to the empty house, so deserted with the long covered tables, the large room looming darkly.

And then it happened, the terrible tragedy which followed so closely on the heels of a happy and joyous celebration. Dieter had gone back to work at the mill. I had planned to be in Spirit River in five days for the beginning of the school term, so we began a busy round of cleaning and packing.. Uncle could not bear to watch all this. Irrational, ragged, starving and unshaven, he appeared in the midst of our activity. With hysterical scenes, falling on his knees, wailing and crying, he pleaded with me to marry him, and declared that he could not face life alone.

Suddenly he rushed to the medicine cabinet and snatched cartridges, which I tried in vain to wrest from him; then he tore the 22 caliber rifle from its hook and ran across the yard. The girls and I screamed, but dared not pursue him. Who knows what a person in that state might be capable of? East of the spruce trees with which the shivaree well-wishers had decorated the fence — some fifty meters from the house —there he lay then, on December 31, 1953, at three o'clock in the afternoon. In a state of terror and confusion, Gerta, eighteen, jumped on Lucie and galloped over to Delfs. Finding no one home,she hurried on to Oltmanns. Within thirty minutes, Johann arrived and loaded the twitching body into his truck and

rushed to Spirit River. Here in the hospital, two hours later, Uncle Horst Richard Anders died.

Now began the whole police investigation; but everyone knew the state of affairs and sad circumstances. It took the neighbours two days, in terrible weather, with pick axes and dynamite, to dig a grave. The pastor lives in a different community (Hines Creek) and could not come for the funeral, so Alfred

Horst Richard Anders

Sellin, a neighbour and pioneer of the settlement stepped in. He spoke of the comrade from the early pioneering days, who was such a part of the community, and who in his generosity, had always been ready to lend a helping hand. He had, even with his limited emotional strength, tried to achieve a place for himself, but had been unable to come to terms with that which he could not change.

All of us, and the whole community, will miss him — he was always called when no one else was available. Why could he not just be our good neighbour, the dear Uncle for the children? The neighbours had often offered to help him finish building his house — just the day before someone had spoken of it. They knew I was leaving, and wanted to help him through this difficult time. I had suggested he could live in our house and look after the remaining four cattle and two horses. We would sometimes be coming home the twenty miles on weekends, and for a change, he could visit us in town.

*Even though everyone is begging me not to, the feelings of guilt and self-blame keep coming back to me. I should have given him **more** compassion and **motherly** love, but lately he would always perceive this as something more, even though I had told him countless times that he could be nothing more than a brother to me. Although I was often nasty to him, he would not give up. It's almost unforgivable that this had to happen in our yard, in the presence of the girls. What all does one have to endure on this earth? Is this too, necessary for my inner person?*

Of course, Horst made no will, and no money is to be found. He must have hidden it because he had just offered me three hundred dollars to help pay for the wedding. Dieter, together with police personnel, had diligently searched the shack and its contents. In summer Uncle had gleefully shown Dieter how he had cunningly hidden seven hundred dollars amongst a mess of soiled old papers in his bed. All the while, he ran around in rags and complained of poverty. An inventory was taken, machinery and the land which had been granted to him through the Veterans Land Act, being the only real assets. How often I had urged him to complete the necessary requirements, so that the land would be legally his, to do with as he wished. He was not far from having enough acres broken. Now it will all go back to the veteran's organization and the trust company which administers and rules in such cases, and there is seldom anything left.

The tools and smaller items are lying around outside under the snow, because he never managed to build even a shed. Often he'd gifted it all to Dieter, but of course there's nothing in writing. Sometimes I had advised him to make a will, since he has so many relatives, but did not wish to appear that I was after his property. So at least in that respect I feel free now. It's just so sad that all that he — and our family with him, had worked for, will now be lost. I had always wished that one of your boys might have taken it over. There'd have been fresh, energetic young blood, and it would have been nice for our Dieter.

Now there'll be a race on for this land. Who will win the draw? I wish there could be something in it for you, Horst's relatives, but that can't be counted on. It's all so bewildering. When Günther died, that too was so sudden and difficult, but everything was settled and we were able to continue. But now I am gripped by apprehension and can't shake the guilt feelings. The neighbours urge and advise me to view this as "a road to freedom."

My friend Helga Andersen writes to me: "The fact that poor uncle now has his tormented life behind him is something that should be viewed with relief. What would otherwise have lain before him? And if you believe that you must harbour guilt feelings, no outsider can be a judge of that. Have you not paid off this blame, and are still doing it now, that by your presence and your efforts to intervene so quickly and without fear, you helped him to achieve his death wish? It was the last favour that you could bestow on him. Be glad that you did it, because it was probably the greatest one that he needed in his life. Imagine, if he'd shot himself over in his shack; think of the hours of suffering he might have undergone. I talked with Uncle for a few minutes at the wedding. He was so dejected and I felt so sorry for him. He who believes that he has lost everything, has no courage and strength left to face life. Why then prolong the torment? Remember him kindly — how poor and bereft his life was compared to yours and mine."

It was hard for Ursel too, who in her quiet manner, always got along best with Uncle. She wrote to me from Wetaskiwin where the newly-wed Delfs had just arrived: "I just hope, Mother, that you will enjoy your new work at the hospital, and that it will help you gradually to forget some of the horror. Please, please, do not blame yourself. It was not your fault, nor was it your wish that things should happen this way. You could have done it no differently with him, and have already sacrificed enough happiness in your life through him."

Mother and the three teen-aged girls moved to Spirit River for the rest of the winter, and lived in two small rooms rented from Chabots. Mother enjoyed her work for the Grey Nuns at the hospital, and the girls attended school just across the street. Dieter went back to his mill job in the bush. Hans and I settled happily into our apartment in Wetaskiwin, where he had a job as a welder. We were all busy enough, and far away enough, to put some of the horror behind us.

When we looked back, the positive aspects of Uncle Horst's presence in our lives could not be denied. Many times he had been "Mr. Fix-it" around the farm and yard; countless times he had been a faithful last-minute baby-sitter — when Mother and Father had rushed to Grande Prairie to lay claim to the river quarter; when Mother was called away in cases of sickness or childbirth; when Mother had to appear in Spirit River for the court hearing to try to gain Father's freedom, and more.

I do indeed remember Uncle Horst kindly. We, as youngsters, did not experience his presence in the same way as our parents — the ever-present "extra spoke," the friction this sometimes caused in our home, from their pioneer beginning, through the depression years and onward. Except for short periods of working out and army service, he considered our house his home, and we were his family. He was never able to muster up enough energy, ambition and desire to establish a home of his own.

During the last year of his life, I remember dropping in to check on him occasionally. His tiny crude shack, perhaps 10' by 10', with a tar paper covered slanted roof, topped by a stove-pipe, stood in the bush on the corner of his V.L.A. property, where Dieter's yard is now. Close by stood the frame of a larger, partially completed house. Uncle sat on his dirty disheveled cot, and invited me to come in and sit on the large round block of wood which fit tightly beside the door. He was so happy to see me and offered me peppermint candy. He tried to hide his unhappiness. "Ach, mein liebes Uschchen" he would declare, trying to tell jokes, even singing — it was always the same few lines — "Es war einmal ein treuer Hussar."

In that winter of '52 – '53 it seems he had reached a level of desperation that had been building for some time. In 1948 he had lost his "rock" and mentor, our father, who, through his years of calm patience, had managed to help Uncle maintain a measure of emotional stability. Then Uncle had been forced to come to the realization that Dieter could not accept him as an example, could not work together with him, and did not wish to be indebted to him in any way. Dieter made his independence quite clear when he left the farm to earn money that winter. Mother, too, had shown that she would make her own way, after taking the Nurses Aide course, then securing a job at the hospital in Spirit River. More devastating to him, she could not possibly comply with his ardent pleas for marriage. The three youngest, Gerta, Heidi and Irma, whom in their younger years he had so often tended, who had played games with him, who had patiently listened to his many tirades, — now they were leaving too, and no longer needed him.

Our wedding celebration seemed to be a final catalyst. His oldest "niece" in whom he had often found a quiet confidante, now had found her own love and happiness, all the very things that had been denied him. All these deprivations and perceived losses seemed to descend upon him and overwhelm him at a time of greatest vulnerability. Feeling totally bereft, he found the long-sought courage to pull the trigger. At the age of fifty-one, the life of our Uncle Horst Anders came to a tragic end.

The V.L.A. land which had been granted to Uncle, now went back to that organization because all the improvement requirements had not been met. The land became available through the public trustee, and since several local farmers were interested in this parcel of land situated on Westmark main road, a draw was held, with the names of all the interested parties. Somehow it felt as if our family should have some preferential right. Had we not worked together with Uncle all these years, sharing machinery and horses, hours of labour and support? Would he not have wanted us to have it? But in legal terms all this meant nothing, and there was nothing in writing. However, to improve chances, two Pankow names went into the draw — Dieter and Gerta. Perhaps justice prevailed when Gerta's name was drawn. She was landowner for a time, until she transferred the title to Dieter, who has developed it into a successful farm.

Much later, in the 1990s when a nephew of Horst Anders and son of Kurt Anders, visited us from Germany, he expressed an interest in the life of his Canadian uncle. In the course of conversation, he made some remarks which left me surprisingly defensive. He asked me for pruning shears, and said he needed them at the cemetery. After spending a half hour, snipping a few wayward caragana twigs, at the grave of the uncle whom he never knew, he commented "Now it looks as if someone cares about his memory." Our family had set the gravestone and looked after the site for nearly fifty years! Later, we were looking at photo albums when we came to a page where a picture had been removed. "That was probably Horst's photo," our visitor said, implying that we had tried to obliterate the memory. For the second time that day, I bristled; this time not in silence. I felt a strong need to set him straight and replied: "Any joy and happiness that your Uncle Horst Anders had in his unfulfilled life – any family life and love that he experienced – he had in our home, and in the interaction with the Pankow family, particularily the five children. Certainly he had more reason to live, more to be thankful for, than for anything that his dysfunctional family in Germany, who had sent him here, ever gave him." After that my guest was silent for a while, and realized that I knew a great deal more about his uncle's life than he did, and that it was not his place to make veiled accusations. I think we were both somewhat taken aback at my defensive attitude. It is a posture I have found myself assuming on more than one occasion, when we, having grown up on our poor remote Canadian homestead, have been in conversation with people from the old "civilized" homeland of our parents. We have a certain pride, and have earned everything we have in a way that they would never really understand.

Chapter 21   Finding Our Way in the Fifties

There were so many adjustments, so many decisions, so very many questions. And Father, in his quiet decisive manner, was not there to help find the answers.

Mother felt that it was not fair to expect Dieter, so young and physically small at seventeen, to have to follow in his father's footsteps. Even if he eventually wished to carry on with the farm, Mother thought he would have more opportunities if he first completed at least high school. Now, as it always had been, a high school education was considered a "must" in our family.

But that fall of '48, Dieter adamantly refused to go back to school. As the only man left in our family, he felt a strong sense of responsibility, a burning need to not let his father down. Such a major decision as selling everything and moving away could not be made so quickly, he reasoned. The cattle and pigs were not ready for market, and that would result in a substantial loss. The livestock consisted of thirteen market hogs, two sows with fifteen piglets; five milk cows, two milked for home use, the other three suckled their calves because veal brought a very good price. There were five yearling calves, two heifers and a steer; five or six horses and some poultry.

Dieter and Else Pankow, Eckhard Kastendieck

Money for our education was not the only need to be considered, and hopes of buying a tractor or a used car had to be put on hold. Our large debt load hung over our family like a dark cloud. The medical expenses of the past winter, (there was no such thing as Alberta Health Care,) and the bank loans that had been made to pay for land clearing, all demanded payment.

During the summer holidays, Father's best friend from internment camp times, Eckhard Kastendieck, (Uncle Dick) his wife and little Irene came to visit us. He had promised Mother he would try to help in any way possible, even though he lived in Saskatchewan. He was positive, that had the situation been reversed, his good friend Günther would have done the same. Together with Mother and Dieter, Uncle Dick rode around the farm and familiarized himself with all the places that had so often come up in camp conversations. That same September, he sent his son Manfred to come and help Dieter with the harvest, and the two young men also repaired and rebuilt the interior of the barn.

Back: Ursula Pankow, Manfred Kastendieck,
Karl Toerper, Dieter Pankow
Front: Gerta, Irma, and Heidi Pankow

That winter we all stayed home. Gerta, Heidi and Irma were still young enough to attend the school in Westmark, where they had a very excellent teacher in Mrs. Arlene Olafson. I enrolled in correspondence courses —Social Studies, Physics, and Art. The former were subjects not available in the U.S. school, and would be required as prerequisites for my grade eleven. So I did not totally lose a year towards matriculation. After harvest we had a nice open fall and managed to get most of the field work done. With the help of Uncle's J.D. tractor, Dieter

Dieter by the Barn

worked many long hours, and we all picked roots and rocks on the many acres of "back-setting," the first plowing back after a fall crop on the breaking, when so many roots are turned up. In the winter there were the usual tasks: hauling out, cutting and splitting firewood, delivering grain and livestock to Woking, crushing grain, taking our turn at the mail haul, and the daily chores of feeding, milking and manure removal. In the evening I did my correspondence lessons.

Mother deplored the lack of social and cultural opportunities for young people, especially her own teen-agers, as she writes Tante Grete:

l. to r: Abbie Sellin, Karl Toerper, Doris Jordan, Dieter and Ursula Pankow, Marlene Sellin, Gerta, Irma and Heidi Pankow, Willie Janssen

Certainly our seclusion here in the bush has its advantages, but there is so little good recreation for young people. And since we won't be able to afford a car for some time, we really don't get out much. To see a nice movie involves so much trouble and expense that you just lose the desire to go. Once in a while there's a dance, but many of the boys don't know how to dance, and usually there's fighting and drinking.

Kay Bice, Elise Egge, Ursula Pankow

Because mother felt this lack of social life for us, she always showed a lot of friendly hospitality and welcomed our visitors. Our home became a favourite gathering place for the young people of the community, and I remember lively games, harmonica and guitar playing, and folk singing in our cozy living room. It was fortunate for me, that because a qualified teacher was not available, a young supervisor had been hired to oversee correspondence lessons for a few

Back: Jasper Toerper, Ursula Delfs, Dieter Pankow, Heinz Toerper,
Margaret Hess, Abbie Sellin, Martha Hess, Karl Toerper, Ursula Pankow,
Hans Delfs, Willie Janssen, Jochen Witte
Front: Barbara and Anneliese Schack, Heidi Pankow, Geesche Glimm,
Gerta and Irma Pankow

months at the Westmark school. Miss Kay Bice from Eaglesham was just a year or two older than I was, and she had room and board at Egge's. We got along well and she was a welcome addition to the young people in our community.Jochen Witte, who had come from Germany and lived with his grandparents, was also a newcomer and became a good friend to Dieter. Martha and Margaret Hess, whose parents had taken over Northmark Store

Ursula Pankow & Martha Hess

from Mortensens, then Albrecht and Marlene Sellin, and our cousin Hansmartin Herrndorf, who had all come from Germany, became a part of the local youth. In addition to new first-time immigrants from Germany, some residents who had formerly homesteaded in Westmark in 1929, returned to Canada. Among these were Eilert and Frieda Pleis with their daughter Helga in '49, and the Charlie Muehrer family in '53.

We four girls at our house began to

**Dieter Pankow, Hartmann Nagel,
Karl, Heinz, Jasper Toerper**

**Barbara Schack, Ursula Pankow,
Ursula Nagel, Ursula Delfs**

1948 Confirmation Class

discover that Dieter, our only brother, seemed to have a lot of friends! Many young neighbourhood boys came to visit! The Toerper boys were, perhaps the most frequent callers, and had a vehicle, so took us places. Their mother Minna was certain that surely one of her four boys would marry one of the four Pankow girls. When she travelled to Germany in '49, my picture was shown around as "Karl's intended." I thought this a bit presumptuous, as I had never thought of him as anything but a friend and pal of my brother.

**1951 Confirmation Class
Back: Reinhold Knoblauch, Jochen
Witte,Victor Delfs, Lawrence Stedel, Arnold
Baum, Ed Hessler, Pastor Wolfram
Front: Gerta Pankow, Anneliese Schack,
Margaret Hess, Doris Backer, Rosemarie
Scriba**

It was during this time that, due to the division within the congregation, Lutheran church services were being held in Westmark School. A large class was confirmed there in 1948. Our pastor Martin Wolfram mentored his young group of Hartmann Nagel, Dieter Pankow, Jasper, Karl and Heinz Toerper, as well as Ursula Delfs, Ursula Nagel, Ursula Pankow, and Barbara Schack. Our younger sisters were confirmed at the new church later, after reconciliation had taken place. It was under the patient guidance and mediation of Pastor Martin Intscher that the Northmark congregation was reunited, and a new constitution was drafted.

Mother showed remarkable strength following the devastating loss of our father, at least in the presence of her children and in the eyes of the public. In the spring of '49, I remember her toiling beside the rock pile by the poplar trees in the yard, a heavy 16-pound hammer in her hand. Not a big or physically strong woman, she pounded repeatedly on each carefully selected field stone, until she had chipped it into a roughly square shape. It seems that each stroke was, perhaps, therapeutic, for she shaped enough stones to create an edging all around Father's grave. They were loaded on the wagon, and along with topsoil from our field, hauled to the riverbank cemetery, where she lovingly planted flowers.

1954 Confirmation Class
l to r: Margaret Oltmanns, Heidi Pankow, Inge Muehrer, Pastor Intscher, Irma Pankow, Sieglind Solty, Peter Glimm

Dieter was trying his best to fill his father's large shoes, and in spite of his small physical stature, he worked with great energy and will. It was almost as though he needed to justify his refusal to go back to school. In the fall of '49 Mother wrote to Tante Anneliese:

> *We are expecting the threshing crew in the next few days. Dieter is driving his own bundle wagon, whereas last year he shared the job with another boy. I still don't like to see him do it. It's very hard work, loading and unloading bundles all day long. And our wagon is one of those old high-wheeled ones — Günther had often complained about it. The rubber-tired wagons are so expensive, but many people have them now.*
>
> *You describe the splendour of autumn. Our valley, too, is beautiful with its fall colours. Unfortunately we have few spruce and pine left to provide the dark evergreen contrast. They were all destroyed by fire, and the dry trunks stand as silent reminders of past glory. One by one, the winds blow these over, and poplar and willow undergrowth covers the windfall.*
>
> *Our summer days are long — in June and July it seems the sun hardly sets. Summer silence and Sunday peace, you say? Yes, perhaps there are rare moments when we enjoy these, but usually we are too hurried, too busy, and then tired.* (Mother was responding, with hard realities, to one of Tante Anneliese's philosophical letters.)

It was during the winter of '49 that Mother took Irma along, and by Greyhound bus they visited Kastendiecks in Hillmond, Saskatchewan, returning that family's summer visit to Woking. They also stopped to visit the widow of Hans Mayer in Vegreville, whose husband, a dairy farmer, had been Father's camp friend. Mother also attended to some business in Edmonton, including a consultation with Dr. Levy, concerning my eyes, and seeing to the transfer of our land from Father's name to hers. This was important if she ever hoped to procure a bank loan.

The winter of 1950 was extreme. Mother wrote to Anneliese in February:

The Pankow Family Goes Visiting "By Ford Tractor"

Thank you for your letter containing the wonderful news of Werner's return from Russia. I had a quick note from him which he wrote from Tante Anna's. Oh, what I wouldn't give to come and see you all! I was surprised that Werner was able to get established again so quickly. I had heard that refugees or displaced persons were not allowed to become independent. What luck for him and his family!

We've almost survived the winter – it was a cruel one. From the 17th of December until now, it's been a constant –40 to –50 degrees below zero. We've never experienced this before in all our years in Canada. Usually there's a chinook somewhere in between. In spite of the weather, Gerta and Heidi attended school faithfully, but Irma was sick for a long time and couldn't shake her cough. The only warm spot was around our big cast-iron heater, and there it was so crowded with children, dog, footwear, socks, mittens, that it was hard to get close. Block after block of firewood made its way into the heater and the pile in the yard got ever smaller. The house is far from cold-proof, with drafts everywhere, and no one has been able to afford storm windows. For our inner "heating" and nourishment, we are on the second pig. We'd prefer beef to pork and it's probably healthier, but steers bring a good market price, and we're counting on that for a down-payment on a tractor.

In 1950 Dieter did purchase a small Ford tractor which made farming easier and more enjoyable for him. He built a box on the back, so that, in the absence of a car, the whole family could travel together without having to hitch up the horses.

In July, 1950, when I was seventeen, we made the decision that surgery should proceed to straighten out my cross-eye problem. Since I had nearly reached my eighteenth birthday, this was the last chance to have the procedure covered under the Mother's Allowance health care. This operation would not improve my sight, but in terms of cosmetic value, it probably did a lot to improve my confidence and self-esteem. I have often been thankful that Mother had the foresight to make this a priority for me.

Near the end of November of that same year, a letter edged in black arrived from Germany. It announced the death, at eighty-six years, of Tante Anna Pankow, our father's aunt, our great aunt. This woman had been a significant factor — a bulwark, a friend, a confidante to the Pankow family over many years. She had helped Father learn the English language, had helped him financially by advancing part of his inheritance, and had written countless letters of encouragement to Canada. A woman of great character and rare wisdom, she would be sorely missed.

> Das reich gesegnete Leben unserer lieben Tante Anna ist sanft erloschen.
>
> ### Fräulein Anna Pankow
> Lehrerin i. R.
>
> starb am 19. November 1950 im bald vollendeten 86. Lebensjahre.
>
> Im Namen aller Angehörigen und Freunde:
>
> **Dr. Werner Pankow,** Zahnarzt
> (20a) Helstorf, Krs. Neustadt a./Rbge.,
> z. Z. Detmold, Heldmannstraße 8.
>
> Die Trauerfeier vor· der Einäscherung findet am Mittwoch, dem 22. November, 11.30 Uhr, in der Kapelle des Landeskrankenhauses in Detmold statt.

In April, after the hard cruel winter of '50 – '51, Mother wrote an update to Uncle Werner:

It is three years ago now, that our good father was taken from us. It is not only the particular day that brings the memory so near. Each spring, the melting snow, with the impassable terrible roads, whether it be in April or later in May, brings the sadness of that fateful time back.

Snow on August 15th, 1950

But life goes on, and every day makes its demands.Thankfully we have been spared from major illnesses since that troublesome winter of '48. Dieter has, it seems, since the removal of his spleen, overcome the circulatory blood problem, and is doing well. Ursel will finish high school in June, and we will try to manage sending her to Edmonton for teacher training in the fall. Gerta has finished her Grade 9 at our little country school and should go to town in September. Heidi, at thirteen, and Irma at ten, can continue at Westmark for now. All the girls help a lot with the chores, as much as school allows.

And their mother got through the winter well. The one kidney, it seems,has adjusted to working for two. I have to be careful to keep warm, especially while travelling. Dieter built a nice closed-in box for the cutter, with a heater in it, so the ten miles to Woking don't seem so bad. The hamlet used to be surrounded by beautiful stands of evergreens. Now that has all burned. Woking is growing, with Ewald Jacobs' large department store at its core. The two grain elevators have had annexes added, because modern brushcutters have made it possible to bring many more acres of land under cultivation in the area. Unfortunately, last year hail, frost and early snow resulted in a total crop failure. But cattle prices were exceptionally high, and saw many farmers through the winter, even though feed and seed had to be purchased.

Ursula Pankow and Ida Rowe at the Oil Rig Campsite

After staying home during the winter of '49 – '50 and taking lessons by correspondence, I resumed high school in Grande Prairie by working for my room and board for two school terms, and achieved matriculation in 1951. Now to advance to the next step and get my teacher training, finances were lacking. But I was lucky. Ida Rowe, who was a long-time camp cook, asked me to work with her for the summer. Ida's brother Sevie had taken me out to a movie, to a dance on a few occasions, and the Rowes were hopeful — the family making friendly overtures. This must have been particularly painful for Mother as she remembered Frank Rowe's behavior during Father's wartime internment. Although I found Frank's son to be a likeable person and always the perfect gentleman, I was not about to let anything serious develop. However, my summer employment as cook's helper with Ida at an oil camp north of Tangent made it possible for me to get my first year of teacher training.

While I was at the oil camp, Dieter managed to have a little change and a break when he attended a week of trial classes for farm boys aged sixteen to twenty-one, at the brand new Agricultural School in Fairview. The purpose was to show off and advertise the new facility, and Dieter was impressed. From Fairview he travelled on to Peace River to visit Herman and Manfred Kastendieck who worked in a garage there. From them he purchased his first car — an old 1929 model, and relished the feeling of driving home in his very own vehicle.

Mother did not give up easily. She was still determined to get Dieter back to school. Perhaps there was another way to get a further education. If not Grade XII, Dieter was willing to consider something else, and she wrote to Uncle Werner, asking his opinion:

> *I had previously mentioned to you, that Dieter is considering joining the Air Force. I got information from Edmonton, and we filled out the preliminary application forms. Now before he goes for his medicals, we'd like to hear how you feel about this. If there were a one or two year conscription, he'd go now without a second thought. But he is required to join for three years, in which time he'd be trained for a specific career. Then he could make further decisions. Pay during the first year is eighty dollars — enough for spending money. Of course everything has two or more sides. It wouldn't be easy, after four years of being his own boss, to submit to military discipline. But that has its advantages. Then, as the only son, he always feels duty-bound towards the family. But if he doesn't undertake something now, he never will.*

Uncle Werner was really not in a position to give much advice on this subject. With the impending harvest and fall work, the idea was put out of mind, and obviously never carried out. The idea of following a family tradition, that of pursuing dentistry, had been abandoned some time ago, as Mother writes:

> *There are few women dentists in Canada, otherwise I would want to persuade one of my girls to take dentistry. They all think it's gross to work around in someone else's mouth. Dieter is totally turned off by it. He hopes that his Uncle Werner will have a son and heir so that the pressure to carry on the family's dentist tradition would be removed from his shoulders. Although at first glance Dieter seems to be his mother's boy, he*

also has a great deal from his father — the long arms and legs, the slim body build, many typical movements and mannerisms.

In December, '51, in her Christmas letter to Uncle Werner, Mother gives another update:

So we have managed to get by again for another year, but it's getting more difficult all the time as the children get older and aspire to finish their schooling. Without it their future is limited. We sorely missed Ursel's help here on the farm this summer as she worked as kitchen help at an oil camp. In two and a half months she earned five hundred dollars, and only in this way was she able to go to University. It would be better if she could take the two-year program, but that's unaffordable. Now she'll find employment in the fall, and have to take two or three summer courses later on, or another year of University to get her permanent certificate. She is a born teacher. (Is it any wonder?) Hopefully she'll find satisfaction in this career. She's having a nice time in Edmonton and I'm glad she can participate in many things for which there was no opportunity here.

Mother was always very stingy in giving any of us direct praise for anything well done. She had little use for "swelled heads" and made sure none of us developed one. But it seems she did, if rarely, extol our virtues to others and it was a complete surprise to me when I read the following in a letter to Uncle Werner:

Ursel is an excellent writer, and I hope and wish that she will progress and perfect herself in this area. It's always a pleasure to read her letters, especially now from Edmonton. Her exams start after Easter and at the end of April she will come home for a short time. In May and June she'll start teaching. Recently she got back a 1000-word essay with nine marks out of ten, and the comment, "You write very well indeed and this piece is first-rate." The instructor was the dean of the faculty of Education.

Gerta is going to school in Spirit River, stays at the dormitory and can often come home for weekends. Twenty-five dollars a month is not a lot but always has to be there. As Heidi will reach this stage next year, we are seriously thinking of moving to town. The rest of the land, which is not already in alfalfa, would be seeded to other clovers and grasses. Then Dieter would be more free and could go out working, which is very important. To live so isolated, as we do here, is not good for young people. And the constant contact with Uncle is making me crazy and is not good for the children either. I hope I can find a way that would be beneficial to all of us. The land, our back-up, will always be there for us.

Others in the settlement had concerns too, and several "signs of the times" are revealed in excerpts from a letter which Reinhold Witte wrote to Hein

I have enclosed a card for Georg and would ask you kindly to send it on to him. We are not allowed to write to him directly from here. Georg's oldest son Joachim has been with us for nearly three years now, has adjusted well to life here, and is a big help to us. Georg knows now that he is here and that Leni and the children want to come over. In the meantime I have reached the age of sixty-eight and my wife is sixty-six. We both suffer from rheumatism and at times we can hardly walk, so the time has come for us to be relieved of the workload. Unfortunately there is great uncertainty as to if and when the Russians will let Georg out. He is in a prison work camp in mid Ural.

Last year Muehrers had commenced their return trip to Canada, but were turned back in Bremen when the consul refused to accept their visa. Six months ago I sent in a new application, but have had no definitive reply. Anyway, at this time it would be impossible for me to come up with their travelling expenses — about sixteen hundred dollars. As you will have heard from Toerpers, we've had another crop failure — the fourth in a row. Yet, for the most part, the elevators are full. I have not been able to deliver a single bushel. Since, in Alberta one third of the crop is still out in the fields, it's hard to understand why the elevators should be plugged. I believe that this is a precautionary measure on the part of the government, so that with the imminent war with Russia, the grain would be well distributed. That war will come in the foreseeable future is expected, as the preparations are going ahead in full force. After all, the gunpowder must be fired sometime, otherwise the factories could not produce more munitions, and high-finance would not make a profit.

Besides, there is already over-production, and massive unemployment would arise, which the incompetent American government (as Hitler once said) could eradicate only by means of a war. I don't believe that the Russians would willingly pull out of Germany, nor would the Poles. England, the German's competitive rival, and France which obviously fears Germany, are hardly concerned about a healthy, strong German nation. So there's little hope. Given a possible war, Germany would likely again be the battleground. According to local news, apparently Russian military power is being assembled with headquarters in Siberia, with plans to overrun Japan and regain possession of Alaska! But enough of that. Russia will not show its cards.

Your children, Albrecht and Marlene, had their eyes opened here! Their education was rather one-sided. They were fortunate, as through Ursel Pankow, they were both able to secure employment with the Hudson's Bay Oil Company. Supposedly they like it there and earn good money — Marlene $200, and Albrecht $250 a month, after room and board. You

*probably have heard other news from here through Toerpers, so I'll close
for today.*

Friendly greetings,
Reinhold Witte und Frau.

It was also in 1952 that Mother tells of another calamity that hit our farm, as though the many crop failures weren't enough:

*You probably have heard, via the media, that foot and mouth disease has
struck Canada for the first time in history. You cannot even imagine what
this means. Suddenly the whole market is dead. No cattle can be exported,
and no beef. The scourge has been found only in a small area around
Regina in southern Saskatchewan, but all Canada is affected. Sometimes I
almost wish that our animals had been stricken and had to be put down
(by federal order) because there is fairly good compensation per head. Now
we sit here and can't sell anything. This national incident has totally upset
our plans, and has shown me again, very clearly, my inability to be
decisive. As you know, I have struggled with the idea for four years, since
Günther's death, of selling the cattle. Now this fall, the best time, we have
"missed the boat." These high prices will never return.*

*The best time was usually May and June, when the winter grain-fed cattle
come on the market. The huge stockpiles of feed led some farmers to
purchase extra feeders. Those people are in a really bad situation because
they have bank payments on top of everything else. But that's small
consolation to me, because I **wanted** to get rid of them all. Imagine, we'd
have sold at high prices in the fall, Dieter could have worked at the oil rigs
and earned $500 to 600 ....but we fed, cleaned barns, milked, all work
that had to be done, and what for!? Actually, once again, we have worked
the whole year for nothing — seeding, making hay, harvesting, just to
maintain the cattle herd and fatten them. Then this happens.*

Mother was obviously very upset, and blamed herself for her lack of decisiveness. Uncle Werner, consoling her, in his reply tried to convince her that she couldn't possibly have predicted or known that foot and mouth disease would strike Canada. But this was just one example of the weighty decisions that Mother had to struggle with in trying to do the right thing for her family.

Community support was still strong, and although decisions ultimately rested with each family, neighbourly empathy helped in any crisis. Visiting was a popular pastime, and birthdays, particularly, were always a reason for celebration, as Mother describes in her April, '52 letter:

*For my forty-fourth birthday, I had more visitors than ever before, in spite
of terrible road conditions. Some still came with sleighs, others thought*

they'd better take the wagon. Cars were out of the question. Imagine, there were forty-eight people, including the children. Luckily it was a warm evening. The little boys played outside in the mud and the straw pile; the little girls upstairs with Irma's dolls, and the older youth danced in the kitchen to the music of mouth organs. Fortunately I had baked enough cake, torten, bread and buns. For supper we had potato salad, cold cuts, cheese, sausage and eggs, with lemon snow for dessert. We had to set for two or three sittings, because there's not enough room or dishes, but that's the same in all our farm homes. For the past few years, many have started serving wieners, also beer and wine, but I don't go along with that, because I can't and don't wish to.

On June 24, 1952, it seems that decision time had come, and we were due for a change. Mother wrote to Uncle Werner:

We have come to the realization that we have to find another way to go on. Hopefully the beginning won't be too difficult and we will find the right place for everyone. There is great unrest in the whole settlement, and many are putting out feelers. Some will leave this valley; only families with sons will be able to expand, and even those prefer to go with the oil industry. Cattle prices have improved somewhat and we've been able to settle our debts. The majority of the fields have been seeded down to Alsike and red clover, so there won't be much spring work, and Dieter will be freer to go out working.

In July '52, Mother made a dream come true when she accepted the invitation from Kastendiecks to travel with them to the Rockies. They visited the Kananaskis valley where Father and Dick had been war-time internees; toured Banff, Jasper and Lake Louise. Mother continued on her own, on a little side trip to the Okanagan in B.C. and fell in love with orchard country.

But on returning to the Peace River Country, she realized that it too, had its charms. Now there were wide fields of grain and prosperous farms, world records in seed and grain production. In

Else Pankow in Okanagan Orchard

spite of all the hardships and disappointments of the early years, Mother found herself defending and extolling this region, and would always be drawn back to it. She wrote:

You know, Werner, I don't believe that we will ever want to live in Germany again. The children don't know it at all, and we don't have the money to come for a trial period. If possible, they should all visit their parents' homeland sometime, and they want to do that. But to make that a reality is another question.

Now the Log House Sometimes Stood Empty

The homestead in the Peace Country remained the "home" to which we would return for years. But the fifties were years of change and transition. There would be times when the old log house stood empty, especially in the winter, as family members sought to further their education, to seek work off the farm, or to get married and establish families of their own. This "dispersal" began in earnest in 1953.

My year of teacher training in Edmonton had culminated in April with the successful attainment of a Junior E teaching certificate. My holiday at home was very short, however, as I had obtained a job for May and June, to complete the school term at Wapiti School near Dimsdale, eight miles from Grande Prairie. This was a rude awakening, from all the University classroom theories to the realities of a nine-grade country school with thirty-plus enrollment. This number included six Grade IX students who, in two-months time, had to write departmental examinations, and some of the big boys were just a year younger than I was!

I had some warning of what lay before me when Lewis Hawkes, chairman of the local school board, met me at the county office to take me to my first teaching position. He eyed me dubiously, shaking his head as he offered his opinion: "You look very young to be taking on that bunch. They've already ousted three teachers this year." This was not exactly an encouraging introduction. I felt apprehensive and vulnerable as Lewis Hawkes dropped me off at the teacherage and drove away. I stood in the doorway of my "home"and surveyed the situation. Both surrounded by a high caragana

Wapiti School Class, Grade 1 to 9. 1952
Look for Heidi and Irma Pankow

hedge, the schoolhouse stood some twenty yards from the teacherage. The nearest farm house was nearly a mile to the north, but was not visible. Alone in a strange community, I was overwhelmed by loneliness and felt totally forsaken.

Somehow I got through the first two weeks of school. My inexperience did nothing to alleviate the multitude of problems, trials and challenges, the indescribable amount of work that lay ahead. There was no one to turn to for help, advice or consolation. Some of the students seemed determined to add a fourth victim to the three they had already vanquished earlier that term. Every night I toiled until midnight, preparing for the next day, because I knew the day would be even worse if I was not organized. Totally exhausted, I fell into bed with very serious misgivings about the career I had chosen. Had I worked so hard, had my family sacrificed so much, for this? If this was teaching, I wanted no part of it.

At the end of the second week, Otto and Minna Toerper, after a trip to Grande Prairie, brought Mother to Dimsdale to visit me. As they prepared to leave the teacherage to drive back to Woking, I would have given anything to go with them. It was very difficult for Mother, too, to leave me, because she could sense my unhappiness as I struggled to keep my composure.

Slowly but surely, from one day to the next, things got better. It seems that, somehow, by tacit agreement, the students had decided that maybe this teacher could stay. Instead of constantly testing and challenging, they had decided to work with me. Together we completed the '51 school year in happy harmony. Now I could face the fall term at Wapiti School with eager anticipation instead of fear and trepidation. After school was out, Gerta came and stayed with me for the last weekend and helped me sort out the library, do some cleaning and tidying of school and teacherage.

Irma, Ursula, (Miss Pankow!) and Heidi at the Wapiti school Teacherage

After a summer at the farm, I did commence my first full term of teaching at Wapiti School. Mother kept Uncle Werner informed:

Ursel is in Dimsdale again, and Heidi, who is in Grade IX, is living with her. So I didn't have to send her to town and could save dormitory costs. Besides, she's a big help, and it's company for Ursel. And Heidi proudly earns eighty dollars for being school janitor. When the two girls returned to Dimsdale after spending the Thanksgiving weekend at home, they were in for a shock. The teacherage had been broken into. All their belongings had been scattered about, blankets, their clock, canned food stolen. Some time later the police found the remains in the bush nearby, but not the perpetrators. Little damage was done, but it was a most traumatic and unnerving experience. Heidi isn't over the fright yet.

Visitors to Wapiti Teacherage
Top Back: Jasper Toerper, Heidi Pankow
Middle: Alice Jordan, Ursula Pankow, Heinz Toerper,Hans Delfs, Dieter Pankow, Christa DelfsFront: Victor Delfs, Karl Toerper, Irma Pankow, Lester & Doris Jordan

In the new year, Irma, now in Grade VII, joined us in Dimsdale, where she became a student in my Wapiti School classroom. Mother was away in Calgary taking her Nurses Aide course. That school year, though certainly not an easy one, remains as a pleasant memory to all three of us. In that farming community we were shown great hospitality and acceptance. Supper invitations from many families were enjoyed and we had fun staging a memorable Christmas concert, with standing room only at the community hall, which many judged to be "the best ever held there." Some Sundays we had visitors from home, and had picnics at Saskatoon Lake. But most importantly, Heidi was able to complete her Grade IX and Irma her Grade VII, without incurring any dormitory expenses.

For it was in December '52 that Mother had received a response to her inquiry to the new school for Nurses Aides in Calgary. The reply came in the form of an application to be filled out! Because of her age, Mother had been dubious, but she was accepted. She wrote to Uncle Werner:

> *This will be a very difficult year, but we want to try it. Our farm home will always be there for us. Since there is such a shortage of nurses, a training program for aides has been developed. The pay is not bad, and there would be opportunities for part-time work, as well as private care jobs. My neighbour Otto Toerper, who this year is expanding his sawmill operations, was quite insistent that I should cook for his crew. I'm afraid he'll not forgive me if I go and take this course.*

Mother did, indeed, make the big decision to go to Calgary, and enrolled in the Nurses Aide course. Certainly this took real courage and a lot of spunk. She successfully completed five months of classes, with the required examinations, then another five months of hospital practicums. At the conclusion of these requirements, she would have liked to stay in Edmonton, but finding a place to live was nearly impossible and rent was incredibly high. So Mother came back up north. There were many things to settle, and she would have no problem finding work at the Grey Nuns Hospital in Spirit River.

But before she could think about her new job, Mother had some other rather important matters which took her full attention and energy. There was a wedding to plan! Hans and I were married on December 28, 1953, with many friends, family and neighbours in attendance at a warm and happy celebration in our log house. Besides the food preparation, decorating, and wedding clothes for the whole family, a wall was removed to make more room. Apart from the physical logistics, there was surely a mother's emotional turmoil when her first child marries. Unfortunately, this happy occasion was followed closely by the traumatic death of Uncle Horst Anders.

Wedding Guests at the Farm Livingroom:
Left: Ursula and Hans Delfs (Bride and Groom), Heidi and Dieter
Pankow, Minna Toerper, Ursula Solty
Right side of Table: Elise Delfs, Otto Toerper, Hermie and Hans Delfs,
Helga Andersen

In January, 1954, Mother's life returned to some degree of normalcy when she started work at the Spirit River Hospital, and her three youngest girls lived with her while attending high school. In the summer she returned to the farm, and in her Christmas letter she gives Uncle Werner an update, as well as expressing some of her frustrations:

The summer was very wet, putting a damper on many activities. But we had an average crop and good harvest weather, allowing us to get the clover combined, and it's high in price (twenty-five cents per pound.) Unfortunately the red clover froze and wasn't worth harvesting. That was supposed to be my Germany trip!

At the present time I have the brushcutters here, and they're cutting and piling the rest of the bush. Dieter absolutely needs more land. One quarter is not enough to warrant the expensive machinery. Nothing has been settled regarding Uncle's land. It's too bad that he didn't have a will. We'd sooner have bought it from the relatives, than have the Trust Company get so much of the money for administration. Dieter wants to continue farming. He feels he's too old and doesn't have the energy to start something else. My greatest mistake was that I didn't rent out the land right away, so he would have had to finish school. Now all these years he's worked here, and believes he can't simply run away from it all.

He was supposed to go to Agricultural school this winter, but harvest was so late, and we hadn't finished threshing when classes started. School would be so good for him. He is not hard-nosed enough. Günther,too, was always so considerate and decent, and Dieter doesn't assert himself in the face of some of the older neighbours. Now he has given Glimm our horses to work with in the sawmill (without remuneration.) When I convert how much more Glimm earns with the horses – I'd have to work myself tired for two months in the hospital, or it's half of my ship's passage. What we lose or suffer because of the weather, we have learned to accept. But what happens because of our own stupidity or inadequacy, or because of "friendly neighbours" makes me very angry. But should I ever intervene, then it's said, "The boy is tied to his mother's apron strings." I would wish for a fatherly friend for him, but everyone is so busy with his own affairs. Mechanization is proceeding at a great pace and we can't keep up. Nevertheless, the sun shines here too, and like the popular song says: "Count your Blessings …."

I'm glad that Hans and Ursel live in Woking (town) now where Hans and his cousin are operating the Massey Harris dealership, along with repair shop and gas pumps. Now this new

**Ellen Louise Delfs,
First Grandchild**

grandmother can enjoy her first grandchild. Ellen Louise is a beautiful baby. The aunts and uncle are totally smitten.

With the coming of the new Lutheran minister, Pastor Martin Intscher, some community spirit was re-awakened in the settlement. In addition to reuniting the congregation of the church, he being very musically talented, also started a choir. All ages participated in four-part harmony and several concerts were staged at the Westmark Hall. German folk songs as well as short plays were performed for audiences from all parts of the Peace Country. One year a rather ambitious cantata was presented at the church for Christmas. In spite of the somewhat rusty amateur voices and the squeaky organ, the whole thing was quite effective and well received. Certainly it was a first in our community. For Mother, participating in the singing practices and the performances, as well as the German picnics held at Dunvegan, were real highlights and

Pastor Martin Intscher

made the fifties decade more enjoyable and meaningful for her and many others.

Martin Intscher Conducting
Front: Hedy Schack, Trudy Glimm, Frieda Pleis
Emilia Sellin, Else Pankow, Ursula Solty;
Male Singers Behind

In the winter of '55 Mother again worked in the Spirit River Hospital. Unable to find a place to live for the family, she stayed in the basement nurses residence at the hospital, Irma at the dormitory, and Heidi worked for her room and board with the Doug Banting family. Gerta was teaching in Gordondale and lived in the teacherage there.

In July '55 Mother travelled to Michigan to visit Rampoldts. They had sent her a return ticket as a Christmas gift. For Mother this was a wonderful trip. The dunes around Silver Lake reminded her so much of the beautiful Kurisches Haff near her beloved Cranz in the homeland. Upon her return, she found life on the farm very discouraging because the crops were poor again, the settlement regarding Uncle's V.L.A. land was dragging out and hard on the nerves. The crops were so bad that she moved to Spirit River earlier than usual, in November, and lived with Heidi and Irma in a small apartment above the old drugstore. It was here that we left baby Ellen for a few days while Brenda was born at Johanna's maternity home in Sexsmith.

In her Christmas '56 letter, Mother describes the agricultural situation as she saw it:

> *During the first years the neighbours all got together and threshed each others grain. Now the only ones who could use a threshing machine would be large families all working together. But the older children are all going out working where they can make a lot more money. Nowadays the small farmer cannot make it. Machinery is too expensive. The grain delivery*

The Homestead House 1962

quota just covers taxes, repairs and expenses. Canada's grain surplus is huge, and the money-making opportunities in the burgeoning industries and building trades are excellent. So everyone is leaving the farm. But Dieter always hopes to get as much fall work done as possible; then by the time he starts job-hunting for the winter, the best jobs are gone. Sad to say, one must work out to support the farm! Only the large mechanized farms have any validity.

We have several quarters of land now, but does it pay to bring them all under cultivation? Certainly, now there are machines to do it, but how high the cost? It would probably be cheaper to purchase cultivated land, but we are so attached to this valley — it is home. I imagine Freddy Brinkmann told you the same thing. It seems he can't get away from here either. Mrs. Glimm is enthusiastically trying to make him her son-in-law. Perhaps she'll succeed.

In the fall of '56 Mother and the three girls moved to Edmonton, where they were able to find a reasonably priced but comfortable basement suite. Gerta attended University to obtain her teacher's certificate; Heidi completed some missing high school subjects and earned her way by working in the hospital. Irma attended the highly-rated Victoria Composite High School. Mother worked as Nurses Aide with chronically ill patients at the Royal Alex Hospital. So the family, except for the two eldest, were all together for another winter.

In summer Mother returned to the farm. As long as Dieter was single, she always felt that it was her duty to help him through summer and harvest. But perhaps this was not always the right thing to do, as she writes to Uncle Werner:

The nurses and patients were reluctant to see me go, and remarked, "If you always go back, your son will never get married!" But the worst of it is — Who would come and live here in the bush, even though it is much more civilized than it was twenty-five years ago? I wouldn't wish it for my own daughters. But as long as I'm always there in the summer, the old log house remains as the hub of the family. Again, I tried to make it as homey as possible. I even bought some suitable country style furniture (used) from a friend in Edmonton — the first time in all my years in Canada!

Outside I planted flowerbeds and window boxes with colourful early annuals which we enjoyed for quite a long time. When either Dieter or the girls took turns with the scythe, our lawn was kept short and tidy, much to the pleasure and amazement of our visitors. And there's no lack of visitors when the girls are home for the holidays.

Gerta taught in Bonanza in May and June after completing her semester in Edmonton, and she came home for July and August. Heidi completed her Grade XII in Edmonton and will commence nurses training at the mental hospital in Ponoka at the end of August. Irma stayed in Edmonton during July and worked in the laboratory of a large hospital. In August I had them all together, even Ursel and her two little ones. They are living on the farm near us again, after Hans gave up the business in Woking,

Back: Dieter, Irma and Heidi Pankow, Hans Delfs
Seated: Gerta Pankow, Mother, Ursula Delfs
Standing on Bench: Ellen and Brenda Delfs

unfortunately with some losses. The town is much too small. So Ursel is teaching in Woking again, this time Grade IX and the principalship.

Since all the children except Heidi are living in the area, I have decided to work at the hospital in Grande Prairie. Irma has already started high school there. I have to think about Mrs. Solty, recently widowed, in a neighbourly way too, and support her as much as I can. Financially, the adjustment won't be as difficult for her as it was for us when Günther died. We had all the medical and land clearing debts. Soltys have a large cattle herd, and along with the sale of machinery, hope to have enough for the down-payment on a small house. It's hard to believe, but a house in town costs much more than a whole farm.

The harvest of '57 had been a very difficult one, after an unusually wet summer. The fields were so soft that tractors and binder got stuck and left deep ruts. Farmers were forced to take extra-ordinary measures. It was in this way that our long-time family friend and neighbour Horst Solty, had his tragic accident. His son Erich, only eleven years old, ran to Oltmanns for help, where only Clara was home. She, to relieve the exhausted and frightened lad, ran to the field where Hans Delfs was working. It took Hans only sixteen minutes with his car to rush the badly injured man to the hospital in Spirit River. But it was too late. Shortly after arrival, Horst Solty died of his injuries.

In 1957, a giant step was taken in the progress of the rural area surrounding Woking, when electricity came in. The organizational meeting had been called in May, 1955, to form a Rural Electrification Association, and after hours and days of labour and many a meeting, the power was turned on in December, 1957. This probably contributed more to the improvement of rural life in our settlement than any other single factor. Because the initial cost of hookup to each subscriber was high, because our old house was now inhabited mainly in the summer, and was some distance off the main road, we did not feel that it was economically feasible to have the power put in. The same was true for our Delfs homestead in the river flat, so we did not enjoy the immediate benefits of this luxury in our community.

Gradually, towards the end of the fifties, our goals of getting an education were becoming a reality. Gerta and I had earned our teaching certificates; Heidi was in nurses training; Irma was completing her last year of high school. Dieter had attended agricultural school and made the decision that farming would be his life. And we were all proud that Mother, too, had received an education — her Nurses Aide certification. This enabled her to fulfill her long-time dream of being a care-giver, and to earn her own pay cheque. Now she could dare to begin thinking seriously, not just dreaming, about a trip to Germany, a visit to her homeland. Several times during the post-war years she had watched quietly and longingly, as friends and neighbours — Minna Toerper, Trudy Glimm, Margaret Hess, Helga

Andersen, Johann Oltmanns, had crossed the ocean, and even visited our relatives. Mother's dream would indeed become a reality, several times over during the next three decades, beginning even before the fifties had come to an end.

Chapter 22   School Days

A human being is not, in any proper sense, a human being till he is educated.

... Horace Mann.

Homesteaders Building Westmark School 1938

It was a beautiful September morning in 1938 when my father went to the barn to harness the horses. "Is it time to go? When can we leave?" Dieter and I asked impatiently, standing by the door with our lunch pails ready. I remember well that first day of school. The log school-house had just been built by the local farmers and we were part of the very first class to use it. My father was chairman of the first local school board, and when the number of school-age children increased, he was instrumental in starting a petition which resulted in the establishment of Westmark School District 4799. Now it was opening day and we left home in a state of great excitement aboard our big rumbling farm wagon. Because of his position, father felt obliged to pick up the teacher and take her to school on this first day. Hazel Coogan had managed to find accommodations in the Otto Delfs house about two miles east of the school because that family was temporarily living in Spirit River. Dieter and I gave the slim, dark-haired young woman our shy appraisal and she would soon win our complete respect and approval.

What trepidation she must have felt! Having faced a variety of classes myself on "first school days," I can more fully empathize with her anxiety and excitement on this morning. Facing her, in eager anticipation in this brand new building, were boys and girls from six to sixteen. My brother and

I, and many others knew not a word of English. German was spoken in the majority of homes in the pioneer settlement. We learned quickly and by the end of that first year we spoke English, and could read it.

I attended this one-room country school for eight more years. Because there were always eight or nine grades, I think we learned not only our own lessons, but those going on around us as well. Some things remain more sharply etched in memory than others. Mrs. Coogan had to make her own report cards and always included the category "Rank in Class." Klara Schulz and I often had a close race for first place in our grade. This competitive aspect may be frowned upon by some in educational circles today, but I do think we were highly motivated.

Our first teacher was quite a disciplinarian. One day a car drove slowly by the school on the rough dirt road. This was a most rare occasion and called for attention. Who could resist a look? Wanting to make sure none of my classmates missed this event, I not only stared in wonder myself, but pointed excitedly "Look, Myrtle, Look!" So I got her into trouble too. We were both sent to stand in a corner — different corners of course — but we could venture a covert peek at each other, making it very difficult to control our giggles. To pass the time in our corner we could always watch the ants as they explored the large cracks in the logs. During the first year or two there was no plaster on the inside and no siding on the outside, just bare logs still redolent with pitch. Of course, there were more serious misdemeanors than looking out of the windows, and harsher punishments than "corner stands." We all knew there was a leather strap in every teacher's desk in those days, but probably served more as a deterrent than an actual weapon.

My other teachers included Robert Hemphill, the bachelor who sometimes fell asleep at school because he couldn't find his way into bed at a reasonable time the night before. In Grade IV he had us singing two-part harmony. We managed a fairly presentable version of "The Crusaders" which pleased parents who were accustomed to real music classes in the old country. The young intern, Pat Weisgerber, worked very hard in his first ever classroom experience and was popular with both parents and students. But he did not complete the '43 term because he was called to serve in the army. Mary Rowe taught in Westmark from 1944 to 1947. Her lot was not an easy one as she rode her big roan mare to school each morning from her husband's farm some three miles to the west.

CANADA INT. OP. 5 CENSORED

Northmark Alberta.
Nov 11 1941.

Dear Daddy,
Now it is getting close to winter. Ernie's horses Eggies horses Uncles horses and two of ours are running on the field of oats that isn't cut. We are having a Junior Red Cross Club in the school. We are going to have a meeting every week. On Monday we voted what each one should be. Aleta Dale is the chairman, Dieter is the wise chairman and I am Secretary. We are each going to get a botton with the red cross on. We are not going to have a Christmas concert at the school, we are just going to have a little party for the children. the small children like Gerta and Heidi can come too. we are going to bring cake and candies. we are going to give presents to each other too. The teacher wrote all the names on a peace of paper and we cut each name out. then we put them all in a cap and each one had to pick a name out of the cap. I got Ursula Delf's name and Dieter got Elma Dales name we have to give them presents

Many greetings
Your Ursula
Gerta, Heidi,
and Irmy.

Letter to Father in Camp

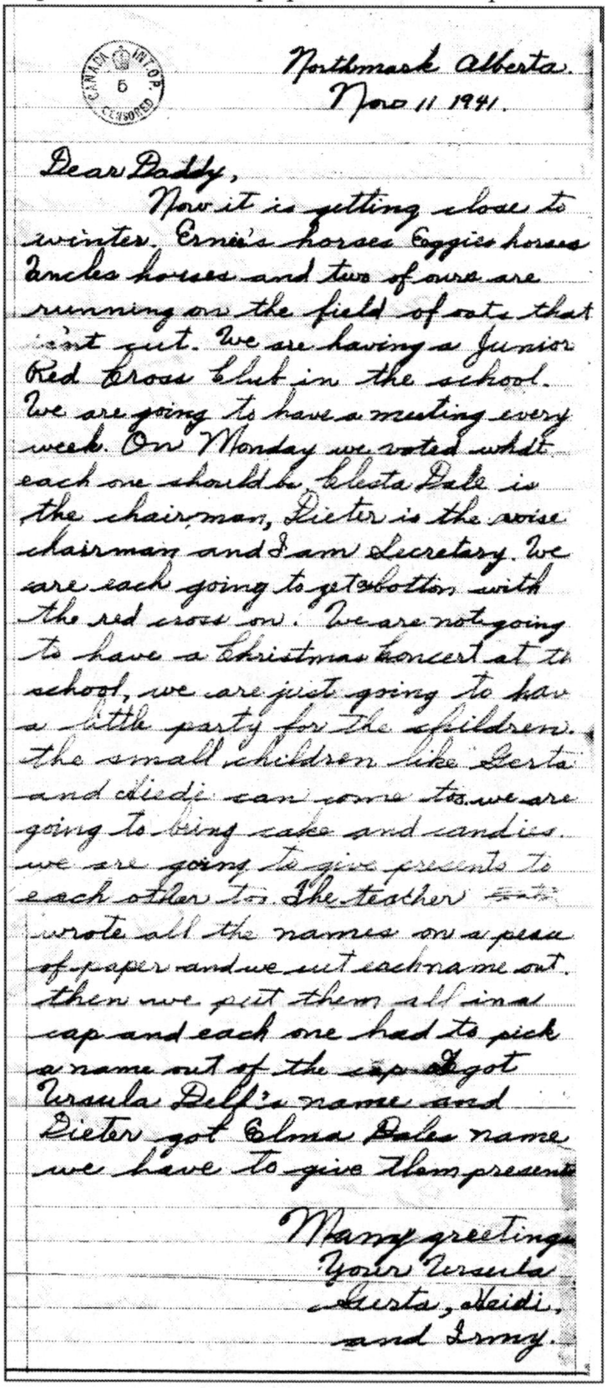

Each morning began with the Lords Prayer, pledge of allegiance to the flag and the singing of our national anthem, performances with no depth and emotion. I remember little about our course subjects in elementary school but a few isolated incidents seem to have left an impression. I can still see myself, with a thin brush, very carefully painting a bright blue Amazon River on a salt and flour relief map of South America. I remember being very enthusiastic about making a bird book in science class, each genus and species painstakingly traced with tissue paper, then shaded with pencil on the back and transposed on to each

page of our booklet, to be colored and written up with biological data. During reading and literature we frequently had poetry memory work, including Longfellow's "Hiawatha" and Kilmer's "Trees," to be recited "with great expression" in front of the class.

We hardly ever had homework. I attribute this to the multi-grade situation. In order for the teacher to get around to each grade the other classes would have to be assigned independent seat-work. Furthermore, when most of our assignments were completed we were allowed to do free reading. What an incentive for book-worms! The Bobbsey Twins, Little Women and Montgomery's Anne books were read many times over. The "library" was minimally stocked!

A large drum heater fed with blocks of wood was the only source of heat for the schoolroom. A small surrounding radius became very hot but the outermost corners remained so cold. On really frigid days, the heater became the focal point and we were allowed to move our desks into a closer circle. As the fire crackled warmly, the aroma of wood smoke mingled with the smell of damp footwear and mittens drying by the stove. A flat surface had been

Part of the 1941-42 Class
Back: Alfred Sloat, Hans Delfs, Helga Delfs, Mildred Sloat.
Front: Henry Sloat, Klaus Delfs, Ursula Pankow, Dieter Pankow, Ingrid Moll, Myrtle Sloat, Helene Schulz

attached to the stove-top. Here, before lunch time, a canner of water with a wire rack in it was heated. Small jars filled with soup or cocoa were retrieved from lunch pails and put on to heat. A hot-lunch program!

I remember my last three years at Westmark School with many mixed emotions. There must have been some learning going on, but the lack of proper discipline made for many undesirable situations. I think that the teacher realized that she was unable to enforce the rules, so tended to pretend that everything was under control. There was never any outside supervision during recesses. During noon hour we would go skiing on the river hill at Sloats and not reappear until two o'clock because "we didn't hear the bell."

Children can be incredibly cruel and there was often a tormenting and "picking on"— the victims changing from time to time, having no one to turn to for help. Some got it for having body odour; it was hard to keep a half dozen little kids "fresh," given the poverty, the sanitation and the size of homes. Some got it because they wet their pants; some were called cheaters when we played games. I was tormented because I was cross-eyed and my younger sisters because others were envious of their pretty "used Red Cross clothes" which had been received during our father's internment. I can remember so well the day Peter and Jürgen delighted in lifting Heidi and Irma up by their pigtails. In a rage, and wanting to protect them, I flew at the tormentors so the little ones could escape. Of course then I became the victim and was whipped with willow switches until my bare legs were covered in red welts. I was allowed to stay home the next day, even if it was to dig potatoes.

Ursula and Dieter
With Syrup Pail Lunches

It was not always so bad. Sometimes we couldn't wait to get outside for recess. A double set of swings had been erected on the east side of the schoolhouse. Here many a competition took place, to see which twosome could "go highest" as they pumped furiously until their feet flew higher than the crossbar. Bystanders at the base roared their encouragement. The boys were especially enthusiastic. What an opportunity to see what color bloomers all the girls wore under those billowing skirts! The games of scrub and softball were fun and we played games like Prisoner's Base, Red Rover, and Fox and Goose. I was always a fast runner and even the big kids would quickly pick me for their side. I was always so happy and relieved when we played games instead of sitting around waiting for trouble to start.

Part of the problem was that there were so many different ages all in one classroom, and some of the students were just not academic types. I can remember Henry and Freddie being on a very soiled Page 75 in their Arithmetic text for a whole month! And the teacher seemed unable to do anything about it. Those fellows really didn't want to be there and couldn't wait to get out.

Our trips to and from school were sometimes an adventure in themselves. During the winter especially, some families, like Dales, Molls and Glimms, drove to school with their cutters and kept the horses in the school barn. On muddy days there were many horseback riders. This would often result in some "betting on the horses." "I bet Kahki can run faster than Lucie!" To put this to the test there would sometimes be a half dozen plow horses galloping at full speed down the slippery wet road, mud flying in all directions. It's no small miracle that there were never any serious accidents.

Most of the time we walked to school, taking the short-cut that followed the west side of the creek through the bush to Egge's and then the main road to the school. This took us about half an hour. Once during spring break-up the water was running across the road west of Egge's so deep that we couldn't get through. I remember Twila Dale with her high gum boots making one trip after another to carry all us little ones safely to the other side. I still get a crawly feeling when I think about walking to school on the bush trail in the summer of '42 when I was ten years old. There was a terrible tent-caterpillar outbreak. The poplar trees were stripped bare and we could hear the critters drop like rain. We could not avoid stepping on them and in places the path was greasy. We constantly checked each others necks for unwelcome crawlers.

During the war there was a shortage of teachers. In 1943 Westmark found itself without a teacher, so many students were forced to make the long trek over to Northmark. Here Mary Rowe was again our teacher and I completed Grade VI. We walked diagonally through the bush to Westmark main road, then down the hill on the Hans Delfs quarter, crossing the river on a log, then up through Tante Minna's land and to the school on Northmark main road. This was an arduous trip for any child. Gerta, who was then in third grade, tried it for part of the term, but was forced to resort to correspondence lessons at home. Dieter and I used to meet Victor and Ursula Delfs at the top of the hill on this side, and then we'd walk together. There came a time when Dieter was sick for a week and I, a not very brave little girl at twelve, was on my own. With great misgivings I set out the first morning, only to turn back after only a few hundred yards. "I hear a strange noise" I stammered to my father. After walking by my side for a few steps, listening, he said "It's only an owl," and with a few kind words of encouragement he sent me on my way. I had missed the Delfs and as I made my lonely way along the top of the hill, I heard eerie sounds in the river valley below. I dared to look down. Three coyotes stood baying mournfully, and I was sure their howls were directed right at me. I ran as fast as my legs would carry me along the snow covered path, my heart pounding, my lungs burning, never stopping until I reached the safety of the Northmark School porch.

There was not always a sense of safety and security at the school that year. A number of boys who shall remain nameless here, were real school-yard bullies. I remember a group of terrified girls being cornered in the cloakroom as this group of would-be studs, armed with baseball bats held in the appropriate positions prodded them mercilessly. These same boors would attack smaller boys returning from lunch, throw them to the ground, and sitting on them with jack-knives poised, threaten to emasculate them. This kind of behavior was a blatant case of sexual assault and nowadays would certainly be reported. We were "educated" in many ways.

Fortunately, when we had Gertrude Bryan for a teacher for part of a year at Northmark, we were left with more positive and pleasant memories. I remember piling into the back of storekeeper Ewald Jacobs' truck together with a number of classmates and heading for the musical festival in Spirit River. We spent the night sleeping on the floor of the Oddfellows Hall because not all the competitions were held on the same day. Dieter was awarded the bronze medal for his vocal solo and I received the silver for mine. I recall being very proud to come home with this kind of recognition. Perhaps that is why I remember the lyrics of that song "The Cuckoo" to this day, and have taught it to my children and many classes. I have a feeling of gratitude towards this teacher for giving us these opportunities.

Christmas concerts were the highlight of the year and provided a welcome change from the day to day lessons. Some would argue that too much time was spent on these preparations, but they did provide opportunity for music, drama and choral speech, which may otherwise have been lacking. We were fortunate that Mother was so handy with a needle and thread and we were always proud of the costumes that she fashioned for us. I particularly remember a white cheese-cloth creation for a star drill. The following year it was dyed blue for an "Alice Blue Gown" drill. Mother often sat up late working by the light of the coal-oil lamp, so that we four girls could have new dresses for the concert.

For three years of Junior High I was back with Mary Rowe at Westmark. During this time my indifference to boys turned into cautious interest, puppy love and my first crush. The object of my affection was in the class just ahead of me, and in spite of my cross-eyes, my long pigtails and awkward posture, I was led to believe that the feelings were mutual. Musical Chairs and Spin the Bottle became favourite games, and Valentine exchanges were awaited with great anticipation.

The end of my Grade IX term brought Provincial Departmental exams.

These were not allowed to be administered in Westmark by our classroom teacher, so we had to go to Spirit River and write them at the school there, meanwhile living in the dormitory. On the first day there I began feeling quite ill. When I reported this to the dorm supervisor, who was a registered nurse, she examined me and gave me the bad news: "You have measles and must be quarantined."

Westmark School in 1978
23 years after closing

So she got special permission to bring the appropriate exam to me each day in my isolation room at the dormitory, and although I was not feeling too well, I managed to complete them all. I was most thankful to this kind lady, because I might have lost a whole year. It always took a long time to get the results from departmental exams, so I was extremely excited when the envelope from the Department of Education finally arrived in the mail in early August.. "It's an A! It's an A!" I shouted, and raced immediately down to the far end of the north field where my father was working, my diploma clutched in my hand. Pleasing him and getting his approval was always very important to me.

This marked the end of my elementary and Junior High school years and the

Rampoldt's House in River Bluff

last days of attendance at Westmark School. Any further connection would no longer be as a child or a student.

Our parents had often regretted the lack of "culture" in our rather "backwoods" community, and as we approached adulthood they thought of possible ways to enrich our lives. Mother's American friend and pen pal Kate Rampoldt had an only daughter Ingrid who was my age. After exchanging letters, our mothers concluded that it would be mutually beneficial if the reserved, somewhat withdrawn girl in Michigan and the culturally deprived Canadian could get together. Before I knew it, plans were complete for me to take my Grade X in the United States.

Ursula Pankow (center) with Rolf. Ingrid, Emil and Eric Rampoldt

As a naive, certainly not worldly fifteen year old, I boarded the train in Woking. I was met in Edmonton by the Arps family with whom I spent a few hours before they put me on the next train east. In Minneapolis-St. Paul, a kind lady from "Travelers Aid" helped me change trains for the last leg of my journey to Chicago. Although I can recall vast stretches of prairie and miles and miles along the Mississippi, these many hours on the rails are a vague, foggy memory. I believe that I had a large-sized lump in my throat during this entire journey. Mother's lovingly packed lunch of brown bread and home-made cookies turned into a never-opened mass of blue mold.

The Rampoldt home was situated in River Bluff, a suburb of Niles on the St. Joseph River in Michigan. Each school day Ingrid, her two brothers Rolf and Eric, and now this Canadian, traveled about ten miles by school bus to Niles. I was indeed introduced to many new experiences, as my parents had hoped. I made a number of good friends and school was interesting and enjoyable. I was at the top of the class in Geometry and probably near the bottom in Home Economics. In English class the teacher told me I should consider journalism as a career and my classmates told me they "just loved my accent." During Biology class we took a number of field trips including one to a fantastic museum of natural history in Chicago. Physical Education classes included volleyball, basketball and social dance. In May my American school days came to an abrupt and sad end when news came of my father's tragic death, then my immediate return home. Mr. Zabel, Niles School principal, reviewed my grades and thankfully gave me an unconditional pass in all subjects, even though I had not completed the year or written final exams.

Ursula with Mr. Payne's Biology Class on a Field Trip to Lake Michigan

That fall of 1948 saw our family with many very difficult decisions to make. We were left without our beloved father and bread winner. There was a heap of medical bills to be paid, as a result of the past years many misfortunes. What now? For mother and her two oldest children, there seemed to be a certain sense of determination, of loyalty and a need to carry on what Father had worked so hard to achieve. Dieter especially felt this and refused to go back to school. As second oldest I shared this feeling, and knew a deep obligation to stand by mother, and help her and Dieter to somehow keep the farm going.

Class of 1950. Look for: Gerta Pankow, Christa Delfs, Jean Dale, Heidi Pankow, Shirley Dale, Anneliese Schack, Geesche Glimm, Mabel Sloat, Hella Delfs, Erika Egge, Dorleen Sloat, Irmgard Pankow, Margaret Oltmanns, Helga Pleis, Sieglind Solty, Victor Delfs, Juergen Moll, Floyd Sloat, Werner Oltmanns, Juergen Glimm, Gerald Oltmanns, Jim Olafson, Wilfred Dale, Hans Egge, Evelyn Olafson, Inge Solty, Gudrun Delfs, Lloyd Sloat, Katie Moll, Ulrich Glimm, Gerhard Delfs, Peter Glimm, Dennis Schulmeister, Ilse Oltmanns, Elke Egge, Teacher Arlene Olafson

But my schooling was not put "on hold" completely. While helping on the farm that year, I took several subjects by correspondence. This took some self-discipline, and the occasional horseback ride to see Mrs. Olafson, Westmark teacher, for help with knotty Physics problems. One Saturday I rode my favourite little horse across the river, and Dixie Mitchell, Northmark teacher, supervised several hours of exams at her house. These came back with good marks so I had now made up the subjects I had been unable to take in the states, and had the prerequisites for Grade XI.

In September, '49 I was determined to continue my high school education — not as simple or straight forward as it would seem. Dormitory costs were out of the question, so we looked for a place where perhaps I could work for my room and board while going to school. Grace Mortensen's friend Pat Campbell owned a florist shop in Grande Prairie, and Pat knew that a new banker and his family were moving to Grande Prairie and were looking for a "slave." However, they were not moving in until October. I was registered to start school in September, and it was generous and neighbourly on the part of Sarah (Mrs. John) Pring to take me in for a few weeks. The widow lived on the northern outskirts of Grande Prairie where she eked out a living as a furrier, altering and repairing fur coats. Her daughter Verna and I walked to classes together, I helped around the house, and tried to get odd jobs so that I could pay for my keep. One Saturday I was hired by Pat Campbell to wash the windows of her large house. All day long I worked very hard polishing countless big windows with many tiny panes, on three floors, inside and out. I was rewarded for my efforts with the tawdry sum of two dollars! This woman went into my memory bank as a person who would never gain my respect.

Perhaps I should have been forewarned. The family who had been recommended by Campbell moved into their house in October, and I occupied a small upstairs bedroom. I remember the next two months as a tension-filled time of trying to please a nervous, high-strung woman with three pre-school children, whose object in life seemed to be to make sure I did enough work to earn my bed and board. During noon hour I rushed many blocks home from the high school, gulped down lunch, washed the dishes, and ran back to school. At the end of the school day she watched the clock to make sure I had not dawdled on the way home. I never felt comfortable or at ease in that home. It was at this time that Mother wrote to Tante Grete:

> Ursel is now going to school in Grande Prairie, but she's strained to the limit. Because she's working for her room and board, she has little time or strength left to do her school work in the evening. She can't take advantage of opportunities for extra-curricular activities with her class-mates. There are school dances where she could learn some grace in movement. Both Dieter and Ursel need this so badly — they're a bit stiff and awkward (like

306

their good father!) Then there are the school choirs. All the children have
quite nice voices, but need some guidance. And it would be so nice if Ursel
could have a few piano lessons, especially if she wants to become a teacher
— and that's definitely her goal. But under the present circumstances she
hasn't the time and I haven't the money.

My position with the banker family became insupportable. Somehow Cora James, the wife of pharmacist Griff James, became aware of my unhappy situation, and thinking she could use some help, was willing to put her trust in me. In January I moved across town and became a part of the James household where I regained my self-esteem. I still hurried home from school to clean house, cook, wash dishes, baby-sit, or whatever needed doing, but the atmosphere was so entirely different from my previous experience. I had a loving relationship with the three young children and they rode on my back as I washed and waxed the floors. The most trying job for me was ironing the many white shirts which the pharmacist changed daily for work. Never-press had not been heard of!

After my experiences in completing my Grade XI, we had decided that I would stay in the dormitory in Spirit River, where the rates were cheaper, rather than trying to work during my final year. However, I found that all the subjects I required for matriculation were not available at Spirit River High School. At the last minute, I felt I had to make alternate plans. My job with the James family in Grande Prairie had been filled by another student because they had not expected me back. But it seems that Cora and Griff still had a soft spot in their hearts for me. It was through them that I found a little attic retreat in the home of Grandma and Grandpa James, Griff's parents.

Making these last-minute arrangements was not without its difficulties, especially for a family living in the backwoods without a phone and without a vehicle. I must have had more pluck and nerve at that time --- or was it just rash youth and a feeling for the great importance of getting an education that had been instilled in us? After having made the arrangements for a place to live, I had to get back home from Grande Prairie to pack and be ready to start school on Monday. I walked up and down Grande Prairie's Richmond Avenue, hoping desperately to see someone from the Woking area. It was with relief, then, that I saw local neighbours. With some trepidation, I approached Glen and L.C.: "Would it be possible for me to get a ride out to Northmark with you?" I asked tentatively. "Sure, why not?" said Glen, "Hop in," and we were on our way in L.C.'s old pickup truck.

It seems that Clairmont Hotel was a customary stopping place on their route home, and this day was to be no different. I sat, rather uneasily, waiting in the truck, until my two cohorts returned, rather more jovial and talkative after a few beers. The drive to Glen's farm was made without incident and he was dropped off, as L.C. and I proceeded on to Westmark, where he had been working as a carpenter on the community hall. In the Burnt River crossing, his pickup came to a sudden halt, — a "getting stuck on purpose" move, it seemed — as in an awkward manner, abetted by alcohol, L.C. became quite amorous! Realizing his intentions, I quickly made my escape and walked the rest of the way home. Perhaps I could be considered ungrateful, but there was a limit to what one could put up with in the attainment of an education!

After this rather uneasy beginning, I remember my Senior year at Grande Prairie High School as a pleasant school term. I lived with the Senior James. My home was an unfinished storage area in the loft of their rooming house,

1951 Grande Prairie High School Graduation Class
Back Row: Daniel Wiebe, Ian Morrison, Mike Sernowski, Jim Moon, John Jackson, Gerald Manly, Gerald McLaughlin, Bill Bickell, Bob Bickell, Jim McNab
2nd Row: Bill Henry, Ray Probst, Shiela Burgess, Eileen Balisky, Lorraine Lemky, Imogene Nelson, Frank Piper, Lyle Kuykendahl.
3rd Row: Doreen Gray, Wilma Cooke, Flora Schmidt, Marion Drysdale, Ruth Leggatt, Elvera Wiens, Ursula Pankow, Gladys Omlid, Evelyn Heggelund.
Front Row: Marg Henderson, Audrey Hanson, Ingrid Pederson, Phyllis Luckey, Dorothy Bryenton, Nieta Wiedeman, Roseanne Dyck, Marjorie Honner

but I felt quite cozy and secure here, doing my homework in peace and quiet. My workload was lighter in the home of this elderly couple, and I was able to earn a little spending money on the side by baby-sitting for twenty-five cents an hour. I did have to do some fairly heavy yard work in the spring, and I remember hiding behind the board fence whenever a group of classmates passed by on the sidewalk. Why would I not want them to see me earning my room and board "by the sweat of my brow" while they enjoyed an after school coke together? In spite of all this, I have pleasant memories of my high school days in Grande Prairie. It still amuses me when I think of teacher Mary Gray holding my hand up in front of the class as an example of "perfect typing fingers." They did hold the class speed record for most of the term! French, English and Social Studies were fairly easy for me, but I struggled with Gavinchuk's algebra and Kujath's physics 30. I was a member of the grad class executive as the secretary, and in June 1951 I graduated with Senior Matriculation. Mother sewed my simple blue taffeta gown and Dieter was my escort to the banquet and dance.

Ever since I was a little girl, Horst Solty had called me "Teacher." I must have made it quite obvious that this was my career goal. In order to earn tuition money, I jumped at the chance when Ida Rowe asked me to go with her, as flunkie, to an oil camp where she was the cook. For two months, July and August, we worked together in a kitchen-dining trailer for the Hudson's Bay Oil Company at a rig site in the bush north of Tangent. The days were long, the work was hard and repetitious — wash dishes, peel vegetables, set tables, wash floors, and then do it all again and again. But it was certainly

Ursula Pankow, Cook's Helper 1951

not dull around camp. I met fellows from all over, seasoned drillers and tool pushes from as far away as Texas, young local farm boys who worked as roughnecks, and the dear Grandpa from Peace River who was the camp attendant. They were all very nice to me and I felt really "popular," an emotion quite foreign to me. But then my only competition was the elderly cook, who each night before she went to sleep, would declare vehemently "I hate men!" The summer passed all too quickly and I had earned a phenomenal five hundred dollars!

To further help me, I applied for and was granted a bursary from the County of Grande Prairie, with the condition that I would teach in that jurisdiction upon the completion of my certificate. In the autumn of 1951 I boarded the N.A.R. in Woking and traveled to Edmonton to begin my teacher training. I stayed in Pembina Hall, a women's residence on campus at the University of Alberta, along with Peace River Country pals Joan, Elvera, Gladys and Phyllis. We were a group of real good friends, supporting each other, studying, attending church, and sharing care packages from home. One Sunday we walked from campus, over the High Level Bridge, down to Jasper Avenue, to the hall where Ernest Manning and his cast originated the "Back to the Bible Hour" heard on radio for years. We were quite thrilled to be in the congregation.

Phyllis Sather, Ursula Pankow, Elvera Wiens and Gladys Omlid at Pembina Hall

I remember few particulars about my classes. Some of them seemed to us to have little relevance to the practical classroom situation. We spent hours making teaching aids such as phonics and arithmetic flash cards, and detailed lesson plans. For our first "practice teaching" assignment, Phyllis and I boarded a bus from Edmonton to Beach Corner. Here Robert Dei met us at the store in his pickup and took us to his family's box-like two-story farm house, our boarding place for the week. An upstairs bedroom became our study, where we made preparations for our next day's teaching. We walked the mile to the two-room Blueberry School each morning, sometimes in the company of our supervising teacher, Mrs. McGinnis who lived further up the road. (It is interesting to note that this school building is still standing and has been converted into a community hall.) Our co-operating teacher was a pleasant, grey-haired, soft-spoken woman who gave us nothing but encouragement, and good marks on our week's practicing.

My second stint at student teaching was not nearly as pleasant. Garneau Junior High, being situated so conveniently close to campus, had been a site for student teachers for years and these teenagers were not particularly interested in whether or not I made a success of teaching them a Social Studies lesson, or passed my student teaching assignment.

At the end of April I left the University of Alberta with a temporary Junior E teaching certificate which would later be made permanent. My teaching career began a week later as I finished out the school term (May and June) at the multi-grade Wapiti School near Dimsdale.

Over the years there was always a certain push on to complete my Bachelor of Education degree. With my responsibilities to family and farm, as well as teaching full time, I was not able to go back to school, but I did take evening and summer courses in Grande Prairie and Fairview. English always gave me the least difficulty and the most enjoyment. So I enrolled in an English Literature course with a sarcastic young professor who flew up from Edmonton once weekly, and later in a Canadian Literature course with Jack Mighton at the new Regional College. These were heavy courses which required a lot of reading and many term papers. For six weeks one summer I took a music course at the college. The instructor was Gerald Nelson, the city's music guru, who patiently guided my hand as he showed me how to conduct. Once a week for two winters I drove across the Peace River to

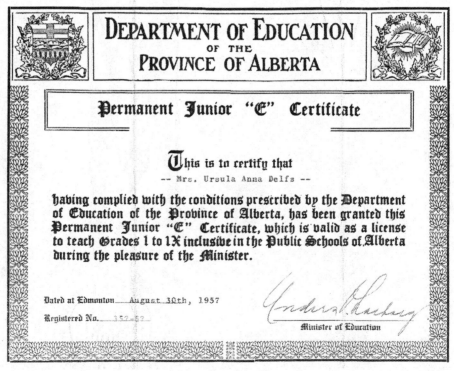

Fairview where I was enrolled in Sociology courses under Bibi Laurie. We were always several teachers traveling together to attend these classes, which made it much easier and more enjoyable. Helen Sideroff, Louise Schulz, Michael Dorval, Lyette Heiligers and Shirley Girling were among my

classmates and fellow travelers. At these times my life was rather full and often hectic and I am most grateful to my family for their help and understanding.

In this way I was able to complete my second year. This resulted in a small increase in salary, but the four-year Bachelor of Education degree was not achieved. I never felt that this was a deterrent to being a good teacher, and never regretted making education my career. I enjoyed working with children and found teaching to be a most rewarding experience. And although salaries were relatively low during my working years, my income helped us through some rough times. It's also a good feeling to have followed a long family tradition. Great Grandmother and Great Grandfather Pankow, Aunt Anneliese, Uncle Ernst, Aunt Kate and several cousins were all teachers. More recently my sister Gerta, our daughter Ellen, nieces Karin and Lisa also chose the same path.

Chapter 23   Dreams Of Nursing Come True

Ever since 1929, when as a young woman, she worked for a short time in a Königsberg Hospital, Mother had felt that nursing was for her. Helping and comforting others in time of sickness and trouble was always important to her. But any thoughts of formal training in this field were abandoned after her engagement, then immigration to Canada.

However, on the northern Alberta homestead, far from doctors and hospitals, she sometimes found herself administering aid, her old "doctor book" close at hand. Perhaps others were even less equipped. When babies were due, Mother served as midwife for many a neighbour. She was often the one to be summoned when sickness or accident struck. At such times she fervently wished that she had some medical training.

So perhaps it should have been no surprise, when, many years later, in 1952, Mother, now a widow with five children, sent to Calgary for information. She wanted to know more about the new school for Nurses Aides. She felt that it was essential for her, somehow, to become a wage earner. The farm income barely covered expenses, the most necessary purchases, and possibly some improvement. Her younger children still required support to complete their education, and Mother had yearned, for some time, to save enough for a trip back to Germany. The training program for a registered nurse (RN) was out of reach, because of its length, expense, and perhaps its level of difficulty, for Mother had no schooling in Canada and the English language. In spite of her own doubts, (she was now forty-four years old,) her application to attend the school for Nurses Aides was accepted.

Nurses Aide Class of '53 --- Else Pankow front left

There were mixed emotions. There was excitement at being accepted. There was apprehension. Can I really do this? And there was pressure. Can I be ready in such a short time, and make arrangements to be away from home for months? Somehow Mother managed it all, and at the beginning of 1953 she was in Calgary, seated in a class of mostly young women, at a modern new school. She sometimes found it difficult, in the midst of an anatomy lesson, to keep her mind from wandering back home to the Peace River Country and the Westmark homestead.

In February, 1953, Mother's belated birthday letter to Uncle Werner had the Calgary postmark on it:

> *Happy Birthday from Calgary! I'm not sure that this is the right thing to do. Will I be able to get through it? At any rate, I'm here in a modern and up-to-date school, studying anatomy, medicine and related subjects for five months. It's not easy for me, but there are several older students besides the twenty-five young girls. The hardest part: the constant thoughts of home and the children. Irmgard and Heidi are with Ursel, Gerta is in Spirit River, and Dieter is working at a sawmill. Horst is, with a heavy heart, looking after the remaining cattle. He almost broke down completely when I received my telegram of acceptance. I am not used to the big city, and at times feel so lonely and forsaken. One day I'll have to look for the German Canadian Club.*

At Easter time, Mother found time to write again:

> *I'm still in Calgary and have become used to city life. The houses lie like coloured building blocks on both sides of the Bow River, and the Rockies glisten in the background. Hopefully I'll be able to find time to visit them for a weekend before I'm sent somewhere to a hospital. It's not easy, after thirty years, to have to write tests and exams again. But the children encourage and cheer me on in each letter, so I mustn't disappoint them. It's best for all of us, and hopefully next winter we can all live together again. Now the children have to be so totally self-reliant.*

> *Heidi and Irma like it very much with Ursel in Dimsdale. The farmers take them along to Grande Prairie and they're invited everywhere for supper, so there's lots more entertainment and social life than at home. Ursel is truly a good person — so much like her father. Recently she wrote me a long letter in German, as though she was the mother needing to encourage her child. The Dimsdale farmers often ask about my progress, so I must keep up my energy!*

> *Gerta goes home from the dormitory in Spirit River on weekends, to clean house, wash clothes and cook for Dieter. She feels very important and it is really nice for both.*

After five months in the classroom in Calgary, it was time to turn her book learning into practical experience. Mother had studied hard to master the medical terminology, and successfully completed her classes and examinations. Then she was sent to the Royal Alexandra Hospital in Edmonton for part of her practicum. For ten weeks she worked in the geriatric wing and lived in the basement of the nurses residence. Again she gave a brief report:

> *It's rather difficult, as an older person, to adjust to everything, and to have young people as superiors. I get along well with the elderly patients, but many are child-like, physically and mentally ill people. Heaven forbid that I should have an old age like this! It's hard work on the morning shift and I get quite tired. Next week I get the three to eleven shift, which isn't as convenient because I can't visit friends during their free time in the evenings.*

> *I hope the children will come in the summer holidays. Dieter has a second-hand car now. I wonder if it can make such a long trip. It's nice though that he can pick up Gerta in Spirit River, and then they go to visit the girls in Dimsdale or go to a show. I miss the children terribly and long for home. And yet I'm afraid that when I'm back there, I'll really be aware of the primitive conditions. It's been twenty-two years that I lived there — it's home. Here I'm often so restless.*

As Mother had hoped, Dieter did, that summer, load his four sisters into the old Meteor and drove to Edmonton. We wanted Mother to be proud of her children, and not embarrassed in front of her peers when we all showed up in the city. Our "good" clothes were carefully packed so they wouldn't become soiled as we slept on blankets beside the car near the river at Smith. As we neared the city, we each disappeared into a roadside clump of trees and changed into "city" duds. Alas, never-press and wrinkle-free materials had not been perfected and we were a rather creased and rumpled group when we appeared before our mother. But she seemed so happy to see us! For two days we were "billeted" with friends and acquaintances — I stayed with Marlene (Sellin) and John Squire at Jasper Place. Certainly we could never

Graduation
Certified Nurses Aide 1953

315

even have considered staying in a motel.

On our way home from our visit to the city, we were all very tired. Perhaps the driver was the sleepiest of all. Near Smith, the old Meteor suddenly veered towards the ditch. Before we knew it, we were stuck, but quite unharmed. While contemplating our dilemma, a pickup load of young people who were on their way to a Sunday School picnic, stopped beside us. In no time they had pushed us out, and thanking them gratefully, we were on our way.

After her stint in the Royal Alex Hospital, Mother was sent to the Charles Camsell Hospital for further practical experience. The majority of the patients here were native Indians suffering from tuberculosis. She would look back on the ten months of classes and internships with a feeling of pride and a sense of accomplishment — and rightfully so. The school, with its youth, then the culmination with a graduation ceremony, were moving and memorable. In her hand was a certificate allowing her to practice in her chosen field, to be a care-giver, to help and comfort the sick.

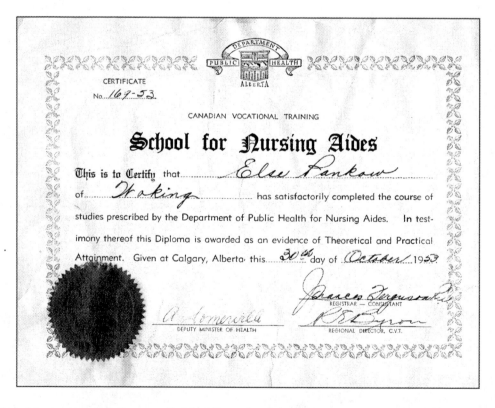

At this point, Mother probably thought of any monetary returns, the resulting wages, in terms of keeping the farm going, and helping her children with their education. But in the long run, this certificate would do much more. Apart from the job satisfaction, it would provide opportunities to work in several different hospitals in Canada and the United States. There was always a demand for this kind of work, and she was able to negotiate many part-time and seasonal positions. This fit her life-style just right. For many years Mother worked in hospitals in the winter, then came to the farm or travelled in the summer. This became a general pattern with many variations.

Mother's first employment as a certified Nurses Aide commenced in January, 1954, at the Spirit River Hospital, under the Grey Nuns. Her three youngest children lived with her. She was very conscious of the great contrast between her past months in the big cities of Calgary and Edmonton, now this small town, as she writes to Uncle Werner:

> *Spirit River is an awful little nest, but the girls' school is practically next door. How would Irma have managed all alone, in this terrible cold (it's -40) to go to Westmark School? And next year she would've had to come to town anyway because there's no grade nine out there now. Here the girls can go skating at the arena, and Gerta, in her senior year, is participating in curling. It's a typical Canadian sport which originated in Scotland. Heavy granite rocks with handles are thrown down a long ice surface, and swept with brooms. I don't know the object or the rules, but next to hockey, it's **the** game, is played by young and old, men and women, in every small town in Canada.*

Nursing in Spirit River
L to r: Else Pankow, Bertha Yany, Anne Suchinsky

> *I had to start work right away, and had to begin with night shift. But I've already earned my first pay cheque (fifty dollars for two weeks) so that's a good feeling. I said to the girls "I wish I could save it all towards my Germany trip." Then I'd be coming soon.*

In the winter of '54 we were all able to spend another Christmas together at the homestead. Mother was glad about this and wrote:

> *For the holiday we will all get together at home. Hansmartin from Grande Prairie is coming too, as well as a couple of homesick boys who came over from Germany recently. Only Uncle is missing. A year has passed, and here too, time has calmed and healed. Without dread and horror, I can now look at the spot by the fence where his twitching body lay writhing in the snow.*

After a summer at home, helping Dieter on the farm, cooking for the men who operated the brushcutters and pilers which cleared more land, Mother resumed her job in Spirit River for the winter. In January, '55 she wrote:

This time I'm working on the men's ward and my special patient is a twenty-seven year-old polio patient, father of three small children. I tend to him with hot compresses, therapy, massage and exercising. In these small rural hospitals we aides are allowed to do everything. I give needles now too, although our school forbids it. The Sisters always looked at me with some uncertainty; now they're happy and can go to their chapel for prayers more frequently and undisturbed.

The crops were so poor that fall of '55 that Mother went back to her hospital job in Spirit River earlier than usual. In November she was working full-time, and especially tired after some hard shifts, she realized that she wasn't getting any younger. Also, the whole issue over Uncle's land was very stressful and she had difficulty achieving peace of mind. Even her Christmas mail remained unwritten that year. In the winter of '56 —'57 Mother moved to Edmonton, and worked with the chronically ill at the

Royal Alexandra Hospital in Edmonton

Royal Alex Hospital. She described her situation in her letter to Uncle Werner:

I find my work on this ward hard and depressing. How nice it was in Spirit River with the nuns, especially since the new hospital is completed. In November we had such beautiful weather that it seemed a crime to sit here in the big city when roots and rocks needed picking at home. But now

we have 30 below and it's cozy and warm in our small but comfortable basement suite. I just need to walk across the street to work, but the girls have to take the city bus. So some of us are together for another winter. We are really homesick for the north, and miss Ursel's little girls.

In 1957 Mother decided that perhaps Grande Prairie should become the "central" for our family, since all except Heidi, training in Ponoka, lived in the vicinity. It would be only an hour away from the farm and from her grandchildren. She managed to rent a small house in the Smith family back yard, and found employment in

**Nurses at G.P. Auxiliary Hospital
Back l. Else Pankow and Friend Craddock**

Grande Prairie. Here in the auxiliary hospital, under matron Nora Shields, she worked on and off for a few winters.

During the summers she returned to the farm, helping Dieter, making a home for her vacationing daughters, and participating, with fun and enthusiasm, in Pastor Intscher's community choir activities.

The summers on the farm during the fifties also provided some other diversions to break the days of hard work. One July Mother had been invited along, by friends, on a trip to the mountains. Heidi and Irma had each visited us in Wetaskiwin. Gerta was taking her short course in Edmonton. Mother felt badly for Dieter, as she wrote to Uncle Werner:

*Only Dieter missed out because "he had no time." But instead, he takes in every dance in the area. It doesn't always suit him that he has to be the big brother to his sisters, but now they often have boyfriends who bring them home. Then he can take his girl home "without accompaniment." Unfortunately he really likes his beer, but I hope this is just a passing phase. **He** certainly needs his father, in every respect. How nice it would have been for them to work together.*

Sometimes Uncle Werner tried to fill this void, even though he was so far away. He addresses his nephew as part of his letter to the family:

You, my dear Dieter, are now the only male Pankow of the younger generation. Surely you must be nearly breaking down under the burden of

319

this great responsibility! I can just extend my hand to you in complete understanding, and say, "You are in the same position as I am. You are surrounded by five women, and I am surrounded by five women. Sometimes you stand in the foreground, sometimes you stand in the background — in the photos, I mean! And besides the five Pankow women — one has since become a Delfs — you surely have a sixth young woman, because at your age one usually has a sweetheart."

I'm sure you'll manage, so that Father Günther would be satisfied with his son, could he observe him. Your mother is sometimes a bit worried about you. It seems that, besides your sweetheart, the beer is also a favourite. Well, with respect to that, I am not worried. Neither the Gesiens nor the Pankows were boozers, and once in a while a tall cool one tastes so good. Dear boy, I also have an understanding for your desire to stay on the farm, in spite of all the weather adversities and market uncertainties.

Although Dieter dated a number of local young ladies, it seems that the right one, the one that Uncle Werner was alluding to, had not yet come along. Mother found it hard to keep her hopes up, as she wrote in December, '56:

I wish he'd find a girl, but who nowadays would want to stay on the farm? Certainly none of the new German immigrants would. Here in Edmonton I have acquaintances who have modern homes, beautiful furniture, televisions and all the comforts. Their husbands are recently immigrated young German engineers with high salaries. How can one expect a young girl to go to a primitive rural area? Perhaps if it were an older established district, it would be different. But for us, there is never any money left for personal amenities. At least it's most encouraging, and high time, that electricity is finally supposed to come to our settlement.

Every time friends or neighbours returned from Germany with enthusiastic stories of their visits, Mother's longing increased. Every crop failure brought discouragement, because again her nursing pay cheque would be needed for

other things — farm expenses, the girls' education. Finally, in July, 1958, she had eked out enough for a ticket, and along with Gerta, she flew back to her homeland and stayed for five months.

The year 1959 was memorable in that it was the year of Gerta's wedding, also the birth of Mother's first

Mother at the Oil Camp

grandson, Eric Otto Delfs, both in August. Early snow and enduring cold made for a long winter. Many in the settlement went to work in the oilfields for a few months, where the big money beckoned. Mother, too, opted for a job change, where she could earn more. For four months, from January to April, 1960, she was second cook at a wilderness oil camp:

> *Just in time for Easter, I returned from the oil camp. This was a new and very interesting experience. But there was disharmony in the cook house as a result of the too-close living and working relationship with the cook. This was very hard on my nerves. I had never known her like this. In April, after a beautiful drive through the wilderness — muskegs, streams, hills and valleys — with one of the truck drivers, I arrived back in Edmonton.*

What happened next was not exactly what Mother needed to recuperate and rest her nerves, but she took it all in stride and helped us through a difficult time. Later, she described the situation to Uncle Werner:

> *When I arrived home on April 25th, we got another shock. Hans and Ursel's house burned down! During a strong wind, sparks from the chimney somehow got into the space between the old house and the later addition. It happened around noon—their table was set for dinner. Ursel rushed to Oltmanns for help. Together with them, and some horseback riders who happened to be passing by, they saved as much as they could. The little ones sat in the car, at a safe distance. For a long time after that, Ellen couldn't go to sleep by herself. With an old log house it can happen so quickly. One doesn't even like to think about what could've been if this had happened at night.*

Beginning of Delfs' new House
Garage is in left Background

So after just getting home, I did some quick rearranging in my house, emptied shelves and cupboards, and made room for the Delfs family. Ursel had committed to teaching in Woking for May and June, so during the day I had the children. Ellen and Brenda (six and four) are already quite sensible, but little Eric (one year in August) is a restless spirit and was especially difficult when he was just between crawling and walking.

Besides driving the school bus, Hans had to travel back and forth from here to put in his crop. In July he immediately began building. This move to the top of the hill had been on the agenda for years, but the finances were always lacking. A garage was built first, and they've just moved into that as their temporary home. Now they're pouring cement for the basement of a new house which they hope to complete in the next year or two. I gathered together some things out of my household to help them get started. Again and again, they are missing things that were not noticed at first. Many children's clothes, bedding, and especially good winter wear, all burned. The local Woking Willing Workers ladies club presented the family with a set of dinnerware for eight, which was very nice.

So we lived together harmoniously for four months and I felt quite lonely when the Delfs family left to move to their own place.

Mother got more news before 1960 was over, and this time it was something she had hoped for. During the winter Dieter had found employment at the plywood factory in Grande Prairie, and here he met Violet Stevenson, a nurse at the hospital. In September, Mother sent these news to Germany:

Dieter is planning to get married! Violet is a farm girl from a very good farming area near Grande Prairie, twenty-four years old, only daughter with two younger brothers. I can't imagine that her parents are too thrilled with her choice, which I can understand. (I hope that at least Heidi and Irma won't marry farmers.) Dieter and Violet won't have an easy life;

Inge and Erich Solty with Else Pankow 1961

neither of them is strong. She is allergic to animals — neither cat nor dog will be in their house. They both have a strong desire to have children, and we will do our utmost to help her feel at home here. Hopefully something of the free, candid nature of our girls will rub off on her, because she is very quiet and reserved.

You can't imagine how the whole community is happy for him. Everyone always felt sympathy for the boy who had to start so young to support a family. This had become so ingrained in his system that his face is already full of worry lines. We all, especially his sisters and I, hope with all our heart, that they will be happy together. The planned date for the wedding is October 29th — probably a big affair because Violet has many relatives in the area. Of course we'll have only friends and neighbours.

After Dieter got married, there was, for Mother, not quite the same sense of urgency and strong obligation to return to the farm each spring. She felt freer to make work and travel plans. It seems that during that first big trip to Germany in 1958, she was "bitten by the travel bug" for she would undertake many more. Since this required money, she always made sure that she landed a Nurses Aide position somewhere for part of each year.

On Boxing Day, 1960, Mother's good friend and neighbour, Ursula Solty died as the result of a stroke, just three years following her husband's tragic fatal accident. Mother was shaken and felt a strong obligation to stand by and help her friend's children. The Soltys had purchased a house in Grande Prairie, where,

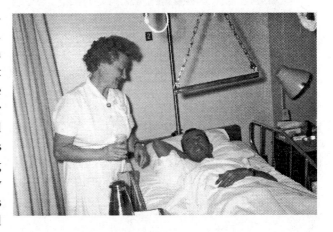

Nurse Pankow on Ward

in 1961, Mother stayed with Inge and Erich during the first sad months of their bereavement. She continued her job at the auxiliary hospital. When a decision had been reached with regard to schooling, Mother returned to the farm. Inge found a home with the Doctor Matheson family; Eric lived with the Eldon Shail family at Hythe, and Siegi was employed as a teacher.

Mother's next job took her far from home and across the border. In late 1962, she commenced work at Mills General Hospital in San Mateo, near San Fransisco. For the first time she spent Christmas far from home, without family, without snow and cold, without the beautiful scent of fresh evergreens. She found the golden, gaudy garlands decorating the hot sunny streets of American cities quite foreign and not at all conducive to acquiring the Christmas spirit. She did visit Hans Herrndorf and his family and spent part of the holiday with them. For eight months in '63 Mother enjoyed her work at the San Mateo Hospital, and this would mark the beginning of many more winters at this facility.

Christmas with the Herrndorfs in California 1962

After Mother had made her way back up north, she wrote a letter to her U.S. friends and colleagues, postmarked September 1963. Excerpts follow:

Nearly two months ago I left San Mateo to see my family in the Peace River Country of northern Alberta. Before going north, I visited for two weeks with my youngest daughter Irma in Lynwood, (L.A.) where she is working as a lab tech. As a confirmed bus traveller, I chose the #99 Highway instead of the scenic #101, and enjoyed it all the way to Seattle. Here I stayed for a few days with our young professor friend, Ernie Kaarsberg, who had just received a call to lecture in Graz, Austria. In Vancouver I visited many old friends who used to farm up north, and we went to see Harrison Hot Springs, lovely mountain lakes, the rich Fraser Valley, and Victoria on the island. The Butchart Gardens were beautiful. The new Rogers Pass sure shortens the way to Calgary. How majestic the Rockies are in Banff!

Now I was back in Alberta and began to feel the excitement of "homecoming." In Ponoka I stayed with my daughter Heidi for the weekend (going back for her first baby in September) and spent a few days in Edmonton. It was terribly hot, and during the bus ride that night we experienced a big downpour and a wonderful thunder and lightning storm. In the morning, coming closer to Grande Prairie, the fields began to look poorer, and the dust was terrible, but nevertheless, the country looked beautiful to me. Everything was so green, the caterpillar-eaten trees had new little shriveled leaves, and the rain showers made the grass lush and

Mother back Home

green. (compared to the grey dry hills around Sacramento.) The temptation was great to continue on to Alaska. The young girl next to me came all the way from Wisconsin to teach Kindergarten with the airforce in Fairbanks.

But I was home now — that is, in Grande Prairie, the city where we shop,

Living Room in the Log House

where the children went to high school, where I worked in the hospital. And my log house, forty miles north, was waiting for me. As soon as I was there, I felt like I'd never been away. I had often wondered, living in residence with all the girls, how I would take the loneliness of the bush country again. But I don't mind it at all, not at this time of year! My daughter-in-law surprised me with a little garden she'd put in for me, so I have the juiciest carrots, peas, beans and fresh potatoes. The multi-coloured daisies, bachelor buttons and poppies are blooming as usual, and the petunias in the window boxes. Everything is as it always had been.

Since there are no bears around this year, I feel a little better at night. My only companions are squirrels and groundhogs, which are really a nuisance, and I should shoot them, since I have no cat or dog. The old home place is one and a half miles from the main road where my son lives, and two and a half miles from my daughter Ursula. They are moving into their new farm home this fall.

For five days I stayed with my daughter Gerta (two little boys) in the Dawson Creek area (Mile 0 on the Alaska Highway.) My son-in-law Peter took us through the picturesque countryside to the new Peace River bridge at Taylor Flats with the big oil refineries, and to Fort St. John, Mile 60. A newly-opened area, with just an oil road leading into it, was very interesting to me, an old-fashioned pioneer, to see this new way of homesteading. They move in with big modern machinery, clear and cultivate hundreds of acres in one summer, which took us nearly a lifetime! But the ministers (Highway, Lands and Forests) are touring the area to investigate. They might close homesteading for a while, since roads and schools have to be built, and Canada has so much surplus grain anyway.

Fall is here. Big flocks of geese are flying south, and thousands of ducks are "harvesting" the fields close to lakes. Night frosts haven't been strong enough to kill cucumbers and tomatoes, which are in abundance this year.

Mother by the Pacific

An early, long and hard winter is predicted, and it's good to hear that the hunting season is longer than usual — probably more moose and deer — so everyone will have a chance to fill the deep-freeze. When an early snowstorm surprises me, I will fly south again, as the birds do, as soon as I can.

This "flying south as the birds do" became a mind set during the sixties. Mother went south nearly every winter and worked as a Nurses Aide in San Mateo. It seems that she first fell in love with this area while on one of her visits to Cousin Hans in Redwood City. The climate, the proximity to the ocean and the city of San Fransisco, were determining factors in choosing to work here. Her days off were often spent exploring this city which she learned to love. Together with her nursing friends, she also visited such places as Sauselito and Lake Tahoe. Although she was not a big gambler, the excitement of taking small chances was titillating. She visited Tante Martha Aragon, Elise Delfs' sister, who had lived in the San Fransisco area since the 1920s; and in Escondida she looked in on the Haglock family, former Northmark homesteaders. She was also able to get together with the Tierneys on occasional weekends off, and enjoyed camping trips with her grandchildren, and visits to places like Solvang and Hearst Castle.

The trips south, then home again in the spring, were seldom "straight forward." Many stops would be made enroute. She seemed to know someone to "look up" in so many places, that we never knew where the next postcard or letter would be postmarked. Several times during this decade, she travelled to Germany instead of returning to the farm. Occasionally when mother returned home, she found changes in the community, some very saddening. She had now lost three friends and close neighbours — Ursula Solty in 1960, then Clara Oltmanns and Elise Egge in 1965. Far away, she received the death notifications, but could not always come to say her final farewells, and grieved in solitude.

Several times during her working years in California, Mother returned to Westmark not only to visit and to help on the farm. Her reasons for coming back were even more important. There were weddings! Hans and I had started it off in 1953; Gerta followed in '59; Dieter in '60; Heidi in '62 and Irma in '64. The Pankow girls all chose to celebrate their marriages in the community of their childhood. For Mother it was an opportunity to have her family all together and to share with neighbours. At times like this our father was deeply missed. Mother also regretted the absence of extended family and would dearly have loved relatives from the "old country" to be present to see her children and grandchildren.

Compared to many of today's elaborate weddings, these celebrations were quite modest and basic, but still involved all the wardrobe planning, decorating and food preparation, and the same stress and emotional involvement. I have often thought that Mother must have had exceptional energy and emotional strength during those years. She was able to combine a job, extensive travelling, and always kept in close touch with her adult children and her young grandchildren.

Mother's Germany letter of October, 1966, included the following:

> *It's good that this mother and Oma was back from her big trip across the ocean, because during the lovely summer days of July, the whole family met at the homestead: Dieter and Vi, Ursel and Hans with Ellen, Brenda and Eric; Gerta and Peter with Norman and Gordon; Heidi and Gordon with Kevin and Trent; Irma and Dennis with little Heidi. My nephew Hans Herrndorf and family also visited from California.*

In an overview of 1967, Mother writes:

> *During the winter months, I worked in the San Mateo Hospital as usual, but resigned earlier than normal. Due to a health problem with my*

**Back: Dieter Pankow, Hans Delfs, Dennis Tierney, Peter Kut
Middle: Vi Pankow, Ursula Delfs, Irma Pankow holding Baby Heidi,
Gerta Kut, Kevin Riggins, Heidi and Trent Riggins
Front: Eric Delfs, Norman & Gordon Kut, Brenda & Ellen Delfs**

bladder, I entered a naturopathic health clinic in Texas in June, where I underwent a four-week fasting and cleansing regime. Of course I lost a lot of weight, and I must admit that it took me quite some time to regain my strength.

Mother just shrugged this experience off in a rather nonchalant way but we, her children, were quite seriously worried and were not impressed with what she had undertaken. Towards the end of her four-week fast, she was

very thin and weakened and we feared for her welfare. Dieter and I worried and debated. What could we do from way up here? Should one of us fly down there? To show our deep concern we wired her, by tele-florist, a large bouquet of red gladioli, for which we were later reprimanded. Fortunately, Uncle Werner Pankow from Germany arrived on his first

M. L. Roppe, Else Pankow, Margaret Ogilvie at Employee Recognition Supper

ever trip to America at a very opportune time, and, in his words: "We snatched Else out of that starvation sanatorium in San Antonio."

Mother and Uncle Werner visited Tierneys and enjoyed the beaches which took them back in time to the beautiful shores of the Baltic at Cranz, East Prussia. After stopping at Herrndorfs in California, Krugs in Vancouver, and Riggins in Claresholm, Uncle was anxious to head north to the main focus of his trip — to see the place where his late brother Günther had established a homestead so many years ago. For two weeks he participated in a steady round of activity: baby Karin Pankow's baptism, a family picnic at Dunvegan, a visit to Kuts in Bonanza and the big Bennett dam at Hudson Hope, a chicken supper at Westmark Hall, and more. All too

Werner Pankow and Else Pankow Holding Heidi Tierney

Oma's Little Grey House

quickly, his time was up and he travelled, via Expo in Montreal to Chicago and New York, back to Hannover.

During that summer, Mother had moved into the little grey house in Dieter's yard. It had previously served as a teacherage which Dieter purchased and had moved. Mother enjoyed making it homey with things from the old log house. She was not so isolated now, close to the main road, and was especially thankful to have electricity. Also in '67, Dieter and Hans each had a Danish exchange worker helping them on the farm for six months from spring to fall. Henning Hansen and Nis Fallesen were pleasant, personable young men to have around. Later, we visited Nis and his family twice while we travelled in Europe.

In 1968 Mother realized that she had three years left in which she could, legally, work in the United States without losing her Canadian citizenship. Also, she would have accumulated the

Back: Dieter Pankow &Baby Karin, Werner Pankow,Ursula Delfs, Nis Fallesen, Henning HansenFront: Siegi Solty, Else Pankow, Brenda, Eric, Ellen and Elise Delfs

necessary forty "quarters" which would make her eligible to receive a small U.S. social security pension. So Mother again headed south, as she reports in a March letter:

The snow drove me south, this time to Florida, where I am working in the hospital at Naples, a quiet but elegant little resort on the Gulf of Mexico. It's close to my friends, the Rampoldts. Here the health spas and resorts spring up like mushrooms. Many rich old people from the north spend their

Irene Young and Else Pankow in Florida

winters here. I work from seven to three, then go to the beach. The ocean air feels so good. I am so thankful that I can spend the winter in this lovely warm climate.

After completing her nursing stint in Florida in February, 1969, Mother travelled to Germany, together with Dieter, in March and April. In May, Tante Lotte Herrndorf came back with Mother, and visited her son Hansi and family in California. Then she spent four weeks in the little grey house with her sister, and became acquainted with her nieces, nephew and their families.

Mother always came back to her home community often enough and long enough that she never totally got away from the old worries about farming and agricultural woes. In November, '69, she writes:

Sisters Lotte Herrndorf and Else Pankow

I am still writing this from my little house on Dieter's farm, before I go south again. It is definitely winter here. In spite of some chinooks, the snow is so deep, that only the heads of the grain are sticking out. Yes, you read it right — most of the crop is snowed under. We had a relatively nice summer, but the rain came in September, just when we wanted to start harvesting, and it wouldn't stop. The fields became so soft, that during the short Indian summer in October, the soil couldn't carry the combines. With many breakdowns and deeply rutted fields, the damp, partly sprouted grain was harvested, and will have to be put through the dryer. The struggle and stress involved is hard to describe. Northern Alberta has been described a disaster area and the ministers are debating how best to help the farmers. The trouble is not just with losses caused by natural disasters. Canada, dependent on exports, can't get rid of its wheat because there is a worldwide surplus. It is to be expected that there'll be a big change in agriculture — just huge farms which will better make use of the big expensive machinery. So again this winter, all the young people are heading for sawmills, oil rigs and other off-farm jobs.

Dieter and Vi moved to Spirit River where she's nursing and he's assessor for the Prairie Farm Assistance Program. Hans is driving school bus and Ursel is teaching. Gerta is teaching in Bonanza.

Again and again it became evident that farmers and farmer's wives had to

331

work off the farm to make ends meet and try to get ahead. No wonder Mother escaped south each winter to work at a job she loved, in a climate so favourable.

In July, 1972, we four Pankow sisters travelled to Europe, together with Mother, who was our experienced tour guide. Understandably, all this was tiring for her, but sometimes we had a hard time keeping up with her pace. In her letter, following this trip, she wrote:

Now the girls have seen Germany and some neighbouring countries and have

L to R: Heidi Riggins, Ursula Delfs, Gerta Kut Irma Tierney, Else Pankow
Front: Cordela Wollesen in Frankfurt

met some of the relatives, but there just wasn't time to accept all the invitations. Not always quite simple, but we five women did it, and I hope my girls will treasure many good memories, and will have the desire, perhaps, to visit again with their own families. But right now it doesn't look good for Alberta farmers (Dieter, Ursel, Gerta) and they may have another hard year ahead of them. An early six to eight inch snowfall in September has ruined another crop — expenses, trouble and hard work, all with no returns.

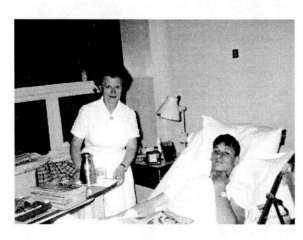

Mother on Ward in Mills Hospital

Again, Mother was able to go south and get away from it all. It took a while to get back into her work routine at the Mills Hospital, after her strenuous trip, then the discouraging conditions at the farm. She was always relieved when she could rest after her eight-hour shifts. She worked there until April, 1973, and it was with a sense of regret that she realized this would be her last employment in the United States. Back in her little grey house in Westmark, she wrote:

> *The acclimatization takes a lot of time. I am suffering from weariness, arthritis, sinusitis, laryngitis and a cough! Tried to take a sun bath, but the mosquitoes wouldn't let me. We have to have a smudge pot to work in the garden. I'm so homesick for California, San Mateo, the hospital, everything.*

Certainly, there were many things Mother would miss, especially her proximity to the many beautiful spots she liked to visit, and the adjustment would not be easy. She fondly remembered and kept in touch with her friends and co-workers — Ogilvie, McRae, Backhaus, Patterson, Boehme, and others. She missed her patients and they missed her. No matter where, in which hospital or ward she worked, she was known for her pleasant bed-side manner, and her exceptional soothing back-rubs. The sick and shut-ins loved her.

And she had many memories. In May she attended her granddaughter Brenda's Spirit River High School graduation, and found this rather interesting on several counts :

> *An unusually large class of eighty students stood on stage to receive their scrolls. It was interesting for me to discover that about half of those young people were "my babies," born while I was nursing in the Spirit River Hospital. On night shift I had to bathe them, and take them to their mothers for the two a.m. feeding — four, five, or six of them neatly laid on the gurney! The good old days! Our doctor was Fong Man Law (Chinese.) We had him for twenty-five years, and it is a pity to see him now, in a wheelchair. He had a stroke with some brain damage. He was delighted to see me.*

Back now in Canada, she had not seriously considered seeking employment. She was ready for a good rest, and her friend Craddock had written that there was a long waiting list to get on at the Grande Prairie Hospital. Helga Andersen, who was receptionist there, confirmed this. Perhaps Mother was not disappointed. She was now sixty-four years old, and more financially comfortable than she had been for years. She looked forward to spending more time with her grandchildren, to becoming a regular part of the home community again. Above all, she could foresee a lot more travel plans, without having to arrange schedules around working hours. But she would never regret that 1952 request for information, which led to her rewarding career as a Nurses Aide.

Chapter 24   Wanderlust

The dictionary definition of "wanderlust" (from the German) is: an impulse to travel; restlessness combined with a sense of adventure. I think our mother had it!

The whole family would have liked to see Mother's dream come true. We all knew how very much she wanted to see her homeland again. She hardly dared hope that it would ever happen, because it seemed something always came up to thwart her plans. She had reached the point where just the bare minimum plane ticket itself would be sufficient. She had even given some

Else Pankow 1958 Passport

thought to purchasing a ticket "on time" with a down payment, and later monthly installments. And she knew it certainly wouldn't be a "rich aunt from America" coming to visit, laden with gifts, but rather a modest, unpretentious little lady with an address book and a packet of photos.

Mother also realized, with regret, that a trip to Germany could not be a true "homecoming." The beautiful beaches and dunes, the stately Villa Kornblume in Cranz would not be accessible to her. For that part of post-war East Prussia (the East Zone) was not open to visitors. Nor would it be a true reunion, for so many loved ones, including her parents, a sister, and a brother, were gone.

Finally, on July 1, 1958, Mother was seated on a plane bound for Amsterdam — Gerta at her side! It's hard to imagine her great excitement and anticipation. Dr. Margarete Boeske had driven them to the airport in Edmonton, and there, Dieter and our friend Otto Theophile, waved goodbye. The flight was most enjoyable, with a brief refueling stop at Frobischer. After landing in Amsterdam, they had a short look at the city together with fellow passenger, Mrs. Drysdale from Clairmont. After an overnight stay in a hotel, another flight took them to Hannover. Here Uncle Werner Pankow welcomed them with open arms.

Else and Grete Pankow,
Helstorf '58

The travel itinerary, and Mother's impressions were contained in a "thank-you" letter which she penned upon her return to Canada:

Five months in Germany after twenty-nine years! I hadn't believed it could become a reality, and now that it's over, it's like a dream. For me it was, for the most part, a journey into the land of my past. All those people who had become so distant with time, have become so close to me again. Now I can identify with each one, can imagine them in their homes, in their struggles and their achievements. We thank you all for your friendly, loving reception, and for the great effort put forth to enable us to see as much as possible. We are truly grateful.

This first visit back to Germany held special significance. It proved that travel was possible without a great amount of money. It reestablished connections, and set the pace for future trips. For this reason, it will be covered in more detail here than later excursions, which were similar, but had, perhaps, a different focus each time.

Because Gerta's time was more limited, visiting as many relatives as possible was given priority. Uncle **Werner Pankow's** home in Helstorf, near Hannover, was the starting point and the "central." Here they participated in bicycle and walking tours through the heath and visited local points of interest. For Mother there was much nostalgic reminiscing. One day they visited Tante **Erika** (Pankow) **Seidler** at the senior's home in nearby Hagen.

In Traben-Trarbach they were welcomed by **Anneliese Jost**, toured wine country and old castles in the valley of the Mosel River. In Boserode, during

**Ida and Werner Gesien, Else Pankow
Augsburg 1958**

their visit at the manse with Pastor **Kurt** and **Hanlyd Anders**, they could look across the barb-wire fortifications and watch -towers (the Berlin Wall) into Germany's "east zone." Munich was extremely busy, with a gymnastics fest and the city's 800th birthday celebrations. Sister-in-law Tante **Anneliese Anders**, a teacher at the Waldorf School there, went out of her way, in spite of fragile health, to show the Canadian visitors around. In Augsburg, **Werner** and **Ida Gesien**, **Bruno** and

Gerta Pankow, Lilo Herrndorf, Else
Pankow. Front: Lotte Herrndorf
1958

Meta Gesien, drove them to some of Germany's most beautiful areas — Wieskirche, Garmisch Parten Kirchen and Salzburg.

The fast train took them northward to Varel, near Oldenburg, to visit Tante **Lotte Herrndorf** and her daughter **Lilo**. In Itzehoe, Mother's sister **Herta** and her husband **Fritz Steputat** treated them to "the most wonderful meals of seafood." In Homberg, there was a short visit and a walk in the woods with **Heinz** and **Ingrid Wollesen**, (Father's niece), then back to Pankow's in Helstorf.

On August 22nd Gerta flew back to Canada, and Mother felt somewhat forsaken, after their joint adventures for seven weeks. Mother notes that she adopted a "more leisurely pace" then, though the next three months could hardly be described as slow-moving. She visited more relatives and friends: her nephew **Gunthard Anders** in Eckernförde; **Doris** and **Herbert Ristedt**, second cousins, in the Bremen area; **Dieter** and **Lisa Anders** in Dortmund. Also on her agenda were reunions with former teachers Fräulein Ewald and Lehrer Senger; and a pleasant visit with her first boyfriend, Ernst Sakuth and his wife Magda near Cologne.

Mother was especially thankful that she was able to visit her sister-in-law **Kate Gesien** and family in the east zone. This "crossing" had previously

Showing Canada Pictures to Ruth Engel
A Scene Repeated Many Times Over

been fraught with difficulty — forms to fill out, money restrictions, and worrisome inspections at the border. But Mother had no trouble, and had such an enjoyable time in Breese that she would have loved to stay longer.

Besides visiting relatives, Mother had received, from neighbours and friends in Canada, many requests to "please look in on ... and convey our personal greetings." Always glad to meet new people, I think Mother didn't turn down a single one of these opportunities!

In Grossenaspe, Holstein, she visited with a sister of Elise Delfs; also Karl and Thea Delfs, brother and sister-in-law of Hans and Otto Delfs and Minna Toerper. She looked up Hans Günther Kirchmann's and Bert Bockholdt's relatives. They, as homesick young German immigrants to Canada, had spent time with us on the homestead. In Singen, she enjoyed a visit with Frau Brommauer, Horst Solty's sister, and in Klein Gerau, she relayed greetings to Mr. and Mrs. Samuel, friends of the Wittes.

In Königsförde, near Kiel, Opa Schuett and Tante Lina, Bernie Schuett's grandfather and aunt, welcomed her warmly. Near Cuxhaven she was part of a family get-together with Elise Egge's siblings, Louis Favreau, Ruth Engel, brother and sister, and Tina Favreau, sister-in-law. In Stuttgart she spent an afternoon with the sister of Otto Kuhn and aunt of Lotte Kuhn, Grande Prairie friends. In Godeshorn, Mother brought greetings to the father of Inge Watzenberg, from his daughter in Edmonton. She was a young friend of Mother's during nursing days in the city.

In Bückeburg, Dr. and Mrs. Michel, Trudy Glimm's parents, and Dr. Jürgen Glimm, Helmuth's brother, were happy to hear about their relatives in Canada. Lotte Theophile greeted Mother warmly in Bad Ratzeberg, treated her to dinner at the town hall and

Mother, Second from left, Visiting Dr. and Mrs. Michel (Trudy Glimm's Parents) in Bückeburg

brought chocolates to the train. Her friendly charm reminded Mother of brother Otto Theophile. In Hamburg, Lilo Brüggemann, Martha Puhlmann's sister, was truly a friend and became Mother's "touch point" for phone and mail communications.

Mother also looked up former residents of Canada, who had gone back. In Schleswig she had dinner with Hein Krog and his wife Käte. He just couldn't get enough of hearing about the old Northmark settlement. He had homesteaded the Minna Toerper quarter. In Stuttgart she visited Karl Götz, a writer who had visited Northmark while researching a book about German homesteaders in Canada. At Bremerhaven, there were excited greetings when Skodda and Bunjes, former Canadian nursing colleagues, spied Mother at the station. Together they attended the theater to hear a flute concert. While in Bonn, it was "an afternoon in Canada" with Harald and Helle Glimm, who had returned to Germany from their Northmark homestead in 1935.

Ferdinand (Freddie) Brinkmann picked Mother and Gerta up in Helstorf and took them to visit his mother in Dielingen, took them through parts of Westphalia, and showed them great hospitality. Freddie had become a good friend and our place was his second home while he worked in the area during his years in Canada.

Although visiting relatives, old friends and former neighbours was the main focus of Mother's trip, she did, especially while Gerta was still with her, take in some of the "tourist spots": the old Heidelberg castle, the Cologne Cathedral, the seat of government in Bonn; the world-famous Reeperbahn in Hamburg. They took a cruise on the Rhine and attended a performance by the Viennese Boys Choir. And of course there were countless "spaziergänge." It seems that "going for a walk" was the German national pastime!

It was in early November, 1958, that Otto and Minna Toerper also visited Germany. They had a surprise when their ocean liner, the Hanseatic anchored at the harbor in Cuxhaven. Else Pankow, their Woking area neighbour stood at the railing to greet them! They had lunch together, and both agreed that this "touch of home" at a distant harbour was quite special.

In December, Mother's thoughts turned towards home, and after much consideration, she opted for a return by sea voyage. In her later letter, she writes:

I never regretted the exchange of my airline ticket for an ocean liner passage. The Italia took us safely, in spite of great storms, from Cuxhaven to Halifax. Without sea sickness, in a wonderful private cabin, this voyage was an adventure in

Else Pankow, right, with New Friends Aboard the Italia

itself. Also the long rail trip through Canada (three days and four nights) was very nice, in the modern Transcontinental with observation car, diner and sleeping cars. As we passed by the beautiful snow-covered landscape, the small towns decked in colorful Christmas lights in the –30 degree cold, I knew that I was home — back in Canada. In Calgary a chinook was blowing. In Ponoka Heidi joined me on the train, and together we travelled to Grande Prairie, where Dieter and Irma picked us up. It was the 23rd of December, the road to the farm was plowed, and we could all spend Christmas together there once more.

After this first long eventful trip to Germany, Mother limited her travels in the early sixties to this side of the ocean. In 1962 she visited the Herrndorfs in California, and Irma in Lynwood, near Los Angeles. Together they attended the World Fair in Seattle. After starting her employment in San Mateo, she took opportunities, on her off days, to visit many of California's beauty spots, and came to love San Fransisco.

In 1966, after completing a winter of work at the Mills General Hospital, Mother undertook another trip overseas. This time she left from Calgary in February, took the C.P.R. to Toronto, then, via Hamilton and Welland, to New York City. Here she boarded the S.S. Berlin and sailed to Bremerhaven, Germany. She had many of the same destinations and visited the

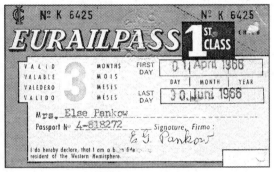

Eurail Pass Ticket

relatives described in her '58 excursion. But this time she had the wonderful Eurail Pass ticket which enabled her to criss-cross Europe at will. Four times the train took her through the majestic Alps. She looked up Siegi Solty who was teaching at the Canadian Armed Forces base in Werl. She sun-bathed on

the beaches of the Spanish Riviera and travelled through southern Germany. The Bodensee and the Island of Meinau were fascinating. A side-trip on a small train along the Neckar River in Odenwald, led to Erbach. In this small town of many artisans, Mother was very pleased to find true hand-turned and hand-painted pottery, which she managed to

Mother on Lido, Venice

transport all the way home! We all treasure these special gifts. On a whim, she took a quick trip to Venice (thanks to the Eurail pass) and would never regret that decision.

On June 21st she sailed for home from Amsterdam on the ocean liner Arkadia, which was overloaded with immigrants. Reaching Canadian shores, it followed the St. Lawrence Seaway to Quebec, landing in Montreal. By Canadian Pacific Railways she came to Calgary, where she took in the world-famous Calgary Stampede. Stopping at Heidi's in Ponoka, she was finally home in Woking at the end of July, just in time for a visit from all her children at the homestead.

During 1967, after working in San Mateo for the winter, Mother was "travel guide" for Uncle Werner for a time. He had come from Germany in June and rescued her from the naturopathic clinic in San Antonio. After visiting Tierneys in Ventura, they made their way up north to the homestead in July. After Uncle's departure, Mother had a short rest period and regained her strength.

That fall Mother was "on the road again." She travelled to Montreal to take in the last three days of Expo, thinking it was something quite special to have a world fair in our own country. She stayed with the Teichert family (related to Hans Teichert who married Gisela Pankow.) In the predominantly German community of Kitchener (formerly Berlin) Mother visited the Intscher family (pastor at Northmark in the fifties.) In Toronto she attended the well-known Royal Winter Fair, enjoyed the horse shows and the R.C.M.P. Musical Ride. A former nursing colleague accompanied her to Niagara Falls. From there she went to Florida and commenced work at the Naples Hospital.

Dieter Pankow and Mother in Helstorf
1969

In spring, after ending her employment in Florida, she set out on a "circle bus tour," which included the Grand Canyon, a visit to Tierneys and friends in California. From there the bus took her to Vancouver, then through the Rockies and home.

In March and April, 1969, before Dieter would have to worry about spring seeding, he accompanied Mother to Germany — his first, her third trip. Their time was spent, for the most part, visiting relatives, and Dieter occupied a dentist chair in Dr. Werner Pankow's practice for a few sittings, as Uncle fit him with dentures. On the return trip, Tante Lotte Herrndorf accompanied them, and Mother took her to California to visit her son Hansi. That summer Mother did more entertaining in her home than travelling. First Tante Lotte stayed for four weeks; then Tina Favreau made Mother's house her headquarters while she visited surrounding Egge relatives. Mother and Tina seemed to be soul-mates, had good times together, and became travel companions. Tina later wrote, "It was so nice, staying at the farm with you. I can still smell the fragrant sweet clover."

In 1970, we the Delfs family, with our Country Squire station wagon and a tent on the roof, travelled all the way to Tia Juana. We took the scenic coastal highway through Washington and Oregon, then through the majestic redwoods. In San Francisco Mother met us on her days off, was delighted to see her grandchildren, and to show us the sights in the city she loved: the cable cars, the crooked street, Fisherman's Wharf, Golden Gate Park, Alcatraz and much more.

Oma Pankow, Brenda, Ursula, Ellen, Eric and Dwayne Delfs in San Francisco

It had taken a lot of planning and some coaxing, but in 1972 the "five-woman trip to Europe" became a reality. Mother and her four daughters, armed with airline tickets and Eurail passes, took the big tour. On the whole, it went amazingly smooth. There were times when it was difficult to get a taxi for five, and accomodations for that many could be a problem. We kept our sense of humour and had many a good laugh, only a few tears. We missed our families and waited anxiously for letters from home. We all dressed in navy blue blazers, making it easier to spot each other should one get lost! We met many Pankow and Gesien relatives, but also did a lot of sight-seeing.

The (nee) Pankow Girls, Heidi, Irma, Ursula, Gerta in a Pub in Rüdesheim on the Rhine

In Bremen we kept tradition alive and drank wine in the "Ratskeller" where our grandparents had celebrated their engagement so many years ago. We took a Rhine cruise that was beautiful and restful, and the old castles provided countless photo opportunities. We ascended the Olympic tower in Munich which was busily preparing for the games. We spent a night in Venice, and were serenaded as we hired a gondola to take us to Markus Square. We travelled through Switzerland, the Black Forest, where we bought clocks; toured the Heidelburg Castle and quaint little shops in Rüdesheim.

In Denmark we visited Nis Fallesen who had lived with us and worked for Hans as an exchange worker in 1967. His whole family went out of their way to show us a good time. Nis and his father drove us from one end of the country to the other, including a visit to Legoland. Nis's mother fed us royally, and confided to me: "I can't possibly make up to you, in such a short time, all the good things you did for our Nis."

Gerta and I had some time left on our Eurail ticket, so we took the train up the coast of Norway, as far as Oslo, and on our return, took the hydrofoil across from Sweden to Lübbeck, Germany. Close to the end of our holiday, we arrived back in Amsterdam, where we took a canal tour, then attended the "Floriade,"one of the world's largest garden shows. Heidi and Irma had flown home earlier. Now Mother boarded her flight to Los Angeles, and Gerta and I flew to Edmonton, where our families welcomed us at the airport.

We would always remember this excursion as a special time with our mother. She was so glad to have the opportunity to introduce her daughters to relatives and friends and to show them many parts of her homeland. One sadness and regret would always linger — the inability to go to East Prussia, her real home, the place of all her childhood memories.

In April, 1973, Mother ended her working days in California and returned to Canada. In that year's Christmas letter, she gives an overview. Excerpts follow :

Again I experienced the northern spring and summer on the farm, with the long days and bright nights; the seeding of field and garden, the miracle of growth. We had a good summer here, a bit dry in August, and then, as happens so frequently, when we want to harvest the rains come. Dieter was happy that he had a lot of fescue, which was harvested early, yielded well, and is up in price. To get the canola and flax, he had to struggle with wet fields. Hans and Ursel couldn't get all theirs harvested, and Gerta and Peter have to put all their wheat through the dryer.

I can't bear to watch this struggle with harvesting wet, muddy fields anymore, so I escaped south for two weeks in October. I visited friends in California, and Irma, especially, was glad to see me. She misses Oma's visits and phone calls. I stopped to see Riggins new house in Maple Ridge, then stayed with Gerta for a week in Bonanza.

I moved into Dieter's old house, and slowly we're getting it fixed up and winterized. I've even got my own phone now, so can talk to my children at any time. Ursel was going to quit teaching, but with Ellen and Brenda in University, and the crop failure, she is going back for another year. It's not easy to drive the twenty miles to work every day in all kinds of weather and road conditions, then to tend to household, garden and family. For Karin, Dieter's oldest, the school bus ride is rather strenuous. From 7:45 till 4:30 the little one is on the go. Barb has Kindergarten twice a week, and Lisa, that energetic little person, would love to go along.

And the world situation? The television brings it all — Watergate scandal, war in the Middle East, inflation, strikes, price increases everywhere, especially food. So Dieter is trying to shoot a moose, but like his father, he's not a great hunter.

In 1974, Mother travelled by Greyhound on an "Ameripass" — two months for one hundred fifty dollars. She took full advantage of this ticket, which took her as far west as Victoria, and north to Alaska, many hundred miles in all.

It seems that in 1975 Mother was "on the go" for most of the year. She saw and experienced so much, visited so many friends and relatives. It started in California, at the home of Wally and Lou, her friends in Desert Hot Springs; the Haglocks in Escondido; nursing friends in San Mateo, and of course, the Tierney family in Ventura. In Florida she spent a few days with the Rampoldts and visited Disney World before heading north. In Brooklyn she visited Dennis Tierney's Aunt Lilly, and also looked up her professor friend,

Ernie Kaarsberg, ex-husband of Martha Hess. In the New York area she visited the Herz family, the daughter of her friend, Tina Favreau, and

viewed the Rockefeller Centre, the United Nations Building, and the Guggenheim Museum. In Niles, Michigan, she visited Irene Dewitt, friend of Rampoldts, in the house where I used to babysit in 1948; and she looked in on Ingrid Rampoldt and her family in Muskegon.

Crossing the border into Canada, she made her second visit to Niagara Falls; saw Toronto City Hall and the beautiful rock gardens in Hamilton. She looked up former Edmonton friends, Richard and Irmgard Struck, also the Martin Intschers in Kitchener. In Ottawa she toured the grounds of the Parliament Buildings, and in that vicinity, looked up Gerda Anderson, (nee Wolfram) and her

Mother Aboard the Russian Ocean Liner Mikhail Lermontov

family. She visited old Montreal and stayed with Martin and Elke Teichert.

As usual, travelling via the trusty bus, Mother went back to New York, and from there, embarked on her fifth trip to Germany. She boarded the Russian ocean liner Mikhail Lermontov, and after what she described as a "wonderful eleven-day voyage," landed in Bremerhaven. Why a Russian ship? I'm not sure, but Mother was always intrigued by things exotic, out of the ordinary. This ship had all the amenities of other ocean liners, music, dancing, entertainment, swimming pool, sauna, sports facilities, international menus with Russian specialties. Mother, like always, had no trouble making new friends on board.

Upon her arrival in Germany, Mother had a flu that she couldn't readily shake during a great heat wave. Tante Lotte in Varel lovingly nursed her back to health,

Three (nee) Gesien Sisters Herta, Lotte, Else 1975

so that in September she was able to attend the reunion of former East Prussians at Pinneberg. Then, activating her Eurail pass, she visited many parts of Germany. In November she took a flight back to Los Angeles, visited Irma, Riggins, then Kuts, before arriving back home in time for Christmas.

1976 had an exceptionally early spring. Seeding was completed in early May, with warm weather and early showers. It was not a big travel year for Mother, but she had the opportunity to have most of her family together again when her oldest granddaughter, Ellen, was married in July. She had hoped that Germany relatives might be among the wedding guests. Many were now taking advantage of the reasonably-priced six-week excursion

flight. In '77 the only trip for Mother was a short visit to Heidi in Maple Ridge. But she quite enthusiastically encouraged and supplied addresses to her grandchildren Brenda and Eric Delfs who took a three-month, back-pack with Eurail pass trip to Europe.

Else Pankow, 2nd from right, and Friends At Cranz Reunion in Pinneberg

Another Cranz reunion was enough reason to go to Germany again in 1978. The gathering brought together some three-hundred former Cranzers in Pinneberg. This time, Mother's long-time friend and neighbour, Johann Oltmanns, accompanied her on the flight, both having kinfolk to visit. Again,

Mother made all the usual stops to see friends and relatives, courtesy of a Senior's Pass and Dieter Anders' car. This time, added to the itinerary, were: Fritz and Anneliese Roblick, (cousin of the Delfs and Toerpers) in Bimöhlen; Henry and Otto Sick (Toerper relatives who had hunted in Canada); Dr. and Mrs. Boness (who had visited Egges in our community); also Olga and Bernhard Jürgens, (Johann

Else Pankow, Johann Oltmanns Ready for Europe

Oltmanns' nephew.) In eight weeks they were back on the 747 Jet which flew from Amsterdam to Edmonton in eight hours.

In 1979 Mother limited her travels to visiting Irma and Heidi. But 1980 was a big year for her again. In June we had a "fifty years in Canada" celebration at the farm, where Oma had her five children, thirteen grandchildren, and one great-grandson, all together. This was a happy occasion, blessed by good weather, with many young people and much reminiscing. We all realized, that were our father alive, this would have been the year for a golden wedding anniversary party.

Little more than two months later, Mother attended a much more somber

Oma and Her Thirteen Grandchildren (1980) and one Great Grandson
Standing: Gordon Kut, Dwayne Delfs, Ellen Bunjevac holding
Anton, Kevin Riggins, Brenda and Eric Delfs, Heidi Tierney,
Norman Kut, Trent Riggins
Seated: Karin and Lisa Pankow, Oma, Barbara Pankow, Brian Tierney

gathering. Uncle Werner Pankow died, September 6, 1980, at the age of eighty-three. He had been considered the head of the Pankow extended family from the time he was just a young man. Many, including our parents, had come to him for advice and support. A man with a passion for family history, he had worked for years to put together a Pankow family archival collection. For the last few years of his life, he suffered from Parkinson's disease, and his handwriting became shakier with each letter. Now in 1980, Mother flew to Germany and attended his funeral in Helstorf, celebrated with full military honors and countless floral tributes. For Mother, the final real link to her beloved Günther was now gone.

The timing was such that Mother was able to attend another Pinneberg homecoming, and again she made many visits in various parts of the country. But on this trip, she was forced to recognize that "this travelling is a strenuous business, and I realized that I'm not a spring chicken. I didn't get to all the people I had planned to visit." She suggested that perhaps sometime they could organize a family get-together in Germany, making it easier to see everyone. And of course, she always stressed that everyone was welcome to come and visit in Canada.

In 1981 Mother did entertain company from Germany — in a change of roles. Our cousin, Elizabeth Anders, after a trip to Nicaragua, visited Irma in California, then Heidi in Vancouver. Here Mother met Elizabeth and accompanied her to Victoria, by ferry to Quadra and Cortez islands. Then by Greyhound they went through the Rockies to Calgary, stopped at Ellen's in Edmonton, then home to the farm. On this trip, our German cousin had her eyes opened in many ways. Mother also had Haglocks from Escondido, Ilse Herz from New York, and Wulfs from Parksville, B.C. visiting that summer. These visitors automatically became ours as well, because Mother would invariably bring them over.

After all the summer visitors, Mother was overseas again in the fall, and in her Christmas letter to Tante Lotte, she wrote :

> *After fifty-seven days in Germany, one has to acclimatize and I got a touch of flu, or maybe it's just jet lag. The flight from Amsterdam to Edmonton was fully occupied. As always at this time of year, we had sunshine all the way, and luckily this greeted me in Edmonton as well. I stayed for a few days with Ursel's daughter Ellen, with the new little great-granddaughter, Marina, and sturdy one and a half year old brother Anton. Ursel was there for a Unifarm convention, and along with Brenda, Eric and Dwayne, I had a great reception back to Canada.*

Just a few weeks later there was a family gathering, in the winter this time, when Tierneys, Riggins, Kuts, Delfs and Pankow families all spent Christmas Eve in the Delfs basement recreation room. For the next few days there was skiing, sleighriding, games, and much visiting.

In 1982 Mother decided to shorten the winter considerably, and enjoyed lots of sunshine. In February she flew to Heidi in Maple Ridge, then by bus to Irma in California, who had booked a flight to Hawaii for her. On the island she stayed for ten days with friends, Dieter Rolinski and family, (originally from Cranz) then for fourteen days in an economy hotel with her friend Else Patterson. Upon her return to California, many bus miles, numerous stops and visits later, she returned to the farm in May.

Again, when Mother returned home, she found changes in the community. Within a few weeks of each other, Elise Delfs, Hans's mother, then Otto Toerper, his uncle, two of the original settlers, had died. In California, too, there was sadness, as within a week, Dennis Tierney lost his grandmother and his father. Mother was thankful that she had, quite recently enjoyed happy times with both.

Oma Pankow in Hawaii 1982

The year 1983 was a year of happy celebrations, also great sorrow. It started out on a positive note as Mother undertook a winter trip to the east --- Florida, New York, Boston, Toronto. She was back in April to celebrate her seventy-fifth birthday, and in May she attended her grandson Eric's wedding in Rycroft.

It was not long afterwards that the tragic news came, of granddaughter

Else Pankow Ready to Board Another Train 1983

Heidi Tierney's death in a car accident. Mother, Dieter and Gerta flew down right away to be at the funeral. Heidi and I went later, when emotional support is also needed so desperately. In July, Mother saw her second granddaughter, Brenda, get married. The Tierneys came to the wedding, though it must have been very difficult for them. Once again, Mother had most of her family together.

In September of that same year, she was off to Germany again, attending another homeland reunion with many guests from Cranz. She was honored with a red rose for having travelled the greatest distance to be there. Besides her usual visits, by train through the beautiful fall-coloured countryside, there was an additional treat this time. For two days she was on Spiekerog Island where Mrs.Stolte operated a bed and breakfast. Mother had previously visited this lady in Vermont, U.S.A. at the home of her daughter Harda Bradford. Though the access by ferry was somewhat awkward, it was worth it. By the end of October, Mother was back on the farm, where Dieter had surprised her with a fresh paint job and new floor covering for her house.

In 1984 Mother went to see a urologist in Edmonton, because she hadn't been feeling real well for some time. She was found to have a tumor in the bladder. This was cauterized, but she would have to return for examination every three months. This, of course, was a great blow to Mother, and certainly it would "cramp her style" especially when it came to travelling.

At Easter time, Mother looked after house and home, dog and cat, while Dieter and his family took a trip to the Toronto area and Niagara Falls. In April when Mother helped Charlie and Lilo Muehrer celebrate their fiftieth anniversary, she realized how few of the old-timers were left.

In early summer, Rick and Winnie Stevenson had come for their grand-daughter Karin Pankow's graduation, and their daughter Vi hosted a golden wedding celebration for them. Three weeks later, her mother was dead of a heart attack. At seventy, Winnie had looked so young, and it was thought that Rick, with two heart operations, great-grandfather Stevenson at ninety-seven, or great-grandmother Whitten, ninety, would be much more likely to go.

In an October, '84 letter, Mother does a little musing about the political situation in our country:

> Were you able to follow the pope's visit to Canada? It was as if God himself had made a visit to earth. The pope berated our province of Alberta, as the richest one, for not giving enough to the Third World. This visit cost Canada more than five million dollars, and then the Queen came! Will the conservative government, and the new prime minister, Mulroney, be able to make any changes, especially regarding unemployment?

In May, 1985 Mother flew to Germany once more, having been granted permission from her urologist. She thoroughly enjoyed springtime there, with the blooming cherry trees, azaleas, rhododendrons and lilacs. But jet lag, her aching joints, Tante Lotte's (now 91) constant chatter, often repetitious, the T.V. always too loud — all this made her irritable. However, they got used to each other and Tante was so very happy to have her younger sister with her. This time, Mother did much of her visiting by telephone from Varel, but she did attend another reunion of East Prussians, this time in Düsseldorf.

She was back in Edmonton in July, for her examination and treatment at the

University Hospital. This was followed by weekly chemotherapy at the Grande Prairie Hospital until the middle of August. This took its toll on her energy and her emotional well being.

Unable to face another fall of terrible harvesting conditions and poor crops, Mother escaped to Riggins, flying down with Vi who attended her father's wedding in Chilliwack. There the weather was beautiful, trees and grass a lush green, and flowers still blooming in abundance. Heidi had holidays in September, and together with Mother, travelled to Edmonton, where we met them at Ellen's. We had come to the city to celebrate my fifty-third birthday with our family, and to escape the depressing weather conditions at home.

Winter set in with a vengeance, with forty below in November. But then a chinook moved in during December and took all the snow. On Boxing Day, 1985, and the days that followed, Dieter combined sixty acres of good wheat! Surely that was "a first."

1986 was a rather eventful year. Mother, now seventy-eight, and her health

"less than optimum," managed it all quite well. In February she visited Irma. In March, the news came, that her sister Lotte was dying. So there was a quick trip to Germany, and Mother was thankful that she arrived in time to be by her sister's bedside before she died. Later she lamented: "I miss her. She was like a

Werner Gesien, Else Pankow, Hans Herrndorf at the Funeral of Lotte Herrndorf 1986

mother to me. Her little apartment in Varel had become a second home and was often the headquarters during my many visits to the old country."

Else Pankow's Farewell to Lisa and Dieter Anders in Edmonton

In May, Dieter and Lisa Anders from Germany arrived in Edmonton. Since they knew no English, our Ellen helped them obtain a rental car at the airport, and got them started in the right direction to drive to the farm. Now Mother could play hostess, and repay the hospitality they had shown on her many visits. After they returned from their foray into Alaska, Mother accompanied them to Vancouver and Expo, then back through the Rockies to Edmonton. This time it was our Brenda who took them to the airport to catch their plane back home.

In July Mother went to Vancouver again, this time by car, with Gerta and Peter, to be together with most of the family. We made Riggins house our headquarters as we attended several days of Expo, at the same time enjoying a family reunion. In August, Mother went to Edmonton with Dieter and his family, to receive, with all the attending ceremony, the Northlands Farm Family Award.

Irma, Heidi, Gerta, Ursula,Dieter and Mother
Else Pankow during Vancouver Expo Reunion

The travel for that year had not yet ended. In September, Mother, along with Heidi, flew east and visited her friend and former colleague, Mary McRae, who lived in Cape Breton. Together they toured the Maritimes and Newfoundland during the beautiful fall colour season.

Somehow, during all this activity, Mother managed, every three months, to keep her appointments for examinations and sometimes treatments in Edmonton. She was quite pleased at how she had "stood up to it all." During '88 she was required to have monthly bladder instillation treatments in Grande Prairie, so could undertake no long trips. But she managed, with airline "specials" to visit Irma and Heidi.

In July, she, with the rest of the family, celebrated the wedding of her grandson, Norman Kut, in Fort St. John. In August she had the opportunity once more, to host Germany visitors, when her niece Reintraud and her husband Jupp Einlechner from the Munich area came. Mother showed them local points of interest, then accompanied them, in their rental car, to Vancouver and Victoria. Mother returned by air, to be back in time for the reunion with Pastor Martin and Rosina Intscher, which was held, for many friends, in our Delfs garden.

Mother's '88 travel year began in February when she flew to Florida with Gerta and Mary Kut, who had an uncle there. They visited Rampoldts, also attended Epcot and Disney World, among other points of interest, before flying back, where Ellen met them at the Edmonton airport.

In September, at eighty years of age, Mother embarked on what would be her final trip to Germany. Because it was the last, perhaps some excerpts from her '88 letter warrant inclusion here:

Mother (left) with Rampoldts in Florida

So I dared to do it once more and booked a flight with Wardair, which has a good reputation and is reasonably priced. At the same time I applied for an entry visa into the DDR (East Germany.) I took the bus to Edmonton, and my granddaughter Ellen took me to the airport where the Jumbo Jet was waiting. Four hundred and fifty passengers were royally treated with excellent service, and in eight and a half hours we landed in Frankfurt. At the main railroad station, I immediately purchased a senior's pass, which would allow train travel at half price. I had put together a big circle tour, with each day carefully planned out.

Else Pankow (l) and Kate Gesien, 1988, Breese, Germany

And indeed it was an extensive tour, with many of the usual stops. At some of these places, familiar faces would, sadly, be missing — especially Uncle Werner, Tante Herta, Tante Lotte. Mother attended her final Cranz reunion, and found it particularly poignant and moving when the attendees were shown a slide presentation of her Cranz, as it was before the war. Her crossing into the DDR went without incident. She was warmly received by all the Gesiens and was part of a big party for her niece Bärbel's fiftieth birthday, that was attended by three brothers and their families. This led Mother to comment: "I was quite touched that my maiden name was so well represented in this area." Still in the east zone, Mother visited Inga, (daughter of Hans Jürgen Pankow) and her husband Wilfried

Kuntze in their lovely apartment in Erfurt, which Mother described as "a beautiful old city which is now being renovated. Always a flower city, my father had ordered seeds from here seventy-five years ago."

Back in West Germany, Mother ended her tour with a visit to Dieter, Lisa, and mother Hanlyd Anders, then Tante Grete Pankow and her daughter Karin, who had just recently moved from Helstorf to the Düsseldorf area. Then it was October 12th, and Mother was homeward bound.

Else Pankow with Niece Inga Kuntze
In Erfurt, Germany 1988

Early in the morning Lisa took me to the train in Frankfurt. At noon the half-full jet soared into the sky. It was a pleasant, comfortable flight. At two o'clock it was Ellen, again, who picked me up in Edmonton. But my journey was not yet ended. On October 6th my son-in-law Peter Kut had been seriously injured in a vehicle accident. Now he was a patient in a Calgary Hospital, with serious burns and a fractured pelvis. So I took the three-hour bus ride from Edmonton to Calgary to visit him and Gerta, who was staying with friends. The following week I took the bus to Grande Prairie, where Dieter picked me up, and finally I was home.

Perhaps Tante Grete expressed it very well, when in her Christmas letter to Mother, she wrote: "I admire you, how calmly you manage all this travelling, always different people around you. May you be granted continued strength and good health, because you are not the type that would take well to having your wings clipped."

In 1989, Mother's travels were not entirely curtailed, but slowed down. In July she attended the Tierney's silver wedding anniversary. She flew down earlier to visit friends in San Mateo, then went to Herrndorfs in Sunnyvale, and together with them, drove to Ventura. Dieter and Vi, Gerta and Peter and I had flown from Edmonton, and Riggins had come from B.C. for the garden party celebration. On the way back, Mother again kept her appointment with Dr. Lakey in Edmonton.

About the time that we thought Mother must have no "travel energy" left, in March, 1990, she took a trip to Hawaii with her friend Tina Favreau. Tina was visiting her daughter Ilse Herz in New York, and then met Mother in

Honolulu. This was a wonderful time for the two old friends. That same summer, Mother's niece, Doris Ristedt and her husband Herbert came to Canada, returning her many visits to their home in Syke.

In 1990, when Mother was eighty-two years old, she could look back, (excluding her initial ocean voyage to Canada,) on twelve trips to Germany. There were two holiday trips to Hawaii, countless trips to California and Florida, as well as other U.S. points from coast to coast, and Canadian destinations from B.C. to Newfoundland. She had attended three World Fairs, in Seattle, Montreal and Vancouver. Then there

Mother in Hawaii 1990

were the numerous more "local" outings — Edmonton, Calgary, and all parts of the Peace River Country.

We all remember Mother stepping off a plane, or more often a bus, her travel bags always crammed "too full." So often she would bring "a little something," especially for her grandchildren and great grandchildren. And how could we forget that address book — worn and dog-eared from much use; thicker each year, with bits and pieces of paper sticking out — someone's precious address on each one; the whole thing held together with a rubber band. This was her directory, a vital part of her travel planning. To lose it would have been devastating to her.

To say that our mother loved travelling would be an under-statement. It was

Else Pankow, World Traveller

almost an obsession. Only her illness forced her to slow down. Then, several albums of photos and postcards allowed her to relive many of her experiences. For some thirty years, our mother enjoyed a serious bout of "Wanderlust."

Chapter 25   The Twilight Years

One must wait until the evening to see how splendid the day has been. ...
Sophocles

Over the years, many people came to know the spunky, courageous woman in a number of different roles. In Cranz, East Prussia, Else Gesien was the petite blonde schoolgirl in Fräulein Ewald's private school. Then she helped as florist and gardener in her father's nursery; and as cook and housekeeper in her mother's large household. Soon Fräulein Gesien was dental assistant at the practice of Dr. Werner Pankow, and became the betrothed of his younger brother.

Two years later she was a young newlywed, Else Pankow, enjoying the excitement and adventure of a honeymoon in the Canadian wilderness. This was followed by motherhood and the challenges of being a homemaker on a northern homestead during the depression years. She was a good neighbour to many. Then came the war and her family was "on the other side." She was left alone with her children when her husband was interned in a prisoner of war camp; so she also had to do the work of a farmer.

After five years she found herself cast in yet another role — the most sorrowful and challenging of all. She was a widow with five young children. In the next chapter of her life she became a nurses aide and dedicated caregiver, loved by many grateful patients. And friends and relatives from many parts of the globe, would remember her as the ebullient traveler, charged with wanderlust.

Other people knew Else Pankow in all these roles. We, her family, knew her for more. She was our mother, grandmother and great-grandmother. We knew her successes and her disappointments, her highs and her lows.

After Father's death, she had to overcome her greatest grief and set new goals for herself and her family. Mother found consolation and enjoyment by participating in Pastor Intscher's choir. She had always enjoyed singing. I remember her harmonizing with Father in the beloved German carols at Christmas time, and she taught her children and grandchildren many a childhood song. Now her strong voice provided leadership in the soprano section of the community singers.

During homestead days and even into later years, Mother's sewing skills were much appreciated. Weeks before Christmas the dolls would disappear, and reappear in a beautiful new wardrobe on Christmas Eve. There were always alterations and makeovers (she could make anything fit), a dress for graduation, wedding or an Oktoberfest; a Hallowe'en costume; last-minute repairs on a bridal veil; and many times, a quick hem on someone's trousers. And for home decore, she fashioned curtains, floor cushions, bed coverings and wall hangings. She was the "ever-ready" seamstress, and seemed glad to be "needed" in this way. She was quite unhappy when, in the summer of '77, her hands became stiff and painful, seriously affecting her skill with the needle and thread. Thankfully, carpal tunnel surgery corrected the problem.

For so many years, Mother had money only for the bare necessities of life (not always that) and truly had to "watch her pennies." Perhaps it was because of this, that even when she later had a pay-cheque, then her pension, she always delighted in finding bargains and special sales. Her favourite stops in California were the "Goodwill" stores and flea markets. She would come home laden with treasures. "I thought this might fit …..," she'd say excitedly. She did find some wonderful "stuff" and it didn't bother her in the least if people knew where it had been purchased.

I think this was just one indication of Mother's confidence, her comfort with who she was. There was no lack of self-esteem, yet certainly no air of superiority. This attitude was quite evident during her many travels. She would strike up a conversation with anyone, male or female, young or old, any nationality, and from any station in life, and would take it for granted that they would want to reciprocate. In this way she got to know so many people, and always had someone "to look up" (and have free lodging!) Her address book got thicker each year. What many of us might consider an

**Oma Pankow Ready for
Westmark Oktoberfest**

imposition, she always viewed as: "They were so happy to see me!" And people did seem to genuinely welcome her. Away from everything, out on the farm, she was dependent on others for transportation. This was a hardship for someone who was seldom content to stay home. One of her greatest regrets was that she had never learned to drive.

In some respects, communication came so easy to her, but in other situations Mother had difficulty, especially within her own family. It was our father who would do the "heart to heart" deeper conversations. When Father was gone, she delegated, as Heidi wrote in her "birthday book" to me:

Do you remember when Mother asked you to tell me about "the birds and the bees?" I had started to menstruate, and she had only handed me "the book." I will always be thankful to you for your explanation, because I thought something was wrong with me.

Mother also found it hard to praise or compliment her family. Perhaps it was her way of discouraging conceit or boastfulness, which she found so distasteful. Sometimes we were hurt by this and felt we could never quite measure up to her expectations. When the judges awarded me a first-place ribbon, and even a "best of the fair" prize, Mother would still find fault: "Yes, but you should have ….." We girls found it particularly irritating when Mother would suggest that "those nice German Holst girls from Hines Creek," or the Andersen girls from Wembley were paragons that we should make every effort to emulate.

It seemed easier for her to give us credit when she could write it in a letter. In 1978 Mother was back from her travels in time for our 40-year Westmark School homecoming celebrations, and enthusiastically described the occasion in a letter to Uncle Werner:

Our school reunion was blessed with perfect weather. Ursel had done an incredible amount of work, starting last year with sending out invitations,

Parents of Westmark Students at Homecoming '78
Georg Witte, Hein Schuett, Helmuth Glimm, Johann Oltmanns, Charlie Muehrer,
Philip Baum, Eilert Pleis
Mary Rowe, Arlene Olafson, Else Pankow, Gertrud Glimm, F.W. Egge, Irene Sloat,
Lilo Muehrer, Frieda Schuett, Else Moll, Emilia Baum, Elise Delfs,
Hermine Delfs, Leni Witte

then making displays of pioneer and baby photos, also school artifacts, which were of great interest to all visitors. She and her committee also planned a program, including a history of the school, which she had written. The school bell summoned past teachers, students and parents to the banquet at the hall across the road, and a dance rounded out the evening.

And again in '85, Mother came back home in time for a major community event, the launching of the Woking community history book, which she describes in her letter:

The community history book has been completed and printed. We had a nice celebration at the Woking School for the launching. There were speeches from dignitaries and organizations, congratulatory messages, and, of course, invitations to purchase, because to have a book like this printed costs a lot of money. The school band, Ukrainian ethnic dancers, vocal soloist Yvonne Floriani, and local thespians provided entertainment on the open-air stage. Ursel, as the editor of the book, was honoured with the first edition, her name engraved in gold on the cover. All committee members and workers were given a hearty round of applause. A big barbecue and dance, then a pancake breakfast next morning, were held at the hall.

Although Mother was enthusiastic about these community celebrations, and seemed to appreciate our efforts, she was never in one place long enough to take an active part, or serve on any committees. She had certainly done her share in the early days of the settlement, for the German Canadian Club, the church and the hall. Now she had her own

Jack Bryan, Ursula and Hans Delfs

special way of making contributions. She purchased a gift copy of "Burnt Embers" for each of her grandchildren.

In 1986, Mother had to hurry home from her travels so that she could participate in a family recognition ceremony. She tells about it in her letter to Germany:

**Dale Cole, Vice President of Edmonton Northlands,
Barbara, Lisa, Violet, Dieter and Else Pankow
Agriculture Minister Peter Elzinga and Constable Grieg**

*In Edmonton we were honoured, along with thirty-two other farm families
from Northern Alberta. The article in our local newspaper read:* **Woking
Family Honoured at Northlands Agricultural Show**, *along with a
family picture, taken with the president of the Ag Show, the Minister of*

**The Pankow Grandchildren
Lisa, Barbara, Karin**

*Agriculture, and an R.C.M.P.
officer in his scarlet dress
uniform. I am very happy for
Dieter, that he got this
recognition, because he does work
hard. And, well, in earlier years,
this Oma contributed too.*

Mother enjoyed her grandchildren.
She had, perhaps, the most
interaction with the Pankow girls,
because of their proximity. This
living in the same yard had its
advantages and its drawbacks. She
could help by baby-sitting when
necessary; she could look after
things when the family travelled;

she had the little ones over for cookies, teaparties, and little Christmases; and she enjoyed watching them grow up. But it also meant she again had the worries she had already been through with her own children. And sometimes it was embarrassing for the young ladies when they returned with their date, only to have Oma standing on her doorstep in her long flannel night-gown, porch light on, checking their safe return! At times, Mother would, perhaps subconsciously, make comparisons, then and now, as she wrote:

> *Karin and Barbara are going to take part in a school trip to France. I can only shake my head and will heave a big sigh of relief when they're safely back home. It's preposterous what the youth today want, and get. But Omas have nothing to say.*

Ring Bearers Eric Delfs and Norman Kut 1964

Flower Girls Brenda and Ellen Delfs 1959

The Delfs grandchildren also lived close enough to get to know their Oma. When they were young, and for several years her only grandchildren, she delighted in seeing "the two little Delfs girls" in their pretty matching dresses, participate as flower girls. This happened at three weddings, when Gerta, Dieter and Heidi chose their nieces, Ellen and Brenda for this honour. When Irma got married the girls were considered too big, so nephews Eric Delfs and Norman Kut served as ring-bearers.

Oma frequently walked to our place, marching to the beat of "The Happy Wanderer" and followed the development of her four "Enkel" with interest. Soon she would be attending their high school graduations and weddings. Later, she found it very helpful to have her granddaughters Ellen and Brenda, living in Edmonton. Over the years they made many a trip to the airport to pick up or drop off their Oma, her friends and relatives. Ellen's

Oma Frequently Walked to the Delfs' House

house was often "headquarters" while she visited friends in the city or took treatments at the hospital. She enjoyed staying there and loved her little great-grandchildren. Anton, Marina and Aaron knew her as "tick-tock" Oma, (from the German Uroma.) She was well served by Ellen and Slavko's generosity and good-nature — their taxi service, room and board, their phone tied up for hours. And, again, Mother felt, in her own way, that she was being helpful, as she wrote to Germany:

I came down with Hans to Edmonton and was able to help Ellen with the children while she visited her mother in hospital.

Great Grandchildren Anton, Marina, Aaron and Left to Right: Oma Pankow, Gordon and Brenda, Laura, Eric and Slavko

Ursel had an operation on her cheek. The biopsy of a lump had been taken previously and was found to be benign. The specialists said the parotid gland had to be removed in order to prevent recurrence. The three-hour operation was performed, and after a nine-day hospital stay, she was released. Today she is giving a slide presentation at the Women of Unifarm convention in Red Deer.

The Kut, Riggins and Tierney grandchildren did not see as much of their Oma, although she visited quite often. Then her visits were very special, and her days with them were "quality time." Special outings and activities would be planned for them to enjoy together. There were times

Dennis & Brian, Heidi and Irma Tierney Oma (middle) at "The Yellow House" Restaurant

when it would have been less worrisome and easier for Mother if she lived farther away from the rest of her children as well. But in her little house in Dieter's yard, she certainly had the advantage of always having help close by, and the feeling of not being isolated and alone.

But this close proximity was not always a good thing. For years, Mother had been forced to be independent, to make decisions for the family, and to be "in charge." Now she sometimes found it hard to relinquish this role. She still had to "have her say," to inspect field and garden; to check into cooking and nutrition; to give unsolicited advice and opinions. Understandably, this was

Gordon Kut Giving His Oma a Ride

Kevin and Trent Riggins with Their Oma

not always welcome or well received. I have often thought that Dieter must have found himself "caught between" — his mother, somewhat controlling, and his wife, who has never found communicating easy. We, his sisters, sometimes felt sorry for our brother in this unenviable position. Maybe it was a good thing that, for many years Mother was home for only parts of each year.

In April 1988, we honoured Mother with an eightieth birthday celebration at Westmark Hall, which was well-attended by many friends and

Marina and Anton Bunjevac at their Great Oma's Eightieth Birthday

neighbours, in addition to most of her family. Irma and Brian had come from California with a thoughtfully created photo collage, and Heidi, who had flown in from Vancouver, came into our still-dormant countryside laden with many fresh flowers, shrubbery blossoms and greenery, which we fashioned into a large bouquet and many table center-pieces. Mother's children, grandchildren and great grandchildren prepared a program of readings, skits and songs, which they presented to the guest of honour, seated in her old rocking chair.

Always a "people person," even when Mother wasn't actually travelling to far-off destinations, she did a lot of local visiting. In Edmonton she spent time with her friend Edith Schulz, also visited Bert and Anne Bockhold, Margarete Boeske and Otto Theophile, to name a few. In Grande Prairie, she looked in on Anne Klukas and her parents, the Yanys, Herta and her brothers, Art and Max Lippelt, who lived by Clairmont Lake. Mother and Johann attended a number of German Canadian Club functions, and enjoyed the fellowship and the German singing. I took her to Wembley to visit Helga Andersen, and Mother was deeply saddened to see how Alzheimer's disease had begun its ravages on her dear friend.

Back in 1954, perhaps in a thoughtful and nostalgic mood, Mother had written to Uncle Werner:

> *When I look back on my life — large family at home; World War I; inflation — always there was **Knappheit** (want, poverty.) Then pioneering in Canada's north during the great depression of the 30s, so infiltrated the system of us "middle-agers" that we still have complexes (I just recently read about this in the paper.) Then came World War II which certainly brought no upturn in prosperity for us — just the opposite. And the fateful 1948, the year of Günther's death, then Uncle's suicide in '53, all had most adverse affects.*

Oma Pankow's House on Dieter's Farm

I think Mother realized, even then, that this much trauma in a lifetime was bound to catch up with her, to leave its mark on the psyche. In her final years, Mother's amazing energy and emotional toughness did wane. It almost seemed as though she had given so much for such a long time, that there was nothing left to give. The many years of "keeping her chin up" had finally taken its toll.

This began to manifest itself in much preoccupation with her health. From the time of her youth in Germany, she had been interested in alternative medicine — natural foods, participation in hiking and exercise programs, attending healthy cooking demonstrations by the Mazdasnan followers (an Eastern holistic movement leaning towards a more natural lifestyle). During the Spartan homestead days, some of these ideals had to be abandoned, out of necessity, but Mother was not happy about it. She was concerned about all the pork, lard, sausage, bread and butter, cakes and puddings that were everyday diet staples, and she deplored the lack of year-round fresh produce.

Oma Made Her Little House Cozy
and Charming

Later, on her own, she resumed a more active interest, and studied books and other literature from not only Mazdasnans, but from such health and nutrition gurus as Gaylord Hauser, Adele Davis and others. And Uncle Werner also sent her "Reform Blätter" (health food literature) from Germany. All this reading led to trials of various diet, fasting and cleansing regimes, and much self-diagnosis. Brewers yeast, lecithin, black strap molasses, juice therapy, vitamin supplements, and much more became part of Mother's vocabulary. We used to tease her that she was keeping the health food industry in business!

But all her home remedies were not effective in calming her colitis, because it was, perhaps not surprisingly, stress related. And her greatest bane was depression. Few were aware that it could exist in this woman whom they saw as the bubbly world traveller, always showing her happy "up" side, her amazing energy. What they didn't see was the physically exhausted, emotionally drained woman who suffered depressions when she returned from her sojourns, to the little house in Westmark. Only her family saw this side, and sought to help her come out of these doldrums — not an easy task.

There were times when we thought Mother might be better off in a senior's home, where she'd be with people all the time. We had made inquiries, even put her name on a waiting list, but she was opposed to this plan because she didn't want to be with "all those old people." She was only eighty-one!

In March, '89 Dieter and Vi had gone to France to visit their daughters Karin and Lisa, studying French there; and also visited many parts of Germany. In a role-reversal, Mother stayed home and looked after house and yard, dog and cat. This was not an easy adjustment for her, as she writes later:

> *Since I didn't get my room in Grande Prairie, I'm still in my little house. Naturally, I'm often very lonely on the snowy farm, especially since I lost my good friend and neighbour, Johann Oltmanns (92). He died of a heart attack. With his little Volkswagen bug we used to drive around the neighbourhood, even to Spirit River. Almost daily he came for coffee, and we watched favourite television programs together; and I miss his frequent phone calls.*

Johann Oltmanns

Mother had been diagnosed with bladder tumors in '84 and had to have check-ups in Edmonton every three months, with occasional cauterization treatment. She showed a calm acceptance and simply planned her life around this turn of events. But the recurring colitis flare-ups, the self-prescribed diet plans, and above all, the bouts of depression, brought about changes in Mother's once up-beat personality.

Her health became her all-consuming concern. She was so convinced that something was very wrong. At first, doctors could find nothing. Twice a supposedly well-respected gynecologist put this eighty-two year old woman under general anesthetic for a misdiagnosed disorder. I remember another day clearly, and I felt so sorry for her. Mother had come home from Grande Prairie, upset and totally discouraged. A doctor had thoroughly reprimanded her and told her rather emphatically, to "go home and live your life. It's all in your head."

By now Mother had been examined by a number of different doctors. And we, her family, seeking to encourage and instill hope, urged her to "believe the doctors. They have found nothing," and intimated that perhaps she suffered from a bit of hypochondria — much to our later regret and shame. Mother knew her own body. Something was not right. And Mother's children, though well intentioned, were wrong.

Oma Else Pankow 1991

For not long after, in September, 1990, Mother found herself in the Edmonton Cross Cancer Institute, where, for thirty days, she received radiation treatments for cervical cancer. She had many hospital visitors — friends, children and grandchildren. Afterwards, back in her little house, Heidi from Maple Ridge, and Irma from California, came to visit her. But a cure was not to be.

During the months that followed, Mother's health deteriorated. We, each in our own way, tried to help her. Heidi and Gordon, with their psychiatric training, attempted, through that channel, to ease her apprehension. Perhaps Irma was the one most suited to administering spiritual comfort. Gerta, always the practical one, cooked, cleaned house, and looked after Oma's clothing. I walked over frequently, and sought to distract Mother's thoughts away from her illness. I reminded her of all the good things she had done in her lifetime — for her family and many patients. This served at least as a temporary balm. Gerta and I alternately had Mother in our homes and patiently dealt with radiation-induced incontinence; the loss of appetite; the mood swings and the depression. Dieter did what he could, by always "being there for her." Because he lived next door, he was the one who listened to Mother on a daily basis, as she told of her fears, and her troubles. He dealt conscientiously with Mother's physical comfort. He shovelled snow, bought groceries, made sure all the utilities were in good order. Seeing our mother steadily failing was very difficult for all of us.

Mother knew she did not have long to live, and we all knew it. But no one ever talked about it. We talked about the weather, the crops and garden, the grandchildren — anything but the immediate circumstances. We never gave her the opportunity, and we avoided the subject of death. Perhaps we couldn't confront our own mortality. As in so many cases when the death of a loved one is imminent, there was "a conspiracy of silence." I have often felt guilty about this.

In March, 1991, and again in April, Mother spent two-week periods in the Spirit River Hospital, and in May she was, very unhappily, in Mackenzie Place for ten days, in a "respite room." She spent Easter with Kuts in Bonanza, and here the Delfs grandchildren visited her. Oma was able to

Oma Pankow (middle) with Daughter Gerta, Great Granddaughter Nicole and Grandson Norman Kut

enjoy her two newest great grand-children, Norman Kut's Nicole and Eric Delfs' Benjamin.

In July, Mother's niece Barbara Gesien arrived from Germany and spent nearly three weeks with her aunt in the little house. It was a good opportunity for Mother to reminisce about her childhood in East Prussia, and at the same time, tell Barbara something about her father Ernst, Mother's brother. Soon the Herrndorfs and the Tierneys arrived from California,

Liza Ostermayer came from Brazil and the Riggins from Vancouver. They had all come for the wedding of Mother's granddaughter, Karin Pankow, which was held at the Centennial Hall in Spirit River on July 20th. Mother was able to get through it all, but it was not easy. Kuts had borrowed a motor home to park beside the hall so she could rest, and Gerta looked after Oma's personal care. The day after the

Oma Pankow (middle) with Laura and Eric Delfs and Great Grandson Benjamin Delfs

wedding, Mother and her five children went, at Brian Tierney's (photographer) request, to the old homestead for black and white "nostalgia" photos.

**Remembering the Homestead Days at the Old House (1991)
Dieter, Mother, Ursula, Gerta, Irma, Heidi**

Less than a month later, Mother suffered a small stroke. Hans and I took her to the hospital in Spirit River. The next morning she was taken by ambulance to Grande Prairie, with a very high white blood cell count. That evening, perhaps mercifully, Mother lapsed into a coma, and thankfully the end came quickly and without pain.

From the time of her last admittance to the Spirit River Hospital, then transfer to Grande Prairie Hospital, until her passing, one or more of her children were by her bedside, day and night. Even though she was no longer aware of our presence, we didn't want to leave her alone. On August fifteenth, 1991, at four o'clock in the afternoon, our mother, Else (Gesien) Pankow died.

On a sunny day, August 19, 1991, her funeral service was held at Westmark Hall, with Pastors Ruby Friesen and Vern Begalke officiating, and Mother's grandsons serving as pallbearers. Oma's oldest granddaughter, Ellen, presented the eulogy, which we her family had prepared. It told of a very full long life, filled with hardships, but also with love and adventure. We buried our mother beside our father at the riverside Northmark Public Cemetery. There were many people who needed to receive death notifications, and the thick, well-used address book served a useful purpose one more time.

Else Pankow's Funeral, August 19ᵗʰ, 1991

The many condolence letters that followed tell of each individual's memory of Mother — whether they knew her as an old neighbour, a traveler, a caregiver or a relative. Kate Rampoldt probably spoke for many when she wrote:

We have so many good memories of hours spent with her. She brought so much fun and zest to our outings. We will never forget the homestead and how we insisted on staying and sleeping there, to get the real feel of the place she loved — her farm. She was so willing to spare no effort to make the experience possible.

And indeed, Mother had, over the years, taken many visitors, from varied places, to show them the spot where she had started her life in Canada. Pastor Martin Intscher, who remembered his years in Northmark with fondness, wrote:

It is not only a dear family member that you have lost. Else Pankow was the soul and driving force of the Westmark settlement. With her, a period of history has also been buried. May she rest in peace. She will live on in our memory.

Dieter Anders expressed his admiration:

> *On the death of your mother, our highly-esteemed friend, we share your sorrow. How fortunate that she could be with us this long. It is granted few people, to leave behind such far-reaching recognition, appreciation and love.*

The Place Where Else Pankow's Life in Canada had it's Beginning

For many Mother was the "bridge" and connection between relatives on both sides of the ocean. Cousin Kriemhild Uihlein wrote:

> *What a responsibility-filled life lies behind her; highs and lows counter-balanced, able to overcome so many complex trials and ordeals. What charisma she radiated, and by overcoming spiritual and physical pain, she mastered her life. We would be happy if your mother's friendly annual Christmas letters could be continued, so that the bond would not be broken.*

So our life went on. Frequently there are reminders of our mother, grandmother and great grandmother. So many fond memories remain —some beautiful, some troubled, some poignant, some humorous — but never dull.

The tide recedes but leaves behind bright seashells on the sand,
The sun goes down, but gentle warmth still lingers on the land,
The music stops, and yet it echoes on in sweet refrains ...
For every joy that passes, something beautiful remains.

(Author Unknown)

One generation passeth away, and another generation cometh; but the earth abideth forever. Ecclesiastes 1:4.

They are gone and we are bereft. But we treasure the memory of our parents, Günther and Else Pankow, the brave and adventurous pioneers who came to Canada so many years ago. Were their hopes and dreams fulfilled? Did all their hard work, perseverance and sacrifice truly lay the foundation, then pave the way to a brighter future? We their descendants can say, with conviction: Certainly !

Our Mother lived to witness many of the results, and to realize some of the rewards of her years of travail. Father was not granted this opportunity. Over these many years, his early death has been a source of sadness and regret for all of us. How often we would have liked to share precious moments with him — the birth of a child, the marriage of a young man or women; our successes in life, and our sorrows. How we have missed him - his guidance, his mentoring, his calm presence.

I believe that our parents passed a legacy of strength, courage and integrity on to their children. This enabled them to meet life's challenges, to go forward and provide an even brighter future for their own families. Dieter, Ursula, Gerta, Heidi and Irma each established families of their own so that

Günther and Else Pankow would have thirteen grandchildren and eighteen great grandchildren. Each sought to build on the foundation, to emulate the values, to follow the examples which had been set for them in such an exemplary fashion.

Now in the year 2003, we, the descendants of Günther and Else Pankow have reason to be thankful and can count our many blessings. Our quality of life has come a long way from the homestead cabin where, in 1929, our father began his life in Canada. Even though we grew up amidst this simplicity, sometimes austerity, I think Father would not be too disappointed if he could see his five offspring and their families as they live today. He would know that all his hard work and sacrifice had not been in vain. And Mother's ardent wishes, as expressed in one of her letters, would come true:

"Our children, how we love and cherish them! To live for them, to nurture and protect them, is our sacred duty. That they may go forward into a brighter future is my constant prayer."

Her prayer was surely answered.

During a family reunion in July, 2003, to commemorate the pioneer spirit of our parents, Günther and Else Pankow, and to assure that their descendents may know the place where a humble beginning in Canada was made, we, their family, erected a bronze plaque at the site of the original 1929 homestead on SE – 10 – 76 – W6.

Epilogue

There is no past we can bring back by longing for it. There is only an eternal now that builds and creates, out of the past, something new and better.

...Johann Wolfgang von Goethe.

During my lifetime and that of my parents, there have been almost unbelievable changes in the community where I grew up. We have gone from kerosene lamps to electric lights; from wood stoves to gas, oil and electric heating with electronic temperature controls; from laundry tubs and corrugated scrub boards to automatic washing machines. In transportation we have gone from slow-moving horse and buggies to fast automobiles, speeding diesel trains and super-sonic jets that streak across the sky. Man has travelled into space. Communications have advanced from the printed page and radio, to television, cell phone and computer e-mail.

If man's goal is progress, and it seems natural for him to strive always upward, then he has come a long way towards achieving his goal. But is progress always good? Unfortunately, it also brings with it some attending downsides. What has happened to the great community spirit, the working together, the joy and satisfaction in simple things; the slower, less hectic pace of living; the absence of greed and envy? And on a global scale, progress has, perhaps because it has not been experienced by all peoples, not led to peace; but has only made the methods of war more devastating and deadly. It is my fervent prayer that my children and grandchildren may live in a world without war.

A pebble is dropped in the water, and its ripples spread on and on. A smile brightens the day of a passerby, and he in turn, smiles at the next person he meets. A child is taught to love, and he responds warmly to those around him. So lives go on touching one human being after another — who knows how far. Our ancestors touch our lives not only by the genes we have inherited, but also by the precepts and values passed down through the years. We, in turn, will influence those who follow us.[1]

Family memories and traditions are the threads that weave generations together. By writing these chapters, I hope I have given you a legacy of memories, a gift of love more valuable than any financial gift. We as humans are happiest when we are creating, and I have found special joy and fulfillment in writing these family memoirs. It is my hope that they may become a precious document that will live in our family for generations.

Ursula (Pankow) Delfs 2003

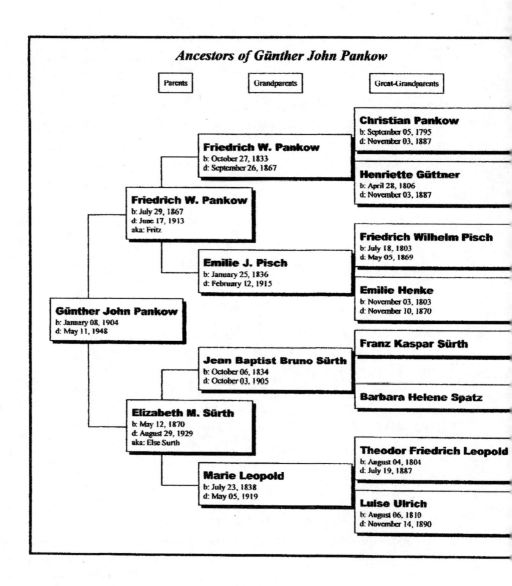

Ancestors of Günther John Pankow

| Parents | Grandparents | Great-Grandparents |

Christian Pankow
b: September 05, 1795
d: November 03, 1887

Henriette Güttner
b: April 28, 1806
d: November 03, 1887

Friedrich W. Pankow
b: October 27, 1833
d: September 26, 1867

Friedrich W. Pankow
b: July 29, 1867
d: June 17, 1913
aka: Fritz

Friedrich Wilhelm Pisch
b: July 18, 1803
d: May 05, 1869

Emilie Henke
b: November 03, 1803
d: November 10, 1870

Emilie J. Pisch
b: January 25, 1836
d: February 12, 1915

Günther John Pankow
b: January 08, 1904
d: May 11, 1948

Franz Kaspar Sürth

Barbara Helene Spatz

Jean Baptist Bruno Sürth
b: October 06, 1834
d: October 03, 1905

Elizabeth M. Sürth
b: May 12, 1870
d: August 29, 1929
aka: Else Surth

Theodor Friedrich Leopold
b: August 04, 1804
d: July 19, 1887

Luise Ulrich
b: August 06, 1810
d: November 14, 1890

Marie Leopold
b: July 23, 1838
d: May 05, 1919

374

Ancestors of Else Gertrud Gesien

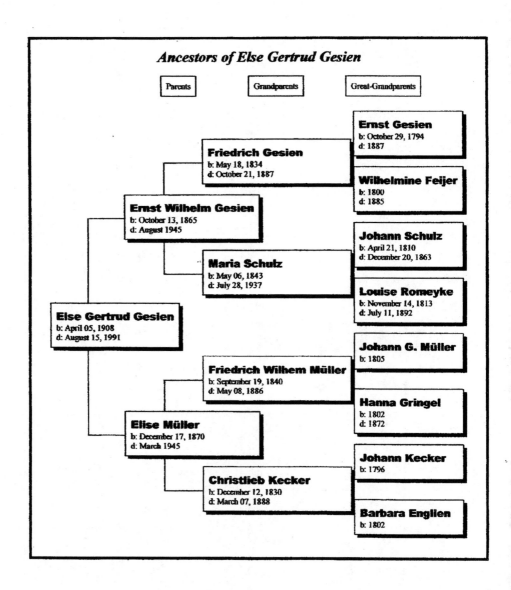

Parents

Grandparents

Great-Grandparents

Ernst Gesien
b: October 29, 1794
d: 1887

Friedrich Gesien
b: May 18, 1834
d: October 21, 1887

Wilhelmine Feijer
b: 1800
d: 1885

Ernst Wilhelm Gesien
b: October 13, 1865
d: August 1945

Johann Schulz
b: April 21, 1810
d: December 20, 1863

Maria Schulz
b: May 06, 1843
d: July 28, 1937

Louise Romeyke
b: November 14, 1813
d: July 11, 1892

Else Gertrud Gesien
b: April 05, 1908
d: August 15, 1991

Johann G. Müller
b: 1805

Friedrich Wilhem Müller
b: September 19, 1840
d: May 08, 1886

Hanna Gringel
b: 1802
d: 1872

Elise Müller
b: December 17, 1870
d: March 1945

Johann Kecker
b: 1796

Christlieb Kecker
b: December 12, 1830
d: March 07, 1888

Barbara Englien
b: 1802

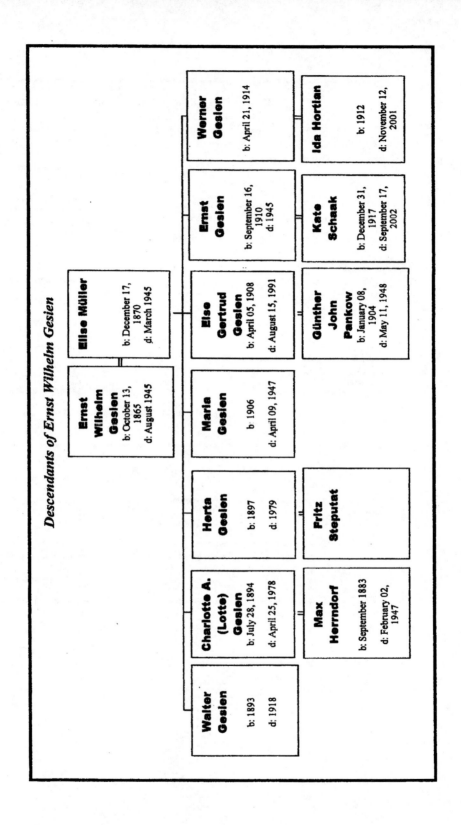

Descendants of Ernst Wilhelm Gesien

Ernst Wilhelm Gesien
b: October 13, 1865
d: August 1945

Else Müller
b: December 17, 1870
d: March 1945

Walter Gesien
b: 1893
d: 1918

Charlotte A. (Lotte) Gesien
b: July 28, 1894
d: April 25, 1978

Herta Gesien
b: 1897
d: 1979

Maria Gesien
b: 1906
d: April 09, 1947

Else Gertrud Gesien
b: April 05, 1908
d: August 15, 1991

Ernst Gesien
b: September 16, 1910
d: 1945

Werner Gesien
b: April 21, 1914

Max Herrndorf
b: September 1883
d: February 02, 1947

Fritz Steputat

Günther John Pankow
b: January 08, 1904
d: May 11, 1948

Kate Schaak
b: December 31, 1917
d: September 17, 2002

Ida Hortian
b: 1912
d: November 12, 2001

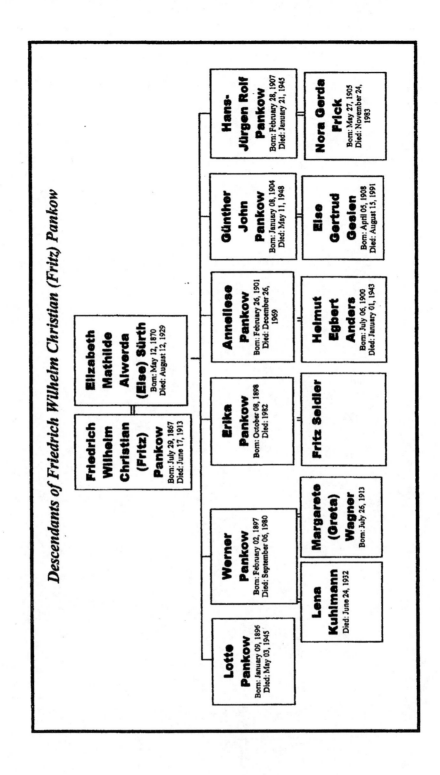

Descendants of Friedrich Wilhelm Christian (Fritz) Pankow

Friedrich Wilhelm Christian (Fritz) Pankow
Born: July 29, 1867
Died: June 17, 1913

Elizabeth Mathilde Alwerda (Else) Sürth
Born: May 12, 1870
Died: August 12, 1929

Lotte Pankow
Born: January 09, 1896
Died: May 03, 1945

Werner Pankow
Born: February 02, 1897
Died: September 06, 1980

Erika Pankow
Born: October 08, 1898
Died: 1982

Anneliese Pankow
Born: February 26, 1901
Died: December 26, 1969

Günther John Pankow
Born: January 08, 1904
Died: May 11, 1948

Hans-Jürgen Rolf Pankow
Born: February 28, 1907
Died: January 21, 1945

Lena Kuhlmann
Died: June 24, 1932

Margarete (Greta) Wagner
Born: July 25, 1913

Fritz Seidler

Helmut Egbert Anders
Born: July 06, 1900
Died: January 01, 1943

Else Gertrud Geslen
Born: April 05, 1908
Died: August 15, 1991

Nora Gerda Frick
Born: May 27, 1905
Died: November 24, 1983

ISBN 141207288-3